VOLUME 652

# THE ANNALS

of The American Academy of Political
and Social Science

*Strengthening Governance in South
Africa: Building on Mandela's Legacy*

Special Editor:
ROBERT I. ROTBERG
*Harvard University*

Los Angeles | London | New Delhi
Singapore | Washington DC

# The American Academy of Political and Social Science

202 S. 36th Street, Annenberg School for Communication, University of Pennsylvania, Philadelphia, PA 19104-3806; (215) 746-6500; (215) 573-2667 (fax); www.aapss.org

**Origin and Purpose.** The Academy was organized December 14, 1889, to promote the progress of political and social science, especially through publications and meetings. The Academy does not take sides in controverted questions, but seeks to gather and present reliable information to assist the public in forming an intelligent and accurate judgment.

**Meetings.** The Academy occasionally holds a meeting in the spring extending over two days.

**Publications.** THE ANNALS of The American Academy of Political and Social Science is the bimonthly publication of the Academy. Each issue contains articles on some prominent social or political problem, written at the invitation of the editors. These volumes constitute important reference works on the topics with which they deal, and they are extensively cited by authorities throughout the United States and abroad.

**Subscriptions.** THE ANNALS of The American Academy of Political and Social Science (ISSN 0002-7162) (J295) is published bimonthly—in January, March, May, July, September, and November—by SAGE Publications, 2455 Teller Road, Thousand Oaks, CA 91320. Periodicals postage paid at Thousand Oaks, California, and at additional mailing offices. POSTMASTER: Send address changes to The Annals of The American Academy of Political and Social Science, c/o SAGE Publications, 2455 Teller Road, Thousand Oaks, CA 91320. Institutions may subscribe to THE ANNALS at the annual rate: $916 (clothbound, $1034). Individuals may subscribe to the ANNALS at the annual rate: $112 (clothbound, $165). Single issues of THE ANNALS may be obtained by individuals for $36 each (clothbound, $49). Single issues of THE ANNALS have proven to be excellent supplementary texts for classroom use. Direct inquiries regarding adoptions to THE ANNALS c/o SAGE Publications (address below).

All correspondence concerning membership in the Academy, dues renewals, inquiries about membership status, and/or purchase of single issues of THE ANNALS should be sent to THE ANNALS c/o SAGE Publications, 2455 Teller Road, Thousand Oaks, CA 91320. Telephone: (800) 818-SAGE (7243) and (805) 499-0721; Fax/Order line: (805) 375-1700; e-mail: journals@sagepub.com. *Please note that orders under $30 must be prepaid.* For all customers outside the Americas, please visit http://www.sagepub.co.uk/customerCare.nav for information.

# THE ANNALS

© 2014 by The American Academy of Political and Social Science

Editorial Office: 202 S. 36th Street, Philadelphia, PA 19104-3806
For information about membership* (individuals only) and subscriptions (institutions), address:
SAGE Publications
2455 Teller Road
Thousand Oaks, CA 91320

For SAGE Publications: Peter Geraghty (Production) and Katherine Chang (Marketing)

From India and South Asia, write to:
SAGE PUBLICATIONS INDIA Pvt Ltd
B-42 Panchsheel Enclave, P.O. Box 4109
New Delhi 110 017
INDIA

From Europe, the Middle East, and Africa, write to:
SAGE PUBLICATIONS LTD
1 Oliver's Yard, 55 City Road
London EC1Y 1SP
UNITED KINGDOM

*Please note that members of the Academy receive THE ANNALS with their membership.
International Standard Serial Number ISSN 0002-7162
International Standard Book Number ISBN 978-1-4833-5874-1 (Vol. 652, 2014) paper
International Standard Book Number ISBN 978-1-4833-5873-4 (Vol. 652, 2014) cloth
Manufactured in the United States of America. First printing, March 2014

Please visit http://ann.sagepub.com and under the "More about this journal" menu on the right-hand side, click on the Abstracting/Indexing link to view a full list of databases in which this journal is indexed.

Information about membership rates, institutional subscriptions, and back issue prices may be found on the facing page.

**Advertising.** Current rates and specifications may be obtained by writing to The Annals Advertising and Promotion Manager at the Thousand Oaks office (address above). Acceptance of advertising in this journal in no way implies endorsement of the advertised product or service by SAGE or the journal's affiliated society(ies) or the journal editor(s). No endorsement is intended or implied. SAGE reserves the right to reject any advertising it deems as inappropriate for this journal.

**Claims.** Claims for undelivered copies must be made no later than six months following month of publication. The publisher will supply replacement issues when losses have been sustained in transit and when the reserve stock will permit.

**Change of Address.** Six weeks' advance notice must be given when notifying of change of address. Please send the old address label along with the new address to the SAGE office address above to ensure proper identification. Please specify the name of the journal.

# THE ANNALS

## OF THE AMERICAN ACADEMY OF POLITICAL AND SOCIAL SCIENCE

Volume 652 March 2014

IN THIS ISSUE:

## Strengthening Governance in South Africa: Building on Mandela's Legacy

Special Editor: ROBERT I. ROTBERG

## FORHCOMING

*Human Trafficking: Recent Empirical Research*
Special Editors: RONALD WEITZER and SHELDON ZHANG

*Family Complexity, Poverty, and Public Policy*
Special Editors: MARCIA CARLSON and DANIEL MEYER

# Preface

The end of apartheid, the empowering of majority politicians and political movements, the return to South Africa of the African National Congress, and Nelson Mandela's assumption of the reborn nation's leadership heralded a sociological, economic, and political upheaval that was assumed at the time to be sustainably transformational. The new dawn suggested by the Freedom Charter and the long struggle for individual human rights had seemingly arrived, and, despite a number of recognizable challenges, Mandela and his close associates, as well as the general public that had been waiting decades for a release from oppression, expected that South Africa's future would be positive, progressive, and fruitful. But as the articles in this volume explain, there is much still to be accomplished to realize the lofty transformational objectives of the 1990s. Twenty years into South Africa's transition, Mandela's iconic legacy has been seriously abraded, and many of the corrosive challenges that confronted his new government and the new nation in 1994 remain seemingly intractable. As President Jacob Zuma's regime tries to satisfy the major needs of South Africans in 2014 and beyond, his people hope, somehow, that they can recover the promises of renewal and revitalization that were central to the final realization of majority rule.

Mandela's passing, as this volume was in press, makes recovering the promise of renewal

*Robert I. Rotberg is the founding director of the Program on Intrastate Conflict, Harvard Kennedy School; president emeritus of the World Peace Foundation; fellow of the American Academy of Arts & Sciences; Fulbright Professor at both the Paterson School of International Affairs (Carleton University) and the Balsillie School of International Affairs (University of Waterloo); and senior fellow of the Centre for International Governance Innovation. His most recent book is* Africa Emerges: Consummate Challenges, Abundant Opportunities *(Polity 2013).*

DOI: 10.1177/0002716213514197

and revitalization that much more urgent. Mandela trusted his people with the truth and led with a moral authority that inspired South Africans to embark on a shared journey of spiritual as well as physical and material reconstruction. But without Mandela, and without his successors having his emotional intelligence, his gift of truly inclusive leadership, South Africa's ability to face the future efficaciously could well continue to erode. The egalitarian and progressive society in which Mandela believed now has to be established in his absence.

This issue of *The ANNALS* is devoted to strengthening governance in South Africa because nothing is so important for Africa, as well as for South Africa itself. Good governance, as explained in the first article, is what Africa and South Africa lacks most. The way forward for both the continent and for South Africa, the continent's most modern and most advanced component, thus follows the path of improved governance through thoughtful educational and medical responses, the creation of abundant jobs, and a thorough remediation of the many other difficult governance challenges facing the African National Congress–controlled government of South Africa.

The articles in this volume—on what must be accomplished to build effectively on the governance legacy of President Mandela—are based on papers initially presented at a conference on constructing better governance outcomes in South Africa. The meeting was held at the Steenberg Hotel, near Cape Town, in May 2013, generously sponsored by the Centre for International Governance Innovation (CIGI) of Waterloo, Ontario, in association with the American Academy of Political and Social Science of Philadelphia, Pennsylvania. Most of the participants in the conference, and the contributors to this volume of *The ANNALS*, are South Africans.

As editor of this volume of *The ANNALS*, I am grateful to David Dewitt, vice-president for programs of CIGI, for his strong support of the research and writing that led to the conference and to this volume. I am equally appreciative of the backing of the Academy, and of Thomas Kecskemethy, its executive director. Emily Wood undertook her usual accomplished editing to create a final publication of which we can all be proud.

—R. I. R.

*Keywords:* governance; new challenges; ANC perils; corruption; energy; water

# Overcoming Difficult Challenges: Bolstering Good Governance

*By*
ROBERT I. ROTBERG

When will South Africa achieve its long-promised renaissance? When will its ruling African National Congress (ANC) abandon "careerism," refuse to be a "predatory elite" looting the "national wealth," shun the temptations of greed, abandon its willingness to tolerate corruption at multiple governmental levels, and begin to act thoroughly in the full national, rather than the party, interest? Timely and harshly relevant today, those were among the many tough challenges put to the ANC in a 1997 speech by none other than Nelson Mandela, its president and South Africa's first leader, posttransition (Mandela quoted in Sampson 1999, 533).

In that speech at a party congress in Mafikeng, Mandela called for a national and a party-led "moral renewal." Without such a moral renewal, he warned, there could be no societal transformation. Mandela worried that the embryonic new nation to which he and other key ANC figures had given birth would fail to flourish if politicians used their positions to help themselves rather their fellow South Africans, and if they failed to be inclusive, generous of spirit, and responsibly to uplift the full nation rather than themselves and the party.

*Robert I. Rotberg is the founding director of the Program on Intrastate Conflict, Harvard Kennedy School; president emeritus of the World Peace Foundation; fellow of the American Academy of Arts & Sciences; Fulbright Professor at both the Paterson School of International Affairs (Carleton University) and the Balsillie School of International Affairs (University of Waterloo); and senior fellow of the Centre for International Governance Innovation. His most recent book is* Africa Emerges: Consummate Challenges, Abundant Opportunities *(Polity 2013).*

DOI: 10.1177/0002716213513542

As the articles in this volume describe in detail, Mandela was right to caution his party and his closest followers to eschew any tendencies to deviate from the path of good governance. He knew instinctively that good governance was primarily the performance of governments—the delivery of essential services to constituents (for detailed explanations, see Rotberg 2004, 3–25; Rotberg, forthcoming). Mandela understood that over the short-, medium-, and long-term the ANC's stewardship of South Africa would be judged on how effectively the ANC-led government transformed the apartheid-mangled country into a fully modern nation providing adequate quantities and high qualities of such fundamental political goods as security and safety; rule of law, transparency, and accountability; political participation, "voice," and respect for fundamental human rights and freedoms; sustainable economic opportunity; and human development, including abundant educational opportunities and medical care (for political goods, see Pennock 1966, 420–26; for the key modern goods, see Rotberg and Gisselquist 2009, 3–7).

In many respects, particularly in comparison to its African neighbors and rivals, South Africa has in fact delivered many of these desired political goods and a welcome post-apartheid dividend.[1] Over its first 20 years, it has provided "steady (if low) economic growth; middle-class prosperity; a massive expansion of tax-financed urban housing, infrastructure and services (as well as social assistance programs)"; and, perhaps, most impressively, "deracialisation" without widespread conflict.[2] Among its significant innovations has been South Africa's development of an edifice unusual for Africa—a social safety net that approximates a broadly expanded, if still embryonic, welfare state. A full 44 percent of all households rely on social grants for everyday subsistence (*The Economist* 2013c).

When the General Household Survey of South Africa was released in mid-2013, it revealed that welfare spending had indeed diminished poverty and that municipal services had become more numerous and accessible. Fewer people than in 2002 reported that they were hungry. More than 50 percent of all persons lived in their own home and only 14 percent in state-subsidized housing. (Eighteen percent of the latter complained, however, that those dwellings had been poorly constructed.) Homes with electricity increased from 77 percent to 85 percent (but there were frequent blackouts). Ninety percent had access to potable water, but 20 percent fetched it from a communal tap. (Fewer people than in 2005, 60 percent, said that water services were adequate, down from 76 percent.) All but 5 percent of South Africans (up from 12 percent) had flush toilets. Two-thirds of all homes had regular rubbish collection, but more respondents than in 2003 complained about its inefficiency and quality. Eighty percent of South Africans owned a television, an electric stove, and a mobile telephone. Only 30 percent owned a motor vehicle. Ten percent had access to the Internet at home.

Despite demonstrable progress, South Africa still lags its own promise. Respondents to the household survey wanted much more than they were receiving. "The standard [people] expect seems to be rising faster than the pace at which the state can improve things" (*The Economist* 2013c). Nasty protests at the lack of water, sanitation, and electric power punctuated much of 2013. The articles in this volume show in compelling and forceful prose how and in what specific domains South Africa's governance deserves to be strengthened. South Africa, a leader in its region and throughout sub-Saharan Africa, has always asked to be held to a higher standard of performance and political consciousness than the run-of-the-mill African state. Mandela elevated the South African model and offered a standard of leadership and a promise of positive governance that transcended that provided by many of his continental peers, predecessors, and successors. As President Thabo Mbeki, Mandela's immediate heir, attempted so assiduously to articulate, the South African experiment was intended to inaugurate an African as well as a local and regional rebirth. Mbeki spoke often of better governance, but provided less and less of it over the duration of his presidency.

Many within and out of the new nation now ask when the much heralded transformation will arrive in a sustainable manner for most South Africans, not just for the well-connected political and economic elite. The promise of a great, glorious, and prosperous country remains strong and certainly realizable. But obstacles remain. This volume thus explicitly looks forward, seeking to chart the key challenges facing South Africa's political rulers, social pioneers, and opinion makers during the remainder of this decade and the decades to come. It also suggests, in the article by Chris Saunders, how South Africa conceivably can help to shape and rebuild the governance of all of Africa.

## Job Creation and Other Crucial Issues

To enhance the possibility of good governance in South Africa, nothing may be as important, overall, as jobs creation. "Social grants cannot make up for South Africa's woeful lack of jobs" (*The Economist* 2013c). South Africa has been growing more slowly economically than it hoped to do in the 20 years since the ANC assumed power. The employment breakthrough on the upside, often forecast, has not yet occurred. As a result, net new formal sector jobs lag population growth, too many young people give up looking for employment, too many depend upon the vagaries of the informal sector, and too many believe that government and society have abandoned them. The articles by Ann Bernstein and Nicoli Nattrass argue strongly for new policies capable of creating the wage employment that South Africa desperately needs.

The perils of joblessness and underemployment will intensify as South Africa grows larger in population over the next several decades and the youth bulge expands as a proportion of the total population. Without significant new thinking, it will be a major challenge to realize a healthy demographic dividend in a timely manner. Even so, policy-makers have yet fully to address the implications of these new numbers and the potential human dissatisfactions that they foreshadow. (The article by Jeremy Seekings draws out the striking implications and suggests how the government of South Africa should address these critical and complex demographic dilemmas.)

The new youth (and their elders) will inhabit cities that in many cases lack well-regarded municipal governance, effective intraurban transport systems, affordable and easily available housing, and other expected amenities. These service and social welfare weaknesses will vex the relevant authorities and trouble citizens and the nation at large. Crime rates, in recent years somewhat lower than they were in the early years of the new republic but still globally high, could soar as the youth bulge impinges on big conurbations, smaller cities, and the enlarging towns. (Elrena van der Spuy and Clifford Shearing's article explores the realities of criminality and weak official responses to it in South Africa.) All of these elements are intimately related to and affected by how and how well the new youth cadres (and others) are to be educated (whether traditionally, with less or more English, and vocationally), how secondary schooling is to be improved, and how the teachers are to be recruited and trained—all pressing and as yet unsolved problems. (Bernstein's article contains a major section on South Africa's educational failings. The article by Saleem Badat and Yusuf Sayed places the nation's acute educational deficit in a social justice framework. Andrew Babson's article argues for more education in English and more vocational training.) In the health field, especially in cities and peri-urban environments, HIV/AIDS will remain a major drain on resources for years to come, but so should drug-resistant tuberculosis, rampant childhood diseases such as diarrhea and pneumonia, malaria, and—paradoxically—the rise of childhood obesity. (Alan Whiteside's article puts those medical problems in context.) As the article by Carol Bower describes fully, all of these issues affect women and children more severely than men. Women and children remain even more at risk across all dimensions than do men in what remains a patriarchically dominated, chauvinist, society.

A shortage of jobs, the youth bulge, social services, crime, educational opportunity, and health services—these are all widely recognized, and difficult to solve or ameliorate, challenges for South Africa. The government may not know exactly how it intends to create more jobs, cope with the influx of urban youth, continue to reduce crime, improve city services, educate its people, and provide medical care. But it at least acknowledges the seriousness, even the potential intractability, of many of these critical concerns.

It also appreciates that its ability to attract new foreign direct investment and even domestic investment and reinvestment, and thus the possibility of new jobs, depends on finding effective answers to those harrowing challenges or employing some of the many innovative solutions offered by the contributors to this volume.

Acute and pressing as they are, however, those are not the only issues to mortgage South Africa's immediate and longer-term futures. South Africa is woefully energy short, having failed until recently to reinvest in plant and machinery. Until the country, albeit the best-served in sub-Saharan Africa, can generate sufficient electrical power from existing and planned hydro, nuclear, and thermal plants, and marginally from wind and solar experiments, and provide the necessary transmission facilities and lines, foreign and local investors will hesitate to bring in new money, the all-important mining industry will suffer, tourism will remain static, and the ordinary consumer and the student attempting to study will suffer from shortages and load-shedding debilitations. Compared to much of sub-Saharan Africa, South Africa is modern and technologically advanced. But adequate supplies of energy constitute an industrial and a governance Achilles heel that limits how far South Africa can expect to progress.

# The Scourge of Corruption

Just as the availability or not of abundant and reliable energy immediately affects an aspiring student in remote Limpopo Province who wants to better himself in school and contribute meaningfully to the national enterprise, and just as the performance of the South African government may be measured by the extent to which it provides essential services (including energy) to that student in Limpopo or to her counterparts in industrial Gauteng, so every aspect of governance is greatly influenced by the extent to which corrupt practices sap the vitality from almost every human transaction and place added costs on all governmental responses to individual and human needs.

South Africa was corrupt before the transition from apartheid 20 years ago. But every independent contemporary account bemoans the insidious spread of corruption to the nearest and farthest nook and cranny of the country. Corruption permeates all levels of government and infects numerous transactions between authority and citizen (see the discussion in Roger Southall's article).

Corruption is the abuse of public office for private gain (Nye 1967; Underkuffler 2009; *The Economist* 2013c). If a person is an elected official or a bureaucrat, accepting a bribe is a corrupt act. So is a decision to ignore regulations to give advantage to a friend or a patron or to shift a tariff category to benefit an importer. Bigger and more damaging are the official awarding of contracts to tenderers who may or may not qualify, and who may or may not have submitted low bids. The procurement business is easily abused, particularly when the putative gains are so substantial for all parties involved. Even a policeman or a nurse may profit by letting petty criminals escape or particular patients jump queues. If a thing needs a permit or a license, money can be made, especially from persons who want results quickly. If expenses or per diems are involved, elected officials or bureaucrats can fiddle the appropriate accounts. Greed, as Mandela warned, is a very human failing. So is the "careerism" he decried, for elected officials are easily tempted to abuse their positions.

Corruption begets more corruption. If leaders permit corrupt practices to begin, tolerate even episodic personal enrichment, or wink and nod only once in a while, the flood gates will soon open. Breaches of norms, sliding norms, or the development of new permissive norms are easily communicated throughout a party or a political system. Leaders are responsible and cast large shadows. What leaders do in this arena matters more than do formal mechanisms of accountability. This is not to deprecate such measures, but to acknowledge that they are insufficient, absent strong leadership, to stanch the normal human tendency to put self-aggrandizement ahead of the national interest, conscience, and morality (Rotberg 2009, 343).

Corrupt practices lower the moral tone of a government and rapidly erode its legitimacy and the legitimacy of its leaders. This loss of credibility and stature makes it hard for a government to be believed, to pursue bold or purposeful initiatives, or to be effective in delivering political goods to constituents. Moreover, corrupt practices significantly distort priorities; politicians and officials begin to make plans not to benefit the nation, but to enrich themselves. As a consequence, roads may not be paved as completely as they should be, military units may enter combat with substandard equipment, and essential pharmaceutical drugs may not reach the persons who need them most. Projects may not be initiated or continued; trains break down; sewers malfunction; and the quality of essential services, and of life, deteriorates.

Economists, moreover, estimate that countries in the developing world on average lose 1 percent GDP per annum per person because of even low levels of corruption (Mahmud 2008; Gyimah-Brempong 2002, 183–209; Pak 2001). In 2013, South Africa's GDP per capita was growing at about 2.7 percent per annum. A growth rate of 3.7 percent would have provided more job possibilities, more wealth opportunities for existing job holders, and monies for family use as well as for governmental service expansion.

To combat corruption, President Paul Kagame of Rwanda, says one must "cut off the head of the snake." "You can't fight corruption from the bottom. You have to fight it from the top" (quoted in Kinzer 2008, 235–36). The more responsible the position and the higher in the official hierarchy the person, the more such actions in this realm speak louder than words. Corrupt persons at the lower levels of the governmental pyramid take their cues from their immediate and then their distant bosses. Everyone along the hierarchy hates to miss out on good opportunities for gain. When persons above them steal, so subordinates steal, whatever the law. Corruption ends up embodying a cascade of individual venalities, each contributing relentlessly to a pervasive atmosphere of sleaze.

Singapore, Botswana, and Mauritius have shown that developing nations need not be corrupt. Indeed, their governance experiences since the 1960s have demonstrated convincingly that it is relatively easy to minimize corruption, both petty and venal. In Singapore, a pirate swamp filled with corrupt and dangerous Chinese gangs before 1965, cabinet ministers and other high officials, even a deputy prime minister, suspected of accepting bribes and falsifying tender procedures were sacked and prosecuted. After a handful of such dismissals and successful trials, persons at the higher rungs of political life in Singapore understood that corruption did not pay. As these individuals fell afoul of the prime minister's zero tolerance for corruption, so their subordinates understood that corruption could end a career. That message was passed rapidly down through the ranks to the lowliest clerk and policeman. Soon none dared risk offending what relatively quickly became the Singaporean norm; a city-state that once rivaled Macao for wildness settled into comfortable, stable, social conformity. It also grew prosperous on the back of consistent attention to good governance, especially the virtual elimination of corruption (see Rotberg 2012, 91–118).

Botswana and Mauritius, with fewer ministerial sackings but equally strong presidential and prime ministerial leadership against corruption, are the African anticorruption exemplars. With the pursuit of good, ethical governance drilled into their dominant political culture DNA by their founders and by those who followed in high office, Botswana and Mauritius (along with Cape Verde) consistently remain the top African performers in Transparency International's annual Corruption Perceptions Index ratings, well above South Africa. Like Singapore, they are small countries in population. Nevertheless, the lessons of these four nations, and of Rwanda and Ghana more recently, might well be learned by South Africa. In all six cases, leadership actions and attitudes made much more of a positive difference than did anticorruption commissions, legislation, prosecutions, and judicial remedies (Rotberg 2013, 102–5).

In South Africa, corruption is at the root of the moral decay against which Mandela warned so presciently. Since the mass of South Africans mostly believe that their leaders are corrupt, that the ANC is corrupt, and that they are surrounded by petty and large-scale corruption daily, the road back for the nation to Mandela's era, to enhanced legitimacy, and to an assumption of probity will be long and arduous. As one commentator suggests, "The criminal justice system has been corrupted to its core, in large part to save Zuma from jail" (Steinberg 2013). The prime task of President Jacob Zuma's government, and of the ANC at all levels, is therefore to restore for the people the promise of a true renaissance—to recapture the possibility of societal transformation. Without any efforts in this regard—without addressing the perceived moral failings of ANC hegemonic governance—it is hard to envisage how South Africa will achieve the material progress that everyone demands and expects. Good governance is neither style nor intention. Rather it puts citizen satisfaction uppermost. It demands—as it has for centuries—meeting the reasonable service delivery expectations of taxpayers and ratepayers.

## The Perils of the ANC

Older ANC stalwarts, even or especially those men and women who were early members of the South African Communist Party (SACP); who were staunch trade unionists; and who were active above and below ground, at home and in exile, campaigning against apartheid, echo these accusations of moral decay. They are as a collection of individuals greatly disturbed that the ANC under Mbeki and Zuma has abandoned nonracialism, more and more preferring to boost the careers within the ANC (as Mandela prophesied) of Xhosa and Zulu speakers. From the perspective of these early ANC members, nearly all still card-carrying members of the party, the ANC has lost its way. At least the ANC that they knew and adhered to, the ANC of Mandela and Joseph Slovo that worked for the downtrodden and was above corruption, seems to be no more. These stalwarts are disillusioned, having hoped for a societal transformation and, instead, today believing themselves the recipients of a wildly corrupt, ill-mannered, self-referential, and incompetent governance apparatus called the ANC[3] (Butler 2013; Habib 2013; see also Southall's article in this volume).

Other South Africans voice similar sentiments. When former University of Cape Town vice-chancellor and former World Bank managing director Mamphela Ramphele launched Agang (Build), a new political party, in mid-2013, she said that 20 years was "too long to wait for jobs . . . too long to wait for quality education." The ANC had failed South Africa and allowed the great promise of transition to fade. South Africa was not in 2013 the country "dreamed of by . . . Mandela, Steve Biko, or Lillian Ngoyi."[4] Corruption, Ramphele said, was one of the main causes of South Africa's dysfunctionality. "Corruption and a culture of impunity have spread throughout the government." She decried stealing textbooks, stealing drugs from persons living with HIV, "stealing thousands of jobs," and stealing billions of rands of investment (quoted in Iob 2013).

On the first anniversary in 2013 of the killings of striking platinum miners at Marikana a year earlier, a union organizer—possibly speaking for other disappointed former ANC backers—said that the ANC was "all about power, not the people." The ANC establishment boycotted the anniversary event. "They are supposed to be here," said the union organizer, "to listen to the problems of the people. . . . But they are nowhere to be seen. They only look after themselves." Another miner said that the ANC had abandoned the people of the country. "They are only looking to make money for themselves" (Polgreen 2013).

## Economic Realities

The economic realities were indeed sobering in late 2013. Earlier in the year the national growth rate had slumped below 1 percent in the first quarter; even the government's forecast of annual growth of 2.8 percent appeared unlikely to be achieved. The Gini coefficient, measuring equality and inequality, indicated that South Africa remained one of the most unequal countries in the world: the top 10 percent with nearly 60 percent of all income, the bottom 10 percent with only 0.5 percent. Unemployment was at least 25 percent—young (15–34), poorly educated blacks (mostly urban-located) accounting for about 70 percent of the total. If discouraged workers are counted, the percentage of unemployed persons of working age climbs to a more realistic figure of 33 percent. A labor aristocracy approach by the Congress of South African Trade Unions (Cosatu), an ANC partner, partly explains the failure to create myriad jobs in the posttransition period. Cosatu believes strongly in a high minimum wage, in a "decent" wage rather than jobs at almost any wage for the unskilled (Bernstein and Nattrass fully articulate the problems associated with Cosatu's approach) (Looney 2013; *The Economist* 2013a, 2013b).

Renewed attention to the rule of law, accountability, and transparency (as well as to strengthened leadership) is fundamental to any redress of moral weaknesses and illicit behavior—possibly even to incompetence. Mandela helped to ensure an advanced and liberal constitution for the new South Africa. As a lawyer, he believed in following the constitution, upholding the rule of law, adjudicating disputes fairly, and in the free flow of ideas, no matter how troubling to a ruling party or an elite establishment. Part of the almost inevitable post-Mandelan malaise that afflicts South Africa comes from less generous leadership views of the role in society of the rule of law, attacks on liberal aspects of the constitution, attempts to preserve governmental secrecy, assaults on the independence of judges and the judiciary, manipulation of the prosecutorial service, and a desire to keep the national police force malleable. (In 2013, nearly fifteen hundred serving police were discovered to possess criminal records, and the Independent Police Investigation Directorate was examining "a number" of officers charged with murder, rape, robbery, assault, and corruption. The appointment of a provincial commissioner of police had to be withdrawn, too, when his pending criminal charges were revealed [Tamukamoyo and Newham 2013; BBC News 2013]). Even Riah Phiyega, the newly installed national police commissioner, agrees that the South African police are "ill-disciplined," the result of inadequate command and control and poor "leadership" at the station level (Phiyega 2013).

To counter these not atypical ways of protecting a dominant political party and a powerful government, South Africa requires a reinforced and reinvigorated free media. Accountability and transparency are obviously enhanced if journalists and editors are watching, investigating, and critiquing. South Africa has an enviable reputation for inquisitive reporting, but with the rise of alternative outlets and the weakening of the traditional press, the capacity of print media to maintain high levels of oversight has been reduced. (Harber's article explains the state of South Africa's contemporary media.) The SABC, the government-owned television and radio broadcaster, is hardly committed to oversight, and the handful of private radio stations and the new community broadcasters have narrower mandates and concerns.

South Africa has a robust and thriving civil society, but even the best financed and best staffed of the many nongovernmental organizations that vie for funding and attention focus only on particular slices of the governance cake. Some, too, have withered away because of government disdain and opacity, as Bower's article makes clear.

Opposition political parties are expected to monitor the government and to ensure that the ANC and its government are accountable appropriately to the people and ultimately to the voters. Led by the Democratic Alliance (DA), the largest and the most active of the minority parties, they do so as assertively and cleverly as they can, and at the national, provincial, and municipal levels. But the DA is handicapped by its small parliamentary size (as compared to the ANC), by its origins as a "white" party, and by the ANC's control of Parliament and parliamentary processes. In many Westminster parliamentary systems, the opposition is able to hold a ruling party to account by the effective use of oral question time in plenary and in portfolio committees, and by chairing critical audit and budget committees. But not in South Africa, where ANC ministers ignore or evade answering oral questions posed by opposition members of portfolio committees, and where both the leader of government business (the national vice-president) and the president rarely appear before the House of Assembly to be questioned orally about governmental decisions or nondecisions. The ANC also controls the order of business and the procedures and proceedings of Parliament, all naturally to its own advantage. The DA is also denied the chair of the Special Committee on Public Accounts, so the ANC's impunity remains comparatively impregnable[5] (Rotberg and Salahub 2013, 13–17; Feinstein 2009, 185–208). Accountability would be well served by new rules for the assembly, and by shifting the South African House toward a more Westminster-like respect for fair play and free exchange of views, no matter how critical of the ruling party. (Readers should consult Southall's article for details on the ANC's control of Parliament, its approach to rule of law issues, deployment of cadres, and more.)

Democracy would also benefit if South Africa shifted from a full proportional representational (PR) system of voting to some modified version of the first-past-the-post system used in so many other democracies. Voting lists of possible parliamentarians in rank order are at the heart of all PR systems. That method gives inordinate power to the party executive, in South Africa known as Luthuli House. The ANC leadership selects those who appear on the party electoral list, and in an order determined by those at the top of the hierarchy. The preferences of local voters and local ANC workers (excluded as they are in South Africa from decisive policy shaping by the absence of real constituencies) are ignored. Parliamentary loyalties naturally flow to the party, not to the constituency (the electorate or a slice of it), and to the party above the state and the nation. (Southall's article makes the workings of the ANC, as a party, evident.)

In South Africa's case, the PR system and how it is used (abused) enables the one-time Marxist-imbued party to "deploy" its personnel, even its top leadership, and to demand that its parliamentarians and its leaders at all levels obey the dictates of the centrally directed party. Cadres, as they are known, are deployed by the party despite personal preferences to the contrary, despite the wishes of the middle and lower ranks of the party, and—sometimes—despite the evident needs of the nation. Party discipline is frequently substituted for the national interest. If the ANC ever democratizes as a party, South Africa may start to put itself back on the path of accomplished and responsible governance.

## Mandela's Legacy?

South Africa in 2014 is weaker than it need be. Given how Mandela brought the rainbow nation together and imbued all South Africans with a sense of belonging to a great, worthy, forward-looking enterprise, its progress over 20 years since 1994 has been underwhelming. Given how responsibly and effectively Mandela launched the transformation of a nation emerging from the brutalizing years of apartheid, adherents of the ANC and wizened idealists with struggle credentials have abundant reason today to be despondent and disillusioned. So does anyone who believes in an Africa where South Africa should be strengthening its own and, by example, the subcontinent's governance.

What Mandela gave South Africa was a leadership example that seemed to know right from wrong, that was loyal to the ANC but resolutely steeped in integrity, that was tolerant of dissent, and that was impeccably inclusive. Moreover,

Mandela persuaded his countrypeople that he held their interests foremost. His successors stepped out of Mandela's shadow, but now give the impression of leading the nation to buttress their own personal power, to solidify support for the ANC, and to ensure as few challenges as possible to their own and their party's hegemony.

As identified by *The Economist*, Zuma "is widely deemed to lack vision and panache" (*The Economist* 2013b; Habib 2013). Moreover, as discussed in later articles in this volume (including one on the leadership factor), Zuma's presidency has been marked by backsliding in a number of social and economic areas. The lives of most South Africans have not improved on his watch. The state has become more incapacitated than before. As the challenges ahead become more stark and sharp, Zuma's ability to lead the nation forward is coming more and more into question.

Courageous, intelligent, bold, and righteous political leadership is required if South Africa is going to build upon Mandela's legacy and address successfully the major problems that engulf the nation now, and for the years ahead. (Bernstein's article echoes this call. So does the final article in this volume, which sets out in some detail the requirements of visionary leadership.) Good governance occurs when astute, fully legitimate leaders mobilize a dejected or demoralized populace behind a vision of promise and coming prosperity. Other leaders in Africa and elsewhere have done so to right their countries. The articles in this volume of *The ANNALS*, mostly written by committed South Africans, explain how South Africa—if it so desires—can strengthen its core governance and mightily improve the lives of its long-suffering people.

## Notes

1. Many of the contributors to this volume helped to critique earlier drafts of this opening article. I am particularly grateful for the trenchant comments and strengthening ideas of Ann Bernstein, Chris Saunders, Jeremy Seekings, Clifford Shearing, Roger Southall, Elrena van der Spuy, and Alan Whiteside.

2. Private communication between this author and Jeremy Seekings, 25 August 2013.

3. Interview with the author, 2013.

4. Steve Biko (1946–1977) founded the Black Consciousness Movement and the South African Students Organisation. He was South Africa's most articulate and committed student activist in the 1970s, and a leading antiapartheid theoretician. Lillian Ngoyi (1911–1980) was a leader of the Garment Workers Union and president of the ANC Women's League. She was among the key ANC activists tried for treason (1956–1961), and later banned.

5. Interviews with author, 2013.

## References

BBC News. 29 July 2013. South African police with records "must be sacked." Available from www.bbc .co.uk/news.

Butler, Anthony. 2013. *The idea of the ANC*. Athens, OH: University of Ohio Press.

*The Economist*. 1 June 2013 (2013a). Muddle through will no longer do.

*The Economist*. 29 June 2013 (2013b). A sad and sorry decline.

*The Economist*. 31 August 2013 (2013c). The dole toll.

Feinstein, Andrew. 2009. *After the party: Corruption, the ANC and South Africa's uncertain future*. London: Verso.

Gyimah-Brempong, Kwabena. 2002. Corruption, economic growth, and income inequality in Africa. *Economics of Governance* 3:183–209.

Habib, Adam. 2013. *South Africa's suspended revolution: Hopes and prospects*. Athens, OH: University of Ohio Press.

Iob, Emilie. 23 June 2013. New political party launched in South Africa. VOA News. Available from http://www.tnatnews.com/new-political-party-launched-in-south-africa/.

Kinzer, Stephen. 2008. *A thousand hills: Rwanda's rebirth and the man who dreamed it*. New York, NY: John Wiley & Sons.

Looney, Robert. 11 July 2013. Where apartheid lives on. *Foreign Policy*. Available from www.foreignpolicy.com.

Mahmud, Quamrul. 2008. *Impact of corruption on economic growth performance in developing countries*. London: Analysees Consulting Group. Available from www.scribd.com/doc/764/analySEES-Report (accessed 21 November 2011).

Nye, Joseph S., Jr. 1967. Corruption and political development: A cost benefit analysis. *American Political Science Review* 61:417–27.

Pak, Hung Mo. 2001. Corruption and economic growth. *Journal of Comparative Economics* 29:66–79.

Pennock, J. Roland. 1966. Political development, political systems, and political goods. *World Politics* 18:420–26.

Phiyega, Riah. 2 October 2013. Public dialogue. *The Sowetan* (Johannesburg).

Polgreen, Lydia. 17 August 2013. Killing of strikers alters South African politics. *New York Times*.

Rotberg, Robert I. 2004. Improving governance in the world: Creating a measuring and ranking system. In *The good governance problem: Doing something about it*, eds. Robert I. Rotberg and Deborah L. West, 3–25. World Peace Foundation Report 39. Cambridge, MA: World Peace Foundation.

Rotberg, Robert I. 2009. Leadership alters corrupt behavior. In *Corruption, global security, and world order*, ed. Robert I. Rotberg, 341–58. Washington, DC: Brookings Institution Press.

Rotberg, Robert I. 2012. *Transformative political leadership: Making a difference in the developing world*. Chicago, IL: University of Chicago Press.

Rotberg, Robert I. 2013. *Africa emerges: Consummate challenges, abundant opportunities*. Cambridge: Polity.

Rotberg, Robert I. Forthcoming. On governance. In *On governance: The national and international dimensions of measuring governance effectiveness*.

Rotberg, Robert I., and Rachel M. Gisselquist. 2009. *Strengthening African governance: The index of African governance, results and rankings*. Cambridge, MA: World Peace Foundation.

Rotberg, Robert I., and Jennifer Erin Salahub. 2013. *African legislative effectiveness*. North-South Institute (Ottawa) Research Report. Available from www.nsi-ins.ca.

Sampson, Anthony. 1999. *Mandela: The authorized biography*. New York, NY: Vintage.

Steinberg, Jonny. 18 October 2013. Hard to lead a party that doesn't want to be led. *Business Day* (Johannesburg).

Tamukamoyo, Hamadziripi, and Gareth Newham. 10 September 2013. How to avoid bad appointments in South Africa's criminal justice system. *New Age* (Johannesburg).

Underkuffler, Laura S. 2009. Defining corruption: Implications for action. In *Corruption, global security, and world order*, ed. Robert I. Rotberg, 27–46. Washington, DC: Brookings Institution Press.

# South Africa's Key Challenges: Tough Choices and New Directions

*By*
ANN BERNSTEIN

The article looks at the "tough choices" (per the National Development Plan) South Africa has to make to be a successful country. It provides policy recommendations and prescriptions for many of the critical issues facing South Africa. The most urgent policy challenges revolve around high levels of unemployment, the regulation of the labor market and the role of unions, the shortage of skills, and the education system. The solutions proposed include the relaxation of labor laws, which hinder entry into the labor market, especially for young people; the introduction of special economic zones; the adoption of an open migration regime for skilled migrants; and the establishment of low-fee private schools and private tertiary education providers. The article calls for bold and visionary leadership in South Africa to ensure that the "tough choices" needing to be made are implemented.

*Keywords:* leadership; South Africa; special economic zones; education; labor market; unions

Creating an inclusive society requires courage, foresight and the ability to make very tough choices.

—Marcus (2013)

Twenty years into democracy, South Africa is in trouble. Achievements have been many since 1994, and much has changed for the better, but now the storm clouds are gathering on many fronts and the country is sliding when compared to global competition and in terms of its own requirements and ambitions.

Crises are evident in local government "unrest," which has taken violent forms and is

*Ann Bernstein is the founder and executive director of the Centre for Development and Enterprise, South Africa's foremost think-tank. Her latest book is* The Case for Business in Developing Economies *(Penguin 2010). She is currently on the board of the Brenthurst Foundation and in 2013 was a public policy scholar at the Woodrow Wilson International Centre for Scholars in Washington, DC.*

DOI: 10.1177/0002716213508913

now almost endemic as a feature of the national landscape; in the quality of judicial appointments to the Constitutional Court and other courts; in the declining capacity of the state in many (not all) departments; in the state of governance and performance in a large number of the country's parastatal organizations; and in the pervasiveness of corruption at the very heart of the government and the ruling party as well as within the private sector. This is to name only a few areas of concern; unfortunately, there are many more.

Democratic South Africa was never going to be an easy country to govern. Visionary leadership was required to end apartheid and its horrendous sins. A different kind of bold leadership is needed to govern a country with such a history and with the enormous diversity of race, class, ethnicity, expectations, and opportunities.

At the root of South Africa's current challenges lies the nature and composition of the ruling alliance. Their overwhelming predominance in South African politics until now has enabled many potentially divisive issues to be put on the back burner or ignored. Until the financial crisis of 2008, South Africa was able to muddle through. Strong and effective fiscal policies and discipline coupled with a positive world economic climate enabled the country to redistribute a lot of resources, encourage some growth in a few sectors of the economy, ensure some measure of progress, and avoid the global commodity boom without too severe a cost. But even without the financial crisis and prolonged austerity among South Africa's leading trading partners in the West, the muddling-through model began to falter badly after 2008. The time for choices by the ruling party loomed ever more strongly.

For South Africa to prosper, to build on all its citizens' skills and talents and provide hope for the vast majority of its people, some vital and hard choices need to be made. A new direction is essential if the country is to move out of what is now increasingly a situation of policy paralysis and decline. These kinds of circumstances are dangerous for any country and particularly in the still-divided realities of South Africa. What is needed is leadership: the kind of quietly confident but effective leadership that can move a democracy forward; a group of leaders who know the direction in which South Africa must move if it is to succeed as an increasingly prosperous, inclusive, and democratic country. Leaders will be needed who have the political will and understanding to build coalitions for fundamental policy change, isolate their opponents, and appoint teams of people who can mastermind effective implementation of new approaches and initiatives. Doing so will require breaking the current bounds of our political and ideological straitjackets. This article illustrates the tough choices regarding economic growth, youth unemployment, immigration policy toward skilled workers, and educational quality that the country has to make.

---

NOTE: This article is based on numerous speeches and articles by the author. All of them arose from policy research, workshops, and publications of the Centre for Development and Enterprise (CDE), South Africa. Much of this work has been done collectively with CDE staff, consultants, and other South Africans.

First and foremost, contemporary South Africa does not have an agreed-upon approach to economic growth. The cabinet reflects different points of view on how to achieve growth, with the result being that the country's economy is stagnating, if not declining. High growth rates are unachievable in part because the economy is dominated by large firms and trade unions in such a way that the growth of smaller firms is inhibited, as is the informal sector. Hence, the nation's overall employment potential is severely limited. The returns from what economic growth is achieved disproportionately favor the organized, the educated, the highly skilled, and the well connected.

At the core of the new direction that South Africa needs to take is a recognition that without higher—and more labor-intensive—growth, the country is heading for big trouble. Extremely high levels of unemployment, particularly among young people, combined with persistent poverty, make addressing growth and labor intensity of particular urgency. The most fundamental choices South Africa needs to make concern the requirements for achieving higher growth and ensuring that jobs become available for young people. These include decisions regarding labor market reform and labor-intensive manufacturing, with a particular focus on lowering the cost of low-skilled employment. South Africa also needs to find a way to ensure that some of the manufacturing jobs currently leaving China come to South Africa and, if necessary, as a means of demonstrating the dramatic and positive effect of changes to the labor market, employing the potential of special economic zones (SEZs) to their full advantage.

The second fundamental area in which tough choices need to be made is education, which is essential for the country, for economic growth, and to create an environment of true empowerment and hope for young people. Key decisions relate to the extent to which South Africa draws on the dynamism of private actors (from profit-driven entrepreneurs to nonprofit NGOs and others) and increased competition among different types of schooling and training providers to strengthen the quality of educational provision at all levels, as well as in training a significantly larger number of teachers (who would then be subject to performance management).

Linking the challenges faced in pursuing faster and more labor-intensive growth, and in reforming the educational system, is the role played by the trade unions, especially those that form part of Cosatu (the Congress of South African Trade Unions), the ANC's tripartite alliance partner. While trade unions are not the only barrier to addressing these issues, defining and enforcing a new deal with the trade unions will be absolutely essential to fundamental and large-scale progress in either area.

A third area in which tough choices must be made urgently concerns how to address South Africa's skills shortage in the short term. A large number of skilled people are needed in a whole range of areas, making a fundamental shift in migration policy vital. South Africa needs an unambiguous, energetic, and proactive approach that will bring skilled people into the country—and what better time than now, with austerity throughout Europe, and uncertainty in many other countries?

These few examples, although critical, are only a subset of the wide range of tough choices that South Africa needs to make. Other important areas include land reform (see Centre for Development and Enterprise [CDE; 2008a, 2008b, 2005] for more information), health care (see CDE [2011b] for more information), the criminal justice system, local government policy, and building an effective state.

At first glance, the 2012 National Development Plan (NDP) appears to provide the kind of new direction called for in South Africa (National Planning Commission 2012). On closer inspection, however, the plan is only a modest and somewhat ambiguous achievement. Although the NDP correctly identifies some of the tough choices South Africa needs to make, it nonetheless conflicts with many other government policy documents and, indeed, with new government policies being proposed.

As one example, the NDP is presented as following on from the Department of Trade and Industry's 2010/2011 Industrial Policy Action Plan (IPAP),[1] and the Economic Development Department's 2010 New Growth Path (NGP) (Department of Trade and Industry 2012; Economic Development Department 2010). In terms of outcomes, all three policies are in broad agreement—South Africa urgently needs to create a large number of jobs. There is far less agreement, however, on how to achieve this.

The primary difference between the NDP, NGP, and IPAP is in the characterization of the trajectory of the South African economy and in the identification of the binding constraints on further development—and by extension, the identification of the economic sectors and activities, and the characteristics of firms, that have the potential to create new jobs. For example, the NDP identifies the South African financial sector as one of the country's key competitive arenas, while IPAP identifies misallocation of resources by a malfunctioning financial sector as a constraint on growth. IPAP and the NGP also argue that South Africa suffers due to an overvalued rand, while the NDP says only that the country should guard against overvaluing the currency through the prudent accumulation of reserves. In addition, the IPAP and the NGP see the principal constraints to South African growth in the macroeconomy (and specifically, in its volatile and overvalued exchange rate and high real interest rates), while for the NDP, the macro constraints are less significant and the key answer lies in the microeconomy.

Although all three policy documents recognize employment creation as a primary aim, there is no agreement on where and how these jobs will be created, and how many. IPAP states that its interventions will result in the creation of 350,000 jobs by 2020 (with another 2.5 million being created indirectly) and that manufacturing will be the driver. The NGP states that if its policy recommendations are followed, 5 million jobs will be created by 2020, primarily in infrastructure, the productive sectors, the new economy, and the so-called social economy. The NDP provides a jobs target of 5.9 million by 2030. It believes that 90 percent of these jobs will be created in the services sector.

These three strategy documents have different perspectives on the trajectory of South Africa's economic growth, on the constraints that confront employment growth, and on where the new jobs will be created. Until the government is able to take a clear and consistent position on these critical issues, a coherent and effective growth policy remains unlikely.

These types of inconsistencies are not limited to these national strategy documents but are also evident in respect to government legislation. For example, in early 2013, controversy emerged about the clear conflict between the NDP's stated aims with regard to the support of small and medium enterprises (SMEs) and the draft Business Licensing Bill released in March 2013. The draft Licensing Bill would have required all businesses to obtain licenses from their municipalities, in addition to all current registration requirements, adding substantially to the already onerous administrative requirements faced by small businesses, as well as greatly increasing the scope for corruption. In addition, concerns were raised that the bill was designed to alleviate perceived "unfair" competition from foreigners, and the associated xenophobic attacks on these foreigners. It was feared that local-level decision-makers would face substantial pressure to discriminate against foreign applicants, making it substantially more difficult for them to succeed as entrepreneurs. In response to widespread criticism of the bill, largely focused on the extent to which it would increase the obstacles already faced by the SME sector, it was redrafted in mid-2013.

At the highest levels of government—within cabinet, as well as within the tripartite alliance—there remains a difference of opinion about what path South Africa should pursue. Until this lack of commitment is addressed through strong and clear leadership, progress is unlikely and South Africa will remain in deep trouble.

This article provides empirical information about the critical challenges South Africa faces and highlights tough choices that need to be made, focusing primarily on growth and unemployment (including of skilled migrants), and on education. Throughout, I highlight ways in which states and markets can be harnessed to ensure that the country makes far better progress than hitherto in addressing these vital challenges. These are not the only challenges South Africa faces, but they are at the core of the country's difficulties, and unless they are addressed successfully, dealing with many of the other challenges will become more and more difficult. Although the state has an essential role to play in providing a secure and stable operating environment, direct solutions to these major challenges are going to be addressed best by allowing market forces and entrepreneurs to play a large role.

## The Challenge of Growth and Unemployment in South Africa

Slow growth and enormously high unemployment combine to form one of South Africa's most destructive challenges. In this section, I describe the nature and extent of this challenge, particularly around youth unemployment, and focus on a range of policy decisions that South Africa could make to address these problems. The policy decisions include reforming the labor market and recognizing that a poorly paid job is still better than unemployment, allowing labor brokers and a youth wage subsidy to support higher levels of youth employment, ensuring that welfare plays an appropriate role to support higher levels of employment, opening up South Africa's borders to skilled immigrants in response to the massive skills shortage, and making use of experimentation and competition to develop genuinely special SEZs.

## Understanding unemployment in South Africa

The first set of tough choices relates to labor-intensive economic growth and employment. In 2013, South Africa had a working-age population (16 to 65) of 33 million people, of whom 18 million (55 percent) were either employed or actively seeking work (Statistics South Africa [Stats SA] 2013a). Employment has risen since 2001, peaking at 13.7 million in 2008 (before the global recession), and now hovering at around 13.4 million. Unemployment, narrowly defined, is around 25 percent (CDE 2013d). The broad rate of unemployment, including those wanting work but not actively seeking it, was closer to 35 percent in 2013 (Stats SA 2013a). The unemployment rate reflects very slow economic growth, and the unusually rapid pace of job destruction during the global recession (CDE 2013d).

Youth unemployment is a particular challenge for South Africa. The 2011 census confirmed that South Africa is a young country—half the population is younger than 25 and two-thirds are under the age of 35. This could be a great asset if properly harnessed for development, but it could become a source of potential destabilization under conditions of rampant unemployment—and youth unemployment in South Africa is at a crisis level (National Planning Commission 2012, 28–29). According to the National Treasury, the unemployment rate among people under the age of 25 who want work is about 50 percent (National Treasury 2011a, 40). Of the 9 million South Africans between the ages of 15 and 25, as many as 3.2 million are unemployed (CDE 2012a).

The main reason for large-scale youth unemployment is the slow pace of job creation in South Africa over the past few decades. The Labour Force Survey indicates that 85 percent of all unemployed respondents said that they were unemployed because they had not been able to find any work. The structure of the South African economy has also changed over the past 20 years, with the most important change being the rapid rise in employment in financial services since the late 1990s and, more recently, in community, social, and personal services. By contrast, over the same period there has been a fall in employment in manufacturing and construction, following on from a sharp, earlier decrease in jobs in the labor-intensive agricultural and mining sectors. These trends have driven and reflect a shift toward a more capital- and skills-intensive economy, with fewer new low-skill jobs being created. In the context of a poorly performing education system, this trend has exacerbated the challenge young people face in finding work. The declining proportion of employment provided by small firms, which tend to pay lower wages but are more likely to hire younger and less experienced workers, has also reduced labor-market opportunities for this group. Levels of self-employment in South Africa are also extremely low by international standards (SAPA 2012).

The weak South African educational system is another major reason that many young people struggle to find employment. The next section explores ways to address the issues in the educational system, but it is important to note here that young people who live in poor neighborhoods with bad schools and little support struggle to access appropriate training opportunities to either improve their employability or set up their own businesses. They have no clear idea how to look for what jobs are available. Many have little or no access to social networks that could link them to job opportunities, partly because many have parents who have themselves been unemployed for substantial periods of time. A growing number of young people are living in environments of multigenerational unemployment. Unemployment at an early age often scars people for life. Young people who are forced to remain jobless for long periods are deprived of on-the-job learning, leaving them with a skills deficit that many will never be able to remedy (World Bank 2007, 99; National Treasury 2011b, 42).

While the unemployed find it difficult to obtain work, employers, on the other hand, often struggle to determine which of the (often numerous) applicants for a particular job is most suitable for the position. As average starting wages and other employment costs are high, and because dismissal and replacement procedures can be onerous, employers tend to see the employment decision as risky, and may be reluctant to employ unskilled, inexperienced people. This is a particular challenge when hiring young people—especially those who have never worked before—and it is compounded by the fact that employers do not regard the qualifications and results achieved by many school-leavers as a reliable signal of the relative merits of job-seekers.

To manage their risks, employers tend to favor those who have been referred by someone working in the business already. They will also usually hire someone with work experience before they hire someone without this experience. In this context, poorly educated young people with no previous work experience and with little connection to the job market through friends and relatives are least likely to find work. Within this group, women have a harder time than men (CDE 2012e).

Employment is vital for South Africa's social, economic, and political development. It is the key mechanism for addressing mass poverty. In addition, many other benefits flow from higher levels of employment. Many of the skills needed to improve a worker's employability—punctuality, discipline, the ability to work with others, and so on—are most easily acquired on the job. This is especially important in South Africa, given low initial skill levels.

The experience of Brazil is instructive. Progress in that country shows that once people are employed, their prospects change quite dramatically, significantly reducing poverty and turning the tide on inequality (CDE 2012d). It also shows that expanding employment numbers can be achieved in a reasonably short period and without fixing everything in a society simultaneously. For example, Brazil's lower middle class has grown by nearly 40 million people in the past

10 to 15 years, and the whole middle class has grown by about 49 million people during the past 15 years. Labor income represents roughly 76 percent of household income, with little variation across income groups. It is likely that improved employment opportunities have made the biggest contribution to getting Brazilians into middle-class income categories. A core reason for improved labor incomes in Brazil is the expansion of economic opportunities for the poor, primarily as a direct result of the economic growth that Brazil has achieved over the past 15 years (CDE 2012d, 2013d).

The very limited employment gains that South Africa has attained to date are largely due to increased state expenditure, which is unsustainable. Sustained employment gains depend on faster economic growth. However, the relationship between economic growth and employment growth in South Africa has weakened over time. In the 1970s, a percentage point of economic growth raised the number of people in jobs by a similar amount. Over the past decade, each percentage point of growth has increased employment by less than 0.4 percent (CDE 2011a). The reasons for this decline are complex but can partly be attributed to rising wages and increased labor market regulations, which have made employers more reluctant to hire workers, particularly those who are young and unskilled. Employers, who might be willing to incur the costs of employing highly productive workers with significant skills, are much more reluctant to do so for workers whose lack of skills and experience mean they will be less productive. This is a key reason why so many young, unskilled, and inexperienced workers are unable to find work.

Unless the employment intensity of growth increases, even very rapid growth will have to be sustained for many years if South Africa is to raise its employment rate to international levels. Unless current trends change, the South African economy is unlikely to generate a significant number of new jobs in the near future, especially not the unskilled jobs that the bulk of the unemployed have a reasonable prospect of securing. While not the sole cause of these trends, South Africa's labor market regime is a key contributor to them.

South African labor market policy has tended to focus on ensuring "decent jobs," unfortunately at the cost of creating jobs at the lower levels. It favors "insiders"—members of established unions and bigger businesses—over "outsiders"—lower-skilled workers in smaller firms and the unemployed.

A case that highlights this challenge has been the conflict over the extension of bargaining council wage agreements to low-cost clothing manufacturers in Newcastle, KwaZulu-Natal (CDE 2013c). Approximately 450 firms, employing some 16,700 workers, came under fire from the National Bargaining Council for the Clothing Manufacturing Industry (NBC) in 2010 for their failure to pay workers at the levels agreed to by the NBC, despite the fact that these firms were not party to the NBC—and despite the fact that paying these higher wages would have forced some of the companies to close and would have led to large-scale job loss. Although the court found in favor of the firms in March 2013, this was a narrow judgment, and the battle seems set to continue.

The Newcastle case shows how, under the guise of promoting "decent work" and the supposed leveling of the playing field for producers, an unholy coalition of a trade union, some employers, and the state can initiate and drive a process of structural adjustment that undermines labor-intensive employment and exports South African jobs to lower wage countries such as Lesotho and China.

South Africa today faces a simple question: Is it better to have a relatively small number of people working at increasingly skilled jobs with good pay and a third of the labor force unemployed, as is currently the case (Stats SA 2013b)?[2] Or would it be better to have as many people as possible employed, even if many of those jobs are—at least initially—poorly paid? Newcastle's noncompliant firms represent the last labor-intensive manufacturing sector in South Africa, and their fate draws attention to the role of labor market institutions and policies in determining the viability of labor-intensive manufacturing in South Africa.

## Labor market reform

South Africa's constitution and labor legislation protect the right to form unions and strike, provide guaranteed minimum conditions of employment, promote redress for historical inequality of opportunity, and finance some skills development and training institutions (CDE 2013d).[3] These are supported by a broad and diverse set of mechanisms and institutions, including bargaining councils responsible for determining conditions of employment among groups of employers, sectoral determinations that shape employment conditions in entire sectors of the economy, and an employment mediation commission responsible for the resolution of employment related conflicts. Because of these conditions, South African labor legislation has the unintended effect of driving up the cost of labor relative to capital, contributing to high unemployment, particularly among the unskilled. This is reinforced by South Africa's approach to industrial development, which has tended to target incentives and subsidies at relatively capital- and skill-intensive industries, sectors, and firms (CDE 2013d).

International surveys, such as the World Economic Forum's *Global Competiveness Report 2012–2013*, suggest that South African labor market institutions perform poorly with regard to cooperation between employers and employees, the flexibility of wage determination, the nature of the rules governing hiring and firing, and the link between pay and productivity. Countries such as Brazil and Malaysia, which have achieved rapid job creation, have typically performed much better in these areas. For example, despite an otherwise byzantine maze of regulation, Brazilian employers can hire and fire at will, which allows their labor market to perform more efficiently and increases labor intensity. By keeping the labor market tight, it also ensures that wages rise with productivity gains (CDE 2013d).

Keeping labor costs from growing creates jobs for less skilled workers. Malaysian labor market policies, which contained wage costs, limited collective rights, and entrenched significant management prerogatives, helped to produce rapid economic and employment growth. Experience in Asia and elsewhere shows that once high levels of employment have been reached, wages begin to rise for a variety of reasons including the tightening of the labor market, increasing endowments of human capital, rising productivity, and firms' moving into markets for more sophisticated goods and services. Together, these processes lead to a rapid rise in workers' incomes and quality of life. It also leads to much higher rates of growth for the economy as a whole.

The gap between the poor productivity of young, unskilled, inexperienced workers in South Africa and their employment costs needs to be addressed. This requires a fundamental reexamination of the labor market regime, with a view to facilitate the emergence of lower-wage industries and businesses that have enabled other countries to drive high and sustained rates of economic growth, and employ a very large number of people. These strategies will create opportunities for unskilled and inexperienced people who would not expect to find jobs in existing industries and firms. Without the development of low-wage companies, South Africa will not be able to create the millions of jobs it needs, or achieve higher rates of economic growth. As small businesses are more likely to hire employees with lower skill levels, fixing the regulatory environment that hampers small business development (such as taxation and business registration) is also essential.

A number of assumptions currently inform official approaches to South Africa's economy growth. At the core of the official approach is the idea that the country needs to move up the value chain, as reflected in the NDP (National Planning Commission 2012, 115). However, if it is to have a more employment-intensive growth path, South Africa also needs to rethink the assumptions that the country should move progressively up the value chain, producing export goods with skilled labor and advanced technology rather than emphasizing goods made by a large number of unskilled workers. Given the low skills and inexperience of most unemployed people, this skills-intensive approach will never create enough jobs. Instead, South Africa should find and fill niches in the global supply chain for goods produced with more basic technology and relatively low-skilled workers.

The imperative to reform the South African labor market derives from our massive unemployment rates, our very low levels of new firm creation, and relatively low levels of investment (foreign and domestic). CDE research has estimated that for South Africa to get close to international levels of employment, about 6 million more jobs are needed immediately (CDE 2011a). Achieving this, even over a longer timeframe, requires government to make policy decisions, and then act decisively to implement them. However, current assumptions about growth, the current role of the unions in the tripartite alliance, and the general approach to small business mean that action is blocked. While these persist, national interests will continue to be subjugated to the interests of organized labor.

Although labor market reform will go a long way to addressing unemployment in South Africa, successfully reducing youth unemployment is likely to require additional, more targeted action.

## Youth unemployment

If South Africa cannot create 6 million jobs in the short term—and the truth is that the country cannot—it should focus on its young people. Young people are the quickest learners. Skills acquired in youth are ingrained in ways that later training battles to replicate. Increasing wage employment in the economy as a whole, which depends on sustained, high economic growth and labor market reform, will increase employment opportunities for young people. In the shorter term, however, more targeted interventions are also necessary.

Effective and efficient mechanisms to link job-seekers to jobs are essential. Particular attention should be paid to ensuring that mechanisms exist to help workers who are least connected to the labor market. Young people with no work experience who come from households in which no one works have a very slim chance of finding a job unless they are assisted in some way. CDE research has pointed to the importance of large, well-established "labor broking" firms, or Temporary Employment Services (TES), in helping "outsiders" to gain a foothold in the world of work, albeit in temporary forms of employment. Labor broking involves outsourcing the hiring of casual labor to a third party—a TES firm—which is responsible for all aspects of a worker's employment, right from initial interviews through to payment. One large TES, Adcorp, places more than twenty-five thousand assignees per day, although many of these are repeat placements (CDE 2012e). Of course, many more people still find jobs through other means, but this is a significant figure nonetheless.

CDE found that government programs such as the National Youth Development Agency's Jobs and Opportunities Seekers' Database (JOBS) placement program (although operating at a small scale) are also helping young people to find suitable forms of employment. People placed in jobs through TES or the JOBS program did not seem to be placed in undesirable jobs, nor were their wages significantly lower than average. TES firms may help to bring excluded households and workers into the economy, making the economy more inclusive.

Despite the evidence for the beneficial role these firms play in the labor market, and particularly for those most excluded from the formal labor market, South Africa has seen extensive opposition to the practice of labor broking. This opposition has been led by Cosatu, which has framed labor broking as akin to human trafficking. Using its close relationship to government, Cosatu has pressured for changes to South African labor legislation to bar labor broking. Although a complete ban on labor broking seemed unlikely in 2013, Parliament does seem likely to limit the duration of employment through labor broking to only three months. Whether this period would provide inexperienced and unskilled workers with sufficient time to develop the kinds of skills that they need to secure permanent employment is unclear. In the South African context of high unemployment combined with low levels of skill and experience, attacking labor broking is counterproductive, and genuinely harmful to the opportunities of the young and unemployed. Cosatu's opposition to the practice stems more from perceived threats to the status of the permanently employed, than from genuine concern about the unemployed. Rather than continuing to allow policy to be shaped by "insiders"— members of established unions and bigger businesses—at the cost of "outsiders"—lower-skilled workers in smaller firms and the unemployed—the South African government needs to take a stand and ensure that policy begins to protect the outsiders.

Another initiative, initially proposed by international advisers to the National Treasury and now a formal proposal from the minister of finance, is to introduce a wage subsidy or employment incentive for young workers (National Treasury 2011a). The logic of this idea is that employers will be encouraged to employ more young and inexperienced workers if the costs of doing so are subsidized. This could also help to reduce the gap between what employers can pay and what young workers hope to earn, thereby getting young people into work while providing them with the pay level they see as necessary to move out of dependence and into adulthood. This will also help young people to gain skills that will raise their productivity. Unfortunately, this proposal has also attracted strong opposition from Cosatu, as well as parts of the ANC, due to concerns that firms may choose to substitute older and more expensive employees with subsidized youth. Although the evidence indicates that in the South African context this is unlikely to happen at substantial levels, and although policy design further reduces this effect, opposition has continued unabated. Although the policy now looks likely to be adopted despite opposition, this comes after a delay of more than three years since President Zuma formally announced the policy. This is another example of labor market insiders—the unions—being allowed by government to shape policy in ways that protect the insiders' interests at the cost of the young and unemployed.

Youth unemployment requires urgent attention, but addressing the issue depends on South Africa being able to stand up for the rights of labor market outsiders and to start to dismantle the barriers to their ever entering the labor market. Decisions need to be taken about facilitating and promoting the growth of low wage industry; supporting job placement services; and subsidizing the employment of the young, inexperienced, and poorly skilled. Employing young people needs to be made easier, less risky, and cheaper. A determined new approach is essential to generating the millions of jobs that South Africa needs, and this approach requires government to stand up to the labor unions and ensure that a new deal is reached with them. As long as the unions continue to hold excessive sway over government, the rights of outsiders will continue to be sacrificed for the rights of labor market insiders. Government must begin to stand up for the outsiders, particularly the young.

## The role of welfare

A well-designed welfare system is another critical component in ensuring that labor market outsiders have both the means, and the motivation, to participate in the formal labor market. South Africa has an extensive, and growing, welfare system. In the 2012/13 financial year, the system cost the government R112.2 billion, which is anticipated to rise to R130 billion in 2014/15 (National Treasury 2013). The previous governor of the Reserve Bank declared this ever expanding welfare bill to be "unsustainable" (Visser 2013). The most widely used social grants in 2012/13 were the child support grant (11.4 million beneficiaries), the old age grant (2.9 million), and the disability grant (1.2 million). The child support grant has grown fastest, rising by 21 percent since 2009/10.

The total number of people now benefiting from social grants in South Africa is 16.2 million, or nearly a third of the population (National Treasury 2013). Indeed, for every 100 people receiving some form of social welfare from the government, there were only 90 employed people (South African Institute of Race Relations 2013).

Evidence from South Africa and abroad indicates that effective social safety nets can make beneficiaries more reluctant to work, leading to claims that the rapidly expanding welfare state (including welfare grants, subsidies for housing, and basic services among others) may be one reason for South Africa's low labor force participation rate. However, the relationship between welfare and unemployment in South Africa is complicated. For example, labor force participation rates were lower in the mid-1990s when South Africa had a far less comprehensive or generous welfare system (CDE 2011a). Access to child support grants might also make it easier for women to leave their children with caregivers and look for jobs, and have been associated with increased labor force participation (CDE 2011a). In addition, working-age men are unlikely to be discouraged from labor market participation by the current welfare system, as they receive no direct state support in any form.

South Africa's welfare programs constitute slightly more than 4 percent of GDP, which places them among the most generous of all developing countries. By contrast, at only 2 percent of GDP, Brazil's welfare payments illustrate that, to be successful, welfare should constitute only a small part of the national budget and be accompanied by an expansion of economic opportunities accessible to the poor. Coupled with an innovative approach to welfare, Brazilians have focused on what they call "productive inclusion"—developing the economy to create income-generating opportunities for poorer and less skilled people (CDE 2012d). Despite South Africa's high, increasingly unsustainable, payments, a very large number of poor people—approximately 45 percent of the population (using a standard $45 per month poverty line)—remain trapped in poverty, without much hope (Bhorat 2013). With very poor education and a capital-intensive economy the vast majority cannot access wage or other income earning opportunities. They therefore remain dependent on the state indefinitely. South Africa will have to make difficult decisions about the balance between the cost of the welfare system and supporting a genuine opening up of economic opportunities to the poor.

## Competition and experimentation: SEZs

SEZs provide another opportunity to increase economic growth, and open up employment opportunities to the unskilled and inexperienced (CDE 2012f). SEZs are specially demarcated geographic areas in which some aspect of the business environment, whether the quality of the infrastructure or the regulatory regime, differs from the norms prevailing in the rest of the country.

Globally, there are currently about three thousand SEZs in operation, spread across 135 countries, and accounting for 68 million direct jobs and $500 billion in trade-related value added (CDE 2012f). SEZs have proven to be a remarkable tool for growth and job creation around the world. The classic example of successful SEZs are those established on China's east coast in the 1980s, which aimed to attract foreign investors who could not penetrate China's closed economy. By offering a radically different investment regime, including strong property rights and freedom to repatriate profits, SEZs encouraged investors to build factories and draw on China's huge labor force, global markets, and impressive infrastructure. Vast investment flows led to massive employment growth. The result has been the most dramatic emergence from poverty in human history. The role of SEZs in Mauritius, Costa Rica, the Philippines, Malaysia, Honduras, and elsewhere has also been impressive, albeit on smaller scale (CDE 2012f).

But not all SEZs are successful. By far the most important reason for this is that many SEZs are not special enough, and fail to make themselves globally competitive in attracting investment. South Africa's three current Industrial Development Zones (IDZs) are examples of this failure. Even the government now acknowledges that they have failed. Investment levels have been low, the number of permanent jobs created small, and many firms located in the zones simply relocated from elsewhere in the country, rather than representing new investment. The same holds true for the five thousand jobs the IDZs account for (Bernstein and Altbeker 2012).

Government is currently drafting legislation to reform the IDZs and establish SEZs; expand their number; and relaunch them as platforms of industrial development, diversification, export growth, and job creation. If this strategy is to succeed, a very different approach is needed this time around. South Africa needs to learn from the IDZ failings and the international experience of success. South Africa should use SEZs to create the kind of environment that will support the emergence of businesses that can employ a large number of unskilled people. Successful SEZs can lead to millions of new jobs, catapult countries out of poverty, and completely transform economies.

South Africa should establish at least two large SEZs focused on low-skill, labor-intensive industries as a matter of national priority. The top priority for South Africa's SEZ program should be to establish zones in which it is considerably easier to establish and run globally competitive businesses—particularly labor-intensive businesses—than it is elsewhere in the economy. These "zones of exception" must be distinct from the rest of the economy, with different economic rules. This approach should be coupled with the use of SEZs as a testing ground for new policy options. Locating such experiments in separate enclaves would allow government to reduce or avoid confrontations with entrenched interest groups opposed to wider reforms. Should these experiments succeed, these approaches could be rolled out to the rest of the economy.

Any new SEZs in South Africa will need to be globally competitive if they are to succeed. They must offer a business proposition that encourages investment and expansion. Exactly how this should be done will depend on the targeted industry or sector, which means that consultation with private investors is essential. Current economic policy is skewed toward high-skill and high-wage methods of production, which do not address the core reasons for South Africa's unemployment crisis. A paradigm shift is required. A new policy instrument such as well-designed SEZs might help to move the country forward from its present impasse. SEZs are a key platform for export-oriented industries, contributing significantly to global trade, attracting vast flows of foreign direct investment, and employing millions of people; South Africa needs to seize such an opportunity to address slow growth and unemployment. South Africa must use SEZs strategically to address the constraints faced by potential employers of unskilled labor. South Africa's SEZs should ensure low labor costs, create more flexible employment relationships, provide efficient access to international markets, ensure easy access to skills, and offer credible guarantees that SEZ policies will be sustained in the medium and long term. International experience also shows that the "demonstration effect" of successful SEZs facilitates wider economic reform, as has been evident in China, Mauritius, Costa Rica, the Philippines, and elsewhere (CDE 2012f).

South Africa needs to experiment with different types of SEZs, and the government needs to make tough choices, overruling vested interests that have so far prevented policy experimentation in SEZs.

### Skills and skilled immigrants

Paradoxically, given the high unemployment rate, South Africa suffers from a serious shortage of skills. Although the policy reforms and changes outlined above—labor market reform, targeted efforts to reduce youth unemployment, building a sustainable welfare system that expands economic opportunities for the poor, and using SEZs—will all contribute to lower levels of unemployment and a more effective and functional labor market, and although the educational reforms discussed in the next section will improve skills supply over the longer term, together they do not address the challenges South African employers face in finding skilled employees in the short term.

Despite the high overall levels of unemployment described previously, unemployment levels for skilled South Africans are extremely low. Among university graduates, in particular, unemployment levels were just under 5 percent in 2011 (CDE 2013b). Black graduates now make up half of all graduates in the labor force—some 600,000—and while they remain somewhat more likely to be unemployed than white graduates, their unemployment rate, at 6.7 percent, is also extremely low (CDE 2013b). Although we do not have information about the quality of the jobs these graduates are obtaining, these data nonetheless provide clear evidence that South Africa's employers are desperate for skills. They also dispel the myth that employers are racist and that black graduates are struggling to find work in South Africa.

There is also substantial evidence that the supply of South African graduates is insufficient to meet the country's current need for skills. Accurate, recent figures on South Africa's skills shortage are extremely hard to ascertain. Estimates indicate that South Africa needs 6,000 more civil engineers just to manage existing infrastructure programs and 22,000 more accountants, book-keepers, and similar professionals (CDE 2010b). Simultaneously, between 1994 and 2006, the number of teachers qualifying in South Africa fell from 70,000 per year to 6,000 (in 2013, to slightly over 9,000), a third of whom do not intend to teach in South Africa; and between 1994 and 2003, South Africa lost about 120,000 qualified professionals to emigration, with the annual number thought to be rising rapidly every year since then. In addition, the World Bank estimates that South Africa has 70 percent fewer researchers per capita than the global norm, and 40 percent fewer than Brazil. These figures all suggest that South Africa's current skills deficit is probably larger than the 502,000 reported in the Department of Labour's National Scarce Skills List for 2008 (CDE 2010b).

Until this critical skills shortage is addressed, South Africa will continue to struggle to attain the level of growth it needs. The long-term solution is obviously to overhaul and improve the country's educational sector, but in the short term South Africa should look to import skills from abroad. South Africa's national interests lie in having a more open migration regime. While the government has been promising to improve the systems under which skilled immigrants enter the country since 2003, progress has not been made.

Since the immigration act was passed in 2002, South Africa's ability to exploit the global market in skills has been hampered by regulations that limit the number of skilled people who can enter the country. This limit is achieved through a cumbersome system of permits and quotas. A measure of the ineffectiveness of this system is that in 2008, the year in which the Department of Labour estimated skills shortages of over half a million, just over 36,000 quota permits were made available for skilled foreigners to enter the country without a job offer. Of these permits, only 1,133 were filled (CDE 2010b). The notion that the state can determine skills needs and provide for them via a quota system is misguided, as is the idea that South Africa needs to impose quotas on skilled immigrants to prevent the country from being flooded by unneeded engineers, doctors, and plumbers. In reality, South Africa needs to welcome, with a minimum of conditions, all skilled people who wish to immigrate. This should include people with entrepreneurial abilities, as well as skilled trainers and educators, all of whom could strengthen our domestic skills production system.

According to Reserve Bank Governor Gill Marcus, it is estimated that for each highly skilled immigrant who comes into the country, between four and eight low-skilled jobs are created (Marcus 2013). The notion of "skills" must be defined widely so that it includes anyone with formal tertiary qualifications from recognized institutions, as well as people with entrepreneurial ability, including proven smaller entrepreneurs. Given the large number of skilled emigrants leaving South Africa, the country is typically portrayed as a victim of the global labor market. Instead, South Africa must explore ways to use the global labor market for the country's benefit. South Africa can draw on the energetic and successful recruitment regimes of countries such as Germany, France, the United Kingdom, the Netherlands, Canada, Australia, and the Gulf states of the Middle East for inspiration. For example, in 2005 and 2006, 130,000 to 140,000 newcomers entered Australia each year, double the numbers of the mid-1990s (CDE 2010b).

Immigrants can spur growth by filling the skilled jobs that firms need to fill to expand; providing the entrepreneurial skills needed to start new businesses; and adding the education, training, engineering, medical, and other skills needed to improve service delivery. With smart leadership and policies that put South Africa first, the nation could reap enormous benefits from welcoming the brave, energetic, people—risk-takers—who choose to migrate to this country in search of a better life. A sensible and pragmatic approach to skilled migration will contribute to South African growth and economic success. The tough choice here is recognizing that high levels of skilled immigration, and by extension changes to South African immigration policy, are essential—despite being potentially unpopular.

# Education

South Africa has achieved real success in promoting access to schooling. The country now has one of the highest rates of access in the developing world, at 98 percent for primary school enrollment (CDE, forthcoming; Spaull, forthcoming; Simkins, forthcoming). The pressing issue is quality of schooling, particularly among poor learners, and in this regard South Africa is struggling badly. This section identifies some of the key challenges facing the South African educational system and identifies a number of policy options with the potential to help solve the crisis. There is particular focus on the potential role that private schooling has to play in strengthening educational quality and on developing a policy environment in which such schools can deliver on that promise. Strategies to attract, motivate, and retain teachers in the South African schooling system—for example, performance-linked pay—are also discussed, as is the importance of increasing the number of teachers South Africa produces, and the role that the private sector can play in this.

The South African education system is large and complex. In 2012 there were more than 12.4 million learners, almost 430,000 educators, and about twenty-six thousand schools in more than seventy districts in nine provinces (Department of Basic Education 2012). It is also very diverse, with huge differences within and among provinces, districts, and schools, and complicated by South Africa's legacy of apartheid and past and current issues of race and politics. South Africa is spending enough on education—5 to 6 percent of GDP—but while minimum levels of funding and resources are essential, they are not in themselves sufficient to transform a schooling system. Expenditure is poorly utilized, and management capacity is an enormous challenge. Effective administration of the very large public education bureaucracy, as well as bold and effective political leadership, will be essential for transformation. Success will require some tough choices.

## Education quality in South Africa

The poor performance of South Africa's educational system is widely recognized, with South African children performing near the bottom of all international measures. Trends in International Mathematics and Science Study (TIMSS) is a cross-national study that tests the mathematics and science knowledge of grade eight pupils in a variety of countries, providing the best opportunity to compare educational outcomes over the period 1995–2011. In South Africa, although math and science performance improved between 2002 and 2011, the overall postimprovement results are still the worst of all participating middle-income countries. The average South African grade nine pupil is two years' worth of learning behind the average grade eight pupil from twenty-one other middle-income countries in mathematics, and 2.8 years behind in science (Spaull, forthcoming). What is more, South African learners perform more poorly on these international tests than those in many low-income African countries such as Mozambique, Lesotho, and Tanzania (Spaull, forthcoming).

In 2013, CDE commissioned two independent, university-based studies of the state of South African schooling. Working separately, these studies arrived at similar conclusions: however one chooses to measure learner performance, and at whichever grade one chooses to test, the vast majority of South African pupils are significantly below where they should be in terms of the curriculum, and, more generally, they have not reached a host of normal numeracy and literacy milestones. Although there have been some improvements, as indicated by an increasing pass rate of the National Senior Certificate (NSC; a standardized exam taken by grade twelve pupils to graduate from high school, and informally known as the "matric" exam), the pass rate fails to address inaccuracies in evaluations or the high dropout rates before grade twelve: of one hundred pupils who start school, only fifty will make it to grade twelve, forty will pass, and only twelve will qualify for university (CDE, forthcoming; Spaull, forthcoming; Simkins, forthcoming).

The 2012 independently administered official Annual National Assessment (ANA) highlights that by grade nine, most pupils are very far behind, with an average mathematics score of just 13 percent. Only 8.1 percent of those tested achieved 30 percent and above, and only 2.2 percent achieved 50 percent and above. There are also vast inequalities within the educational system. The average grade nine pupil in the poorest 40 percent of South African schools is three years' worth of learning behind the average student in the most affluent 20 percent of schools in mathematics and four years behind in science. Provincially there is also a discernible variation, with the average pupil in the Eastern Cape being 2.2 years behind the average pupil in the Western Cape in mathematics and 3.2 years behind in science (Simkins, forthcoming).

The indicators of school performance in South Africa reflect a deep-rooted teaching incompetence in the great majority of schools, especially in mathematics. This incompetence will not quickly be remedied. Yet mathematics schooling is a key determining variable for entry into higher education and qualification for most types of modern, knowledge-intensive work. South Africa's ability to develop as a modern knowledge economy is dependent on improving basic literacy and numeracy, and the overall quality of the state's educational system. It is also essential to remedy youth unemployment and to ensure South Africa's ongoing stability.

A 2010 study on mathematics and science performance in South African schools commissioned by CDE, and based on comparative statistical analyses of

Senior Certificate and National Senior Certificate (NSC) results over the past decade, showed that the number of university entrance level passes in 2008 doubled over the previous year. However, many capable learners do not take subjects that qualify them for university entrance. For example, a full 40 percent of the ninety-five thousand learners capable of passing mathematics in 2008 did not write that subject—instead opting to study and be examined in the rather easier subject of mathematical literacy.[4] This, however, means that they do not qualify to study technical subjects at the university level.[5] This outcome means that about 40 percent of the potential of the South African schooling system to produce university entrance passes in mathematics and science is still being wasted. The study also found that half of university entrance level passes in mathematics are produced by only 6.6 percent of schools, and half of science passes by only 5.5 percent of schools. Thus, while some progress has been made with respect to mathematics and science, and should be acknowledged, some 90 percent of South African schools are still failing to meet minimum performance standards in these subjects (Simkins 2010).

The quality of teaching and teachers is a central determinant of student performance. Teacher quality cannot be reduced to formal qualifications, which often have little impact on student results. Many teachers, especially in mathematics and science, are not teaching well, partly because many of them have been badly trained. According to one official evaluation in 2010, only about a third of the institutions currently training teachers should qualify for accreditation (CDE 2011c). This result has grave implications for the quality of their graduates. Teachers are also often poorly utilized. For example, despite the shortage of mathematics teachers, many qualified mathematics teachers who want to teach mathematics are not currently doing so—they are teaching other subjects. Teacher absenteeism is a major problem, and teachers spend too little time in the classroom. Government studies have shown that many teachers often come late, leave early, and spend only 46 percent of their time teaching each week—hardly teaching at all on Fridays (CDE 2011c). South Africa is also producing too few teachers—only about a third of the twenty-five thousand new teachers the country needs every year (CDE 2011c).

In a context of poor-quality education, affordable private schools offer an alternative schooling option in poorer communities. A growing number of parents are looking for a different schooling ethos or for a better standard of schooling instruction (or both). Private schools play a vital role in addressing the issues of educational quality in South Africa, specifically private schools for the poor (which are a global phenomenon). "Edupreneurs" are emerging to meet local needs.

## Private schooling in South Africa

Internationally, between 1991 and 2003, the average growth in private primary education was 58 percent, compared with a 10 percent growth in the public primary school sector (CDE 2012b). In developing countries such as India, Pakistan, Chile, Ghana, Kenya, and Colombia, most of this expansion has been in private schools for the poor, which make schooling accessible for disadvantaged communities and marginalized groups (CDE 2013a). In South Africa, private schools have a long history, and they have grown in number since the transition to democracy. If private schools are registered and meet certain criteria, they are eligible for some subsidies from the state.

The emergence of private schooling for the poor in South Africa has been insufficiently recognized. Between 2008 and 2010, CDE surveyed and visited all the private schools in six high-poverty areas across three provinces (CDE 2010a). Principals and teachers were interviewed, grade six learners were assessed using a standardized test, and focus group sessions were conducted with parents. In the six areas that CDE surveyed, more than 30 percent of the schools were private—far more than the official national estimate for 2008 of 4.3 percent. Furthermore, in the period 1994 to 2009, more private schools were established than public schools.

There are strong indications that private schools are expanding at an accelerating rate, while the public school sector in South Africa is actually shrinking. Between 2000 and 2010 the number of public schools declined by 9 percent, while the number of known independent schools (albeit from a much smaller base) grew by 44 percent. There has also been a changing demographic and socioeconomic shift for those attending private schools in South Africa. In 2010, 72 percent of learners at private schools were black. Additionally, the majority of the private schools became mid- or low-fee (mid-fee schools charge between R10,500 and R30,500 per annum, and low-fee schools charge less than R10,500 per annum), making the schools accessible to a growing working and middle class (CDE 2013a).

CDE research focused on the lower-fee end of South African private schools. Researchers asked focus groups why parents elected to send their children to very-low-fee private schools, and even unregistered schools. Most parents explained that they chose these schools because they achieve better results and use English as the medium of instruction; paying school fees made these private schools more accountable to parents. Although varying in quality, the vast majority of these schools were valued by parents, accountable to those parents, staffed by dedicated teachers who often work for low salaries, and run by principals and owners determined to provide the quality of schooling sought by local people. Although teacher qualifications and salaries are generally lower in the private schools, so are levels of teacher absenteeism. As fee-payers, parents monitor the schools more closely and hold them accountable for delivery. Principals and teachers are always aware that parents will take their children to another school if they do not produce satisfactory results (CDE 2012b).

South African government policy has been progressively extending free schooling in the country. Although the initial goal was for 60 percent of South African public schools to be no-fee schools, this figure is now more than 80 percent. Almost 70 percent of South African learners now attend a no-fee school (South African Institute of Race Relations 2012, 450). The extent to which paying fees makes private schools accountable to parents raises the question of whether the extension of free schooling should be a policy priority. Rather than removing the leverage that parents gain from being customers of a school, it may be more beneficial to assist struggling families on an individual basis. If dissatisfied parents had the option of removing their children from public schools and enrolling them in low-fee private schools, it would act as a powerful incentive to principals and teachers in state schools to improve performance or face job losses—as long as state schools face financial and other penalties when parents vote with their feet by taking their children out.

Although public schools have played, and will continue to play, a key role in ensuring that all South African learners have access to schooling, they are not the only viable option for educating poorer people. Low-fee private schools should be seen as a vital part of the South African educational environment. It is in everyone's interest that the private schooling sector continue to expand, offering access to better quality schooling to as many South Africans as possible. Public policy should aim for three complementary outcomes: increasing the number of high-quality private schools to which poor children have access; widening educational choices for parents and learners in all communities; and ensuring that the regulatory environment is enabling and creates a level playing field on which both public and private schools can constantly strive to improve. The South African regulatory regime needs to be reassessed in light of these objectives. The government needs to be persuaded to act decisively to embrace private schools and create an environment in which schools of all types can improve.

## The policy environment for private schooling in South Africa

In South Africa, generally supportive foundational legislation has been eroded by ill-considered secondary legislation with which many private schools struggle to comply. Private schools have far more quality checks than public schools and have to deal with considerable red tape to qualify for state subsidies (CDE 2012b). Private schools charging high fees do not receive state subsidies, but the lowest-fee schools can receive to up to 60 percent of the average provincial cost per learner in ordinary public schools. This fee structure threatens the two pillars of private schools' survival: having enough independent "space" to follow their different missions and having sufficient resources to be viable.

This threat is compounded by poor policy implementation at lower levels of government. There are increasing reports of and investigations into significant delays in payment of subsidies, and of unexplained subsidy cuts (CDE 2013a). The policy environment seems to have become disabling for private schools, especially low-fee ones. It is in the public interest that private schools should meet reasonable registration conditions and be held accountable for public subsidies received. However, good results are not always dependent on state registration and certification: some low-fee private schools have unqualified teachers but achieve better results than equivalent, local, public schools. Competition is an important force for improving school performance. Creating a regulatory environment where competition motivates principals to improve and expand their schools should be seen as an effective and not very costly way of improving the quality of schooling.

There should be improved accountability for all schools, both public and private. To ensure that school choice exerts pressure on public and private schools to improve their performance, parents need credible information about the schools that they are considering. In this respect, South Africa's introduction of the Annual National Assessments (ANAs) is to be welcomed. An easily administered assessment system that involves parents in the assessment process, and applies to all schools, both public and private, is also required. Public schools need greater freedom to respond to competition from other schools, and schools that fail to respond to competition need to be penalized. Public schools that fail to produce results and attract learners should run the risk of closure.

A more supportive regulatory framework is essential. This could allow for a probationary period, with provisional registration, during which private schools can work toward compliance. An international trend worth noting is the movement toward more choice and delegated authority for quality assurance. For example, in the Philippines, an Accreditation Federation comprises different school accreditation boards. Each of these boards has to meet certain standards, after which they are allowed to accredit the schools under their jurisdiction (CDE 2012b). Public-private partnerships must also be developed. In some countries, special agencies can be created to manage private schools and manage the flow of funds from the government to privately run public schools, as well as to enforce qualifying criteria and regulations (CDE 2012b).

Finally, support for and investment in private schools, from all stakeholders, is critical. Public-private partnerships allow government, private philanthropists, corporations, financial institutions, and education specialists to support private schools. Private-sector organizations could establish a special loan facility at a favorable interest rate, and with a relatively lenient repayment schedule, which private schools could access with no or limited collateral. Private funders and experts could also explore and help to set up more efficient business models within the low-fee schooling sector. Parents and community organizations could become involved in effective advocacy. The country needs concerted and sustained pressure from all those interested in promoting school choice as a means of improving the quality of education available to the poor. A change of attitude is required if South Africa is fully to embrace the potential and dynamism of low-fee private schooling to provide choice where there is none, improve quality, and, through competition for scholars and funding, have a beneficial impact on public schools.

## Teacher pay for performance and training

In addition to creating an environment in which private schools can contribute to improved educational quality, sustained schooling reform also requires a new approach to the teaching profession. As indicated earlier, not only is there a shortage of teachers, but many South African teachers are not performing at a high enough level. According to a 2007 study, only 32 percent of grade six mathematics teachers have desirable levels of mathematics content knowledge. This is compared to the average of 42 percent across fourteen African countries (Spaull, forthcoming). Teacher training programs are not providing the knowledge needed for quality teaching. Based on a review of teacher educational programs by the Higher Education Quality Committee in 2007, only six of fifteen Bachelors of Education programs and seven of twenty-two Post Graduate Certificate in Education programs were deemed worthy of full accreditation (CDE 2011c).

Countries with effective high-performing school systems tend to value highly the importance of teachers, and in those countries teachers see themselves as professionals and behave accordingly. With up to a quarter of newly trained teachers not even taking up teaching posts in South Africa, special efforts are required to retain teachers, who have many other options in the economy and overseas. Despite perceptions among teachers and the general public that teachers are not paid well, research over the past decade confirms that teachers in South Africa are more than adequately paid compared to their international counterparts (CDE 2012g). However, when it comes to experience and years of tenure, teachers at the top end are underpaid, whereas teachers at the bottom end are overpaid, providing little incentive for teachers to perform.

A review of global evidence on teacher pay for performance commissioned by CDE in 2012 revealed an upsurge of interest in this topic in recent years. Globally, education systems are increasingly being held to account by their various stakeholders with regard to the cost of their inputs and the efficiency of their processes and outcomes. There is, therefore, a global swing in educational policy toward outcomes and outputs and away from input-based interventions, such as salaries traditionally based on qualification and years of service. Internationally, the results of pay-for-performance incentives schemes are variable but broadly positive, particularly in developing countries (CDE 2012g). The design of incentives is of paramount importance, with more sophisticated incentives that avoid perverse effects or shortcuts being more likely to achieve proven effects upon student scores.

In South Africa, a well-conceived and properly implemented pilot pay-for-performance experiment would go a long way toward establishing whether and how the country's exceptionally low learner achievement could be addressed using an incentive scheme. The potential benefits of a pilot study are many: not only would it provide a clearer idea of the size and form of incentives to be used and performance criteria, but it would give a clearer idea of the cost implications of a full-scale program and its possible relationship to other schooling reforms.

The design of pay-for-performance programs is an all-important consideration. Basic goals and criteria need to be clear and simple, and mechanisms need to be fair and credible. Special care needs to be taken with the issue of fairness: if only some teachers are eligible for incentives, it is important to ensure that this bias does not produce adverse effects of decreasing motivation and undermining collegiality in the teacher corps. Teachers, principals, and education officials all need to be incentivized, and the involvement of teachers' unions may be crucial to public sector implementation of such reforms. A new social compact will need to be negotiated by the government that ensures that the national interest in better performing schools trumps minority interests.

In addition to reforms in teacher remuneration, changes also need to be made in teacher training. The South African teacher training system needs to produce an additional fifteen thousand teachers per year. Although the government has increased its bursaries for student teachers in the past few years, the increase is insufficient to meet the country's needs. Too few candidate teachers are being trained in scarce subjects, such as mathematics, science, and African languages. This deficit can only be remedied by even more bursaries, and better and more diversified teacher training. South Africa cannot continue to rely solely on current predominantly public institutions to train more and better teachers (CDE 2011c).

Although the government has acknowledged that South Africa lacks a sufficient number of good teachers, and has begun initiatives to fill this gap, the public sector alone cannot address this national need with sufficient scale, quality, and speed. Public tertiary institutions are currently producing about one-third of the required number of new teachers. Additionally, given that only a small proportion of formally trained mathematics and science teachers can teach competently, there are concerns about quality control at the institutions that train them. South Africa cannot rely solely on these state institutions. A new response is required, drawing on the best of global experience as well as all the country's resources, both public and private. Teacher training and retraining should be opened up to market forces. Private players and public institutions should compete for public funds in the training arena.

Brazil provides a clear example of how successful this type of approach can be. In response to a rapidly increasing number of students in the early 1990s, Brazil reluctantly opened up its higher education sector to private providers. To date, approximately twenty-five hundred private higher education institutions have been created, and the private sector now accounts for three-quarters of higher education institutions. This growth came despite the fact that these institutions receive no significant government subsidies. Contrary to the fears of many Brazilian officials and experts, private providers have not lowered the standard of education. While there is variability across private institutions, private students fared as well as public students in assessments and perform well in national exams. The majority of the best one hundred institutions are now private. This approach enables Brazil to provide a far higher number of students with higher education at a reasonable cost (CDE 2012c). Such an approach, if well implemented, could enable South Africa to train a far greater number of highly skilled teachers.

To deliver on the promise of its constitution and to equip itself to face its economic challenges, South Africa has a vital interest in improving the quality of education generally and especially for poorer South Africans. The fundamentals of schooling reform are well known. The challenge is to take account of local context—politics, unions, and economics—and devise an effective approach that will deliver results. Teachers need to be in class, on time, and teaching, but words and intentions are not enough. Bold political leadership and a new social compact led by the state and involving principals, teachers, parents, and private donors on quality schooling are urgently required. The country needs firm resolve, as well as much better outcomes. Tough choices must be made—about allowing the private sector and competition to play a greater and more effective role in education delivery, ensuring that teacher pay and productivity are closely linked, and ensuring that national interests receive precedence over special interests.

# Conclusion

In this article, I have used some important examples to show why South Africa is in trouble. Dealing with the constraints to progress in these and other arenas of national development will require bold, democratic, and visionary leadership. South Africa needs leadership that sees a future built together with all the country's people, and using their talents, as well as recognizing that growth matters above all. Growth alone will not solve all South Africa's problems, but without it, it is hard to see how to govern this society and make the progress required to build a new South Africa that provides hope and trust across the country's many divides. Sustained growth, of the kind that South Africa requires, demands a new growth strategy, based on expanding opportunities, growing the economy, and using interim redistribution initiatives to help poor people access the economy and education. This departure from current practice will need to be supported by the development of a new political coalition around these goals and by the breaking up of the ruling tripartite alliance—which no longer makes any sense and often serves simply to block the decisive and directed action that is required to deal with poverty and unemployment. A successful South Africa requires a vision of the country firmly focused on the future; beyond race, and transcending the wounds of the past.

*To govern is to choose.* National interests now need to trump sectional interests. Visionary and cohesive leadership need to emerge that can see the hard choices that so urgently need to be made and can successfully build coalitions around these choices. The government has a primary responsibility to provide this leadership but is currently failing dismally in this regard. This failure does not let other leaders in our society off the hook, however. Business leaders, in particular, need to think hard about a strategic direction for the country, and how they can play a more strategic, more effective role in placing South Africa on a better path. The same goes for other interests and groups in civil society. Shouting louder can only take a society so far. Demanding that more money is spent is often counterproductive when value for money is far from being achieved. Demanding more and more from a weak, corrupt, and divided state is often not a compelling strategy.

The time for romanticism is over. The "people" comprise many different groups and interests. Organizations often represent small minorities with loud voices. Pragmatic and sober realism about the state of the nation, the power of markets and competition, and the hard choices that have to be made is now essential. South Africans 20 years after the introduction of democracy need to think anew about who speaks for the excluded, the poor, and the unemployed; and how best to build the inclusive society that will ensure a prosperous and stable democracy.

# Notes

1. A revised report is released every year.

2. According to the latest Quarterly Labour Force Survey released by Stats SA, the unemployment rate in South Africa in the first quarter of 2013 was 25.6 percent. However, if one had to include discouraged work-seekers (those who are willing to work, but have given up looking for a job), South Africa's unemployment rate is 34.1 percent, meaning a third of the labor force is unemployed.

3. Key legislation governing employment in South Africa includes the Labour Relations Act (1995), which protects the right of workers to form unions and to strike. It also established a number of key labor market institutions, such as the Commission for Conciliation, Mediation and Arbitration (CCMA), and a system of bargaining councils. The Basic Conditions of Employment Act (1997) sets out minimum standards for work, such as working hours and overtime, as well as leave and health and safety standards across the economy; the Employment Equity Act (1998) aims to compensate for historical inequality of opportunity by prohibiting discrimination and increasing opportunities for "designated" groups, including women, black men, and disabled people. In addition, there is the Skills Development Act (1998) and the Skills Development Levies Act (1999), which use a payroll levy distributed to Sector Education and Training Authorities (SETAs) to run skills development and training programs within their sectors. Section 23 of the Constitution also guarantees employees a number of rights, including the rights to form and join a trade union, to participate in the activities and programs of a trade union, and to strike.

4. In South Africa, someone is considered to have "written a subject" if they have sat for the final examination.

5. South African learners can choose to take mathematical literacy instead of mathematics on the NSC. Mathematical literacy is about the application of math in real-world scenarios rather than the technical aspects of mathematics. It is also a much easier subject to pass but does not qualify learners to study technical subjects at a university.

# References

Bernstein, Ann, and Antony Altbeker. 8 August 2012. Get SEZs right and cash in on Asia's rising labour costs. *Business Day*. Available from http://www.bdlive.co.za.

Bhorat, Haroon. 28 July 2013. Economic inequality is a major obstacle. *New York Times*. Available from http://www.nytimes.com.

Centre for Development and Enterprise (CDE). 2005. *Land reform in South Africa: A 21st century perspective*. Johannesburg: CDE. Available from http://www.cde.org.za/images/pdf/Land_Reform.pdf.

CDE. 2008a. *Farmers' voices: Practical perspectives on land reform and agricultural development*. Johannesburg: CDE. Available from http://www.cde.org.za/images/pdf/Farmers_Voices.pdf.

CDE. 2008b. *Land reform in South Africa: Getting back on track*. Johannesburg, CDE. Available from http://www.cde.org.za/images/pdf/Land%20Reform%20in%20SA%20full%20report.pdf.

CDE. 2010a. *Hidden assets: South Africa's low fee private schools*. Johannesburg: CDE. Available from http://www.cde.org.za/images/pdf/Hidden%20Assets.pdf.

CDE. 2010b. *Skills, growth and borders: Managing migration in South Africa's national interest*. Johannesburg: CDE. Available from http://www.cde.org.za/images/pdf/SKILLS%20GROWTH%20AND%20BORDERS%20Research%20report%2017%20Full%20report.pdf.

CDE. 2011a. *A fresh look at unemployment: A conversation among experts*. Johannesburg: CDE. Available from http://www.cde.org.za/images/pdf/A%20fresh%20look%20at%20unemployment%20Full%20Report.pdf.

CDE. 2011b. *Reforming healthcare in South Africa: What role for the private sector?* Johannesburg: CDE. Available from http://www.cde.org.za/images/pdf/REFORMING%20HEALTHCARE%20IN%20SA%20full%20report.pdf.

CDE. 2011c. *Value in the classroom: The quantity and quality of South Africa's teachers*. Johannesburg: CDE. Available from http://www.cde.org.za/images/pdf/VALUE_IN_THE_CLASSROOM_full_report.pdf.

CDE. 2012a. *Coping with unemployment: Young people's strategies and their policy implications.* Johannesburg: CDE. Available from http://www.cde.org.za/images/pdf/COPING%20WITH%20 UNEMPLOYMENT_Young%20peoples%20strategies%20and%20their%20policy%20implications .pdf.

CDE. 2012b. *Promoting school choice for the poor: Practical ideas from international experience.* Johannesburg: CDE. Available from: http://www.cde.org.za/images/pdf/PROMOTING_SCHOOL_ CHOICE_FOR_THE_POOR_Practical_ideas_from_international_experience.pdf.

CDE. 2012c. *Public reform and private education: The development of higher education in Brazil.* Johannesburg: CDE. Available from http://www.cde.org.za/images/pdf/PublicReformandPrivate Expansion_TheDevelopmentofHigherEducationinBrazil.pdf.

CDE. 2012d. *Reflecting on Brazil's success: How durable? What lessons for South Africa.* Johannesburg: CDE. Available from http://www.cde.org.za/images/pdf/REFLECTING%20ON%20BRAZILS%20 SUCCESS_How%20durable%20What%20lessons%20for%20South%20Africa.pdf.

CDE. 2012e. *Routes into formal employment: Public and private assistance to young job seekers.* Johannesburg: CDE. Available from http://www.cde.org.za/images/pdf/ROUTES%20INTO%20 FORMAL%20EMPLOYMENT%20_Public%20and%20private%20assistance%20to%20young%20 job-seekers.pdf.

CDE. 2012f. *Special economic zones: Lessons for South Africa from international evidence and local experience.* Johannesburg: CDE. Available from http://www.cde.org.za/images/pdf/SEZs%20full%20 report.pdf.

CDE. 2012g. *Teacher pay for performance: Lessons from other countries.* Johannesburg: CDE. Available from: http://www.cde.org.za/images/pdf/TEACHER_PAY_FOR_PERFORMANCE__Lessons_from_ other_countries.pdf.

CDE. 2013a. *Affordable private schools in South Africa.* Johannesburg: CDE. Available from http://www .cde.org.za/images/pdf/Affordable%20Private%20Schools%20in%20South%20Africa.pdf.

CDE. 2013b. *Graduate unemployment in South Africa: A much exaggerated problem.* Johannesburg: CDE. Available from http://www.cde.org.za/images/pdf/GRADUATE%20UNEMPLOYMENT%20 IN%20SOUTH%20AFRICA%20_A%20much%20exaggerated%20problem.pdf.

CDE. 2013c. *Job destruction in the South African clothing industry: How an alliance of organised labour, the state and some firms is undermining labour-intensive growth.* Johannesburg: CDE. Available from http://www.cde.org.za/images/pdf/Job_Destruction_in_the_South_African_Clothing_Industry.pdf.

CDE. 2013d. *Rethinking South Africa's labour market: Lessons from Brazil, India and Malaysia.* Johannesburg: CDE. Available from http://www.cde.org.za/images/pdf/RETHINKING%20SOUTH%20 AFRICAS%20LABOUR%20MARKET_LESSONS%20FROM%20BRAZIL%20INDIA%20AND%20 MALAYSIA.pdf.

CDE. Forthcoming. *Complacency and systems inefficiency in mathematics education.* Johannesburg: CDE.

Department of Basic Education. 2012. *School realities.* Pretoria: Department of Basic Education.

Department of Trade and Industry. 2012. *Industrial Policy Action Plan 2011/12–2013/14.* Pretoria: Economic Sectors and Employment Cluster.

Economic Development Department. 2010. *New growth plan.* Pretoria: South Africa.

Marcus, Gill. 2013. *Employment and the economics of job creation.* Available from http://www.politicsweb .co.za.

National Planning Commission. 2012. *National Development Plan 2030: Our future – make it work.* Pretoria: The Presidency.

National Treasury. 2011a. *Confronting youth unemployment: Policy options for South Africa.* Discussion Paper. Pretoria: National Treasury. Available from http://www.africaneconomicoutlook.org/fileadmin/ uploads/aeo/PDF/Confronting%20youth%20unemployment%20-%20Policy%20options.pdf.

National Treasury. 2011b. *2011 budget review.* Pretoria: National Treasury. Available from http://www .treasury.gov.za/documents/national%20budget/2011/review/chapter%203.pdf.

National Treasury. 2013. *Estimates of national expenditure, 2013.* Pretoria: National Treasury. Available from http://www.treasury.gov.za/documents/national%20budget/2013/ene/FullENE.pdf.

Simkins, Charles. 2010. *The maths and science performance of South Africa's public schools: Some lessons from the past decade.* Johannesburg: CDE.

Simkins, Charles. Forthcoming. *Performance in the South African educational system.* Johannesburg: CDE.

South African Institute of Race Relations. 2012. *South Africa Survey 2012*. Johannesburg: South African Institute of Race Relations.

South African Institute of Race Relations. 28 June 2013. More people on social welfare than with jobs. *MoneyWeb*. Available from http://www.moneyweb.co.za.

South African Press Association (SAPA). 2 October 2012. South African youth entrepreneurship lagging. *The Times*. Available from http://www.timeslive.co.za.

Spaull, Nicholas. Forthcoming. *South Africa's education crisis: The quality of education in South Africa 1994–2011*. Johannesburg: CDE.

Statistics South Africa (Stats SA). 2013a. *Quarterly Labour Force Survey, Quarter 1 2013, Statistical Release P0211*. Pretoria: Stats SA.

Stats SA. 2013b. *Quarterly Labour Force Survey, Quarter 2 2013, Statistical Release P0211*. Pretoria: Stats SA.

Visser, Amanda. 28 June 2013. South Africa faces potent crisis over social welfare, warns Mboweni. *Business Day*. Available from http://www.bdlive.co.za.

World Bank. 2007. *World development report 2007*. Washington DC: World Bank. Available from http://www-wds.worldbank.org/external/default/WDSContentServer/WDSP/IB/2006/09/13/000112742_200 60913111024/Rendered/PDF/359990WDR0complete.pdf.

# Democracy at Risk? Politics and Governance under the ANC

*By*
ROGER SOUTHALL

The negotiated settlement of 1994 established South Africa as a constitutional democracy. Under Nelson Mandela, the new democracy basked in a glow of national reconciliation, early growth, and optimism. Subsequently, however, the national sense of collective well-being has declined. Racial inequality has narrowed, but the fundamental features of the apartheid economy remain, including a significant section of the population living in absolute poverty, despite the efforts of the government to combine economic growth with redistribution. Given the continued entrenchment of white economic power, the African National Congress (ANC) has sought to use its capture of the state to promote the empowerment of blacks. However, having assumed the characteristics of a "dominant party" assured of successive election victories, the ANC now presides over a party-state whose accountability leaves much to be desired, providing opportunity and scope for corrupt and predatory behavior by significant elements of the party's elite. Further merging of party and state challenges constitutionalism and threatens the rule of law. It is only when the ANC's electoral hegemony is eroded that we will discover whether, if faced by loss of power, it will obey or disregard its democratic heritage.

*Keywords:* African National Congress; constitutionalism; party-state; dominant party

South Africa is correctly celebrated for the triumph of its constitutional settlement of the years of 1990–1996 whereby the country moved from apartheid, a legislated form of white minority racial oppression, to democracy. Constructed around negotiations conducted principally by the former ruling National Party (NP) and the predominant liberation movement, the African National Congress (ANC),

*Roger Southall is a professor emeritus in sociology at the University of the Witwatersrand in South Africa and was the Van Zyl Slabbert Visiting Professor in Politics and Sociology at the University of Cape Town in 2013.*

DOI: 10.1177/0002716213508068

the outcome reflected something of a stalemate between historically contesting forces.

The result was a negotiated constitution that could scarcely have been imagined 20 years prior, at a time when it was not uncommon for many analysts to predict a descent into civil war. Rather than chaos, what emerged was a settlement that committed South Africa to becoming a "constitutional state": that is, one in which laws passed by parliament or actions taken by a government might be judged by a Constitutional Court as not conforming to the constitution and hence would be subject to rejection as unconstitutional. Thus it was that the "interim" constitution of 1994 provided for a constitutional democracy that embodied a founding set of constitutional values; a Constitutional Court at the apex of an independent judiciary; a Bill of Rights, protective of an array of individual rights (including the right to own property); commitments to redress the legacy of apartheid's racialized socioeconomic disparities; and a separation of powers between the executive, legislature, and judiciary. In turn, this constitution was to be revisited by a first democratically elected parliament, a resulting "final" constitution having to be approved by the new Constitutional Court in accordance with the previously negotiated constitutional values.

South Africa embarked on its democratic journey under the leadership of Nelson Mandela, a global icon whose five-year presidency, marked by a commitment to racial reconciliation, can retrospectively be characterized as an era of relative post-apartheid goodwill and social harmony. However, thereafter, under the successive presidencies of Thabo Mbeki (1999–2008), Kgalema Motlanthe (2008–2009), and, as of this writing, Jacob Zuma, the glow of optimism that accompanied the country's initial democratic progress has dimmed. While the ANC's management of the economy has arrested the long decline witnessed under the last decades of NP rule, the growth trajectory pursued has confirmed past patterns and failed to address fundamental features of the apartheid legacy; indeed, while the racial shape of inequalities has changed, notably with the development of a black elite and middle class, massive socioeconomic disparities between classes and races remain. In turn, the ANC itself, faced by the temptations of ruling, has found its good intentions increasingly overwhelmed by the predatory behavior of elites at the national, provincial, and local levels. These elites have come to dominate its structures and have rendered major organs of the state increasingly dysfunctional. Correspondingly, failure to meet the raised expectations of its popular constituency has resulted in a surge of political and industrial protest from below, which the ANC has met with a mixture of promises, passing the buck, and brutal police power. In short, 20 years down the road, South African democracy seems at serious risk.

In what follows, I attempt to sketch out the logic of the ANC's degeneration, before concluding with some speculations about possible future directions. Prior to that, however, it is necessary to turn to both the difficult economic legacy that the ANC inherited and the legacy that it brought to government as a liberation movement.[1]

# Background to Democracy

Following South Africa's transition, Jan-Erik Lane and Svante Errson provided a highly cautious assessment of the prospects for democracy. In the tradition of Seymour Martin Lipset, they focused on the structural conditions likely to determine the probability of democratic success, including such factors as income distribution, economic inequality, ethno-linguistic diversity, religious divisions, rate of population growth, rate of urbanization, human development ranking, and so on. Suffice it to say that, while they argued that the mode of political interaction had moved from confrontation and large-scale repression to bargaining and mutual respect, their ultimate conclusion was pessimistic: "Neither the social conditions nor the political in South Africa at the moment are strong enough to carry the democracy in the long-run perspective" (Lane and Errson 1997, 15). My personal response to such arguments was that although they were cogent, there was danger of their becoming self-fulfilling, and that those who lived in South Africa had to insist that the future was open to more optimistic alternatives. Indeed, while the country undoubtedly faced major dilemmas, the early post-apartheid years suggested that South African democracy was "acquiring a basic, rude strength" (Southall 2000, 168).

In retrospect, the question remains whether an "optimism of the will" can counter the structural deficits that continue to blight South Africa's democratic prospects. However, although space is too short to provide anything approaching a comprehensive analysis of the country's broader socioeconomic trajectory, any focus on the specifically political aspects of ANC rule should take into account three fundamental economic factors underlying the party's governance.

## Economic factors

First, the ANC gained control in South Arica in 1994, but it left white domination of the economy largely intact. South Africa's corporations, although extremely wary of the ANC, had been preparing for political change since the early 1980s. External factors (the oil crisis of 1973, external sanctions, and political pressures on international corporations to disinvest) had combined with an upsurge in black protest to thrust the country into an extended economic decline. As foreign corporations fled, domestically owned conglomerates bought up their subsidiaries, and the ownership structure of South Africa became increasingly concentrated. However, unable to operate outside the boundaries of the country's immediate hinterland, corporate profits faltered and future prospects became increasingly dependent on the removal of the constraining political conditions.

In so far as the ANC in exile espoused a socialist future, the corporate sector preferred to remain with the white NP devil it knew, but once regional conditions changed (notably with the end of the Cold War and the collapse of Soviet support for the liberation struggle), the terrain was transformed. Thus, while it was the political negotiations for democracy that dominated the global headlines, these were matched by behind-the-scenes dealings among the ANC, the corporate sector, and international financial institutions. As a result, whereas the ANC's popular constituency hungered for socialism, the party's elite quietly conceded a refurbishment of capitalism. White domination of corporate structures would be largely maintained, although diluted by the creation of a black subaltern capitalist class through share deals, board appointments, and increased recruitment of blacks to senior management positions. The accompaniment would be that the economy would be opened up by an incoming government's adoption of the neoliberal macroeconomic mantras of the day: free markets, abandonment of protections, financial deregulation, tightened fiscal discipline, and privatization of state industries.

Once the 1994 election was out of the way, the broad thrust of this policy was to be achieved by the ANC's replacement of its social democratically inclined Redistribution and Development Programme with its promarket Growth, Employment and Redistribution strategy (GEAR) in 1996. Although prompted by a necessary response to a post-transitional crisis of indebtedness, the shift from one policy orientation to another was equally a signal of the party elite's ideological abandonment of its previous socialist commitments. Although the ANC leadership was disinclined to say so openly, it now evinced the desire to become capitalistic.

Alongside the ANC's acceptance of capitalism, there was a second economic factor that underlay the transition. Under successive white governments since the 1920s, but with added emphasis under the NP from 1948, the state itself had come to assume a significant ownership role within the economy. Centered on four major state-owned enterprises (SOEs) (Telkom, Eskom, Transnet, and Denel), the late apartheid state was directly responsible for something around 15 percent of gross domestic product (GDP). Furthermore, the parastatals employed well over 300,000 people. In short, although the ANC was compelled by circumstances to accept that white dominance of the private sector would remain for the foreseeable future, the extent of state ownership it would inherit offered some considerable recompense. In consequence, just as the public service was soon to be subjected to a major process of "transformation," the SOEs were swiftly placed under largely black managerial control. While offering the ANC considerable economic leverage, the parastatals were also to serve as a major platform for black managers aligned with the ANC subsequently to move into high positions within the private sector. It was scarcely surprising, against this background, that the one aspect of the neoliberal mantra that never really took off was privatization. Although GEAR originally embraced privatization, the ANC was eager to link any sell-off of state assets to what it regarded as the decolonizing strategy of Black Economic Empowerment (BEE): that is, sales should seek to promote black capital ownership. However, because, for historical reasons, few blacks combined managerial experience with the capacity to purchase such assets, even if they were to be sold by the state at a generous discount, the government's enthusiasm for outright privatization rapidly diminished and was replaced by a concerted attempt by SOEs to steer procurement to emerging black companies. As a result, the ANC government soon opted instead for a "restructuring" (i.e., commercialization) of state firms. While in a few instances this involved the sale of minority shareholdings to large corporations (as in the cases of Telkom and South African Airways—deals that were later reversed for market reasons), outright privatization was otherwise largely limited to the disposal of a handful of "noncore" assets.[2]

Third, and finally, while ANC policies have freed the economy of the immediate constraints of the later apartheid years, the benefits of modest growth have remained highly skewed. Overall, interracial disparities have been reduced, as the concerted movement of blacks into public service has provided the major dynamic behind the growth of the black middle class. Against this gain, just as neoliberal growth internationally has seen a widening of social inequalities, so too have the overall levels of economic inequality between rich and poor remained extreme, and little, if at all, better than under apartheid. Furthermore, the ANC era has seen the proportion of the economic pie going to corporate profits increasing relative to that going to wages, while in turn the growth trajectory has failed to provide any effective antidote to the appallingly high levels of unemployment (between 25 percent and 40 percent of the age-defined workforce, according to the definition employed) (SAIRR 2012, 258–62). Hence, although the ANC has, with justifiable pride, presided over a massive expansion of the country's social security and pension system—thus providing a major protection against the worst deprivations of poverty for many millions of people—the sustainability of this expansion (given the country's narrow tax base) is increasingly being questioned.[3]

Continued white domination of the economy, increasing class differentiation within the majority black population, and widespread dependence for livelihoods upon state grants have all combined with popular expectations raised by the ANC's promise of "a better life for all" to provide a volatile background to the country's political life. In addition, however, ANC governance has been profoundly influenced by its legacy as a liberation movement.

### The liberation movement legacy

The banning of the ANC and the rival Pan-Africanist Congress (PAC), after the regime had brutally crushed a rising tide of peaceful protests, turned both movements toward a strategy of armed struggle. With much of their leadership jailed and their internal structures smashed by the state, what was left of the ANC and PAC was forced into exile. Once mass-based movements, they were forced to transform themselves into "liberation movements." Over the years the PAC, torn apart by squabbles, was effectively going to implode, leaving the ANC to dominate the international terrain. Subsequently, although scholarship (e.g., Ellis 2012) has established that the ANC's political activities in exile were far more successful than its military actions in eroding NP power, the militarist identity and modes of operation it developed as a liberation movement were to make a marked impression upon its character when it became a ruling party.

Despite difficulties concerning how a "national liberation movement" (NLM) should be defined, it is possible to identify a political culture that to a greater or lesser extent characterized the different southern African NLMs, the ANC among them. First, although it is often claimed (e.g., Saul 1994, 2008) that the various liberation struggles (in Angola, Mozambique, Namibia, Zimbabwe, and South Africa) had expansive objectives, from the overthrow of capitalism to the establishment of gender equality, they were above all struggles to replace white minority with black majority rule. This does not mean that in the case of the ANC, for instance, the NLM disregarded other dimensions of democracy—such as individual rights and racial equality—but it does point to a strong tendency to interpret democracy in a narrowly majoritarian fashion. Second, NLMs have displayed a pronounced tendency to identify themselves as the embodiments of "the nation," with the consequence that they tend toward the delegitimizing of and labeling those opposing them as aliens or traitors—a mode of thinking that can have disastrous implications for human rights, opposition movements, and ethnic minorities. When combined with a glorification of militarism and the armed struggle, this approach leads to "reinvents of history" that eliminate the contributions to anticolonial and democratic struggle of other forces in society and proclaims the right of NLMs to rule in perpetuity. Third, the NLMs propose in one form or another that what they describe as the "seizure" of political power will prove meaningless unless it leads to a more fundamental restructuring of their respective societies. This thrust is embodied in the theory of the "National Democratic Revolution" (NDR), developed in its most advanced form by the ANC in partnership with its long-established ally, the South African Communist Party (SACP), whose influence over the ANC's armed wing, Umkhonto we Sizwe, during the period of exile, was critical.[4]

Central to the ANC's theory of the NDR was its conception of its liberation struggle as being fought against a "colonialism of a special type." Whereas the national liberation struggles in other territories had been waged against colonial rule, the struggle in South Africa was fought by the oppressed nation against a white minority (or nation) that controlled a sovereign state. The struggle for liberation was thus simultaneously one for "national democracy" in which formerly oppressive white settlers would become citizens as individuals, rather than as a separate nation. Yet in recognition of its alliance with the SACP, national liberation had to be envisaged as a two-stage project. First, the triumph over the minority regime would inaugurate democracy. However, because this result would leave oppressive structures untouched and the black nation still subject to economic oppression, there would be a need for an NDR to realize racial redress. Thereafter, national democracy would give way to a second stage of development, that of socialism.

Twenty years after the inauguration of the NDR, the goal of socialism, while not theoretically having been abandoned, has been endlessly postponed. It is not necessary here to elaborate on the limitations of the theory of the NDR as a construct (save to mention, perhaps, that it left the timings and mechanisms of the transition from national democracy to socialism remarkably vague). However, it is relevant to note that the NDR has retained its salience for two reasons. First, in maintaining "revolution-speak," it constantly reiterates the ANC's radical credentials, thereby serving an important goal of keeping its capitalist and nationalist elements in alliance with its socialist ones and with the SACP. Second, it provides an historical justification for the ANC's steady extension of its control over state and society. Thus, in one of its early post-1994 "Strategies and Tactics" documents, the ANC committed itself to a "transformation" of the state that entailed: "First and foremost, extending the power of the NLM over all levers of power: the army, the police, the bureaucracy, intelligence structures, the judiciary, the parastatals, and agencies such as regulatory bodies, the public broadcaster, the central bank and so on" (ANC 1998).

To be sure, we need to recognize that the postliberation ANC engages in much political theatre at its major conferences, playing to its popular constituency (in the tradition of bread and circuses). Consequently, the extent to which the ANC government actually implements the policies prescribed by its party documents is debatable. Nonetheless, the ANC's strategy of extending power over all "levers of power," notably by the "deployment" of party loyalists to positions in and out of government, has been crucial, and has proved to have been deeply at odds with the separation of powers and the supremacy of the constitution.

## The ANC as a Dominant Party: Elections as the Road to State Power

Given its inability to overthrow the apartheid government by armed struggle, the ANC's road to power lay through negotiations, and subsequently by winning inaugural elections and thereafter confirming its electoral hegemony.

The interim constitution had provided for the first democratic elections to be conducted under a national list system of proportional representation (PR), adopted in preference to a plurality-style constituency system that would have led to numerical underrepresentation of political minorities in parliament. In contrast, the PR system adopted eschewed any requirement for political parties to obtain a minimum proportion (threshold) of the vote to obtain representation in parliament, allowing for maximum representativeness. With the election administered by the newly established Independent Electoral Commission, the ANC gained 62.7 percent of the vote—a sweeping victory, but one that fell short of the two-thirds majority that would have enabled it to finalize the constitution-making process without the support of minority parties. With the NP obtaining 20 percent and the Inkatha Freedom Party just over 10 percent of the vote, the grounds were laid for their inclusion in an initial Government of National Unity (as required by the 1994 constitution), while the liberal Democratic Party (DP), ahead of a clutch of minor parties, was left as the principal opposition party after gaining less than 2 percent of the vote.

In subsequent elections (1999, 2004, and 2009), all judged to have been largely free and fair, the ANC has continued to enjoy a large proportion of the popular vote, climbing to as high as just under 70 percent in 2004 before falling back to just under 66 percent in 2009 (Daniel and Southall 2009, 234, Table 1).

This popularity is still based on the ANC's deliberately calculated reputation as the party that overthrew apartheid, supplemented by its adroit use of patronage to secure the support of people of influence such as traditional leaders, who continue to exert significant control over the communal areas (the former homelands); its massive expansion of the social security system, which today covers well over 16 million people out of a population of nearly 50 million; and its development of a highly effective electoral machine based on an elevated level of mobilization of its supporters, all backed by ample funding provided by a mix of officially ordained sources, investments, donations from businesses, and cozy relationships forged with SOEs.[5]

With the ANC dominating the electoral arena, only around a third of the vote has been up for grabs by opposition parties. Beyond that, while the composition and ranking of the three largest parties has changed since 1994, together they have shared the overwhelming proportion of the vote, leaving minor parties to fight for the scraps, with between five and ten such competitors sharing meager spoils (Schulz-Herzenberg 2009).[6] At the same time, the opposition Democratic Alliance (DA) has emerged as the significant challenger to the ANC, first outpacing the New National Party (NNP) by presenting itself as a more effective champion of the rights of minorities, and second, since 2004, combining its reputation as a robust critic of government in parliament with its role as an effective government of the Western Cape and the Cape City municipal council. For other parties, however, the terrain of opposition has proved perilous.

Ultimately totally demoralized (yet desperate to cling to low-hanging fruits of government), the NNP folded itself into the ANC in 2005. The Inkatha Freedom Party (IFP) of Chief Mangosuthu Buthelezi, which had secured a bare majority vote in KwaZulu-Natal to emerge as the leading partner in an IFP-ANC coalition in KwaZulu-Natal in 1994, proved incapable of shedding its image as a party of chiefly domination and rural ethnicity. Although it continued to lead the provincial government after 1999, it lost control to the ANC in 2004, and in 2009 its support was decimated by the election of President Jacob Zuma, who played strategically to his Zulu ethnicity. Under Zuma, the ANC appears to be completing the job of securing the support of the chiefs and winning the rural vote, leaving little option but for a post-Buthelezi party to either throw in its lot with the ruling party completely or to consign itself to irrelevance. Otherwise, breakaways from the ANC (by Bantu Holomisa, former military leader of the Transkei homeland, to form the United Democratic Movement in 1997 and by the Congress of the People, formed by ANC rebel supporters of Thabo Mbeki after he had been ejected from the state presidency in September 2008), tend to experience a vigorous start before collapsing into self-induced disarray. Other parties, ranging from the Freedom Front Plus (expressive of right-wing Afrikaner elements) to the African Christian Democratic Party, have struggled to resonate with more than a tiny fraction of voters.

Hence it has been the DA, drawing on its rich heritage of parliamentary know-how and benefitting from adroit leadership, that has established itself as the leading force of opposition and, to all intents and purposes, that has managed to transform South Africa into a de facto two-party system. Under its leader Helen

Zille, who speaks fluent Xhosa, and who since 2009 has doubled-up as premier of the Western Cape, the DA has embarked on a strategy of moving beyond its minority base among whites and Coloureds to appeal to Africans. It has campaigned vigorously in black African townships and appointed Lindiwe Mazibuko, a black African woman, to lead it in parliament (Southern and Southall 2011). However, the obstacles to its moving beyond its historic image as a party merely for whites and other racial minorities remain formidable; indeed, its bid for the disillusioned ANC black vote was contested in 2013 by Agang, a new group established by Mamphele Ramphele, a leading independent African personality.

Dominant parties are supposedly democratic, in that they regard themselves as vulnerable to electoral upsets and even as replaceable at the polls. Yet party dominance also opens the way for parties to fall prey to undemocratic temptations, and the significant analysis of Herman Giliomee and Charles Simkins (1999) suggests that this result is more likely to occur in less developed countries than in industrialized democracies. Hitherto, to be fair, the ANC has passed the electoral test, accepting junior roles in the Western Cape and KwaZulu-Natal provincial governments in 1994, following contests in which, in the first case, its minority role had been proven; and in the latter case, it was forced by the ANC at the national level, to the chagrin of its provincial wing, to collaborate in the new arrangements with an IFP that had played a spoiling role in the last two years of the post-1994 transitional process and had been a reluctant, last-minute participant in the first national elections.[7]

More importantly, the ANC accepted the outcome of the 2004 and 2009 provincial elections in the Western Cape in which the DA secured majorities, and in alliance with smaller parties proceeded to form the provincial government there. Notwithstanding the bad grace of its provincial wing, the ANC at the national level has, on the whole, worked constructively with Zille's provincial government in a manner that, in future years, may possibly be seen to have laid a basis for a more genuinely federally based political system. However, the ANC has yet to face the dilemma that, eventually, seems to confront all ruling parties at a national level—being defeated at the polls (if not, in Africa, being ejected by the military). As illustrated by the refusal of President Robert Mugabe's ZANU-PF to give way to the opposition MDC in Zimbabwe, to which it lost the National Assembly (and if the truth be known) presidential elections in 2008, a liberation movement's insistence on the party of liberation as the true representative of the people can prove hugely problematic to democracy. Meanwhile, the ANC has sought to put off that day in South Africa by consolidating its dominance, not least by extending its control over parliament.

## The ANC as a Dominant Party: The Subordination of Parliament

The classic role of parliaments is threefold: to provide recruits for high political office; to debate, pass, amend, or reject proposed legislation; and to hold the executive accountable. These functions, and the separation of powers that they signify, were all to be spelled out in the 1994 and 1996 constitutions in South Africa. However, although the ANC is by no means alone in the modern world in exerting executive control over a legislature, the ANC has systematically used its dominance to subvert the autonomy of parliament.

Recruitment to parliament is via the political parties' electoral lists. Hence the ANC, for instance, will nominate candidates for election to parliament in rank order, the eventual number of candidates entering the House of Assembly being calculated proportionately according to the party's vote. Parties have different procedures for selecting candidates, with the ANC going through a lengthy internal process that features nominations from the branch level upward, culminating in provincial list conferences. Nominees are forwarded to the party's National Executive Committee (NEC), which makes the final selection of candidates. The list-making process is enormously political, with the NEC having intervened historically to ensure that an adequate number of candidates from racial minorities gain electable positions. The ANC wants credibly to claim that it is demographically representative of the entire population, while also intervening in numerous factional disputes that continuously arise in the provinces (see Butler 2009, 71–72, for the process in 2009). Meanwhile, parties also have to recognize that although they may want to secure election of individuals close to their communities, doing so can be problematic if it results in the election of candidates whose capacities to undertake the job of members of parliament (MP) or provincial legislatures are compromised by their lack of formal education (in a country where the black population has historically been comprehensively disadvantaged). There is no overview of the educational levels of MPs since 1994, although Francis (2011, 114–23) has tracked how the educational level of members of provincial legislatures (MPLs) in KwaZulu-Natal increased significantly from the first to the second election, with new entries to the legislature increasingly likely to have a diploma or initial degree.

Nonetheless, there are generic complaints that many MPs and MPLs lack the capacity to undertake their roles adequately; generally, legislatures are less effective today than they were at the dawn of democracy. In turn, this lack of efficacy has serious implications for the pool of candidates available for selection as cabinet ministers by the president or provincial premiers. Although there has been no study of such a tendentious issue, there is enough informal evidence to indicate that some ministers lack the competence that their posts require.

Part of the problem is that a position in a legislature is widely viewed as a job rather than a career. With national unemployment having remained at an astoundingly high level, politics is widely seen as a route to achieve wealth by gaining access to state positions, rather than as a means to further ideals or the public interest. This tendency has been exaggerated by the lack of autonomy accorded to MPs. In a first-past-the-post system, MPs have a base in their home constituencies, which may provide them with an independent platform for contesting the authority of party bosses. In contrast, in South Africa, MPs who flout party discipline are at risk of being expelled from the party, in which case they may no longer remain in parliament. Meanwhile, ANC party bosses have the capacity to "redeploy" their MPs out of parliament (perhaps to appoint them to another state position) and replace them with candidates from the party list who missed out on being elected at a previous poll. Unsurprisingly, the continuous entry and exit of MPs and MPLs through the revolving doors of legislatures does nothing for the continuity of business, undermines parliamentary capacities, and detracts from legislatures' public reputation.

The suffocating grip that party bosses have over MPs and MPLs translates into strict control of the parliamentary agenda by the executive, thus compromising the quality of debate, the legislative processing of bills, and the ability of parliament to hold the government to account. Generally, there are severe limits on the time allowed for opposition parties to comment, the very legitimacy of the opposition quite regularly being brought into question (with the DA in particular accused of being a vehicle of white interests). Furthermore, the opposition's capacity to insert its own priorities into the parliamentary agenda is very limited. In late 2012, for instance, when the DA called for the scheduling of a vote of no confidence in the government (following media revelations of massive expenditure of public funds on Zuma's private Nkandla residence in KwaZulu-Natal), the motion was refused; and when the DA went to court, the court ruled that while parliament was obliged to accede to the DA's request, it had no right to dictate to the Speaker when the debate should be held.

More alarmingly, ANC control of parliamentary procedure has been used to clamp down on the investigative powers of parliamentary committees, the most notorious example being the clipping of the wings of the Select Committee on Public Accounts (SCOPA) when, among others, ANC MP Andrew Feinstein was leading a charge to investigate massive corruption in the notorious 1998 arms deals between the incoming ANC government and a clutch of international arms companies (Feinstein 2007, 154–234). A disinclination on the part of ministers to provide answers to questions asked by the opposition has been matched by a tendency to refuse to impart information on the grounds of state security.

All these impediments do not mean that the government is impermeable to criticism. Parliamentary committees remain a forum in which ministers and senior civil servants can be called to account; and, when subject to criticism, especially if it is backed up by significant lobbying by interest groups outside parliament, ministers do withdraw bills for amendment and consideration. For example, during 2012, a Protection of Information Bill (dubbed the "Secrecy Bill" by critics), whose passage would have had major implications for the right of the media to expose corruption and official malfeasance, and which aroused passionate criticism from outside parliament, was withdrawn for amendment. However, it was later returned to parliament in a form that would still allow enormous ministerial discretion to declare "official" information out of bounds. With the ANC majority voting to drive the bill through parliament, the executive again evinced a general inclination to place major spheres of state beyond the reach of public accountability.

# The Merger of Party and State

No strategy of the ANC has been more controversial than that of the "deployment" of so-called cadres. This is the practice whereby the party appoints party loyalists to positions of state and wider public office. In making appointments, party loyalty trumps qualifications, relevant experience, and competence; the constitutionally required independence of various bodies is thereby seriously undermined, and the functionality of numerous institutions (and the commercial health of parastatals) is severely compromised. Fundamentally, critics argue that deployment blurs the distinction between party and state, and subordinates the latter to the former. "Cadre deployment" argues Davis (2010), "is unique to political parties (like the ANC) steeped in the Leninist tradition of democratic centralism. This principle commits every cadre to defending and implementing the will of the party leadership . . . even if it means acting outside the Constitution and the Law." In defending itself, the ANC argues that the deployment of party officials to senior state positions occurs in virtually all political systems, democratic and despotic alike; furthermore, the South African state inherited after apartheid was totally unsuited to serve the needs of all South Africans in that the leading posts in the public service were dominated by NP loyalists.

Booysen (2011) has tracked the development of the deployment policy, stressing how its formalization after the ANC's 50th National Conference at Mafikeng in 1997 followed up on its earlier practices in exile. A National Deployment Committee was established in late 1998, with provincial and local deployment committees to follow. However, thereafter the history of the deployment process is very much one of messy battles around deployment committees at all levels of the party, the intensity of the struggles suggesting that the deployment committees wield very real powers of appointment. Furthermore, although the rationale has remained that of the need for placing revolutionary cadres in strategic positions, even the ANC's own documentation laments the extent to which deployment has become an instrument for selective patronage, material accumulation, and upward mobility.

Deployment excites enormous debate, most of it severely critical of the ANC. To be sure, as noted by Naidoo (2013), much of this debate tends to be rather hysterical and ignores any wider international comparative referent as to how governments elsewhere manage their relations to their public services. Against this absence, however, a major aspect of the problem is that there is a lack of systematic data regarding the workings of deployment because the ANC's deployment committees operate behind very firmly closed doors. Furthermore, although it is difficult in practice to disentangle deployment from the ANC's determination to ensure that a previously white minority-dominated public service should be rendered demographically representative of the population, there is little doubt that the ruling party has used the powers granted to it by such instruments as the Employment Equity Act of 1998 (dedicated to promoting equity in the workplace) to place loyalists in multiple posts throughout the public sector at all levels of government. Thus, while political affiliations constitute no part of the official criteria for appointment to state positions under the constitution, there is manifestly an overlap between "historical disadvantage" and alignment to the ANC.

That deployment can be problematic has been acknowledged, even by the ANC government. Indeed, in 2010, the government offered de facto recognition that its effect had led to a major deterioration in the capacity of numerous local governments to perform even their most basic functions by passing a Municipal Systems Amendment Act, which prohibited municipalities from employing local party officials (Booysen 2011, 373–78). The act was an acknowledgement that at the local level, deployment by local ANC structures had largely degenerated into patronage and cronyism. Yet this conclusion begged the question of whether practices at higher levels of the public sector were or are seriously different.

## The ANC Party-State and the Threat to the Rule of Law

Deployment has been the instrument whereby the ANC has eroded the independence of key state institutions as envisaged under the constitution. This erosion has had alarming consequences for the rule of law. The constitution has been assaulted following the 1998 arms deal. Moreover, the ANC has sought to compromise the independence of the judiciary.

### The arms deal

The arms deal saga defies condensation in a short article (but see Holden 2008). Suffice it to say here that it has its origins in agreements concluded between the then-new ANC government and international arms companies at an extravagant cost (originally R30 billion, that figure later rising). The deal was soon alleged to have involved massive corruption, with huge "commissions" passing to the then-minister of defense, various other ANC-related figures, and very probably to the ANC itself (to fight the 1999 election). By 2003, Jacob Zuma, Mbeki's deputy president, had himself been accused of accepting bribes in return for his assisting a French company in the deal. By this time, however, Zuma had fallen out with Mbeki and become the champion of the ANC's allies, the Congress of South African Trade Unions (Cosatu) and the SACP. Alienated by the government's macroeconomic policy, Cosatu and SACP joined other elements (such as the ANC Youth League) to lend Zuma their support. Subsequently, his prosecution by the authorities was to become embroiled in a tumultuous battle for the party leadership, which culminated in Zuma's victory over Mbeki at the ANC's Polokwane conference in December 2007.

Given the Mbeki government's insistence that any corruption of individuals was incidental to the conclusion of legitimate negotiations, and the matching determination of Zuma's supporters to prove that his prosecution for corruption was politically motivated, the consequences for the body politic were enormous. In sum, in its bid to close down any enquiry into the arms deal, the ANC stamped down on the independence of SCOPA, severely compromised the autonomy of constitutionally appointed investigative and prosecutorial bodies, and embroiled those bodies in the party leadership's factional battles. The arms deal fall out culminated in the eventual abolition of the Scorpions, the National Prosecuting Authority's investigative arm (its evidence had provided ammunition under Mbeki's watch for the attempted prosecution of Zuma); the use of a High Court's judgment of doubtful standing (later overturned on appeal) to secure the removal of Mbeki from the state presidency; and the dismissal, on the flimsiest of grounds, under President Motlanthe, of an unduly independent public prosecutor and his replacement by an acting successor who was chivied into dropping all charges against Zuma, clearing the latter's way to become president. Later, too, to smooth his way to reelection as ANC president at the party's Mangaung conference in Bloemfontein in December 2012, Zuma preempted a likely ruling by the Constitutional Court in favor of an appeal by civil society activists at long last to have the arms deal subject to a fully independent investigation by appointing a Judicial Commission of Enquiry under Judge William Seriti on Zuma's own terms. Alas, the judge's subsequent activities suggested a craven subordination to the ANC—the hot potato of corruption in high places may yet be thrown back by activists into the lap of the Constitutional Court.[8]

## The ANC and the judiciary

It is understandable that the ANC should want to render the judiciary suitably responsive to the democratic era. Equally, the NP and liberals were eager to entrench constitutional supremacy and the independence of the judiciary. The outcome of this debate in 1994 was the establishment of a Constitutional Court at the apex of a judicial system. At the same time, however, the constitution stated that the composition of the judiciary should reflect the racial and gender composition of the national population. For the Constitutional Court, this challenged balancing the need for "transformation" against the integrity of the rule of law.

R.W. Johnson (2009, 153) has argued that, from the start, the ANC did its best to pack the Constitutional Court and that its eleven members always included "a safe pro-government majority." Other commentators are less strident, with leading constitutional lawyers citing major cases where the Constitutional Court has decided against the government. The arguments are complex. Theunis Roux (2012) argued that although during the period from 1994 to 1996 the interests of the ANC were aligned with the Constitutional Court in stabilizing the new constitutional order, that rationale fell away with the passage of the 1996 constitution. Thereafter, he maintains, the ANC's interest in the court shifted to its role in overseeing the party's agenda of social transformation.

The ANC, given the Constitutional Court's special status, has been particularly circumspect in its efforts to deploy its personnel to the judiciary. Consequently, the ANC has emphasized a need for the bench to become demographically representative. There has been a significant shift in the composition of the judiciary, which, 97 percent white male in 1994, was, by 2008, 36 percent African,

7.5 percent Coloured, 8.5 percent Indian, and just 48 percent white (SAIRR 2009/2010, 686).[9] However, particularly notable have been the ANC's efforts to change the composition of the Constitutional Court. Its judges may serve no more than 12 years or until they reach the age of 70. They are appointed through a process of open hearings conducted by the Judicial Service Commission (JSC), chaired by the chief justice, and otherwise composed of a mix of twenty-two political and legal representatives. In effect, the ANC, as the government, enjoys a plurality with the power to appoint six representatives from parliament to sit alongside the minister of justice and four other appointees of the president, who also appoints two practicing attorneys and two practicing advocates. Critics claim that the JSC is ANC-dominated, and, indisputably, the impression has spread throughout many quarters of the legal profession that race and political fealty are more important criteria for appointment than legal ability and record. Particularly controversial have been the JSC's rejections of the applications for appointment to the Constitutional Court of a number of white candidates, despite each person having outstandingly progressive track records.

The sense that the ANC is bent on clipping the wings of the judiciary has been strengthened under Zuma, whose serial legal battles predisposed elements of his supportive coalition to regard the courts with suspicion, if not outright hostility. Particularly controversial was the appointment of a new chief justice in 2011. Initially, Zuma had sought to extend the expiring term of Chief Justice Sandile Ngcobo, but was faced with indications that if he did so, he would face legal challenges about the constitutionality of his action. Ngcobo got him off the hook by announcing that he would decline any extension to his term. Now it was Zuma's responsibility to nominate a chief justice after consulting the JSC and leaders of parties represented in the National Assembly.

Leading jurists considered Judge Dikgang Moseneke, deputy president of the Constitutional Court, an outstanding candidate for the position. A former protégé of the PAC, Moseneke indicated openly that if he were appointed to the court, his duty was to the constitution rather than to the ANC. Zuma bypassed Moseneke, settling on Judge Mogoeng Mogoeng. The choice was immensely controversial. For a start, opposition party leaders complained that Zuma had failed to consult them and was breaking with constitutional convention by nominating only one candidate for consideration by the JSC. More particularly, Mogoeng's qualifications were widely regarded as suspect. None of his past judgments had broken new legal ground, and he was deemed to have taken deeply conservative positions in cases regarding the rights of homosexuals and women. Nor did Mogoeng, an ordained minister in the local branch of a Nigerian evangelical Christian sect, convince earthly critics when he averred that he had been chosen for the position by God. Thereafter, prompted by divine guidance, the de facto ANC majority of the JSC recommended his appointment to Zuma. Against the background of recent comments that Gwede Mantashe, the ANC secretary-general, had made about the Constitutional Court tending to act as if it were the opposition, and that the judges tended to be "counterrevolutionary," the appointment of Mogoeng seemed to signal the president's intention to appoint a chief justice who would favor the executive.

# The Party-State and the Rise of Corruption

The late apartheid state was structurally conducive to the encouragement of corruption and criminality. Corruption ranged from South African Defense Force involvement in wildlife poaching to a series of scandals regarding the misuse of public funds encouraged by the "embourgeoisiement" of Afrikaner political culture. Meanwhile, involvement of the private sector in "sanctions-busting" encouraged illegal means of doing business to gain access to world markets. The installment of a democratic order in 1994 was intended to put a stop to such activities and, where they continued, to provide the state with the means to control and prosecute them.

Despite such intentions, corruption under the ANC has billowed. Although space constraints forbid any effort to validate this contention, it is argued that the systematization of corruption has followed from the logic of the ANC's party state.[10] In condensed form, my argument is as follows.

First, the structure of the democratic settlement—a white minority retaining economic dominance while an incoming ANC elite acquired political power—set up a situation where the corporate structure and the new politicians required each other. To acquire access to government goodwill and business, corporations fell over themselves to curry favor with the ANC by offering share deals and appointments to influential party personnel. The ANC reciprocated by responding positively to private sector pleas for the maintenance of a capitalist economy. Subsequently, strategies of BEE have been implemented by the ANC that, while at times leading to contestation with large scale business, have institutionalized a crony-style relationship between the ruling party and most of South Africa's largest corporations.

Second, given the historical disadvantage in opportunities to gain education and wealth, along with white domination of the private sector, employment in the public sector—facilitated by the ANC's capture of state power—has become the preferred (and often the only) route to a regular income for many black South Africans. Furthermore, given a widespread sense of entitlement (on the grounds of the injustices of the past and the sacrifices endured in the struggle against apartheid), the public sector (and the largesse to which it can give access) has become transformed into a major site for class formation and material accumulation.

Third, given that it is the ANC's capture of state power that facilitates access to public employment, political position, and subsequent allocation of resources (notably the award of contracts via a state tendering system that is widely abused), it follows that membership of and, in many cases, donations to the ruling party, at its national, provincial, and local levels, proves critical for the acquiring of political goods. Hence "tenderpreneurship," the award of contracts to cronies or relatives, has become a major phenomenon, from Zuma down to the local government level.

Fourth, despite announced good intentions and the best efforts of the Treasury and various other official agencies, the political will and capacity to control corruption is often absent, at best spasmodic, and consistently limited. In financial year 2011–2012, for instance, only 22 percent of the 536 national and provincial government entities audited received clean audits, 55 percent received financially unqualified audit opinions, and 14 percent qualified audit opinions (while 31 entities failed entirely to submit reports). Furthermore, R438 million worth of contracts were identified as awarded to suppliers whose employees had an interest, and R141 million worth went to forty-two entities in which family members had an interest. Overall, these results recorded a decline in the performance of the government's financial control system. Meanwhile, the situation at the local government level is worse, with only 5 percent of all municipal entities receiving clean audits. Although remaining upbeat about official intentions, Auditor-General Terence Nombembe has lamented not just the widespread lack of financial skills but the tardy and lackluster efforts by political leaders to exert control.[11] Political instability within many local authorities (a product of vicious battles for control of resources characteristic of many municipalities), he argued, has been combined with a lack of corrective disciplinary action against key officials guilty of misconduct.

Nombembe points to the government's effective toleration of corruption and a widespread perception that prosecution, when it happens, is often politically selective. This approach was illustrated by the fall of former ANC Youth League leader Julius Malema. After backing Zuma for the ANC presidency in 2007, he subsequently launched a campaign to have him unseated at Mangaung in 2012. Thus, the message sent by Malema's expulsion from the ANC, his pursuit by the authorities for unpaid taxes, and his arraignment in court for corruption in his home province in Limpopo was as much a consequence of his crossing the president as it was of his actual malfeasance. Overall, the message of the government's political and disciplinary failures is that, on the whole, corruption pays, and the chances of getting caught and prosecuted are minimal, unless one falls foul of elements within the ruling party.

The massive extent of corruption is regularly deplored in ANC statements. Recently, the government committed itself to a major cleanup in a bid to forge a "capable state."[12] Consequently, in mid-2013, Lindiwe Sisulu, minister of public service and administration, announced the creation of an anticorruption bureau. However, as noted by Paul Hoffman, a lawyer and prominent anticorruption warrior, the new bureau would join thirteen state institutions already formally charged with countering corruption, thus far with little effect. The problem, he argues, is that the state lacks any will to tackle corruption and that it has systematically undermined constitutional requirements that anticorruption bodies be adequately protected from political interference and properly resourced.[13] In other words, given, first, that the party itself is led by a man who is widely viewed to have been caught up in the massive corruption of the arms deal and to have used the presidency financially to benefit his personal circle of family and friends; and second, that the ANC has institutionalized rent-seeking by its forging an incestuous financial relationship with government parastatals, the prospects of the ruling party turning on the emergent "party-state bourgeoisie" (which it has itself created) are minimal.

# Democracy at Risk?

South Africa is undoubtedly a far better place than it was under apartheid, and for that the ANC deserves much credit. The legacy that the ANC inherited was unenviable, and ANC rule has provided for significantly improved life chances for the majority of the population. In considerable part, their doing so has been a result of the deal struck with business at the onset of democracy: in return for corporations granting greater access to segments of the population previously largely excluded from the private sector, the ANC would pursue policies facilitative of capitalist growth within the context of a rapidly changing global economy. Increasingly, however, questions are being raised about whether the economic deal struck in 1994 can remain viable: on one hand, business complains loudly that the ANC's political management is inhibiting greater competitiveness and efficiency; on the other hand, many critics join the ANC in alleging that corporate commitment to profitability too often comes at the expense of domestic investment and social welfare. Above all, the combined failures of ANC economic management and corporate expansion to bring down the unemployment level, and the enervating poverty a paucity of jobs brings in its wake, arouse popular antipathy and feed a disillusionment with the democratic outcome. Hence come ever louder calls for the ANC to transform South Africa into a "developmental state"—one in which the state would become the senior partner to business in pursuing growth and development, notably via a parastatal-led drive for the expansion and upgrade of infrastructure.

Even if we allow for the idea that South Africa requires a major shift in state economic policy, we come up against significant factors that suggest that the ANC's capacity to manage such a change faces obstacles of its own making and, equally, may put democracy at risk. Above all, we may point to the clash between the values of constitutional democracy and those of the ANC's commitment to the NDR. While the former implies that constitutionalism is fundamental to political freedom, the ANC's liberationist theorizing proposes the necessity of extending its authority over all sites of power, authorizes deployment as the means for doing so, tends toward the delegitimation of political opposition, and diminishes democracy by asserting "majoritarianism." Increasingly, the ANC seems to feel that it owns South Africa and that its political monopoly is historically justified. It is thus a moot point whether its ownership provides more for the erection of a predatory state under a rapacious party-state bourgeoisie than enables a developmental state under a technocratically oriented and pragmatic political leadership capable of forging a productive developmental partnership with large-scale capital.

This argument presumes that ANC political dominance will be entrenched for decades to come. Yet appearances are not always what they seem. As the NP was to find to its cost, South Africa is a highly complex society that is not easy to rule. There are, in short, actual and incipient countertendencies to ANC domination. Here, I briefly focus on four.

First, although the ANC rules in partnership with the SACP and Cosatu via the Tripartite Alliance, it is also subject to the significant influence they each wield within the party itself, notably the ability of Cosatu to get its members onto the streets in protest against particular government policies. Indeed, Pitcher sees the SACP and Cosatu as having played a major role in diluting the ANC's post-GEAR commitment to privatization and various other aspects of neoliberalization. At the same time, she sees the ANC having to balance internal alliance pressures from Cosatu against those of the expanding black middle class, with South Africa becoming an exemplar of "high-quality democratisation" (Pitcher 2012, 188). From the analysis presented in this article, her conclusion is regarded as rather too optimistic, not least because it can be argued that the leaderships of both SACP and Cosatu have themselves increasingly participated in the processes of class formation and, similarly, are increasingly socially distant from their constituencies. Nonetheless, Pitcher is undoubtedly correct in arguing that Cosatu, in particular, has, to some extent, powers of constraint.

Second, ANC transformational policies face the inherent contradiction that they promote state incapacity. On one hand, it is now notorious that while the ANC inherited an appalling educational deficit among the majority population, its oversight of the public schooling system has been severely deficient, a problem that feeds upward into the higher educational system (which itself faces multiple challenges) (for a recent review, see Motala 2013; see also Badat and Sayed, this volume; Babson, this volume). This educational deficit translates into a shortage of appropriately trained and equipped personnel available for recruitment into the public sector, where, despite high levels of unemployment, there are numerous unfilled positions. On the other hand, transformation of the public sector has translated into a rapid class formation that fosters adherence to a bureaucratic culture under which innovation and integrity are subordinated to political authority, and one which is strongly linked to the perception that state positions are a route to material accumulation. As a result, while there are undoubtedly sites of excellence within the government machinery, the state is highly dysfunctional in many areas—notably in the poorer provinces and within the smaller municipalities.

As a result and third, the government is facing mounting problems of service delivery, ranging from an inability to spend capital budgets through to equipping schools and providing basic sanitation and household services to local communities. Again, the developmental problems are huge, but the government's achievements in rolling out housing, water, and electricity to poorer segments of the population have been, overall, commendable. However, in such spheres, resources are never enough, especially when ANC electoral rhetoric boosts popular expectations. Thus, when delivery of services is compromised by officials' incompetence, often allied to corruption, the outcome is social upheaval. In a context of high levels of unemployment and poverty, among communities where popular memory recalls the ANC's bid in the 1980s to render the NP's South Africa ungovernable, and where officialdom is often viewed as impervious to complaint, riot is viewed as an effective way of securing political attention. The result has been an upsurge of local protests, which observers date from around 2004 and 2005 (when there were some six-thousand-odd such events that have continued at a similar rate from year to year). These disturbances are often inchoate and are sparked by disparate demands, but they are usually centered on forms of collective action that go beyond marches to tire-burnings, destruction of public property, and attacks on public officials. They regularly result in violent confrontations with the police. In turn, the state has responded with a militarization of the police; the most notorious result of this militarization has been the gunning down of striking mineworkers at Marikana in August 2012.

However, fourth, there is no automatic translation of social protest into organized oppositional politics. Indeed, contradictorily, protest regularly transforms itself into a vote for the ANC at election times, with Booysen (2011), for instance, viewing protest and voting as different repertoires of the relationship to the ruling party. That argument has some strength. Nonetheless, high levels of social protest could well contribute to a lasting countertendency to ANC domination. Certainly, there are major structural barriers to the consolidation of any unified opposition. For a start, the ANC, Cosatu, and the SACP, all of which claim to be movements of the poor, remain highly ambivalent toward emergent social movements. The ANC and the SACP tend to dismiss them as hostile or irresponsibly "ultra-Left"; Cosatu remains torn between joining their cause and seeking to control it. Meanwhile, the social movements are themselves highly divided along lines of class, race, ideology, and interest (Veriava and Naidoo 2013). Most particularly, they tend to scorn the ANC while regarding the DA as beyond the pale; yet they seemingly defy attempts by activists to forge an alternative. For its part, the DA recognizes that its growth requires it to expand among black communities, yet it needs to convince the nation at large that it can attract the active support of more than Coloured voters and a small segment of the black middle class. Nonetheless, for all that this analysis indicates that the ANC is under no immediate threat, the existing immense social fluidity, along with subterranean changes in electoral attitudes and behavior (Schulz-Herzenberg 2009), suggests that that the foundations of ruling party hegemony are inexorably being undermined.

Only time will tell whether the ANC will confirm the fears of doomsayers by resorting to political authoritarianism or whether it will fulfill the demands and hopes of democrats by accepting—sometime—electoral rebuke.

## Notes

1. I draw on Southall (2013), from which detailed referencing for much of the analysis pursued here can be obtained.

2. Pitcher (2012, 204) records that by 2005, just 9 out of 300 SOEs (or just 9 percent of state assets) had been privatized. See Southall (2007) and Maylam (2013) for discussions of how this process emulated models of ethnic empowerment pursued by NP governments in an earlier era.

3. Treatments of South Africa's economic trajectory under the ANC abound. Two useful discussions of different aspects are provided by Mohamed (2010) and Forslund (2013).

4. For more detailed discussion of the liberation movement's political culture, see Southall (2013, 69–77).

5. On the relationship with the SOEs, see Jolobe (2010).

6. The three largest parties shared 93.6 percent of the vote in 1994 (ANC, NP, and IFP), 84.5 percent in 1999 (ANC, DA, and IFP), 89 percent in 2004 (ANC, DA, and IFP), and 90 percent in 2009 (ANC, DA,

and the Congress of the People). The number of parties represented in the assembly was eight in 1994, thirteen in 1999, twelve in 2004, and thirteen in 2009.

7. The IFP's 50.5 percent majority at the provincial level in 1994 was almost certainly negotiated (with vote counting disappearing from national television for several hours). Unfortunately, the full story has yet to be told.

8. Illustrative of Seriti's supine posture has been his supposed inability to track down Fana Hlongwane, a key advisor to Joe Modisi and important facilitator of the arms deal, for interview. However, on one occasion the *Mail & Guardian* was able to ascertain Hlongwane's whereabouts by simply phoning him. On a later occasion, he was seen dining with a member of the ANC's NEC in Sandton, Johannesburg. The commission has also come under massive criticism for its failure to summon the ANC, on the grounds that it was not implicated in corruption related to the arms deal, a conclusion that activists who have supplied huge reams of evidence to Judge Seriti find incredible.

9. The magistracy has been similarly transformed.

10. Although see Picard (2005).

11. Results of the auditor-general's reports on national, provincial, and local governments for 2011–2012. See *Business Day*, 12 March 2013; *Daily Maverick*, 31 March 2013; *Mail & Guardian*, 15–21 March 2013.

12. See *Business Day*, 20 December 2012.

13. Hoffman (2013) notes how the specialist police unit (the hawks) established to replace the highly effective scorpions (who had led the anticorruption charge against Zuma, only to be disbanded when he gained power), has been located within rather than outside the police service, and thus under the authority of the minister of police and police commissioner (the latter, always effectively a political appointment). An important judgment in the Constitutional Court (the Glenister judgment in 2011) ruled that the status of the hawks failed to fulfill constitutional requirements that it be politically independent, and instructed the government to amend the situation. Hoffman regards the government's proposed amendment bill as only tinkering with the situation and, if passed, likely to lead to another challenge to the hawks constitutionality in the Constitutional Court.

# References

ANC. 1998. The state, property relations and social transformation. *Umrabulo* 5 (3).

Babson, Andrew. 2014. Developing possibilities for South African youths: Beyond limited educational choices. *The ANNALS of the American Academy of Political and Social Science*, this volume.

Badat, Saleem, and Yusuf Sayed. 2014. Post-1994 South African education: The challenge of social justice. *The ANNALS of the American Academy of Political and Social Science*, this volume.

Booysen, Susan. 2011. *The African National Congress and the regeneration of political power*. Johannesburg: Wits University Press.

Butler, Anthony. 2009. The ANC's national campaign of 2009: *Siyanqoba!* In *Zunami! The 2009 South African elections*, eds. Roger Southall and John Daniel, 65–113. Johannesburg: Jacana Media.

Daniel, John, and Roger Southall. 2009. The national and provincial electoral outcomes: Continuity with change. In *Zunami! The 2009 South African elections*, eds. Roger Southall and John Daniel, 232–69. Johannesburg: Jacana Media.

Davis, Gavin. 19–25 November 2010. An independent cadre is a contradiction in terms amid party loyalty. *Mail & Guardian*.

Ellis, Stephen. 2012, *External mission: The ANC in exile*. Johannesburg and Cape Town: Jonathan Ball Publishers.

Feinstein, Andrew. 2007. *After the party: A personal and political journey inside the ANC*. Jeppestown: Jonathan Ball Publishers.

Forslund, Dick. 2013. Mass unemployment and the low-wage regime in South Africa. In *New South African review 3: The second phase—Tragedy or farce?* eds. John Daniel, Prishani Naidoo, Devan Pillay, and Roger Southall, 95–118. Johannesburg: Wits University Press.

Francis, Suzanne. 2011. *Institutionalizing elites: Political elite formation and change in the KwaZulu-Natal provincial legislature*. Boston, MA. Brill.

Giliomee, Herman, and Charles Simkins, eds. 1999. *The awkward embrace: One-party domination and democracy*. Cape Town: Routledge.

Hoffman, Paul. 25 June 2013. Anti-corruption bureau: Just another toothless agency. *Cape Times*.

Holden, Paul. 2008. *The arms deal in your pocket*. Jeppestown: Jonathan Ball Publishers.

Johnson, R.W. 2009. *South Africa's brave new world: The beloved country since the end of apartheid*. London: Allen Lane.

Jolobe, Zwelethu. 2010. Financing the ANC: Chancellor House, Eskom and the dilemmas of party finance reform. In *Paying for politics: Party funding and political change in South Africa and the Global South*, ed. Anthony Butler, 201–17. Johannesburg: Jacana Media.

Lane, Jan-Erik, and Svante Errson. 1997. The probability of democratic success in South Africa. *Democratization* 4 (4): 1–16.

Maylam, Paul. 2013. Fragile multi-class alliances compared: Some unlikely parallels between the National Party and the African National Congress. In *New South African review 3: The second phase—Tragedy or farce?* eds. John Daniel, Prishani Naidoo, Devan Pillay, and Roger Southall, 61–75. Johannesburg: Wits University Press.

Mohamed, Seeraj. 2010. The state of the South African economy. In *New South African review 2010: Development or decline?* eds. John Daniel, Prishani Naidoo, Devan Pillay, and Roger Southall, 39–64. Johannesburg: Wits University Press.

Motala, Shireen. 2013. Equity, quality and access in South African education: A work very still much in progress. In *New South African review 3: The second phase—Tragedy or farce?* eds. John Daniel, Prishani Naidoo, Devan Pillay, and Roger Southall, 221–38. Johannesburg: Wits University Press.

Naidoo, Vinothan. 2013. Cadre deployment versus merit? Reviewing politicization in the public service. In *New South African review 3: The second phase—Tragedy or farce?* eds. John Daniel, Prishani Naidoo, Devan Pillay, and Roger Southall, 261–77. Johannesburg: Wits University Press.

Picard, Louis. 2005. *The state of the state: Institutional transformation, capacity and political change in South Africa*. Johannesburg: Wits University Press.

Pitcher, M. Anne. 2012. *Party politics and economic reform in Africa's democracies*. New York, NY: Cambridge University Press.

Roux, Theunis. 2012. *The politics of principle: The first South African Constitutional Court*. Cambridge: Cambridge University Press.

SAIRR (South African Institute of Race Relations). 2009/2010. *South Africa Survey*. Braamfontein: SAIRR.

SAIRR. 2012. *South Africa Survey*. Johannesburg: SAIRR.

Saul, John. 1994. The Southern African revolution. In *Recolonization and resistance: Southern Africa in the 1990s*, ed. John Saul, 1–34. Trenton, NJ: Africa World Press.

Saul, John. 2008. *Decolonization and empire: Contesting the rhetoric and reality of resubordination in Southern Africa and beyond*. Johannesburg: Wits University Press.

Schulz-Herzenberg, Collette. 2009. Trends in party support and voting behaviour, 1994–2009. In *Zunami! The 2009 South African elections*, eds. Roger Southall and John Daniel, 23–46. Johannesburg: Jacana Media.

Southall, Roger. 2000. The state of democracy in South Africa. *Commonwealth and Comparative Politics* 38 (3): 147–70.

Southall, Roger. 2007. The ANC, black economic empowerment and state-owned enterprises: A recycling of history? In *State of the nation: South Africa 2007*, eds. Sakhela Buhlungu, John Daniel, Roger Southall, and Jessica Lutchman, 201–25. Cape Town: HSRC Press.

Southall, Roger. 2013. *Liberation movements in power: Party and state in southern Africa*. Pietermaritzburg: UKZN Press.

Southern, Neil, and Roger Southall. 2011. Dancing like a monkey? The Democratic Alliance and opposition politics in South Africa. In *New South African review 2: Old paths, new compromises?* eds. John Daniel, Prishani Naidoo, Devan Pillay, and Roger Southall, 68–82. Johannesburg: Wits University Press.

Veriava, Ahmed, and Prishani Naidoo. 2013. Predicaments of post-apartheid social movement politics: The anti-privatisation forum in Johannesburg. In *New South African review 3: The second phase—Tragedy or farce?* eds. John Daniel, Prishani Naidoo, Devan Pillay, and Roger Southall, 76–89. Johannesburg: Wits University Press.

# The Social and Political Implications of Demographic Change in Post-Apartheid South Africa

JEREMY SEEKINGS

The cohort of young people born between the early 1980s and early 1990s consitute a demographic bulge in the South African population. The sheer size of this cohort renders it especially important in terms of the changing political, economic, and social life of the country. The cohort grew up for the most part after apartheid had ended, entered the labor market at a time of high unemployment, is having children as marriage is in decline, and reached voting age just as the African National Congress's (ANC's) moral stature began to decline. All these factors might be expected to result in distinctive disaffection and a propensity for dissent. In terms of their attitudes and behavior, however, this cohort looks much like older (or immediately preceding) cohorts of South Africans. Where this cohort is likely to leave its mark is in entrenching some of the social, economic, and political changes that, until recently, might have appeared transient.

*Keywords:* childhood; youth; unemployment; violence; transition to adulthood; demographic change; South Africa

## Introduction: "Perfect Window" or "Perfect Storm"?

South Africa's 2011 Population Census confirmed that the country's population had broken through the 50-million mark, reaching an estimated 51.8 million people. This figure depicts growth of 28 percent since 1996, when the population had been 40.6 million (Statistics South Africa [Stats SA] 2012, 14). Although South Africa's 2012 National Development

*Jeremy Seekings is a professor of political studies and sociology and director of the Centre for Social Science Research at the University of Cape Town, and a visiting professor at Yale University. His most recent (coauthored) book is* Growing Up in the New South Africa: Childhood and Adolescence in Post-Apartheid Cape Town *(Human Sciences Research Council 2010).*

DOI: 10.1177/0002716213508265

70

ANNALS, *AAPSS*, 652, March 2014

Plan (NDP) worried that fertility rates might not continue to decline and that total population might rise to 60 million by 2030 (National Planning Commission 2012, 77), World Bank data on future growth suggest that population growth will continue to slow, reaching about 55 million sometime between 2040 and 2050.[1]

Continuing population growth at the same time as fertility declines is typical of Africa, but the age structure of South Africa's population is distinctive in that the largest cohort is not the youngest, but is the cohort born in the mid- and late 1980s, aged between 20 and 29 at the time of the 2011 census. This cohort is larger, in absolute numbers, than both preceding and following cohorts. This bulge in the age structure is due to the rapidly declining fertility rate as well as to AIDS-related mortality, especially in the late 1990s and early 2000s, among both children and working-age adults.

The existence of this unusually large cohort of young people has already had major implications for the schooling system, through which the cohort passed in the late 1990s and early 2000s. Additional schools had to be built and teachers employed. The cohort has now entered the labor market, increasing the number of job-seekers during a global (and local) economic downturn and subsequent slow growth in job creation. The young men and women in this cohort are look-ing for work, and their consumption preferences are transforming demand. They are trying to raise their social status and to find their own homes. They account for a large proportion of both perpetrators and victims of crime and violence, compose a large proportion of the electorate, and are having—and raising—children of their own.

The effects of this demographic bulge are compounded by urbanization. Whereas Gauteng's population grew by 57 percent between 1996 and 2011, and the Western Cape's by 47 percent, the other seven provinces combined grew by only 17 percent. The population of the Free State may even have begun to decline (Stats SA 2012, 14–15). The NDP noted that "it is likely that almost all of South Africa's net population growth until 2030 (an estimated 8 million) will take place in urban areas, especially in major cities" (National Planning Commission 2012, 84).

The demographic data point also to a third important trend: the slowly rising number of elderly, both in absolute numbers and as a proportion of the total population. Between 1996 and 2011, the proportion of the total population aged 65 or older rose from 4.8 percent to 5.3 percent. Models predict that this popula-tion will grow from about 2.3 million (in 2010) to 5.7 million by 2050.[2]

The 2012 NDP paid careful attention to these demographic trends. The bulge in the working-age population opens a "window of opportunity" in terms of inclu-sive economic growth:

> South Africa has arrived at the "sweet spot" of demographic transition. The population has a proportionately high number of working-age people and a proportionately low number of young and old. This means that the dependency ratio—the percentage of those over 64 and under 15 relative to the working-age population—is at a level where there are enough people of working age to support the non-working population. (National Planning Commission 2012, 78)

The NDP reported that the age-related dependency ratio will have stopped declining by 2020, as the rising number of elderly offsets the slowly declining number of children.

In the South African case, however, dependency is much more of a challenge than the age structure alone suggests. "The caveat in South Africa's case is that unemployment and HIV/AIDS have produced many more dependents than would normally be the case," the NDP noted. "Although statistically South Africa is in a position to cash in on a demographic dividend, the challenges of HIV/AIDS and joblessness are a burden on those who are working." The large working-age population might be a "major asset," but only if "the challenge" of "putting this working-age population to work" is tackled successfully (National Planning Commission 2012, 78).

The challenge is, of course, social and political as much as economic. The NDP warned that, if the working-age population is not put to work, "the perfect window could be the perfect storm" (National Planning Commission 2012, 78). A large number of unemployed young men are, the NDP suggested, a recipe for "social disorder, widespread political unrest and increased crime" (National Planning Commission 2012, 86). As trade union leader Zwelinzima Vavi, among others, has said, unemployed youth represent a "ticking time-bomb" (see Institute for Justice and Reconciliation [IJR] 2012).

The demographic data feed into a long-standing anxiety in South Africa about the country's youth. Young men, especially poor and black young men, have long been a source of anxiety not only for privileged elites but also for many poor and black people themselves. The image of the "youth" has sometimes had a positive dimension, associated with energy and perhaps a commitment to transforming society for the better. But its negative dimensions have generally predominated: violence and crime, alienation and aggression, irresponsibility and idleness, disaffection and disrespect. If youths do not have opportunities to become responsible, work-oriented "adults," the stability of society will be threatened. If they pass their norms and attitudes onto their children, the strain in the social fabric will worsen further.

In the early 1990s a moral panic erupted over anxiety that South African youth might derail the pacted transition to representative democracy (Seekings 1995, 1996). In the early 2000s, attention shifted to the more "ordinary" experiences of young people (Seekings 2006). In the late 2000s and 2010s, however, anxiety over the youth resurfaced in the media, driven by a concern that their disappointment and frustration with the slow pace of social and economic change would threaten South Africa's fragile democracy. Unemployment, crime, violence, and declining social cohesion would feed each other. Widespread, often violent protests over service delivery and governance, and a rising tide of violent strikes, were reminiscent of the tumult of the 1980s.

The usual source of anxiety over the youth is that, during an incomplete transition to adulthood, youths' behavior is unconstrained by the practical, moral, or social constraints or responsibilities that order the lives of adults. More precisely, in a world in which there are many facets to the transition to adulthood, failure to complete any one of these transitions reduces the likelihood of young people behaving in the ways associated with the completion of other transitions. In this view, for example, if unemployment delays the completion of someone's transition to the "adult" role of worker, this person is less likely to behave in the ways associated with other adult roles, such as citizen and community participant, spouse, parent, or household manager. Conversely, a failure to transit successfully into adult familial roles might impede the transition into work. The recent comparative literature on transitions to adulthood suggests that the duration of transitions from childhood to adulthood has lengthened across much of the global south (Lloyd et al. 2005).

As the comparative literature also concludes, however, youths do become, eventually, adult workers, citizens, community participants, spouses, parents, and household managers. Although the precise form of a "successful" transition varies among societies—for example in terms of differences regarding the balance between individual autonomy and ties to larger households and communities— most young people do make a successful transition (Lloyd et al. 2005). The behaviors, norms, and attitudes associated with youths are generally age-specific, giving way to different ones as young people enter full-time employment, form independent households, marry and have children, and participate in community activities. Indeed, the kinds of youth who are viewed as social problems may be visible but almost always comprise a small and diminishing proportion of even their own generation.

Are there circumstances in which a significant proportion of the young people in an age cohort or generation might permanently fail to complete one or more of these transitions to adulthood? This is the spectre raised by the concept of a "lost generation," but that rarely (if ever) seems to be realized. One common version of this spectre points to children who were denied or deprived of education, which makes it harder for them to become responsible workers, citizens, or family members. In the South African case, the generation of adolescents born in the late 1960s and even early 1970s was, according to some commentators (see Seekings 1996), socialized on violent streets rather than in functional schools, rendering them "lost" in terms of both economic growth and social order. However, empirical research findings tend to undermine this view (Seekings 1996, 2006). Is the generation born between the early 1980s and mid-1990s different? What happens when an unusually large cohort of young people enter their 20s at a time when their employment opportunities are scarce, when social relations are in flux, and when political loyalties are eroded and grievances sharpened? In the South African case, has the combination of a demographic bulge and the contemporary economic, social, and political context resulted in a situation unlike even past periods of anxiety? Might some combination of background, numbers, and context serve to render transitions permanently incomplete, with consequences for the rest of society?

This article explores three key dimensions of the experiences of this generation. My focus is on its experiences in the late 2000s and early 2010s, after most of the adolescents involved had exited the schooling system. I focus on entry into the labor market, household formation, and the exercise of citizenship, arguing that the lives of many (but not all) young people are characterized not so much by a protracted or incomplete transition to adulthood, but rather by quick immersion into a novel kind of adulthood that is characterized by economic, social, and political fluidity.[3]

## Entry into the Labor Market

The labor market is at the core of the challenge of incorporating this cohort of young people into full citizenship. Exceptionally high rates of unemployment among young people in South Africa are widely seen as an important foundation of many of the country's social problems: violence and crime, alcohol and drug abuse, widespread gangs, the decline of marriage, and the fragility of community. It would be surprising if young people's unequal experiences in the labor market did not have enduring consequences for their life chances in many other respects as well.

The generation of young South Africans who entered the labor market in the late 2000s and early 2010s had high, but orthodox, aspirations. Adolescents in Cape Town aged 18 in 2002—that is, born in 1984—were asked (as part of the Cape Area Panel Study [CAPS]) about their future expectations. Asked what work they expected or planned to be doing at the age of 30—12 years later—most of the 18-year-old adolescents in poorer neighborhoods said that they expected to be professionals, businessmen, or in other high-earning occupations, with jobs that were well-paid and enjoyable. Some expected to be working three years later; most of the others said that they would still be studying then. Even in poor or very poor neighborhoods, between 40 and 50 percent of adolescents put their chances of getting a well-paid job as "high" or "very high." Many other indicators (in CAPS and other surveys) reveal a similar picture of optimism and even a high degree of perceived control over life among young African men and women in post-apartheid South Africa (Bray et al. 2010, 217–23, 296–300). These high aspirations were generally matched by enrollment in school. In 2010, as many as 93 percent of 16-year-olds, 86 percent of 17-year-olds, and 71 percent of 18-year-olds attended educational institutions (Hall 2012, 96). Few South African adolescents leave school at a young age to work. Even when adolescents experience difficulties in progressing through school or finding employment after leaving school, expectations often remain high (Bray et al. 2010; Roberts 2011).

Although most young people spend longer than previous generations in school, most learn too little and many leave with limited skills. In the 2011 Annual National Assessment, the average score in Grade 3 numeracy was 28 percent, and in Grade 6 mathematics it was 30 percent. Cross-national educational assessments show that South African schools perform disastrously, especially in mathematics. Performance varies massively between better schools, mostly in rich neighborhoods, and weaker schools, invariably in poor areas (Branson and Zuze 2012; van der Berg 2007, 2008). Basic literacy rates have risen over time, but it is unlikely that the same is true of numeracy (given South Africa's very low numeracy rates).[4]

FIGURE 1
Employment Status by Age, Men

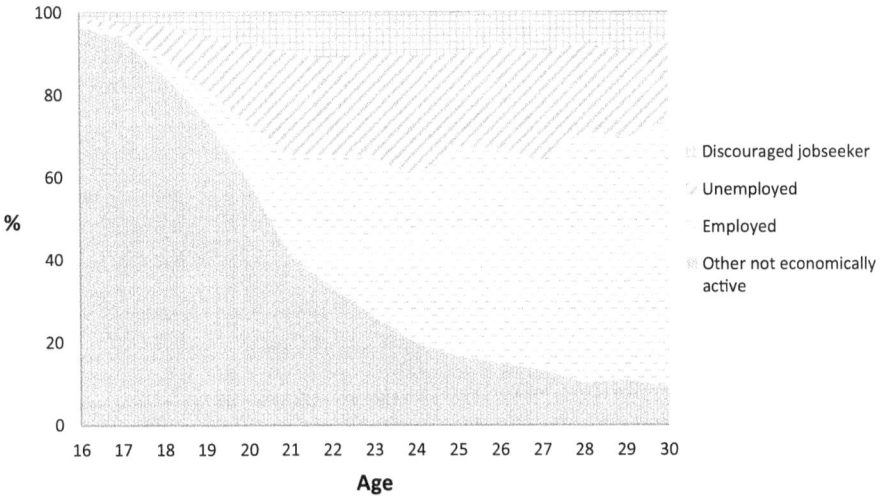

SOURCE: Author's calculations using the Labour Force Survey (LFS) for the second quarter of 2010.

Leaving school with very limited skills was especially important because the demand for low-skilled workers was declining at the same time as unemployment was rising. Indeed, unemployment is high despite steady (but underwhelming) economic growth in large part because of the collapse in demand for unskilled and even semiskilled workers in the formal sector. Data on the skill composition of the workforce are fragmentary, and insufficiently disaggregated between formal and informal, public and private, tradable and nontradable sectors. But the trend is clear: the demand for unskilled labor in the formal sector, and especially in tradable sectors, has fallen dramatically (Bhorat and Oosthuizen 2006). The general problems of entering the South African labor market were compounded at the end of the 2000s by the global economic downturn. Close to one million jobs were lost in 2009–2010, and unemployment rates rose sharply (Yu 2012).

The magnitude of the employment crisis facing young men and women in South Africa is evident in Figures 1 and 2. In 2010, almost all 16- and 17-year-olds were still in school, and were therefore classified as "other not economically active." By the age of 21 (for men) or 22 (for women), more than one-half of young people were in the labor market. By their late 20s, about 10 percent of young men, and about 25 percent of young women, were neither working nor wanting work. But many young people who had left school and wanted work could not find it. Six out of every ten young people in their early 20s who had not completed secondary school and wanted work were

FIGURE 2
Employment Status by Age, Women

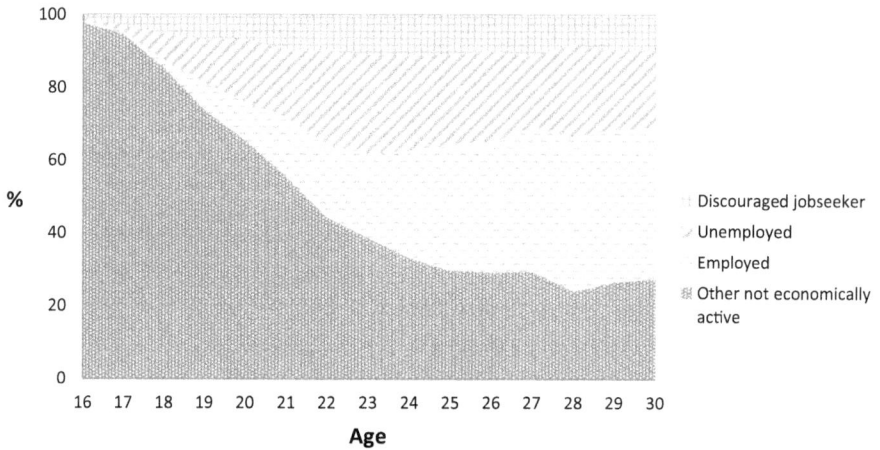

SOURCE: Author's calculations using the LFS for the second quarter of 2010.

unemployed. The corresponding proportion for young people in their late 20s was about 50 percent. Young people who had completed secondary school or (especially) had some tertiary education were much more likely to find work. By their late 20s, young people who completed secondary school have an unemployment rate one-third lower, and young people with some tertiary education have an unemployment rate two-thirds lower, than their less educated peers.[5]

Unemployment rates are higher among women than men, but the difference is modest due to the dramatic feminization of employment. Working women in their mid- and late 20s were, on average, earning much the same as their male peers, and the proportion of young women who had ever worked was only a little lower than for young men.[6]

In previous work, we identified three broad clusters of classes in South African society at the end of the twentieth century (Seekings and Nattrass 2005). One in seven households was in what we called the "upper classes." About 38 percent of households fell into a "middle" set of classes, comprising the lower middle class and formally employed (rather than informally employed) working classes. Almost one-half (48 percent) of all households fell into a lower tier of classes, comprising the more marginal sections of the working population, together with what we called the "underclass" (comprising households effectively shut out of the labor market). Some of the young men and women who entered the labor market in the late 2000s found stable employment and entered the upper or middle clusters of classes. Many, however, swelled the lower cluster of marginal classes, either unemployed or with precarious and

FIGURE 3
Unemployment Rates, by Age and Year

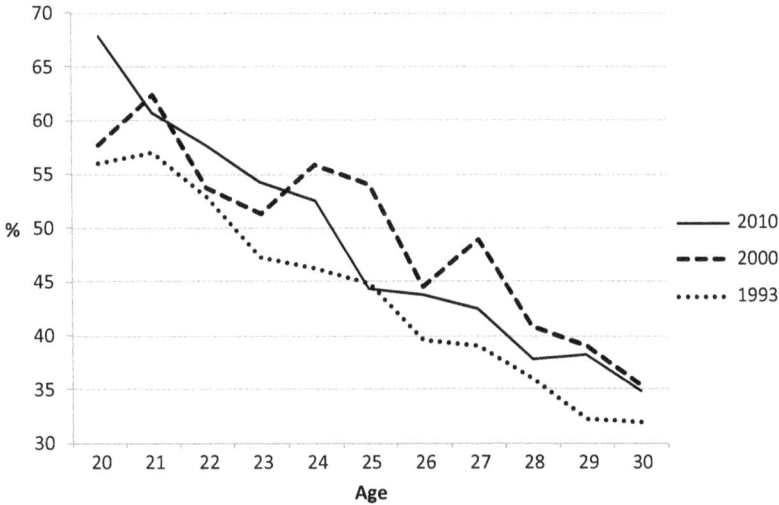

SOURCE: Author's calculations using the LFS for the second quarter of 2010; LFS, February 2000; and 1993 PSLSD (Project for Statistics on Living Standards and Development) survey.

poorly paid work in the informal sector or in the most marginal corners of the formal sector (such as domestic and agricultural work). These young people are "outsiders," typically lacking social capital (i.e., useful connections through kin, friends, or neighbors), cultural capital (including both knowledge of how labor markets work and the conventional aesthetic markers of success), financial capital, and educational credentials. They struggle to find employment; if they find work, they often struggle to retain it, and if they lose it, they battle to find new employment.

Our in-depth interviews with these individuals provide a depressing picture, with considerable evidence for depression and passivity. Only a minority of jobless adolescents are actually looking for work at any one time. It is usually assumed that not looking reflects the perception that looking is futile, that is, that the unemployed have been discouraged from active search because of its futility. But it seems that this discouragement is often fuelled by psychological depression, which saps initiative.

Is the experience of this generation very different from the experience of previous generations? Figure 3 shows unemployment rates for young people from the ages of 20 to 30, in 1993, 2000, and 2010.[7] The rates by age in 2000 and 2010 were higher than in 1993, but the differences are not large; and the rates in 2010 were, at least from the age of 24, a little lower than in 2000. Chronic unemployment and underemployment have been problems since the 1970s.

# The Transformations of Families and Care

Young South Africans are shaped by their familial backgrounds and, in turn, shape the next generation through arranging the kinds of families in which their children grow up. In many parts of the developing world, families are undergoing profound change, but these processes are especially dramatic in the South African context. A declining number of children grow up with regular contact with their fathers or even living in households where there is a stable or enduring adult male presence. Marriage has declined rapidly, and unmarried chronic cohabitation has only partially taken its place. Extended family ties have weakened, especially on the paternal side, with the decline of patrilineal culture. Many households are characterized by fluidity (Ross 1996, 2003; Seekings 2008).

The fullest data on the backgrounds of the generation born in the 1980s and early 1990s is from CAPS. The CAPS data cover only young men and women living in Cape Town, and a major metropolitan area should not be taken as representative of the country as a whole. Nonetheless, the CAPS data reveal important features of the national experience, not least because many young people in Cape Town grew up in poor, rural areas of the Eastern Cape before migrating to the city.

Among adolescents born in the mid-1980s and living in Cape Town in 2002, three-quarters had always lived with their mothers but less than one-half had lived with their fathers for their entire lives. Children from poor families were least likely to have coresided with their parents, while children from rich families were most likely to have done so. Physical separation need not mean a complete absence of contact between parents and children, however. Many fathers continue to play a role in the lives of their children, even when they live apart (Richter and Morrell 2006; Bray et al. 2010). Overall, however, paternal absence is associated with reduced contact and weaker relationships between children and their fathers. Some physically absent, emotionally distant fathers do fulfill their material roles as providers, but many absent fathers fail to play even this role. Some adolescents growing up apart from one or both parents form close attachments to other kin (and even nonkin), calling them "mother" or "father." While almost all adolescents have mother figures in their lives, a significant proportion of young men and women grow up without any regular father figure (Bray et al. 2010). How much this matters, or for what, is not clear. There have been few South African studies that trace the enduring consequences of parental absence and behavior for young people in later life. One study of male perpetrators of violence, using CAPS data, found a significant positive bivariate relationship between paternal absence during childhood and perpetrating violence against strangers in later life. The relationship ceases to be statistically significant when one controls for other characteristics of the childhood home, such as the prevalence of drinking or drugs or the young adult's own drinking practices (Seekings and Thaler 2010). In short, it seems likely that the kind of environment in which a child grows up and in which he (or she) later lives seems more important than the fact of paternal presence or absence in itself.

The declining presence of fathers might not itself be associated with subsequent pathologies, but it is unlikely that relationships between kin will stop evolving and even less likely that they will revert to the kinds of relationships that existed in the past. This has important consequences for society as a whole in that current trends in patterns of care and obligation are likely to become permanent. Perhaps the most striking characteristic of kinship in the early 2000s is its diminishing salience and reach. Kinship was famously defined by the anthropologist Meyer Fortes as "binding," creating "inescapable moral claims and obligations" (Fortes 1969, 242). In South Africa, kinship has ceased to be binding, and the obligations considered inescapable in the past are now often negotiable. Across much of South Africa, claims on paternal kin have declined dramatically, and maternal kin recognize a narrower range of responsibilities than in the past. Obligations between a mother and her children seem to have remained generally sacrosanct, but support between siblings is often conditional, and support between more distant kin even more so. The elderly are generally financially independent, on account of the country's old-age pension, and children are almost always cared for by kin. But the claims made by working-age adults on kin can and often are denied and are, at least, open to negotiation (Harper and Seekings 2010). The rise of chronic unemployment has clearly played a major part in this transformation of norms. The generation born in the 1980s and early 1990s will play a crucial role in determining whether the norms associated with diminished responsibility become entrenched and hegemonic. The evidence points in different directions. On one hand, there are plenty of young people who contest the diminution of kinship obligations and who support a range of kin, if and when they can. On the other hand, both quantitative and qualitative research suggests that the radius of responsibility is generally (although unevenly) shrinking (Harper and Seekings 2010; Mosoetsa 2011).

At the core of the transformation of kinship is the decline of marriage. By the age of 25, only 10 percent of young people are (or have ever been) married; another 9 percent are currently cohabiting without being married. By the age of 30, these proportions have risen to 25 percent and 15 percent, respectively. Even at the age of 30, only a minority of young men and women are married or cohabiting.[8] In 1996, only 36 percent of women aged 30 to 34 had never married. By 2007, this proportion had risen to 46 percent. The equivalent figures for men are 41 percent and 53 percent, respectively. In other words, the proportion of men and women who were married in this age range fell by, on average, 1 percentage point per year. Any increase in cohabitation had failed to offset the decline in marriage (Moore 2011).

There are numerous likely factors in the decline of marriage. A growing minority of young people believe that marriage is an outdated institution. Among some young women, marriage is associated with abuse. It has also become increasingly accepted to have children outside marriage. Bridewealth is expensive. Unemployed men struggle to provide at all, while many women are educated, working, and economically and culturally less dependent on male breadwinners (Hunter 2010). Unemployment is associated with delays in marriage and independent household formation (Klasen and Woolard 2009). More than a quarter of all 30-year-olds are living with one or both parents, and only over half are the heads of their own households (or are the partners of the household head).[9] While young employed people live in separate, small households, young unemployed people tend to live in large households.

The decline of marriage does not mean that young men and women have no children. Rather, they have children outside of marriage, and often outside of any cohabiting relationship. The median age of first birth among African women is 22 (Moore 2011). By the age of 30, almost all young women have had children, and most of these mothers live with their children.[10] There are no national data on the proportion of men who are fathers by age (see Posel and Devey [2006] for a discussion of the dearth of data on fathers). It is likely that a majority of young men have fathered children by the age of 30, but only a minority actually live with any of their children. These data are reflected in data on children. Of the current generation of children, only one in three lives with both parents, with another 40 percent living with their mother but not their father. One-quarter live with neither parent; only a minority of these are orphans (Meintjes and Hall 2012, 83). Paternal presence is the exception rather than the rule. It is not clear whether, or how much, any of this matters. But regardless of their consequences, it is difficult to see these trends being reversed.

## Political Attitudes and Behavior

The youth were widely considered central to the "township revolt" of the 1980s—when many of South Africa's townships exploded in protest against the apartheid state (Seekings 1993)—and to political instability in the early 1990s (Seekings 1995). A generation later, (now former) ANC Youth League president Julius Malema came to personify the threat supposedly posed by restless, frustrated young men. Malema's appeal was generally attributed to the combination of the age-specific frustrations of his youthful constituency, the pall cast on democracy by persistent unemployment and inadequate public services, and the declining moral legitimacy of the ANC itself. In this view, young people have brought with them their usual proclivity for rash action, and have arrived at a political context marred by widespread disappointment and general disillusionment.

The 1980s cohort of young men and women became adults in a political system with apparently strong institutions of representative democracy. Elections are free, fair, and regular. The constitution provides for some separation of powers among the executive, legislature, and judiciary, and the judiciary has imposed constraints and obligations on the government in terms of the Bill of Rights and other constitutional provisions. South Africa has a set of somewhat independent and sometimes effective statutory watchdogs, as well as an energetic press.

In practice, however, many of the checks and balances in the constitutional architecture of democracy are weakened by the dominance of the ANC. Power is highly centralized within the ANC, and the ANC's leaders have been effective in co-opting dissidents and neutralizing defectors. The result is that it is difficult for citizens to hold the government to account. The ANC-led government, for example, has won four successive national elections despite being judged by a majority of the electorate to have performed poorly on the most important issues facing the country, that is, unemployment followed by crime.

Many young people are outsiders in (or from) the labor market. They often live in neighborhoods where there are few employment opportunities and know few people who can help to find them work elsewhere. They typically lack strong educational qualifications and work experience. And they often lack the cultural capital to have a good understanding of what might help them find work, what kinds of work are realistically available, and even how to perform satisfactorily in any work that they do get. At some point in their early 20s, as the prospect of returning to school recedes, most must realize that they are unlikely ever to achieve their aspirations for success. Their current lack of success is demeaning and debilitating; many experience prejudice or stigma from friends and family. The government has not done well in terms of addressing these issues. A pervasive culture of crass consumerism and conspicuous consumption (Posel 2010) might be expected to amplify the grievances of the excluded.

This economy and culture might seem to offer a setting that is conducive to an alienation from democratic politics. We might expect to find that young people have turned away from elections and, perhaps, mobilized by demagogues such as Malema, turned to direct action. This does not appear to have been the case.

Using data from a series of cross-sectional studies of political opinion, Mattes (2011) finds that young people are no less interested in politics, they do not discuss politics any less, and they do not read newspapers any less often than older generations. They are less likely to vote or to attend community meetings, but it is not clear that either rates of voting or community activism among young South Africans are low by global standards. Political participation might not be as high as the level in 1994, but it is likely that it was the moment of democratization that was exceptional. Mattes also finds that young people might have been slightly more likely than older adults to participate in protests in the early 2000s, but any age differential had disappeared by the mid-2000s. The IJR, using a second series of cross-sectional studies of public opinion, also finds little evidence that young people are politically distinct. Young people are only slightly more likely than older adults to report that they participate in protests or demonstrations, and there has been no clear trend over time in participation in protests or demonstrations (IJR 2012, 25). Young people are marginally less respectful of the law than older adults, but the difference is very modest, and the trend over time seems to have been one of rising, not falling, respect for the law. Age makes no difference to confidence in public institutions or trust in political leaders (IJR 2012, 22–24).

Mattes does find that "as far as democracy goes, the post-*apartheid* generation remains as 'lukewarm' as their parents and grandparents. . . . Whatever advantages might have accrued from the new political experiences of freedom, liberty and self-government seem to have been neutralized by the disadvantages of enduring unemployment, poverty and corruption" (Mattes 2011, 19). This result is worrying given that, among South Africans in general, commitment to democratic norms is narrow and shallow in post-apartheid South Africa. As Mattes writes, "South Africans—of all races—pay minimal lip service to the idea of democracy, and that significant minorities would be willing to countenance one party rule or strong man dictatorship especially if these regimes would promise economic development (or may simply believe erringly that those regimes are consistent with democracy)" (Mattes 2011, 3; see further Mattes 2001). Intolerance is widespread (Gibson and Gouws 2003), and South Africans exhibit "the highest levels of xenophobia measured anywhere in the world" (Mattes 2011, 3; Mattes et al. 2000). Violence, including against women, is pervasive. Hopes that the generation of young men and women who came of age after apartheid—the "born frees"—would have a stronger and more positive commitment to democracy have been disappointed. In their attitudes toward democracy, young people exhibit the same diversity as older generations, and their attitudes seem to be shaped by their experiences of, for example, corruption, unemployment, or poverty. Age or generation by themselves seem to have little effect.

Social attitudes show the same pattern. A culture of consumerism seems hegemonic even among poor young people (Schenk and Seekings 2013). Attitudes toward race are changing, with rising levels of reported interracial contact (although less so among the poor). Young people are a little more open to some interracial interactions than older people, but there is still widespread disapproval of interracial marriage; there do not seem to be significant differences between younger and older people in terms of their attitudes on most aspects of racial integration (IJR 2012, 42–45). Whether attitudes among young people are reassuring or worrying, they tend to mirror similar attitudes among older people.

Might very high rates of unemployment among young men fuel South Africa's very high rates of violence and crime, even if they have little observable effect on political behavior? Our interviews in poor neighborhoods of Cape Town find general popular support for the view that unemployment is linked to violence. The unemployed are said to have time on their hands, and unemployed men are also said to hit their girlfriends out of anger and frustration with their own marginalization, especially if women make them feel like failures for not providing. This popular explanation mirrors analyses of a crisis of masculinity, with respect to the 1980s by Campbell (1992), and more recently by Wood and Jewkes (2001), Bruce (2007), and Barolsky et al. (2008). In these accounts, unemployment and the consequent inability to perform the role of male breadwinner undermine the status of young men, who seek status in other ways through sexual success and interpersonal violence.

More systematic research provides mixed findings on the relationship between unemployment, violence, and crime. At the aggregate level, Demombynes and Özler (2005) matched district-level data on crime with social and economic data, and found positive and significant correlations between unemployment rates and armed robbery and murder (but not rape). At the micro level, Leoschut and Bonora (2007, 93–95) found in interviews that young criminal offenders frequently mentioned a lack of employment opportunities and poverty as reasons to commit crimes. They also found, however, that young offenders, when pushed, revealed that many of the financial rewards from their crimes were spent on material status symbols such as brand name clothing and cellular phones, rather than basic necessities (see also Centre for the Study of Violence and Reconciliation [CSVR] 2008a, 2008b). In a second study comparing youth offenders and nonoffenders, Burton, Leoschut, and Bonora (2009, 31) found no significant difference in employment rates between offenders' and nonoffenders' households.

Our analysis of data from CAPS suggests that unemployment plays some role in some forms of violence, but perhaps not as much as the popular view suggests. We found no significant direct relationship between being unemployed and the perpetration of violence against strangers, although some other measures of poverty did have a positive effect. It is other factors—notably drinking—as well as some aspects of current poverty that have the most marked effects on violence against strangers, girlfriends, or family members (Seekings and Thaler 2010). Drinking is a consistent predictor of most forms of violence (see also Burton, Leoschut, and Bonora 2009; Jewkes et al. 2006). One reason why the relationship between unemployment and violence is not stronger is that the relationship between unemployment and drinking is not strong. Drinking heavily, and often, requires resources that the unemployed lack. Poverty inhibits drinking, and therefore had indirect inhibiting effects on violence (offsetting other, more direct and probably positive effects). Many young men with work (and some money) are violent (Seekings and Thaler 2010).

# Conclusion

Most studies of young people see "youth" as a transitional stage between adolescence and adulthood. Empirical studies of young people across the contemporary Global South find that the duration of transitions to adulthood has extended, as young people take longer to form independent households, find permanent employment, marry, have children, and so on. In South Africa, as in many other societies, these transitions also appear to have been extended. By or at the age of 30, only one in four South African young people is (or has ever been) married. While more than one-half of the 30-year-old population claims to vote, fewer attend civic meetings, and very few engage in protest demonstrations. Although most young people have worked by the age of 30, only just over one-half are currently working at that age. In short, there are many 30-year-olds who are not workers, are not married, are not household heads (or the partners thereof), and do not vote or otherwise engage in politics. Among men of this age, many are not fathers, and only a minority live with their children. If we think of youth in terms of a transition to an orthodox form of adulthood, a large number of young men and women in South Africa have not completed this transition, even in their early 30s.

It is not clear, however, that it makes sense to think of these experiences in terms of an extended transition to some full adulthood to be achieved sometime in the future. Many of the characteristics of "youth" in South Africa might not be markers of transition so much as the characteristics of a new form of adulthood.

Many young people in their 20s are already living the kind of life that they will probably lead for the rest of their lives: in precarious, intermittent employment; raising children outside of marriage or even cohabitation, in complex, multigenerational households; engaging fluidly with both formal and informal politics, guided by norms and beliefs that indicate very uneven adherence to democracy and the rule of law. In terms of their attitudes and behaviors, most young South Africans may be as adult as they will ever be by their early and mid-20s.

The men and women born between the early 1980s and early 1990s do not seem to be especially prodemocratic or antidemocratic; nor are they distinctively violent or attracted to direct action. They are not pioneering the decline of marriage or the rise of more fluid and contingent relationships. Above all, they are following in their predecessors' footsteps in terms of finding mostly intermittent and precarious employment. This generation is not unimportant, however: the large size of the cohort born between the early 1980s and early 1990s means that its experiences of politics, violence, marriage, parenthood, and employment are very likely to become entrenched and even more powerful than ever.

## Notes

1. See http://datatopics.worldbank.org/hnp/popestimates.

2. Ibid.

3. This is not to say that such an experience is universal in South Africa: some young South Africans do experience a transitional phase—often extended—as they move from childhood to the kind of adulthood that was more common among their parents' and previous generations. Nor is it abruptly novel: immediately preceding cohorts experienced some of the same circumstances.

4. Unfortunately there are (as far as I am aware) no good and comparable data on the numeracy of successive age cohorts at the same age, so we cannot determine whether the cohort born between the early 1980s and early 1990s was any more or less numerate than its predecessors were at the same age.

5. LFS 2nd quarter 2010, my calculations.

6. Ibid.

7. My calculations using the LFS 2nd quarter 2000 and the 1993 PSLSD (Project for Statistics on Living Standards and Development) survey.

8. LFS 2nd quarter 2010, my calculations. Elena Moore points out to me that surveys might underestimate the extent of partial cohabitation, among men and women who have separate residences but in practice spend a lot of time together.

9. My calculations, using the General Household Survey (2009). See http://www.statssa.gov.za/publications/P0318/P0318June2009.pdf.

10. My calculations, using National Income Dynamics Study, wave 1 (2008). See http://www.datafirst.uct.ac.za/catalogue3/index.php/catalog/175/overview.

## References

Barolsky, Vanessa, Catherine L. Ward, Suren Pillay, and Nadia Sanger. 2008. *Case studies of the perpetrators of violent crime*. Report by the Human Sciences Research Council on behalf of the Centre for the Study of Violence and Reconciliation (CSVR). Johannesburg: CSVR.

Bhorat, Haroon, and Morné Oosthuizen. 2006. Evolution of the labour market: 1995–2002. In *Poverty and policy in post-apartheid South Africa*, eds. Haroon Bhorat and Ravi Kanbur, 143–200. Pretoria: Human Sciences Research Council.

Branson, Nicola, and Tia Linda Zuze. 2012. Education, the great equaliser: Improving access to quality education. In *South African child gauge 2012*, eds. Katherine Hall, Ingrid Woolard, Lori Lake, and Charmaine Smith, 69–74. Cape Town: Children's Institute, University of Cape Town.

Bray, Rachel, Imke Gooskens, Lauren Kahn, Susan Moses, and Jeremy Seekings. 2010. *Growing up in the new South Africa: Childhood and adolescence in post-apartheid Cape Town*. Cape Town: Human Sciences Research Council.

Bruce, David. 2007. To be someone: Status insecurity and violence in South Africa. In *Someone stole my smile*, ed. Patrick Burton, 57–68. Cape Town: Centre for Justice and Crime Prevention.

Burton, Patrick, Lezanne Leoschut, and Angela Bonora. 2009. *Walking the tightrope: Youth resilience to crime in South Africa*. Cape Town: Centre for Justice and Crime Prevention.

Campbell, Catherine. 1992. Learning to kill? Masculinity, the family and violence in Natal. *Journal of Southern African Studies* 18 (3): 614–28.

CSVR. 2008a. *Adding insult to injury: How exclusion and inequality drive South Africa's problem of violence*. Report to the Secretariat for Safety and Security. Braamfontein: Centre for the Study of Violence and Reconciliation.

CSVR. 2008b. *Case studies of perpetrators of violent crime: A report by the Human Sciences Research Council on behalf of the Centre for the Study of Violence and Reconciliation*. Report to the Secretariat for Safety and Security. Braamfontein: Centre for the Study of Violence and Reconciliation.

Demombynes, Gabriel, and Berk Özler. 2005. Crime and local inequality in South Africa. *Journal of Development Economics* 76:265–92.

Fortes, Meyer. 1969. *Kinship and the social order*. London: Routledge.

Gibson, James, and Amanda Gouws. 2003. *Overcoming intolerance in South Africa: Experiments in democratic persuasion*. Cambridge: Cambridge University Press.

Hall, Katherine. 2012. Children's access to education. In *South African child gauge 2012*, eds. Katherine Hall, Ingrid Woolard, Lori Lake, and Charmaine Smith, 95–97. Cape Town: Children's Institute, University of Cape Town.

Harper, Sarah, and Jeremy Seekings. 2010. Claims on and obligations to kin in Cape Town, South Africa. Centre for Social Science Research Working Paper 272, University of Cape Town.

Hunter, Mark. 2010. *Love in the time of AIDS: Intimacy, gender and rights in South Africa*. Bloomington, IN: Indiana University Press.

Institute for Justice and Reconciliation (IJR). 2012. *Ticking time bomb or demographic dividend? Youth and reconciliation in South Africa*. SA Reconciliation Barometer Survey: 2012 Report. Cape Town: IJR.

Jewkes, Rachel, Kristin Dunkle, Mary Koss, Jonathan Levin, Mzikazi Nduna, Nwabisa Jama, and Yandisa Sikweyiya. 2006. Rape perpetration by young, rural South African men: Prevalence, patterns and risk factors. *Social Science and Medicine* 63:2949–61.

Klasen, Stephan, and Ingrid Woolard. 2009. Surviving unemployment without state support: Unemployment and household formation in South Africa. *Journal of African Economies* 18 (1): 1–51.

Leoschut, Lezanne, and Angela Bonora. 2007. Offender perspectives on violent crime. In *Someone stole my smile: An exploration into the causes of youth violence in South Africa*, ed. Patrick Burton, 89–111. Cape Town: Centre for Justice and Crime Prevention.

Lloyd, Cynthia, Jere R. Behrman, Nelly P. Stromquist, and Barney Cohen, eds. 2005. *The changing transitions to adulthood in developing countries: Selected studies*. Washington, DC: National Academies Press.

Mattes, Robert. 2001. Democracy without the people: Institutions, economics and public opinion in South Africa. *Journal of Democracy* 13 (1): 22–36.

Mattes, Robert. 2011. The born frees: The prospects for generational change in post-apartheid South Africa. Centre for Social Science Research Working Paper 292, University of Cape Town.

Mattes, Robert, Donald Taylor, David McDonald, Abigail Poore, and Wayne Richmond. 2000. South African attitudes to immigrants and immigration. In *On borders: Perspectives on international migration in Southern Africa*, ed., David McDonald, 196–218. New York, NY: St. Martin's.

Meintjes, Helen, and Katherine Hall. 2012. Demography of South Africa's children. In *South African child gauge 2012*, eds. Katherine Hall, Ingrid Woolard, Lori Lake, and Charmaine Smith, 82–85. Cape Town: Children's Institute, University of Cape Town.

Moore, Elena. 2011. Beginning a family in South Africa. Unpublished paper.

Mosoetsa, Sarah. 2011. *Eating from one pot: The dynamics of survival in poor South African households.* Johannesburg: Witwatersrand University Press.

National Planning Commission. 2012. *National Development Plan 2030: Our future, make it work.* Pretoria: National Planning Commission.

Posel, Deborah. 2010. Races to consume: Revisiting South Africa's history of race, consumption and the struggle for freedom. *Ethnic and Racial Studies* 33 (2): 157–75.

Posel, Dori, and Richard Devey. 2006. The demographics of fathers in South Africa: An analysis of survey data, 1993–2002. In *Baba: Men and fatherhood in South Africa*, eds. Rob Morrell and Linda Richter, 38–52. Cape Town: Human Sciences Research Council.

Richter, Linda, and Robert Morrell, eds. 2006. *Baba: Men and fatherhood in South Africa.* Cape Town: Human Sciences Research Council.

Roberts, Gareth. 2011. Youth employment in South Africa and the persistence of inflated expectations. Unpublished paper.

Ross, Fiona. 1996. Diffusing domesticity: Domestic fluidity in Die Bos. *Social Dynamics* 22 (1): 55–71.

Ross, Fiona. 2003. Dependents and dependence: A case study of housing and heuristics in an informal settlement in the Western Cape. *Social Dynamics* 29 (2): 132–52.

Schenk, Jan, and Jeremy Seekings. 2013. Locating Generation X: Taste and identity in transitional South Africa. In *Generation X goes global: Mapping a youth culture in motion*, ed. Christine Henseler, 51–72. London: Routledge.

Seekings, Jeremy. 1993. *Heroes or villains? Youth politics in the 1980s.* Johannesburg: Ravan.

Seekings, Jeremy. 1995. Media representations of youth and the South African transition, 1989–1994. *South African Sociological Review* 7 (2): 25–42.

Seekings, Jeremy. 1996. The "lost generation": South Africa's "youth problem" in the early 1990s. *Transformation* 29:103–25.

Seekings, Jeremy. 2006. Beyond heroes and villains: The rediscovery of the ordinary in the study of childhood and adolescence in South Africa. *Social Dynamics* 32 (1): 1–20.

Seekings, Jeremy. 2008. Beyond fluidity: Kinship and households as social projects. Centre for Social Science Research Working Paper 237, University of Cape Town.

Seekings, Jeremy, and Nicoli Nattrass. 2005. *Class, race, and inequality in South Africa.* New Haven, CT: Yale University Press.

Seekings, Jeremy, and Kai Thaler. 2010. Socio-economic conditions, young men and violence in Cape Town. Centre for Social Science Research Working Paper 285, University of Cape Town.

Statistics South Africa (Stats SA). 2012. Census 2011, Statistical Release PO301.4. Pretoria: Stats SA.

van der Berg, Servaas. 2007. Apartheid's enduring legacy: Inequalities in education. *Journal of African Economies* 16 (5): 849–80.

van der Berg, Servaas. 2008. How effective are poor schools? Poverty and educational outcomes in South Africa. *Studies in Educational Evaluation* 34 (3): 145–54.

Wood, K., and Rachel Jewkes. 2001. Dangerous love: Reflections on violence amongst Xhosa township youth. In *Changing men in Southern Africa*, ed. Rob Morrell, 317–36. Pietermaritzburg: University of KwaZulu-Natal Press.

Yu, Derek. 2012. Youths in the South African labour market since the transition: A study of changes between 1995 and 2011. Stellenbosch Economic Working Papers 18/12, University of Stellenbosch, South Africa.

# Meeting the Challenge of Unemployment?

*By*
NICOLI NATTRASS

South Africa has one of the highest rates of unemployment in the world. Job creation is a national priority, yet labor-intensive options are derided by the trade union movement as an unacceptable throwback to the "cheap labor" policies of apartheid, and effectively ruled out by the government in its recent National Development Plan (NDP). Instead, minimum-wage setting in South Africa continues to contribute to job destruction (as evidenced most recently in the clothing industry). Policy-makers hope that support for high-productivity firms and rapid economic growth will make up for job losses and solve the unemployment problem. Unfortunately, South Africa's economic performance has been comparatively disappointing and constrained by negative investor sentiment, especially with regard to the labor market. The NDP has called for a social accord between labor and capital. But the prospects are not promising, and unemployment is likely to remain a significant feature of the South African economic landscape.

*Keywords:* South Africa; unemployment; economic growth; Brazil; BRICS

South Africa has one of the highest unemployment rates in the world. According to data compiled by the International Labour Organisation (ILO), of the ninety countries for which comparable labor force survey data exist, South Africa's unemployment rate is three times higher than the median, is similar to that in the West Bank and Gaza Strip, and is exceeded only by the war-torn regions of Kosovo and Macedonia. South Africa's poor track record is reflected also in its relatively low ratio of employment to working-age population (see Figure 1).

*Nicoli Nattrass is a professor in the Centre for Social Science Research at the University of Cape Town. Her recent research has focused on labor market, economic, and health policy in South Africa, the clothing industry, AIDS denialism and conspiracy theory, and human–wildlife conflict.*

DOI: 10.1177/0002716213511189

88

## FIGURE 1
## Unemployment: South Africa in Comparative Perspective (2010)

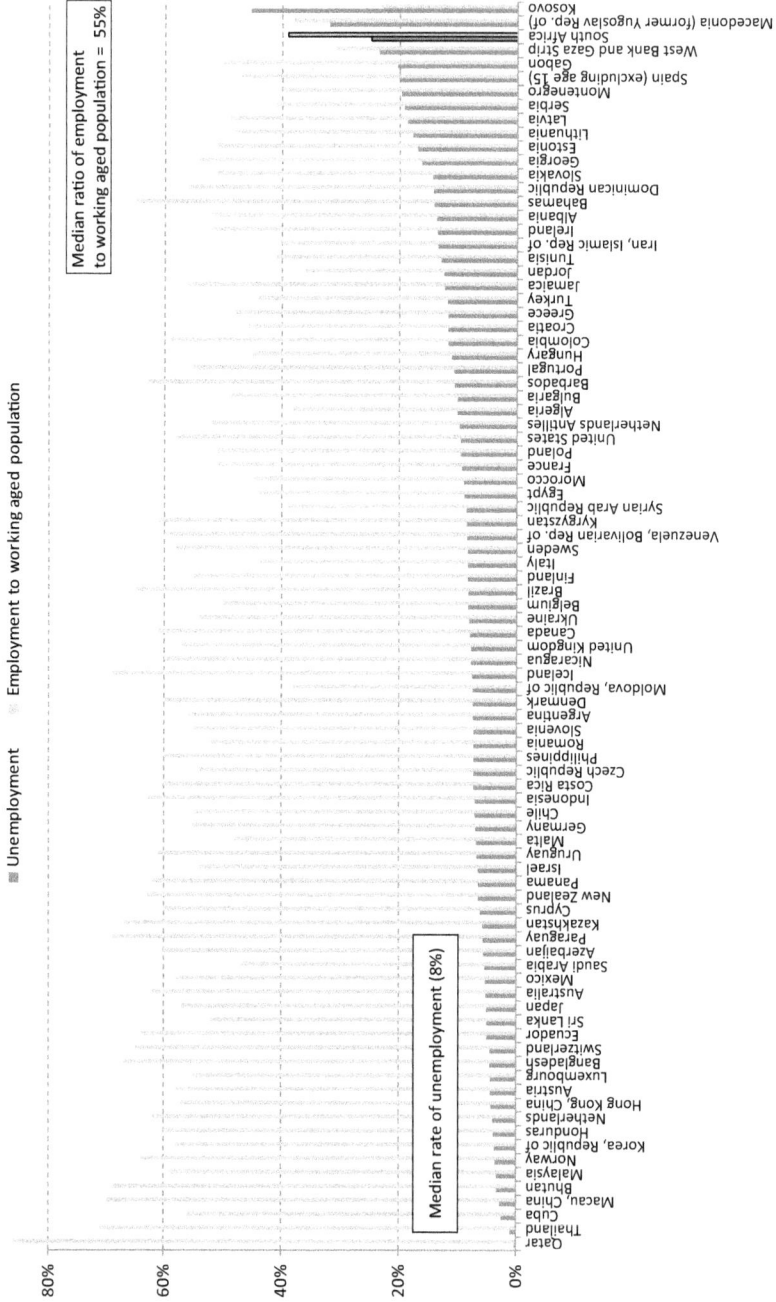

■ Unemployment ▨ Employment to working aged population

Median ratio of employment to working aged population = 55%

Median rate of unemployment (8%)

Kosovo
Macedonia (former Yugoslav Rep. of)
South Africa
West Bank and Gaza Strip
Gabon
Spain (excluding age 15)
Montenegro
Serbia
Latvia
Lithuania
Estonia
Georgia
Slovakia
Dominican Republic
Bahamas
Albania
Ireland
Iran, Islamic Rep. of
Tunisia
Jordan
Jamaica
Turkey
Greece
Croatia
Colombia
Hungary
Portugal
Barbados
Bulgaria
Algeria
Netherlands Antilles
United States
France
Poland
Morocco
Egypt
Syrian Arab Republic
Kyrgyzstan
Venezuela, Bolivarian Rep. of
Sweden
Finland
Italy
Brazil
Belgium
Ukraine
Canada
United Kingdom
Nicaragua
Iceland
Moldova, Republic of
Denmark
Argentina
Slovenia
Romania
Philippines
Czech Republic
Costa Rica
Indonesia
Chile
Germany
Malta
Uruguay
Israel
Panama
New Zealand
Cyprus
Kazakhstan
Paraguay
Azerbaijan
Saudi Arabia
Mexico
Australia
Japan
Sri Lanka
Ecuador
Switzerland
Bangladesh
Luxembourg
Austria
Hong Kong, China
Netherlands
Honduras
Korea, Republic of
Norway
Malaysia
Bhutan
Macau, China
Cuba
Thailand
Qatar

80%
60%
40%
20%
0%

SOURCE: National Labour Force Survey data from ILOSTAT (http://www.ilo.org/ilostat/) and World Development Indicators (http://data.worldbank.org/indicator/SL.EMP.TOTL.SP.ZS). Data from 2010 or 2009.

TABLE 1
Unemployment in South Africa, Third Quarter 2012

|  | Total | Percentage |
| --- | --- | --- |
| Employed formal nonagricultural | 9,611,000 | 70.8% |
| Employed informal nonagricultural | 2,205,000 | 16.2% |
| Employed in agriculture | 685,000 | 5.1 % |
| Employed in private households | 1,076,000 | 7.9% |
| 1. Total employed | 13,577,000 | 100% |
| 2. Unemployed work seekers | 4,501,000 | 29% of work seekers are under 25 |
| 3. Unemployed discouraged work seekers | 2,257,000 |  |
| Other (not economically active) | 12,794,000 |  |
| Unemployment rate (official) = 2/(1 + 2) | 24.9% (50.9% for those aged 15–24) | |
| Unemployment rate (broad) = (2 + 3)/ (1 + 2 + 3) | 33.2% | |

SOURCE: Quarterly Labour Force Survey, Quarter 4, 2012, Statistical release PO211, February 2013. See http://www.statssa.gov.za/publications/P0211/P02114thQuarter2012.pdf.

Table 1 reports labor force data for the third quarter of 2012 for South Africa. It shows that a quarter of the labor force is unemployed, that is, without work and actively seeking it. This official rate of unemployment is twice as high for young people (i.e., those aged 15 to 24). Note that if one uses an expanded definition of unemployment that includes the so-called discouraged work seekers who are no longer actively engaged in a job search, South Africa's unemployment rate rises from a quarter to a third of the labor force.

It is, thus, unsurprising that the recent "diagnostic report" of South Africa's National Planning Commission (NPC) concluded that the country's number one failing was that "too few people work" (NPC 2012, 24). The NPC's 2012 National Development Plan (NDP) subsequently proposed a strategy to "roll back poverty and inequality" through a "combination of increasing employment, higher incomes through productivity growth, a social wage and good quality public services" (NPC 2012, 25–26). The hope is that this combination of initiatives will more than double economic growth rates from around 2 percent per annum currently to 5.4 per year until 2030, and that this skill- and capital-intensive growth path will be sufficiently labor demanding that unemployment will fall to 6 percent. Job opportunities for the less skilled are assumed to come from growing the small- and medium-enterprise sector, a revamped rural development program, and an expanded public works program. A wage subsidy to encourage firms to hire young unemployed people is also proposed, albeit in the face of strong opposition from organized labor.

India's National Rural Employment Guarantee Scheme has demonstrated that developing-country governments can provide a significant number of jobs for poor people (Shankar, Gaiha, and Raghbendra 2011). But minimum wages are much higher in South Africa than in India (see Table 2), and there is strong

TABLE 2
South Africa Compared to the Other BRICS and Chile

| | Brazil | Chile | China | India | Russia | South Africa |
|---|---|---|---|---|---|---|
| GDP per capita, purchasing power parity (PPP) (current international $ 2012) | $11,640 | $17,270 | $8,400 | $3,650 | $21,921 | $10,960 |
| Share of agriculture in GDP (2011) | 5.5% | 3.4% | 10.0% | 17.6% | 4.3% | 2.4% |
| Share of industry in GDP (2011) | 27.5% | 39.1% | 46.6% | 26.7% | 37.0% | 30.6% |
| Share of services in GDP (2011) | 67% | 57.5% | 43.4% | 55.7% | 58.7% | 67.0% |
| Average annual real GDP growth (1990–2011) | 2.8% | 5.2% | 10.1% | 6.5% | 0.7% | 2.6% |
| Gross fixed capital formation as % of GDP (average: 1990–2011) | 17.6% | 22.5% | 36.8% | 26.2% | 20.1% | 17.2% |
| Gross Domestic Savings as % of GDP (average 1990–2011) | 18.6% | 26.9% | 44.3% | 26.3% | 32.3% | 19.0% |
| Wage employed as % total employed (most recent data) | 66.4% | 72.8% | | 18.1% | 92.7% | 84.5% |
| Percent vulnerable employment as % total employment (most recent data) | 25.1% | 24.4% | | 80.8% | 5.7% | 10% |
| Most recent GINI | 54.7 | 52.1 | 42.5 | 33.4 | 40.1 | 63.1 |
| Unemployment rate (most recent) | 8.3% | 7.1% | 4.1%[a] | 9.3% | 6.6% | 24.9% |
| Employment rate (most recent) | 64.8% | 56.1% | 70.9% | 53.6% | 52.8% | 39.3% |
| Firing costs (weeks wages) 2009 | 46 | 52 | 91 | 56 | 17 | 24 |
| Lowest government-set minimum monthly wage (U.S. dollars) | $272.5 (2011) | $287.6 (2011) | $81.1 (2010) | $36.8 (2011) | $138.3 (2009) | $124.2[b] (2011) |
| Trade union density | 28.7 | 13.6 | | 41.1 | | 27.7 |
| Collective bargaining coverage | 35% | 23.6% | 22.3% | 60% | | 42.5% |
| Level of bargaining | Firm and industry | Firm level | Firm level | Firm and industry | | Industrial |

SOURCE: World Development Indicators; see http://databank.worldbank.org/data/; http://www.ilo.org.

NOTE: BRICS = Brazil, Russia, India, China, and South Africa.

a. This is not a Labour Force Survey estimate.

b. Domestic workers in rural areas.

ideological opposition to the very notion of low-wage work. As discussed below, relatively low-wage labor-intensive production is derided by the trade union movement as an unacceptable throwback to the "cheap labor" policies of apartheid and regretfully ruled out by the NDP. Instead, the NPC effectively relies on industrial, educational, and infrastructural policy to transform the economy so successfully that it creates millions of high-productivity jobs.

The idea of mobilizing state resources to revolutionize a country's economic structure has a long vintage in development economics. In its contemporary form, it ranges from those who suggest that industrial policy is important but that policy interventions should be in line with comparative advantage (Lin 2012), to those emphasizing that industrial policy in China, South Korea, and Japan was successful precisely because it "defied" national comparative advantage by facilitating the shift into new industries in capital- and skill-intensive sectors (e.g., Chang 2002, 2012). But as Lin (2012) points out, even in the cases of China, South Korea, and Japan, government policy was working with "latent comparative advantage" in that the existing industrial base and physical and human capital provided the springboard for launching into new areas (pp. 76–78). And while it is certainly true that Korean and Chinese industrial policies facilitated industrial upgrading prior to the exhaustion of the supply of cheap labor from agriculture, it is nevertheless the case that both countries were also highly successful at absorbing a significant number of workers in labor-intensive industries. South Africa, by contrast, has wage-setting institutions that actively harm labor-intensive production. For example, minimum wages in the clothing industry are set in the National Bargaining Council for the Clothing Manufacturing Industry (NBC) through collective agreements between the South African Clothing and Textile Workers Union (Sactwu) and various employer organizations. As Sactwu has 50 percent of the votes (it is the only union) on the NBC, it needs the agreement of only a single employer association to obtain a collective agreement. Such agreements have routinely been "extended" by the minister of labor to all firms in the industry—to the detriment of employment in low-wage, labor-intensive firms outside of urban areas, very few of which are represented in the NBC (Nattrass and Seekings 2012a, 2012b, 2013).

This article begins with a brief history of unemployment and then turns to a discussion of economic policy in the post-apartheid period. I argue that the ruling African National Congress (ANC) effectively ceded labor market policy pertaining to minimum wage setting to the trade union movement and conclude that a more differentiated approach than the current approach is needed—one that supports high-productivity activities while also tolerating low-wage job creation. Unfortunately, the prospects for this are limited given continued opposition from organized labor.

## The Origins of South Africa's Unemployment Problem

One of the reasons for South Africa's comparatively high unemployment rate is that there is no significant subsistence agricultural production or peasant sector, and very little informal (i.e., unregulated) employment (see Table 1). Table 2 presents comparative data for Chile as well as Brazil, Russia, India, China, and South Africa (the BRICS). It shows that South Africa has a comparatively high proportion of wage workers and a low proportion of "vulnerable" jobs in total employment—both indicators of a generally low level of informality.

South Africa's welfare system is premised on full employment in that it assumes that able-bodied working-aged adults will be able to provide for themselves through work. Means-tested welfare is available only for the young (child support grants), the old (old-age pensions), and the disabled (disability grants). Unemployment insurance is limited to contributors (i.e., the previously employed) and is available only for a single six-month period. In 2011/12, a mere 706,000 people received unemployment insurance payouts, averaging a paltry R8,000 per recipient (Department of Labour [DOL] 2012, 97). Most unemployed people thus fall straight through South Africa's supposed welfare net (see also Bower, this volume).

The anachronistic notion that able-bodied adults will be able to support themselves in the labor market was inherited from the apartheid era, when full-employment for whites was ensured by labor market policies that included job reservation, and when (in the early apartheid period) the mines and farms suffered from persistent shortages of labor. Open unemployment only became a significant and sustained feature of the South African economy in the early 1970s when a perfect storm of global recession, disruptions to the supply of migrant labor to the mines, unionization, and rising real wages resulted in the demand for jobs dramatically and obviously outstripping supply (Seekings and Nattrass 2005). By the time that South Africa made the transition to democracy in the mid-1990s, subsistence agriculture had almost entirely collapsed and unemployment had become a key driver of poverty and inequality. Despite subsequent improved growth and some job creation in the 2000s, unemployment remains a persistent feature of the South African economic landscape. The income gap between the employed and the unemployed is as much a determinant of South Africa's high level of inequality as the gap between low and high earnings (Leibbrandt et al. 2010).

## Post-Apartheid Economic and Labor Policies

Soon after being released from prison in 1990, Nelson Mandela called for the nationalization of the mines and monopoly industry, a long-standing demand of the ANC. But by the following year, at the World Economic Forum in Davos, Mandela reassured international investors that nationalization would not happen. This about-turn was part of a marked shift in the content and tone of ANC economic policy during the early 1990s. As the ANC's policy documents became increasingly market-friendly (see Nattrass 1994), left-leaning local critics accused it of forging an elite pact that would leave existing power structures intact (e.g., Bond 2000). But as Cyril Ramaphosa, a leading ANC negotiator who has since become the party's deputy president, noted of the time, an ideological ground-swell was evident, and "many people were beginning to feel more and more comfortable with a mixed type of economy" (quoted in Green 2008, 339). Even so, the ANC had a job to do to convince the business community that it was serious. During negotiations over the interim constitution, Maria Ramos, a key ANC economic advisor and subsequent Director General of Finance, argued for an independent Reserve Bank in large part to gain credibility with investors: "We really felt that if we had a sound and rational and appropriate set of institutional arrangements around fiscal policy, and fiscal policy management and Central Banking . . . that in itself would give us a lot of credibility" (quoted in Green 2008, 382).

The ANC's "Reconstruction and Development Programme" (RDP) election manifesto sought to reassure the business community and the labor movement while also addressing the need for redistribution. It did so by promoting the idea of a "strong, dynamic and balanced economy" that would "eliminate poverty . . . meet basic needs . . . [and] . . . create productive employment opportunities at a living wage for all South Africans" (ANC 1994, 79, para. 4.2.2). It portrayed wage pressure as a necessary tool for economic transformation, ascribing the weakness of the manufacturing sector to its "undue dependence upon low wages" (ANC 1994, 76, para. 4.1.3) and calling for "a decisive break with the exploitative cheap-labour policies of apartheid" by moving "toward education, training, skills, a living wage, and collective bargaining as the *basis* for enhanced productivity in the economy" (ANC 1994, 81–82, para. 4.2.10-1 [emphasis added]; see also the RDP White Paper, para. 3.2.6). The RDP also called for the reduction of minimum wage differentials between urban and rural areas (ANC 1994, 113, para. 4.8.5) and for collective agreements between unions and employer organizations in bargaining councils to be "extended through legislation to all workplaces in that industry" (ANC 1994, 114, para. 4.8.8)—both of which would have had the effect of driving up minimum wages across industries and putting pressure on relatively low-wage jobs in nonmetro areas.

The intellectual argument that higher wages could be the basis for growth, that is, a tool for forcing firms to improve productivity, is associated in South Africa with the Industrial Strategy Project (ISP), a trade union–linked think-tank that supported the use of labor market interventions to "encourage restructuring up the value chain rather than restructuring towards low-wage, low-productivity forms of production" (Joffe et al. 1995, 213). The ISP explained that organized labor's approach to industrial restructuring was "premised on the need to move South African firms out of their low-wage, low-skill, low-productivity vicious circle in which they are out-competed by the second-tier newly industrialising countries" (Joffe et al. 1995, 214). In other words, the claim here is that South Africa either cannot, or should not, try to compete internationally on the basis of low wages—and that deliberately shifting the economy away from low-wage work will ultimately be good for productivity and employment growth. These ideas were subsequently incorporated into South Africa's industrial policy, which has consistently promoted capital- and skill-intensive development (e.g., Department of Trade and Industry [DTI] 2011).

FIGURE 2
Key Economic Trends

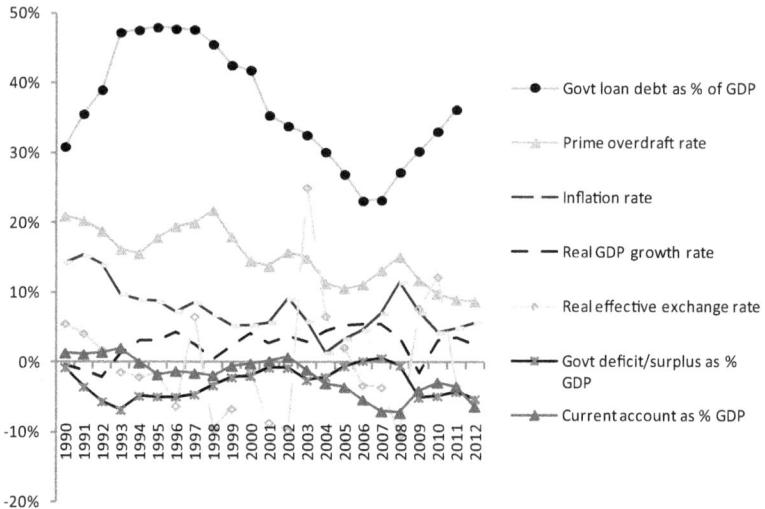

SOURCE: Data from the South African Reserve Bank; see www.reservebank.co.za/.

But organized labor was less successful in shaping macroeconomic policy. The Congress of South African Trade Unions (Cosatu) favored expansionary Keynesian policies, but this option was explicitly ruled out by the RDP. Rather, it argued that to avoid inflation and serious balance of payments problems, government spending should be redirected rather than increased as a share of the GDP. The early ANC economic policy-makers drew this line in the sand because even before the political transition, it was becoming clear that government finances were out of control; the budget deficit had ballooned from 1.5 percent of GDP in 1990 to 7.3 percent in 1993 (see Figure 2). When the RDP was revised and published as a government white paper in late 1994, it warned explicitly about the already "unacceptably high government debt" and the need for a "progressive reduction of the overall deficit" by maintaining "fiscal discipline" because "excessive government deficits [would] result in higher inflation, higher real interest rates, balance of payment problems and lower economic growth, thereby undermining the RDP" (RDP White Paper 1994, 20, para. 3.3.2; 30, para. 4.1.2).

Figure 2 shows how South Africa's debt to GDP ratio skyrocketed in the early 1990s. The especially sharp increase from 1993 to 1994 was driven primarily by the transfer of debt from the former homeland governments to the national government. This transfer, coupled with rising interest rates, raised the grim possibility of a debt crisis. Fortunately, the new government was able to curb the deficit by improving the efficiency of tax collection, restraining the growth of government expenditure while redirecting it, and adopting a more sophisticated approach to borrowing than had been in existence under apartheid. The deficit narrowed steadily and the debt burden fell (up until the 2007/8 financial crisis when it started rising again as the government adopted Keynesian policies to reflate the economy).

ANC policy-makers were particularly sensitive to the power of adverse market sentiment to affect the economy—as evidenced by the fall in the value of the rand when Trevor Manuel became the first ANC minister of finance in 1996 and the difficulties experienced by the new government in selling bonds (Green 2008, 426, 435–36). The 1996 economic policy document known as the "Growth, Employment and Redistribution" (GEAR) strategy (Department of Finance [DOF] 1996) sought to address this problem by spelling out a coherent macro-economic strategy that, they hoped, would send positive signals to investors and would generate jobs.

GEAR argued that the most sustainable and effective way of boosting investment and employment was through investor-friendly policies, trade liberalization, improvements to the social and economic infrastructure, and—in sharp contrast to the RDP—some reforms to South Africa's wage-setting machinery. It articulated the challenge facing labor market policy as being "to promote dynamic efficiency, skill enhancement and the expansion of reasonably remunerated employment—while at the same time supporting a labour-intensive growth path which generates jobs for the unemployed, many of whom are unskilled and have never had previous employment" (DOF 1996, 19). With regard to labor market policy, the recommendation was clear: "Government recognises that industrial agreements which reach across diverse firms, sectors or regions should be sufficiently flexible to avoid job losses and should be extended to non-parties only when this can reasonably be assured" (DOF 1996, 19). GEAR also proposed a "national social agreement" to avoid "a vicious circle of wage and price increases leading to instability in the financial markets and a decline in competitive advantage" (DOF 1996, 21).

Such proposals are social-democratic in nature. Yet Cosatu responded to GEAR by successfully framing it as a neoliberal betrayal of the revolution (Nattrass 2013). The ANC quickly backed away from all proposed amendments to the wage-setting machinery, effectively ceding the Ministry of Labor to the union movement. Although this approach served the ANC's immediate political needs by offering an olive branch to its alliance partner, the result was an entrenched oppositional relationship between macroeconomic and labor market policymaking at the heart of the state. Whereas the national Treasury was and continues to be staffed by economists concerned about macroeconomic balance and the sustainability of government borrowing, the director general of labor and the deputy director general in charge of labor policy and industrial relations are both long-standing trade unionists, and the current and previous ministers of labor were ex-chairpersons of the Cosatu Women's Forum and the head of the national teacher's union, respectively. Successive ministers of labor have routinely extended collective bargained agreements across industries.

Unsurprisingly, the "vicious circle" that GEAR had warned about between wages, prices, and interest rates materialized as predicted. For example, inflation increased in 1997, in large part because of a public sector wage deal in 1996 that

FIGURE 3
Real per Capita Income: South Africa in Comparative Perspective

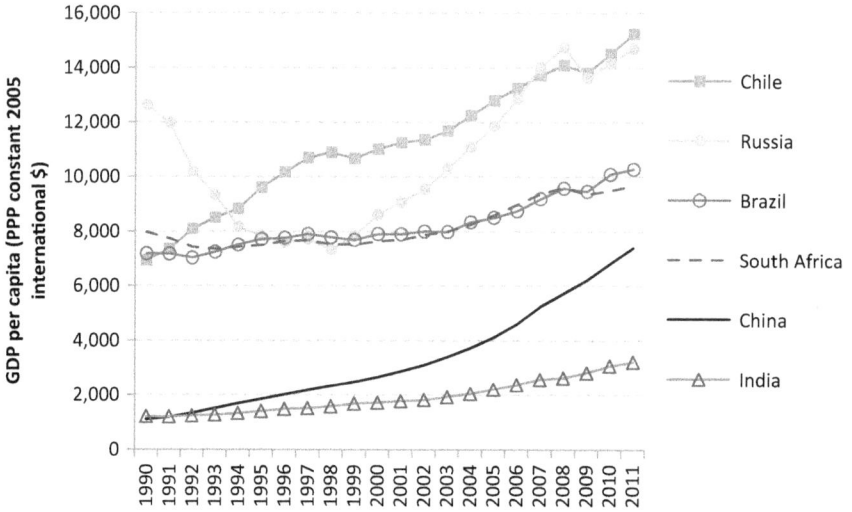

SOURCE: World Development Indicators; see http://databank.worldbank.org/data/.

increased wages in health and education by 15 to 20 percent. The Reserve Bank responded by increasing interest rates, thereby slowing growth and reducing the fiscal space for redistribution. Doing so put pressure on employers, particularly those in markets previously protected by tariffs. As is typical of other countries that liberalized their trade regimes under rigid labor market conditions and fiscal austerity (OECD 1999, 156–59), South Africa's uncoordinated economic policies were costly in terms of employment, especially of unskilled labor.

South Africa's macroeconomic policy was also challenged by severe fluctuations in the exchange rate (see Figure 2), as money flowed into developing-country markets in 1997 and then out again following the 1998 Asian crisis. But as the 2000s dawned, the economy was buoyed by growing international demand. Economic growth picked up, real interest rates declined, and the budget deficit was brought under control. Even so, South Africa's performance was far from stellar in international terms. Real per capita income growth was slower than in comparable middle-income countries such as Chile and Brazil, and significantly slower than in China and India (see Figure 3 and Table 2).

Figure 4 shows that employment stagnated and fell during the 1990s, only picking up sluggishly and erratically in the 2000s. Average labor productivity (output per worker) rose as firms shed unskilled labor and substituted machinery for labor. The result was higher real wages for those who kept their jobs, but increased hardship for the growing number of unemployed. The corporate sector benefitted from a rising share of profit (as labor productivity growth exceeded that of real remuneration). This proved crucial for investment, particularly post-2008. As shown in Figure 5, gross capital formation has relied on corporate

FIGURE 4
Employment, Productivity, Profitability, and Real Remuneration in South Africa

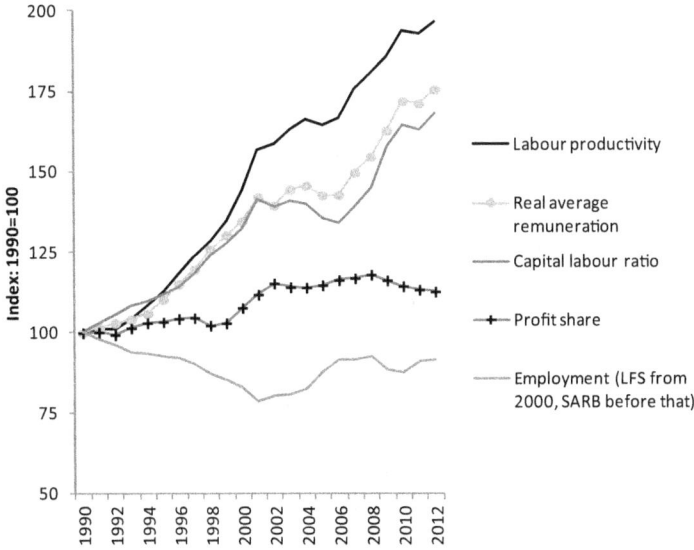

SOURCE: Data from the South African Reserve Bank and from the Labour Force Surveys (Statistics South Africa). See www.reservebank.co.za/; www.statssa.gov.za.

FIGURE 5
The Financing of Gross Capital Formation

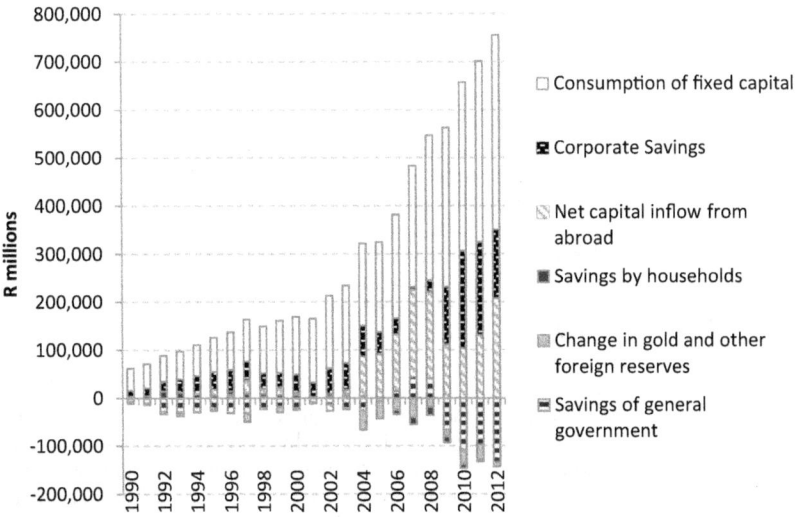

SOURCE: Data from the South African Reserve Bank; see www.reservebank.co.za/.

savings and capital inflows in a context where the household sector and government have been net borrowers.

Many factors have contributed to South Africa's poor employment record, including uncertainty over mineral rights and land tenure (which exacerbated job shedding in mining and agriculture), and trade union militancy. Industrial policy encouraged capital intensity (Kaplan 2007) and labor legislation raised the direct and indirect costs of employment labor (e.g., Moll 1996; Nattrass 2000; Nattrass and Seekings 2012). Even policies designed to improve the machinery of labor-dispute resolution, notably the introduction of the Commission for Conciliation, Mediation, and Arbitration (CCMA), had the unintended effect of burdening employers further by operating in an unnecessarily legalistic way (Bhorat and van der Westhuizen 2009).

According to the 2012/13 World Economic Forum's *Global Competitiveness Report*, South Africa ranked 52 out of 144 on the Global Competitiveness Index (GCI). This index is a weighted average (varying across countries depending on levels of development) of various subindices of quality of institutions, infrastructure, macroeconomic environment, health, primary education and higher education and training, goods market efficiency, labor market efficiency, financial market development, technological readiness, market size, business sophistication, and innovation. The subindices are based on a combination of objective measures (e.g., school enrollment, HIV prevalence) and opinion surveys of business executives in each country. The *Global Competitiveness Report* sums up South Africa's position:

> South Africa is ranked 52nd this year, remaining the highest-ranked country in Sub-Saharan Africa and the third placed among the BRICS economies. The country benefits from the large size of its economy, particularly by regional standards (it ranks 25th in the market size pillar). It also does well on measures of the quality of its institutions and on factor allocation, such as intellectual property protection (20th), property rights (26th), the accountability of its private institutions (2nd), and its goods market efficiency (32nd). Particularly impressive is the country's financial market development (3rd), indicating high confidence in South Africa's financial markets at a time when trust is returning only slowly in many other parts of the world. South Africa also does reasonably well in more complex areas such as business sophistication (38th) and innovation (42nd), benefitting from a good scientific research institution (34th), and strong collaboration between universities and the business sector in innovation (30th).
>
> These combined attributes make South Africa the most competitive economy in the region. However, in order to further enhance its competitiveness, the country will need to address some weaknesses. South Africa ranks 113th in labour market efficiency (a drop of 18 places from last year), with rigid hiring and firing practices (143rd), a lack of flexibility in wage determination by companies (140th) and significant tensions in labour-employer relations (144th). Efforts must also be made to increase the university enrolment rate in order to develop better its innovation potential. Combined efforts in these areas will be critical in view of the country's high unemployment rate. . . . In addition, South Africa's infrastructure, although good by regional standards, requires upgrading (63rd). The poor security situation remains another important obstacle to doing business in South Africa. The high business costs of crime and violence (134th) and the sense that the police are unable to provide sufficient protection from crime (90th) do not contribute to an environment that fosters competitiveness. [See also van der Spuy and Shearing, this volume.] Another major concern remains the health of the workforce,

which is ranked 132nd out of 144 economies, the result of high rates of communicable diseases and poor health indicators more generally. [See also Whiteside, this volume.] (Schwab 2012, 37, 41)

Figure 6 focuses on the GCI labor market efficiency subindex and some of its components. It is an index made up of the four reported measures (cooperation in labor-employer relations, flexibility in wage determination, pay and productivity, and hiring and firing practices) as well as some other measures/indicators, such as redundancy costs, reliance on professional management, brain drain effects, and women in the workforce. It shows that South Africa performs extremely poorly with regard to the overall index, and especially with regard to cooperation in labor-employee relations, wage flexibility, hiring and firing practices, and pay and productivity.

The GCI has been criticized for its strong reliance on opinion data. For example, Paul Benjamin (2012) is dismissive of the data, arguing that there is a "disjuncture between perception and labour market reality," notably when it comes to hiring and firing costs (p. 38). He argues that "South Africa's labour laws, including protection against dismissal, are not particularly onerous when compared to other middle-income countries; hence South Africa's low score on the hiring and firing practices is undeserved" (Benjamin 2012, 38). As can be seen in Table 2, South Africa's firing costs, in terms of weeks' wages to be paid out, are indeed relatively low. But this is a very limited metric of firing costs. That is why the GCI includes retrenchment costs as just one of the elements of labor market efficiency and puts considerable store on how business executives answered the more general questions listed in the notes to Figure 6. The question on hiring and firing is explicitly broad, asking respondents how they would characterize the hiring and firing of workers in their country, with "1" being impeded by regulations, and "7" flexibly determined by employers. This general question clearly invites respondents to think beyond simple short-term costs, such as weeks' wages paid out to retrenched workers, and to consider costs arising from the process of dismissal and hiring. Workers can now easily take employers to the CCMA, and they do: the number of dismissal cases rose from three thousand a year in 1994–95 (before the CCMA was put in place to improve access to dispute resolution), to more than one hundred thousand as of this writing (Benjamin 2012, 38). This easier access to dispute resolution ties up executive time and raises the costs of dismissal higher than any retrenchment package.

The opinion data reported in Figure 6 capture the perceived "hassle factor" of employing labor as well as the disquiet many executives feel over the lack of control at the firm level over wages and productivity. As described earlier with respect to the clothing industry, minimum wages in manufacturing are set in South Africa by trade unions and employers' associations in bargaining councils, and these wages are then routinely "extended" by the minister of labor to other firms in the industry. Where workers are not organized (for example, in domestic work and agriculture), wages are set by the Employment Conditions Commission. In other words, minimum wage setting is primarily at the industrial or national level rather than the firm level. It is thus not surprising that the executives

FIGURE 6
Labor Market Efficiency: South Africa in the Global Context

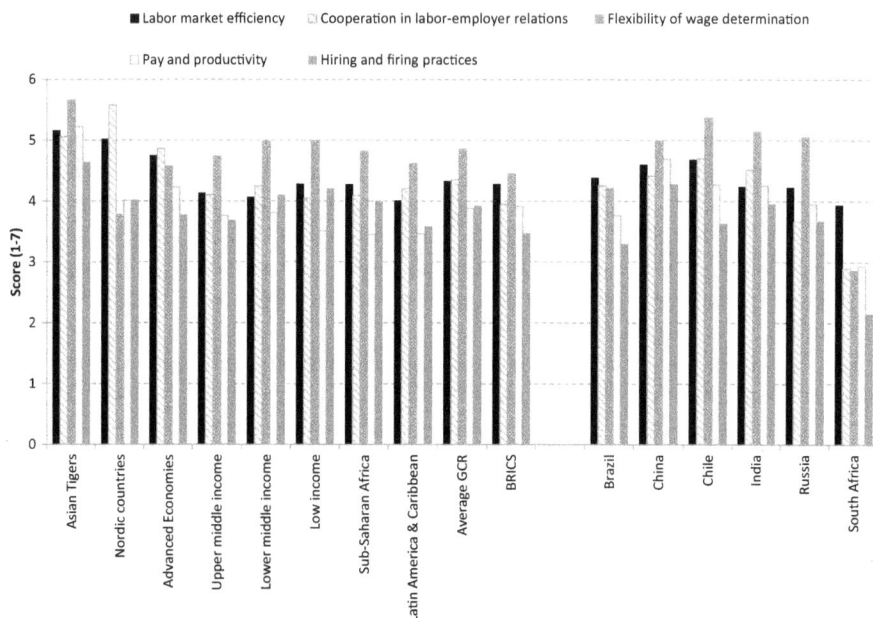

SOURCE: See http://www.weforum.org/issues/competitiveness-0/gci2012-data-platform/.
NOTE: Questions asked: How are wages generally set in your country? 1 = *by a centralized bargaining process*, 7= *up to each individual company* (flexibility of wage determination); How would you characterize the hiring and firing or workers in your country? 1 = *impeded by regulations*, 7 = *flexibly determined by employers* (hiring and firing practices); How would you characterize labor-employer relations in your country? 1 = *generally confrontational*; 7 = *generally cooperative* (cooperation in labor-employer relations); To what extent is pay in your country related to productivity? 1 = *not related to worker productivity*, 7 = *strongly related to worker productivity* (pay and productivity).

surveyed for the GCI gave responses that were closer to the value of 1 than 7 to the question on wage flexibility. South Africa's score is appropriately lower than the scores for Brazil, China, India, and Chile, given that these countries use firm-level or mixed-firm and industry-level bargaining rather than industrial-level wage setting systems (Table 2).

As discussed earlier, the South African trade union movement is committed to industrial-level bargaining and to using the minimum wage to force firms to move up the value chain. It is unsurprising that this approach, combined with adversarial labor-relations and industry-level bargaining, encourages executives to complain about the lack of labor-market flexibility in South Africa. Their perceptions are rooted in this reality and need to be taken very seriously as they discourage new and old firms from investing, especially in labor-intensive sectors and activities.

# The Way Forward?

The NDP recognizes that South Africa has a serious problem with regard to labor-employer relations and argues that "there is now an urgent need to craft a social contract that will enable South Africa to achieve higher growth and employment" and increase investment and savings (NPC 2012, 475). The NDP is thin on details about how to achieve this happy result, but calls for workers (except the very low paid) to agree to accept lower wage increases than their productivity gains would dictate, and calls on business to reinvest profits in ways that boost employment and growth rather than fuelling executive remuneration. Government is supposed to assist this process by lowering the cost of living for workers (e.g., keeping inflation and import tariffs low) while facilitating skills development and productivity growth (NPC 2012, 475–76). The NDP acknowledges that neither business nor labor trusts each other to keep its side of the bargain and that "state capability issues bedevil the chances of success"; but it ends with the following appeal:

> Even as negotiations continue government should invest more on social and economic infrastructure and deliver an expanding social wage to the poor, business should take a longer term perspective by investing more and increasing employment and training. Labour has to recognise that some wage moderation is required and efforts to raise productivity are essential. (NPC 2012, 477)

The key question going forward is, How is this result to be achieved? GEAR suggested revisions to the extension of collective agreements to nonparties and reduced employment protection for new employees, whereas the NDP merely proposes entry-level wage flexibility, simplifying dismissals procedures, and reviewing regulations and standards for small and medium enterprises (NPC 2012, 134–45, 143). The NDP talks in general terms about "the competing interests of reducing mass unemployment, raising living standards and closing the earnings gap" and about how "in the early phase of the plan, emphasis will have to be placed on mass access to jobs while maintaining standards where decent jobs already exist" (NPC 2012, 132). But no labor-intensive growth-promoting changes are suggested with regard to the wage-setting machinery in industry.

Indeed, the NDP appears to have given up on labor-intensive manufacturing, declaring,

> South Africa's manufacturing strength lies in capital-intensive industries. In the context of high unemployment, growth would ideally be sourced through expanded contribution of labour. However, to compete, the country's cost structure requires an emphasis on productivity, products and logistics. (NPC 2012, 147–48)

Essentially, the power of organized labor, assisted by the bargaining council system, to drive up wages is taken as an unchangeable part of the country's "cost structure," akin to geography. Low-wage manufacturing is simply assumed to be likely to gravitate to South Africa's neighboring countries, such as Lesotho, rather than providing any basis for significant job creation for South Africa's unskilled unemployed.

There are three obvious problems with regard to South Africa's growth and employment strategy. The first is that the country has serious skill shortages, as reflected in its relatively poor ranking by the *Global Competitiveness Report* with regard to basic education and the supply of skilled labor and university graduates. The NDP accordingly places great emphasis on education and training, but to embark on such a skill-intensive growth strategy, before first achieving a sufficient platform of human capital to do so, is bold to the point of folly. Second, the country is reliant on capital inflows and retained corporate earnings out of profits to fund investment (see Figure 5). This reality means that any rapid process of capital accumulation will quickly come up against a balance of payments constraint—especially if rising remuneration drives down the profit share. Third, it is highly unlikely, particularly in the current global recession, that South Africa will be able to grow at anything close to 5.4 percent per annum between now and 2030; hence, the chances of unemployment falling below 20 percent in the medium term are vanishingly small. A strategy that also allows for significant expansion of relatively low-wage, labor-intensive activities is thus needed.

How could this goal be achieved? Expanding the public works program is one way, but encouraging labor-intensive growth is a necessary adjunct. And a simple first move in this direction would, as originally proposed by GEAR, be to stop destroying existing low-wage jobs through the extension of collective agreements to nonparties. However, those who defend the destruction of low-wage jobs argue that if these low-wage jobs are not destroyed, there will be a "race to the bottom," as such jobs will necessarily undermine "decent," higher-paying jobs elsewhere.

Such claims fail to take into account the highly differentiated nature of most manufacturing production. The clothing industry, for example, ranges from labor-intensive production of simple mass market items, to skill-intensive, fast-fashion and bespoke tailoring. Relatively high- and low-wage clothing firms have existed together in South Africa for over a century because they have different wage-productivity ratios and compete in different product markets (Nattrass and Seekings 2012a, 2012b, 2013). Destroying jobs in the low-wage, labor-intensive, mass-market part of the industry does not help firms in the high-productivity niche markets—it merely benefits competitors in low-wage countries and denies unskilled South Africans the opportunity to work, albeit at low wages.

There is a strong case for taking a more differentiated policy approach to the labor market, such as requiring the minister of labor to consider potential employment losses before extending collective agreements, or even scrapping the extension mechanism altogether. Organized labor, however, has implacably resisted all such proposals.

Which brings us back to the issue of a social accord. The NDP is correct to focus on the need for wage restraint and to develop more trusting labor-employer relations, but this resonates as rather utopian given organized labor's persistent demands for higher wages and for more expansionary macroeconomic policies

FIGURE 7

Consumption, Investment, and Savings in South Africa and Brazil

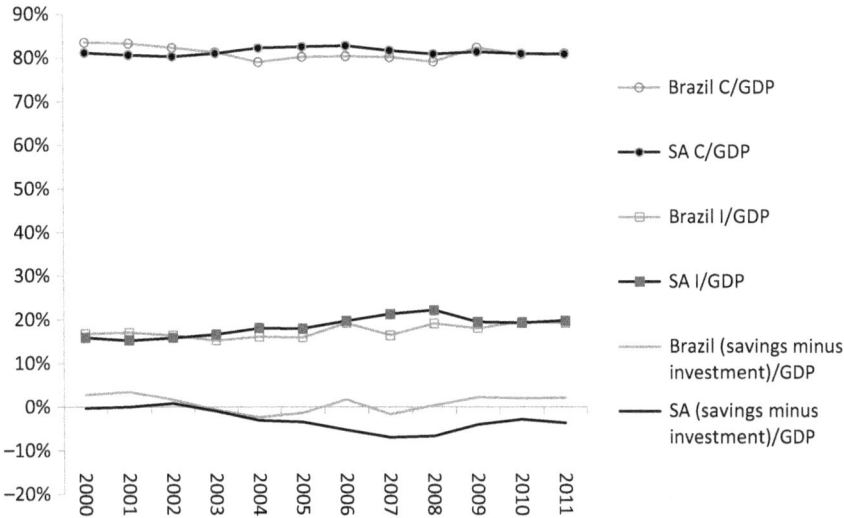

SOURCE: World Development Indicators; see http://databank.worldbank.org/data/.

(e.g., Cosatu 2010, 2012). Indeed, organized labor has recently called for a national minimum wage, justifying it in part by referring to the Brazilian case, the so-called Lula moment when economic growth benefitted from increased minimum wages and social security payments during President Ignacio Lula da Silva's second term of office (2006–2010). Left-inclined intellectuals aligned with Cosatu (e.g., Coleman 2012) accordingly portray wage pressure as being good at the micro level (productivity enhancement) and at the macro level (boosting demand and thereby investment).

There is evidence that rising minimum wages and social security payments in Brazil helped to cushion the effect of the global economic crisis, create jobs, and lower inequality and poverty (ILO 2011; Serrano and Suma 2011). Could South Africa do the same? Figure 7 shows that the share of consumption and investment in South Africa is already comparable to that of Brazil, so there is not obviously much space for future consumption-led growth. Furthermore, the impact of higher wages on profits, investment, and the balance of payments is a very real constraint in South Africa. Unlike Brazil, where investment was financed out of exports and domestic savings, South African investment is reliant on retained earnings out of profits and capital inflows (as evidenced by the negative "savings minus investment/GDP" ratio in Figure 7). The idea that South Africa can embark on a wage-fuelled consumption boom without generating an investment and balance of payments crisis flies in the face of these realities.

In short, there are no easy, quick-fix solutions to the challenge of economic growth and job creation in South Africa. A first step toward any realistic social accord has to be the intellectual recognition on the part of all parties that there are important trade-offs in the relationships among wages, profits, investment, and job creation. Whether the NDP can initiate a meaningful dialogue in this regard remains to be seen. As things stand, the counternarrative about higher wages being good for productivity and economic growth is standing in the way of the kinds of class compromise required in South Africa.

# References

African National Congress (ANC). 1994. *The RDP: The Reconstruction and Development Programme.* Cape Town: ANC.

Benjamin, Paul. 2012. Labour law beyond employment. *Acta Juridica* 2012:21–40.

Bhorat, Haroon, and Carlene van der Westhuizen. 2009. A synthesis of current issues in the labour regulatory environment. DPRU Working Paper 09/136. Available from http://www.commerce.uct.ac.za/research_units/dpru/WorkingPapers/PDF_Files/WP_09-136.pdf.

Bond, Patrick. 2000. *Elite transition: From apartheid to neoliberalism in South Africa.* London: Pluto Press.

Bower, Carol. 2014. The plight of women and children: Advancing South Africa's least privileged. *The ANNALS of the American Academy of Political and Social Science*, this volume.

Chang, Ha-Joon. 2002. *Kicking away the ladder.* London: Anthem Press.

Chang, Ha-Joon. 2012. Debate: Should industrial policy in developing countries conform to comparative advantage or defy it? In *New structural economics: A framework for rethinking development and policy*, ed. Justin Lin, 113–40. Washington, DC: World Bank.

Coleman, Neil. 2012. Towards new collective bargaining, wage and social protection strategies: Learning from the Brazilian experience. Concept paper presented at the University of Cape Town Conference on Strategies to Overcome Poverty and Inequality, 4 September, Cape Town, South Africa.

Cosatu. 2010. *A growth path towards full employment: Policy perspectives of the Congress of South African Trade Unions.* Available from http://www.polity.org.za.

Cosatu. 2012. *11th COSATU Congress secretariat report.* Johannesburg: Cosatu. Available from http://www.COSATU.org.za/docs/reports/2012/report.pdf.

Department of Finance (DOF). 1996. *Growth, employment and redistribution: A macroeconomic strategy.* Pretoria: DOF.

Department of Labour (DOL). 2012. *Annual report 2011–12.* Pretoria: DOL. Available from https://www.labour.gov.za.

Department of Trade and Industry (DTI). 2011. *Industrial policy action plan 2011/12–2013/14.* Pretoria: DTI.

Green, Pippa. 2008. *Choice, not fate: The life and times of Trevor Manuel.* Johannesburg: Penguin Books.

International Labour Organisation (ILO). 2011. *Brazil: An innovative income-led strategy.* Geneva: ILO.

Joffe, Avril, David Kaplan, Raphael Kaplinsky, and David Lewis. 1995. *Improving manufacturing performance in South Africa: Report of the Industrial Strategy Project.* Cape Town: University of Cape Town Press.

Kaplan, David. 2007. The constraints and institutional challenges facing industrial policy in South Africa: A way forward. *Transformation* 64:91–111.

Leibbrandt, Murray, Ingrid Woolard, Arden Finn, and Jonathan Argent. 2010. Trends in South African income distribution and poverty since the fall of apartheid. OECD Social, Employment and Migration Working Papers No. 101. Available from http://dx.doi.org/10.1787/5kmms0t7p1ms-en.

Lin, Justin. 2012. *New structural economics: A framework for rethinking development and policy.* Washington, DC: World Bank.

Moll, Peter. 1996. Compulsory centralisation of collective bargaining in South Africa. *American Economic Review Papers and Proceedings* 82 (2): 326–29.

National Planning Commission (NPC). 2012. *National development plan 2030: Our future—Make it work.*

Pretoria: NPC. Available from http://www.info.gov.za/issues/national-development-plan/.

Nattrass, Nicoli. 1994. Politics and economics in ANC economic policy. *African Affairs* 93:343–59.

Nattrass, Nicoli. 2000. Inequality, unemployment and wage-setting institutions in South Africa. *Studies in Economics and Econometrics* 24 (3): 129–42.

Nattrass, Nicoli. 2013. A South African variety of capitalism? *New Political Economy*. doi:10.1080/135634 67.2013.768610.

Nattrass, Nicoli, and Jeremy Seekings. 2012a. Differentiation within the South African clothing industry: Implications for wage-setting and employment. Centre for Social Science Research Working Paper No. 307, University of Cape Town. Available from http://www.cssr.uct.ac.za/pub/wp/307.

Nattrass, Nicoli, and Jeremy Seekings. 2012b. Institutions, wage differentiation and the structure of employment in South Africa. Centre for Social Science Research Working Paper No.309, University of Cape Town. Available from http://www.cssr.uct.ac.za/pub/wp/309.

Nattrass, Nicoli, and Jeremy Seekings. 2013. Job destruction in the South African clothing industry: How an unholy alliance of organised labour, the state and some firms is undermining labour-intensive growth. Centre for Social Science Research Working Paper No. 323, University of Cape Town. Available from http://www.cssr.uct.ac.za/pub/wp/323.

OECD. 1999. Labour market performance and the OECD jobs strategy. *Economic Outlook* 65 (June): 142–61.

RDP White Paper. 15 November 1994. White Paper on reconstruction and development. *Government Gazette* 353 (16085), Cape Town.

Schwab, Klaus. 2012. *The global competitiveness report 2012–2013*. Geneva: World Economic Forum. Available from http://www.weforum.org/issues/global-competitiveness.

Seekings, Jeremy, and Nicoli Nattrass. 2005. *Class, race and inequality in South Africa*. New Haven, CT: Yale University Press.

Serrano, Franklin, and Ricardo Summa. 2011. *Macroeconomic policy, growth and income distribution in the Brazilian economy in the 2000s*. Washington, DC: Center for Economic and Policy Research.

Shankar, Shylashri, Raghav Gaiha, and Jha Raghbendra. 2011. Information, access and targeting: The national rural employment guarantee scheme in India. *Oxford Development Studies* 29 (1): 69–95.

van der Spuy, Elrena, and Clifford Shearing. 2014. Curbing the killing fields: Making South Africa safer. *The ANNALS of the American Academy of Political and Social Science*, this volume.

Whiteside, Alan. 2014. South Africa's key health challenges. *The ANNALS of the American Academy of Political and Social Science*, this volume.

# The Plight of Women and Children: Advancing South Africa's Least Privileged

*By*
CAROL BOWER

Despite South Africa having ratified several international and regional women's and children's rights treaties, and having one of the most admired constitutions in the world, the plight of women and children after 20 years of democracy remains, in many respects, dire—especially in rural communities. South Africa is a deeply conservative and patriarchal society, with high levels of violence in general and gender-based violence in particular. It has failed to create sufficient employment opportunities and to sustainably address intergenerational poverty, the latter of which impacts most severely rural women and children. HIV/AIDS has wreaked its most adverse effects on women and children. This context is exacerbated by breakdowns in the health, education, justice, and security sectors; the relative inaccessibility of services (such as health care, schooling, and housing); and the frequently poor quality of services when they are available.

*Keywords:* women; children; gender-based violence; abuse; patriarchy; poverty; HIV/AIDS

For women and children in South Africa, not much has changed since the first democratic elections in 1994 and the presidency of Nelson Mandela. Progress toward the full realization of the rights of women and children has been unacceptably slow, given the extent of available resources and the commitments the country has made in its own legislation.

The patriarchal and traditional view of women and children as inferior to men prevails, with more men in positions of power and influence than women. Although the Constitution and legislation are clear about the equality of all citizens, I show in this article that the government, the economy, and civil society are run by

*Carol Bower has been actively involved in protecting the rights of women and children since 1976, and is especially committed to protecting them from sexual violence and harsh discipline. She has worked extensively with child rights issues, prevention and early intervention, and in the development of law and policy to protect children.*

DOI: 10.1177/0002716213512086

men who frequently show scant regard or understanding for the rights of women and children.

Violence against women and children in South Africa is endemic. As is shown below, there are as many as 180 to 265 rapes each hour of every day; four women die every day at the hands of their intimate partners; and more than two children are murdered every day, with the same number being the victims of attempted murder every day.

Women and children have borne the brunt of the HIV pandemic, in a country with the dubious distinction of being at the epidemic's epicenter; and they are hardest hit by poverty (see below). Women in rural areas remain among the most vulnerable and marginalized in the country.

## International, Regional, and Domestic Obligations toward Women and Children

South Africa has made serious commitments to protecting and enhancing the rights of women and children, placing obligations on the country to ensure the realization of these rights. At the international level, the new South Africa moved swiftly to lay the groundwork, and ratified both the Convention to End All Forms of Discrimination against Women (CEDAW) and the Convention on the Rights of the Child (CRC) in 1995, just over a year after the dawn of democracy.

At the regional level, South Africa is one of the nine Southern African Development Community (SADC) countries that has signed and ratified the SADC Protocol on Gender and Development (the SADC Protocol); it has also signed and ratified the African Charter on the Rights and Welfare of the Child (the African Charter), the African Charter on Human and Peoples' Rights, and the Maputo Declaration on Sexual and Reproductive Health and Rights.

Domestically, the Constitution, passed by Parliament in 1996, contains a comprehensive Bill of Rights in Chapter 2. It is unequivocal that neither the state nor anyone else "may ... unfairly discriminate directly or indirectly against anyone on one or more grounds, including race, gender, sex, pregnancy, marital status, ethnic or social origin, colour, sexual orientation, age, disability, religion, conscience, belief, culture, language and birth."[1] The Bill of Rights also contains an entire section on the additional rights of children, in Section 28.

In addition to its Constitution, South Africa has a number of laws that are (mostly) proactive and protective of women and children, in particular the Domestic Violence Act (no. 116 of 1998), the Children's Act as Amended (no. 38 of 2005), and the Criminal Law (Sexual Offences and Related Matters) Act (no. 32 of 2007).

Despite these positive steps, though, South Africa remains a country in which "to be a child ... is to walk a fragile path to adulthood" (UNICEF 2013b) and to be a woman is, for far too many, to be poor, disempowered, and vulnerable to appallingly high levels of sexual violence. The gap between the principles espoused on paper and the reality on the ground is profound.

# A Profoundly Patriarchal Society

The patriarchal nature of South African society has an enormous impact on the lives of women and children in South Africa, contributing significantly to perceptions of the roles and rights of women and children, to the high levels of sexual violence, and to the poverty and inequality that characterize their lives.

More than 80 percent of South Africans belong to one of the three major religions: Christianity, Islam, and Judaism (South African Government 2013a). The latter two provide endless and well-documented justification for regarding women and children as the possessions of men. With regard to Christianity, South Africa has a long Calvinist tradition, and widespread adherence to biblical and Calvinist perceptions of the role and status of women as inferior to that of men within families and societies (Landman 2009). This is true also among the non-Calvinist branches of Christianity.

Further evidence of the patriarchal nature of South African society is provided by the preponderance of males in positions of power within government, the business community, and public life in general despite multiple and repeated commitments at all levels for gender parity. Despite the fact that South Africa has one of the highest proportions of female cabinet ministers globally, the current gender breakdown across the Cabinet (ministers and deputy ministers) is 39 percent female and 61 percent male; 43 percent of cabinet ministers are female (*Gender Links* 2010).

According to the 2011 Businesswomen Association (BWA) South African Women in Leadership Census, women hold only 4.4 percent of CEO/MD positions, 5.3 percent of chairperson positions, and 15.8 percent of all directorships; in the public service, women hold 35 percent of all senior managerial positions (Skillsportal 2012). Colleen Lowe Morna, CEO of Gender Links, reports that research done by her organization indicates that only 5 percent of media decision-makers—producers, managers, and owners—are women, and that women are underrepresented as hosts, guests, and callers to radio talk shows, a popular form of information and entertainment in South Africa (Charles Stuart Mott Foundation 2006).

The patriarchal nature of South Africa is further evidenced by the very traditional nature of large sections of the population. Indeed, the principles of gender equality that are now part of South Africa's Constitution were won in the face of rigorous opposition from the Congress of Traditional Leaders (Schäfer 2013). The traditional leaders are chiefs who, under the apartheid regime, enjoyed a certain amount of power and authority in the so-called homelands. This power and authority has continued into the new South Africa, and in 2013 a controversial bill to consolidate the National House of Traditional Leaders Act[2] and the Traditional Leadership and Governance Framework Act[3] was on the table giving traditional leadership even greater authority. In addition, a Traditional Courts Bill seeks to introduce a parallel legislative system that reverses women's rights and gives traditional chiefs significant power over their "subjects" without any democratic checks or balances (Awino 2013). The 2011 census indicated that women make up 52 percent of the South African population. Almost half (47 percent) live in rural areas, which fall under traditional leadership (Bobo 2011).

The resurgence of traditional leadership, which had been discredited and was weak and ineffectual by 1994, is in part the "fault" of Mandela himself, with his insistence of the inclusion of traditional leadership in the CODESA process and his deference to traditional leadership as president. However, there is increasing evidence that pre-colonial, pre-missionary, and pre–slave trade Africa held views of more equitable roles for women in society (Sesanti 2011) to those reflected in 2013. Perhaps this heritage should be explored further to stem the tide of gender-based violence.

## Perceptions of women and children

In general, it is fair to say that women and children are regarded as being "owned" by the men in their lives—fathers, husbands, boyfriends, brothers, and even sons (in the absence of anyone else). Women who work in civil society organizations, for example, routinely report that their work is discredited if they are not married or at least in a clear relationship with a male partner.[4] This is true no matter what age they are or the extent of their experience. In rural areas, especially those parts of South Africa that formerly constituted the infamous homelands, it is commonly found that, when a man dies, his house (in which his wife and children may be living) is inherited by his nearest male relative (no matter how distant), and his wife and children lose all their rights to it and to any other property.

This situation is exacerbated by the fact that President Jacob Zuma is a deeply patriarchal man and a polygamist. He has been married six times and currently has four wives, several "girlfriends," and at least twenty-two children. He was charged with rape (in 2005), although he was acquitted after admitting to "consensual," unprotected sex with an HIV-positive family friend; subsequently he claimed that he had sought to minimize the risk of HIV infection by showering. At the time, he was the head of the South African National Aids Council (BBC News 2006).

Similarly, Zuma's personal views on the role and rights of women stand in stark contrast to his more politically correct official public statements about women's rights and rape. For example, in August 2012 (coincidentally and ironically Women's Month in South Africa), speaking of the marriage of one of his daughters, he stated that marriage was desirable for all women and that "kids are important to a woman because they actually give an extra training to a woman, to be a mother" (Davis 2012).

Of perhaps greater concern was the response of the ANC Women's League (ANCWL) to Zuma's pronouncements—they leapt to his defense, claiming that his comments were "taken out of context" (Pillay 2012). The ANCWL also backed Zuma's bid for reelection as ANC President in December 2012. Gone are the days when the ANCWL was a staunch and outspoken advocate for the protection of the rights of women.

*Gender-based violence*

The deeply patriarchal nature of South African society is also reflected in the social constructions of masculinity and femininity, which feed directly into high levels of gender-based violence. Femininity is still seen as inextricably linked to motherhood and dependence on a man, while masculinity is defined by sexual activity and conquest.

Research that Community Information, Empowerment and Transparency (CIET) Africa has undertaken has found that young South Africans measured "successful masculinity" in terms of whether one was in at least one sexual relationship, while "successful femininity" was measured in terms of being in a relationship at all (note, not necessarily a sexual relationship) (Andersson et al. 2004). It is in the cross-hairs of a man's need to be in a sexual relationship and a woman's need to be in a relationship that innumerable women and girls become vulnerable to rape and domestic violence.

The Medical Research Council (MRC) has found that much of the sexual violence in South African society can be attributed to a sense of male entitlement, not just poverty as some researchers suggest (Jewkes et al. 2011). For example, in a large sample of mostly rural young men, rape was more commonly committed by those who came from relatively better economic backgrounds (Jewkes et al. 2006). This indicates that it is a sense of entitlement arising out of their relative advantage and within a context in which few can realistically attain high levels of material "success" (Jewkes et al. 2006). Based on their findings, Jewkes et al. (2006) concluded that "the most common motivations for all types of rape stemmed from ideas of sexual entitlement, a further measure of which [was] that 45 percent of men indicated that they had felt no guilt about their act of rape" (Jewkes et al. 2011, 9).

According to Jewkes et al. (2006) several scholars have shown how, in general, certain social constructions of masculinity serve to legitimize unequal and violent relationships with women. Research from South Africa, a setting characterized by high levels of gender inequality, indicates that these intractable masculine ideals emphasize heterosexual performance, toughness, and strength, and rely on an ability to "control" women (Jewkes and Morrell 2010).

Perhaps the least subtle expression of patriarchal heterosexist violence is corrective rape, which has become a particular problem in South Africa since 1994. Corrective rape most often involves multiple perpetrators (i.e., gang rape) who rape and sometimes kill black lesbians to "correct" their behavior. Statistics for corrective rape are not collected in South Africa, but a South African nonprofit set up to "fight corrective rape" estimates that more than ten lesbians are raped or gang raped weekly and that at least five hundred lesbians become victims of corrective rape every year (Luleki 2011). The Cape Town-based Triangle Project (LGBTI) organization reported in 2008 that 86 percent of black lesbians in the Western Cape lived in fear of being raped (Di Silvio 2011).

# Violence

Violence underlies and informs every aspect of the lives of women and children in South Africa. South Africa has arguably the highest rates of sexual violence in the world. For example, in an article in the *Daily Maverick*, a local daily e-newspaper, eleven incidents of violence against women and children were reported during February 2013, including rape, gang rape, and murder of victims ranging in age from two years to 101 (Davis 2013).

The media seldom draws together in one report all incidents of sexual violence, even if it reports them at all. In reality, violence against women and children occurs at such a high rate that individual cases are often not even particularly newsworthy unless they are especially brutal or involve a high-profile perpetrator. Indeed, the Institute of Race Relations claimed recently that "if data for all violent assaults, rapes, and other sexual assaults against women are taken into account, then approximately 200,000 adult women are *reported* as being attacked in South Africa every year" (Davis 2013, emphasis added). Sexual violence is so pervasive that it is easy to defend the claim that it has been normalized in South African society.

## Rape and sexual assault

Between April 2011 and March 2012, 64,514 rapes were reported to the South African Police Services (SAPS)—in excess of 170 a day (SAPS 2012). There is widespread agreement among those who work with the victims of rape that it is seriously underreported. The MRC estimates that as few as one in twenty-five is reported (Genderlinks and Medical Research Council 2013). The police themselves have suggested a rate of only one in thirty-six rapes being reported (SABC 2012).

A more accurate estimate of the actual number of rapes can be made by a simple extrapolation from the estimated reporting rates: between 1,612,850 (at MRC rate) and 2,322,504 (at SAPS rate) women and children were raped in South Africa last year. At the MRC rate, there are more than 4,000 rapes a day, at a rate of roughly 180 an hour. If the police are correct, the figures are even more horrific, with around 265 rapes an hour taking place. Wherever the true number lies, these are statistics that indicate a very serious problem.

## Intimate partner violence

Reliable statistics on domestic violence in South Africa are hard to come by. Although the number of reported cases is high, as with rape, many go unreported. The problem is exacerbated by the fact that the police do not keep separate statistics on assault cases perpetrated by intimate partners. However, the World Health Organisation reported in 2012 that around sixty thousand women and children in South Africa were victims of domestic violence every month—the highest reported rate in the world (Hunter-Gault 2013).

In 1997, the Department of Justice estimated that one out of every four South African women was a survivor of domestic violence (Blaser 1998). According to People Opposing Woman Abuse (POWA), a Gauteng-based advocacy and service organization dealing with gender-based violence, one in six women who die in Gauteng Province is killed by an intimate partner (Mathews et al. 2004), and it is estimated that a woman in South Africa is killed by her intimate partner every six hours (Mathews et al. 2004).

### Corporal punishment of children

Corporal punishment by parents is still legal in South Africa. The link between gender-based violence and parental corporal punishment has become increasingly clear in recent times. While corporal punishment is not obviously a form of discrimination against girls (as both girls and boys are corporally punished), it is directly linked to other forms of gender-based violence, particularly domestic violence, and is used to control and regulate girls' behavior much as intimate partner violence aims to control women's behavior (Global Initiative to End All Corporal Punishment of Children 2013). Childhood experience of corporal punishment for girls has been reliably linked to a life of violent victimization by authority figures and family members. There is also a demonstrated relationship between experiencing corporal punishment as a child and an increased likelihood of men perpetrating violence against partners and children as adults (Contreras et al. 2012).

High levels of acceptance of parental corporal punishment contribute to the overall ethos of violence and bolster notions that women and children are inferior. According to the 2011/2012 crime statistics released by SAPS, nearly eight hundred children were murdered in South Africa and a further nearly eight hundred were victims of attempted murder during that period (News 24 2012b). Unfortunately, statistics on the perpetration of these crimes are not disaggregated. Most of these crimes are perpetrated by a parent (biological or otherwise), and, according to Childline South Africa, they are frequently the result of parental corporal punishment "gone wrong."[5]

# Unemployment, Poverty, and Inequality

South Africa has high levels of deep intergenerational poverty. Poverty impacts most negatively women and children. In his 2013 State of the Nation Address (SONA) (South African Government 2013b), President Zuma highlighted what he called "the triple challenge" facing South Africa: that of unemployment, poverty, and inequality, "which persists in spite of the progress made. Africans, women, and the youth continue to suffer most from this challenge" (Gumede 2012).

### Unemployment

Officially, the unemployment rate in South Africa is 25 percent and has hovered around this figure for a number of years (TradingEconomics.com 2013).

The true figure is regularly at least 10 percent higher than that if the unemployed who are not actively seeking work are also taken into account (Posel, Casale, and Vermaak 2013).

Although there is significant emphasis on employment creation in South Africa, efforts have been hampered by the global recession, and the impact on the costs of basic goods and services and the steep increases in fuel and energy costs. South Africa loses more jobs each month than it creates (Hazelhurst 2013). According to the Quarterly Labour Force Survey (QLFS) produced by Statistics South Africa, unemployment increased by 4.3 million during the first quarter of 2010; the formal sector lost 140,000 jobs and the informal sector an estimated 100,000 between the last quarter of 2009 and the first of 2010. The agricultural sector lost 25,000 jobs in the same period (UNDP 2013a).

The unemployment rate for women is higher than the national average (UNDP 2013a). Only four out of ten South African women are employed; for black South African women, the figure is 50 percent; and for young black South African women, it jumps to 70 percent (Education and Training Unit [ETU] 2013). Many women who are employed work the in agricultural and domestic sectors—the most exploitative categories of work (ETU 2013).

These high levels of unemployment also impact children—approximately 38 percent of households are headed by women in South Africa (UNDP 2013a), and almost 40 percent of South Africa's children live in such households (Hall et al. 2012). This is particularly so in rural communities, where the number of female-headed households is relatively larger than in urban areas. For example, the highest proportion of female-headed households is found in the three most rural of South Africa's provinces: 49 percent in Limpopo, 45 percent in Eastern Cape, and 44 percent in KwaZulu-Natal. More than 25 percent of female household-heads are older than 60 (UNDP 2013a). Female-headed households are, therefore, by their very nature, more likely to exist as lower-income households and be more vulnerable to hunger.

## Poverty

Statistics relating to the number of poor women are not disaggregated in South Africa. Mostly, the available information is based on household surveys; they tell us how many households are poor, but not how many women are (Southern Africa Regional Poverty Network [SARPN] 2008). The more detailed information related to children and poverty that is available, however, gives insight into the situation of women also.

Nearly 67 percent of South African children live in poverty, and 35 percent of all children live in households where there is no employed adult (Hall et al. 2012); 43 percent of female-headed households do not include a single employed person (Statistics South Africa 2010). This lack of adequate income compromises the health of children and women and their access to services. It frequently leaves them in situations where their physical safety is threatened (Hall et al. 2012).

*Inequality*

South Africa has the dubious distinction of being one of the most unequal societies in the world, reflected in its high Gini coefficient of .65 (the measure between 0 and 1 of the degree of inequality, where a coefficient of 1 is equal to total inequality). The 2011 census found that, while the income of black South African households has increased by 169 percent in the last decade, whites still earn on average six times more (Conway-Smith 2012). So, although South Africa has managed to build a much larger black middle class than was the case in 1994, the majority of black people have not found that their lives have improved over the last two decades. Though absolute income poverty has decreased in the 2000s, income inequality has actually increased (Sharma 2012). Indeed, the assertion by then–Deputy President Thabo Mbeki in 1999 that South Africa was "two-nations divided by poverty and inequality" remains largely true in 2013.

For women (and also for their children) the situation is exacerbated by significant gender inequality. For example, researchers from the University of the Witwatersrand stated that "culturally, the patriarchal status quo remains relatively unchanged, and unless the mind-set behind gender discriminatory practices is challenged through debate, media campaigns, education, etc. nothing much is going to change" (Skillsportal 2012).

The Millennium Development Goals (MDGs) provide a useful framework for the assessment of progress toward a more equitable society. These are eight development goals agreed to by all 191 UN member states in 2000, to be achieved by 2015. Goals 1 through 6 are of particular relevance for this article. They are, in order: eradicate extreme poverty and hunger; achieve universal primary education; promote gender equality and empower women; reduce child mortality; improve maternal health; and combat HIV/AIDS, malaria and other diseases.[6] South Africa's progress toward the 2015 MDGs is uneven, with women and children bearing the consequences of unmet promises (UNICEF 2013b). Nevertheless, some progress has been made.

*Goal 1: Eradicate extreme poverty and hunger*

South Africa has introduced an impressive social grants system, which research indicates is achieving its aim of reducing hunger and poverty (Studies in Poverty and Inequality Institute 2008). Since 2012, all children (under the age of 18) are eligible for a child support grant (CSG), provided their caregivers pass a means test. Currently, just over 11 million children are in receipt of a means-tested CSG. The uptake of the CSG almost doubled between 2005 and 2012 (Hall et al. 2012).

In addition, in 2012, 572,903 children were in receipt of the foster child grant (available to foster parents who have a child placed in their care by court order), and a further 117,256 were in receipt of the care dependency grant (available to caregivers of children with severe disabilities, or whose chronic illness has become disabling) (Hall et al. 2012).

There is clear and significant evidence that grants facilitate the realization of children's right to social assistance and improve their access to food, education, and basic services, including health care (Hall et al. 2012). Nevertheless, in 2010, the Children's Institute reported that one in five South African children go hungry (Hall 2010).

## Goal 2: Achieve universal primary education

South Africa is on track to achieve the MDGs on universal primary education, and access to education for children from previously disadvantaged backgrounds has improved significantly since 1994. As of 2012, 96.9 percent of children aged 7 to 17 were enrolled in an educational institution (Hall et al. 2012). Girls' education has been prioritized, resulting in almost as many girls being enrolled in primary school as boys. In secondary school, girls outnumber boys (UNICEF 2013b). The poorest children pay no school fees; in 2010, 60 percent of all public schools, (14,567 of 24,532 schools) were no-fee schools (News 24 2012a).

As of this writing, only 16.9 percent of children under the age of five have access to day care, crèches,[7] preschools, and early childhood development centers. Government has prioritized early childhood development and substantially increased funding for this sector (UNICEF 2013b). The government is also committed to offering grade R (reception year for children aged 5–6); in 2013, enrollment stood at 50 percent in both public and private schools (UNICEF 2013b).

Despite the high enrollment and significant budgetary investment in education by government, South African scholars consistently score low on international literacy, reading, and numeracy assessments (UNICEF 2013b). The poor quality of education undermines children's ability and desire to learn. For many children, regular attendance at school is fraught with absent teachers, underqualified teachers, a lack of books and other resources, teenage pregnancy, and abuse and violence in and around schools; 27 percent of public schools do not have running water, 78 percent have no libraries, and 78 percent do not have computers (UNICEF 2013b). The Legal Resources Centre found one or more of "a lack of basic furniture, intolerably over-crowded classrooms, crumbling buildings, teacher shortages, and filthy or non-existent toilet facilities" at each of the eleven rural schools that they visited recently in the former Transkei (Ganesh 2013).[8]

## Goal 3: Promote gender equality and empower women

As noted earlier in this article, South Africa has a way to go in terms of gender parity in government and the private sector; the number of men outweighs the number of women in every sphere. However, there has been some progress.

- In August 2012, the Women Empowerment and Gender Equality Draft Bill was published for comment in the Government Gazette.[9]
- The number of girls in school is high; at primary school level, there are slightly more boys enrolled than girls, but at secondary and tertiary levels, the number of girls outweighs the number of boys (UNDP 2013b).

- In terms of the representation of women in government at the national level, about a third of the members of parliament are women, and 43 percent of cabinet ministers are women. At the provincial level, five of the nine provincial premiers are women, and three of the six major metros are led by women. In the private sector, though, the figures are much less encouraging (as shown earlier).

Women are not only unequitably represented in the different employment sectors, but women with the same levels of education as their male counterparts earn about 80 percent of what men do (UNDP 2013b).

However, it must be remembered that "gender equality has both public and private aspects" (Skillsportal 2012). While the public aspects (such as legislation promoting gender equality) are relatively easy to measure, what happens in the private sphere is far less clear. It is possible to have good laws and a progressive constitution and not observe an appreciable improvement in gender equity in the private sphere because the gender dynamics operating within society are more difficult to observe and measure directly. Comments made by political role-players often highlight a high degree of dissonance between what is espoused as policy and individuals' actual views on the issue (for example, the comments that President Zuma made, mentioned above).

## Goal 4: Reduce child mortality

Child survival is the gold standard for measuring the likelihood of achieving the MDGs. In South Africa, the under-five mortality rate for children has remained almost the same over the past two decades. One in fifteen children dies from diseases that could be prevented, such as intestinal infection, influenza, pneumonia, and HIV-related illnesses. Twenty-two percent of under-five deaths occur during the first month of life (UNICEF 2013b). The target for this MDG is to reduce child mortality (as measured by the infant and under-five mortality rates) by 2015 by at least two-thirds of the 1990 rate.

The 1990 infant mortality rate (IMR) was 54 deaths per 1,000 live births (UNDP 2013b); the IMR rose to 58.88 deaths per 1,000 live births in 2000, but dropped to 42.67 in 2012 (Index Mundi 2012a) The 1990 under-five mortality rate (U5MR) was 59.8 per 1,000 live births and dropped to 56.6 in 2010 (Index Mundi 2012b). For the IMR, this represents a decrease of approximately one-fifth over a 22-year period; for the U5MR, the decrease over a 20-year period is in the order of 5 percent. It is clear that progress is slow and that the target of reducing child mortality by two-thirds by 2015 will not be reached.

## Goal 5: Improve maternal health

This MDG targets a 75 percent reduction in the maternal mortality ratio (MMR) and the achievement of universal access to reproductive health by 2015. Children need healthy mothers for their own optimal health and growth.

Maternal mortality in South Africa is high and on the rise. The latest UN figures estimate that one in 250 women dies during pregnancy or childbirth. AIDS-related diseases account for 23 percent of all maternal deaths, followed by complications of pregnancy-related hypertension (UNICEF 2013b). The UNDP estimates that the MMR per 100,000 live births was 369 in 1994 and had risen to 625 by 2010 (UNICEF 2013b). The MDG target would be 38 per 100,000 live births by 2015; it is clear that this is unlikely to be achieved. Primary health care is free for pregnant women and for children under the age of six in South Africa. Despite high rates of coverage for antenatal care, the fact that 95 percent of women give birth in hospitals and other medical facilities, and 100 percent of women receive prenatal care, pregnant women are still dying (UNICEF 2013b).

# HIV and AIDS

MDG 6 relates to combating HIV/AIDS, malaria, and other diseases (including tuberculosis). HIV's most devastating effects are reserved for the most vulnerable and marginalized groups—in this case, women (especially women living in rural areas) and children.

After a tragic period of AIDS denial under President Thabo Mbeki, the South African government made a historic shift and began to implement treatment and prevention programs. In 2009, it committed to accelerating the national AIDS response and to meeting the targets of the HIV and Infectious Disease Surveillance (IDS) and Sexually Transmitted Infections (STI) Strategic Plan by 2011 (UNICEF 2013b). South Africa now has the largest antiretroviral treatment program in the world, with almost 800,000 adults and 76,000 children under the age of 15 receiving free treatment by mid-2009 (UNICEF 2013a; see also Whiteside, this volume).

Since then, HIV prevalence has been declining among children and teenagers. For example, HIV prevalence among children between 2 and 14 decreased from 5.6 percent in 2002 to 2.5 percent in 2008, likely because of several successful HIV-prevention measures such as prevention of mother-to-child transmission (PMTCT) (UNICEF 2013b).

Although HIV-prevalence rates appear to have, at last, stabilized at 17–18 percent over the 2008–2010 period (Hall et al. 2012), they are still high. Infection rates are higher in rural provinces, which can be attributed in part to inequitable power relationships between men and women and between men and children in those areas (UNICEF 2013b). An apparent increase in relationships that expose young girls to HIV because of gender power inequalities and older male sexual partners are also of concern (UNICEF 2013b).

Around 5.6 million South Africans are living with HIV—this is roughly 11 percent of the population (South African Institute of Race Relations [SAIRR] 2009). Five million (89 percent) are adults aged 20 to 64, and 2.93 million (53 percent) are women between the ages of 15 and 49; youth aged 15 to 24 account for 731,000 (13 percent), while children 14 years and under account for

454,000 (8 percent) (SAIRR 2009). Women under 25 are between three and four times more likely to be HIV-infected than men in the same age group (Amnesty International 2008). Sex with older men—an important risk factor for HIV infection—has increased substantially, from 18.5 percent of teenage girls in 2005 to 27.6 percent in 2008, and surveys have reported that accurate knowledge about HIV transmission is rare (UNICEF 2013b).

Michel Sidibé, executive director of UNAIDS, stated in 2009 that "this epidemic unfortunately remains an epidemic of women" (UN News Centre 2010). Not only are women infected with HIV at higher rates than men, but HIV also has other negative effects for women. For example, disclosure of HIV status may bring about stigmatization, rejection, domestic violence, abuse, and abandonment (IDASA 2002). Once symptoms begin, women are often in increasingly dependent positions and frequently cannot obtain employment (IDASA 2002).

The impact of the HIV pandemic on South African children, then, has been devastating. Beside children becoming infected (primarily during the birth process because their mothers are infected, and some through breastfeeding), and thus becoming ill or dying, a large number of children are orphaned. According to the 2010 General Household Survey, there were approximately 3.84 million orphans in South Africa, 21 percent of all South African children (defined as a child without a living biological mother, father, or both parents) (Meintjes and Hall 2012). This represented a 28 percent increase since 2002 (Meintjes and Hall 2012). About half of these children have been orphaned by AIDS; it is estimated that 150,000 children are living in child-headed households in South Africa (UNICEF 2013a).

It must be noted, however, that the idea that there is a generation of children raised without parents and overwhelming the country with crime has no foundation. The majority of the children orphaned by HIV are not in fact living in child-headed households, but mostly in extended kinship care. And most children living in child-headed households are not orphans: the 2006 General Household Survey found that only 8 percent of children living in child-headed households were parentless, while 61 percent had two living parents and 80 percent had a living mother (Meintjes et al. 2009).

## Access to Services

South Africa has a sound legislative and policy framework for protecting the rights of women and children. However, the gap between policy and practice is huge, more so in some areas than in others. Access to basic services, adequate housing, educational facilities, and health care is often challenging, especially in rural provinces; access to prevention and protection services for vulnerable women and children is patchy, to say the least; and the criminal justice system routinely fails the victims of, in particular, sexual crimes. The problem is aggravated by the fact that service providers frequently do not understand their role and legal obligations nor the laws that they are supposed to be implementing and upholding.

## Basic services

Information on women's access to basic services is not readily available, but the information available on the situation for children is revealing.

## Potable water

Access to clean water is vital for human survival; an individual needs 20 liters of fresh water per day for hygiene, drinking, and cooking (Ban 2007). Young children are particularly at risk without adequate access to sufficient clean drinking water, with gastrointestinal infections directly linked to the high infant and under-five mortality rates (Hall et al. 2012). Nearly 7 million children live in households without access to clean drinking water. Nearly 36 percent of South Africa's children (Hall et al. 2012) cannot easily find clean water. This situation has improved only marginally since 2002, when 40 percent of children were in this lamentable situation (Hall et al. 2012).

## Sanitation

Access to adequate sanitation is an important component of disease prevention and health promotion, and its absence is directly linked to cholera, malaria, bilharzia (schistosomiasis), worm infestations, eye infections, and skin disease. Although access to adequate sanitation improved between 2002 and 2010, a third of South African children live in households without basic sanitation (Hall et al. 2012).

## Adequate housing

According to the UN Committee on Economic, Social, and Cultural Rights, "adequate housing" includes reasonable access to work opportunities, clinics, police stations, schools, and childcare facilities (UN Office of the High Commissioner of Human Rights [OHCHR] 1991). Thus, services and facilities should be well distributed, even in less populous areas. In South Africa, while access to services and resources in urban areas is relatively good, this is not the case in rural areas. The South African Constitution provides that all South Africans have the right to adequate housing—a right that was upheld in the landmark Grootboom case, in which the Constitutional Court confirmed that the state is obliged to ensure shelter for children in situations where their parents are unable to do so, in fulfillment of section 26 of the Constitution (IDASA 2002). Women's access (or lack thereof) to adequate housing is complicated by a context of historic, economic, and social inequality.

Historically, the restriction of black urbanization by both the colonial and apartheid regimes disproportionately affected women's access to housing, and this has spilled into the new South Africa, with nearly half of South African women residing in rural areas. Economically, women earn, on average, far less than men, and fewer of them are employed. In addition, women and girls older than 10 spend an average of 216 minutes per day on unpaid housework, care work, and community work, compared to an average of only 83 minutes for men (Budlender, Chobokoane, and Mpetsheni 2001). These activities inhibit women's capacity to find and hold employment and add to their relatively lower incomes. Socially, the fact that patriarchal norms and values underpin gender relations, discriminatory customary and religious laws and practices (such as patrilineal succession under customary law), domestic violence, and HIV/AIDS—all of which disproportionately affect women—constrain women's access to adequate housing.

In 2010, just over 10 percent of South African children were living in informal housing, mostly in informal settlements around the major cities; nearly 17 percent of children were living in traditional housing in the rural areas of the country; and just over 23 percent of children were living in overcrowded conditions (Hall et al. 2012).

### Educational facilities

South Africa has a high level of enrollment in educational facilities; however, nearly a quarter of children live more than 30 minutes from their school. As is the case with other services, this situation is worse in rural areas (Hall et al. 2012). And mere attendance at a school is no guarantee that a child will learn. In addition, the closure of a number of rural schools since 2002 has exacerbated the lack of access to educational facilities, especially for rural children (Hall et al. 2012).

### Health care

Although primary health care has been free for all South Africans since 1996, access to health care facilities is often challenging. In 2002, just over 36.4 percent of children (6.4 million) lived more than 30 minutes away from the nearest health facility; by 2010, this number had risen to 36.7 percent (6.8 million) (Hall et al. 2012). However, in the more rural provinces of Limpopo, KwaZulu-Natal, and Eastern Cape, 40 percent of children remain far from a clinic. Eighty percent of South Africans are dependent on public health care (Taylor 2012). Access to appropriate health care is made more challenging by the fact that the quality of available care is very mixed. For example, in the Eastern Cape, in 2012, it was reported that insufficient doctors and chronic shortages of life-saving medicine were putting patients' lives at risk (Child 2012). In addition, medical personnel complain about the administrative chaos that bedevils some provincial health departments (Taylor 2012). The impact of these inadequacies on women and children can clearly be seen in the high rates of infant and maternal mortality discussed above.

### Prevention and protection services

Prevention and protection services are especially critical in light of the high levels of sexual violence to which women and children in South Africa are subjected. Despite the extent to which an enabling legislative environment has been put in place that addresses violence against women and children, it is of grave concern that many of these legislative and policy-driven interventions have not been put into effective practice, and that implementation has, "at best ... been patchy" (Smythe et al. 2007).

The truth is that most prevention services for women and children are provided by nonprofit organizations, most of which live on the edge of precarious funding and most of which are based in the major metropolitan areas. To overturn the deep-seated and entrenched patriarchal ethos found in South Africa will require higher levels of resourcing and commitment from government, including in particular the funding of sustained training and awareness-raising activities concerning gender-based violence.

Of particular issue is the lack of therapeutic and recuperative services for woman and child victims of sexual violence, and this lack is particularly problematic in rural communities. Many of the harmful and lasting psychological impacts of sexual violence may be prevented or minimized with structured interventions and the provision of psychological support post-rape (Sexual Violence Research Intitiative [SVRI] 2011). Again, it is of concern that these services are provided largely by civil society organizations. Post-traumatic stress disorder (PTSD) is a significant threat to mental health, especially that of children. Untreated PTSD may lead to a host of problems in children and youth, including criminal and antisocial behavior, alcohol and drug abuse, future dependence on welfare, psychiatric problems, academic deficits, school dropouts, health problems, relationship problems, sexual acting-out, and sexually transmitted diseases including HIV/AIDS (Freyd et al. 2005).

The cold reality is that the vast majority of woman and child victims of sexual violence never access the therapeutic services that could facilitate their healing, and this has long-term consequences for their health and well-being.

*Criminal justice system*

The criminal justice system in South Africa is notoriously victim-unfriendly, especially with regard to victims of sexual violence. In the 2000s, it was marred by questionable decision-making, resulting in the closure and then reinstatement of specialist services. The Family Violence, Child Abuse, and Sexual Offences (FCS) units within SAPS were closed in 2006, and in 2013 were being reinstated. Similarly, the specialist Sexual Offences Courts (SOC) were closed; in March 2013, the minister of justice announced the roll-out of fifty-eight SOCs and admitted that "these dedicated courts are necessary. When there are these dedicated courts, the conviction rate goes up, but when we stopped them, the conviction rate went down" (MSN News 2013).

The reporting rate, arrest rate, and the number of reported cases that actually go to court in sexual offence cases are low (Smythe et al. 2007). Less than 7,000 of the 66,196 cases reported in 2010/2011 resulted in court appearances. And the conviction rate is a small percentage of the reported cases; in 2011/2012, only

6.9 percent of reported cases resulted in a conviction. Effectively, in South Africa, rape is a risk-free activity.

Despite vigorous lobbying by civil society organizations when the Sexual Offences Act (SOA) was passed, it included troubling sections. Such sections include the retention of the cautionary rule in the case of child witnesses and the exclusion of the automatic right for child witnesses to give evidence *in camera*. Nevertheless, provisions in the SOA relating to the widening of the definition of rape to include sexual penetration of the vagina, anus, or mouth with any object or body part (previously rape was defined specifically as involving only penis-vaginal penetration) were applauded.

# Recommendations

It is critical that the challenges to women and children in South Africa be addressed in a comprehensive and coherent way, not in isolation from one another. Doing so will require a far greater degree of cooperation between government departments, and government and civil society, than has hitherto been the case.

### Addressing violence against women and children

The government should:

- Prohibit corporal punishment in the Third Amendment to the Children's Act and commence a countrywide, sustained awareness-raising campaign to promote positive parenting and highlight the dangers of corporal punishment. It should increase support to civil society organizations providing training and support to parents to discipline their children without violence.
- Increase support to civil society organizations providing counseling and therapeutic services to the survivors of sexual violence.
- Provide that rape and gender-based violence no longer be "risk-free" activities.

### Addressing patriarchy

The government should:

- Commence a countrywide, sustained, awareness-raising campaign to promote the equality of women and the rejection of notions that women are inferior. It should revoke legislation that gives power and control over women and children to traditional authorities and structures.
- Reexamine the historical antecedents of the subjugation of women in Africa.

*Addressing unemployment, poverty, and inequality*

The government should:

- Improve access to and the quality of primary health care and education, including quality early childhood development services.
- Continue the social grants system, and place far higher emphasis on the creation of sustainable and adequately remunerated employment opportunities.
- Reconsider the Growth, Employment and Redistribution (GEAR) plan, the basic macroeconomic policy of the South African government. There is growing consensus that GEAR has failed to deliver the promised economic and job growth or significant redistribution of income and socioeconomic opportunities for the poor. The Congress of South African Trade Unions (Cosatu) claims that GEAR, which focuses on stringent monetary and fiscal targets, operates against the goals of the Reconstruction and Development Programme (RDP), where growth is based on sustainable job creation, meeting people's needs, the reduction of poverty, and the more equitable distribution of wealth (Knight 2001; Puri 2012). Women and children are most affected by these failures.
- The government should create sustainable employment opportunities and prioritize rural women.

## Notes

1. Constitution of the Republic of South Africa, Chapter 2, s9, 1996.
2. No. 22 of 2009.
3. No. 41 of 2003.
4. Interview with Sipuka, Nokuku, Director, UCARC, 2010.
5. Interview with Van Niekerk, Joan, National Training and Advocacy Manager, Childline SA, 2010.
6. Goals 7 and 8 relate to environmental sustainability and the development of a global partnership for development and are not considered in this article.
7. This is a place where small children are looked after while their parents are working or shopping, for example.
8. Transkei is a former homeland in southeast South Africa.
9. Available from http://www.info.gov.za/view/DownloadFileAction?id=173252.

## References

Amnesty International. 18 March 2008. South Africa: Rural women the losers in HIV response. Available from http://www.amnesty.org (accessed 10 March 2013).

Andersson, Neil, Ari Ho-Foster, Judith Matthis, Nobantu Marokoane, Vincent Mashiane, Sharmila Mhatre, Steve Mitchell, Tamara Mokoena, Lorenzo Monasta, Ncumisa Ngxowa, Manuel Pascual Salcedo, and Heidi Sonnekus. 2004. National cross sectional study of views on sexual violence and risk of HIV infection and AIDS among South African school pupils. *British Medical Journal*. doi:10.1136/bmj.38226.617454.7C.

Awino, Okech. 2013. A defining moment for South Africa: The Oscar Pistorius case. *Pambazuka News*. Available from www.pambazuka.org (accessed 6 March 2013).

Ban, Ki-moon. 2007. *Children and the Millennium Development Goals: Progress towards a world fit for children*. New York, NY: UNICEF.

BBC News. 2006. SA's Zuma showered to avoid HIV. Available from http://news.bbc.co.uk (accessed 6 November 2013).

Blaser, Dawn. 1998. *Statistics on violence against women in South Africa and internationally*. Cape Town: National Institute for Crime Prevention and Rehabilitation of Offenders (NICRO).

Bobo, Thabiso. 2011. *Challenges of rural women*. East London, South Africa: Masimanyane Women's Support Centre.

Budlender, Debbie, Ntebaleng Chobokoane, and Yandiswa Mpetsheni. 2001. *A survey of time use: How South African women and men spend their time*. Pretoria: Statistics South Africa.

Charles Stuart Mott Foundation. 20 August 2006. *Women in South Africa still seek equality*. Flint, MI: Charles Stewart Mott Foundation. Available from http://www.mott.org (accessed 6 March 2013).

Child, Katherine. 2012. Healthcare crisis looms. *Times Live*. Available from http://www.timeslive.co.za (accessed 9 March 2013).

Contreras, Manuel, Bria Heilman, Gary Barker, Ajay Singh, Ravi Verm, and Joanna Bloomfield. 2012. *Bridges to adulthood: Understanding the lifelong influence of men's childhood experiences of violence, analyzing data from the International Men and Gender Equality Survey*. Washington, DC: International Center for Research on Women (ICRW). Available from http://www.icrw.org/files/publications/Bridges-to-Adulthood-Understanding-the-Lifelong-Influence-of-Men%27s-Childhood-Experiences-Violence.pdf (accessed 5 March 2013).

Conway-Smith, Erin. 2012. South African census shows continuing racial inequality. *Globalpost*. Available from http://www.globalpost.com (accessed 7 March 2013).

Davis, Rebecca. 31 August 2012. Et tu, ANC Women's League? *Daily Maverick*. Available from http://www.dailymaverick.co.za (accessed 5 March 2013).

Davis, Rebecca. 25 February 2013. Lost in Oscar Pistorius frenzy, the horrific violence against women and children continues. *Daily Maverick*. Available from http://www.dailymaverick.co.za (accessed 25 February 2013).

Di Silvio, Lorenzo. 2011. Correcting corrective rape: Carmichele and developing South Africa's affirmative obligations to prevent violence against women. *Georgetown Law Journal* 99 (5): 469–515.

Education and Training Unit (ETU). 2013. *Gender and development*. Johannesburg: ETU. Available from http://www.etu.org.za (accessed 5 March 2013).

Freyd, Jennifer J., Frank W. Putnam, Thomas D. Lyon, Kathryn A. Becker-Blease, Ross E. Cheit, Nancy B. Siegel, and Kathy Pezdek. 2005. The science of child sexual abuse. *Psychology* 308 (5721): 501.

Ganesh, Aravind. 12 March 2013. Among school children in the Transkei. *Daily Maverick*. Available from http://www.dailymaverick.co.za (accessed 12 March 2013).

Gender Links. 8 November 2010. South Africa cabinet reshuffle—How did women fare? Available from http://www.genderlinks.org.za (accessed 5 March 2013).

Genderlinks and Medical Research Council. 2013. *The war at home: Preliminary findings of the Gauteng Gender Violence Prevalence Study*. London: Medical Research Council. Available at www.mrc.ac.za/gender/gbvthewar.pdf (accessed 12 June 2013).

Global Initiative to End All Corporal Punishment of Children. 2013. Ending violent punishment of girls: A key element in the global challenge to end all violence against women and girls. Brief. London: Global Initiative to End All Corporal Punishment of Children. Available from http://www.endcorporalpunishment.org/pages/pdfs/briefings/Corporal%20punishment%20of%20girls%20CSW.pdf (accessed 5 March 2013).

Gumede, Vusi. 17 February 2012. Facing SA's real "triple challenge." *Mail and Guardian*. Available from http://mg.co.za (accessed 6 March 2013).

Hall, Katherine. 2010. Nutrition—Child hunger. Children Count. Available from http://www.childrencount.ci.org.za (accessed 5 March 2013).

Hall, Katherine, Ian Woolard, Lori Lake, and Charmaine Smith. 2012. *South African child gauge 2012*. Cape Town: Children's Institute, University of Cape Town.

Hazelhurst, Ethel. 2013. Stats SA records first fourth-quarter net decline in jobs. IOL. http://www.iol.co.za (accessed 5 March 2013).

Hunter-Gault, Charlayne. 2 March 2013. Will the Pistorius case change South Africa? *New Yorker*. Available from www.newyorker.com (accessed 5 March 2013).

IDASA. 2002. The Grootboom case and women's housing rights—Budget brief. IDASA. Available from http://www.idasa.org/media/uploads/outputs/files/Budget%20Brief%20111.pdf (accessed 6 March 2013).

Index Mundi. 2012a. South Africa—Infant mortality rate. Index Mundi. Available from http://www.index-mundi.com (accessed 10 March 2013).

Index Mundi. 2012b. South Africa—Mortality rate. Index Mundi. Available from http://www.indexmundi.com (accessed 7 March 2013).

Jewkes, Rachel, Kristin Dunkle, Mary P. Koss, Jonathan B. Levin, Mzikazi Nduna, Nwabisa Jama, and Yandisa Sikweyiya. 2006. Rape perpetration by young rural South African men: Prevalence, patterns and risk factors. *Social Science & Medicine* 63 (11): 2949–61.

Jewkes, Rachel, and Robert Robert Morrell. 2010. Gender and sexuality: Emerging perspectives from the heterosexual epidemic in South Africa and implications for HIV risk and prevention. *Journal of the International AIDS Society* 13 (6): 1–11.

Jewkes, Rachel, Yandisa Sikweyiya, Robert Morrell, and Kristin Dunkle. 2011. Gender inequitable masculinity and sexual entitlement in rape perpetration in South Africa: Findings of a cross-sectional study. *PLoS ONE* 6 (12): e29590. doi:10.1371/journal.pone.00.

Knight, Richard. 2001. South Africa: Economic policy and development. Available from www.richardknight.homestead.com/files/sisaeconomy.htm (accessed 12 June 2013).

Landman, Christina. 2009. Calvinism and South African women. *Studia Historiae Ecclesiasticae* 35 (2): 89–102.

Luleki, Sizwe. 2011. South African lesbians at risk for "corrective rape." *Contemporary Sexuality* 45 (7): 8.

Mathews, Shanaaz, Naeemah Abrahams, Lorna Martin, Lisa Vetten, Lize Van der Merwe, and Rachel Jewkes. 2004. Every six hours a woman is killed by her intimate partner: A national study of female homicide in South Africa. Medical Research Council Policy Briefs. Available from http://www.mrc.ac.za/policybriefs/woman.pdf (accessed 5 March 2013).

Meintjes, Helen, and Katherine Hall. 2012. Orphanhood. Children Count. Available from http://www.childrencount.ci.org.za (accessed 6 March 2013).

Meintjes, Helen, Katherine Hall, Double-Hugh Marera, and Andrew Boulle. 2009. *Child-headed households in South Africa: A statistical brief*. Cape Town: Children's Institute.

MSN News. 2013. SA to roll out dedicated rape courts. MSN News. Available from http://news.howzit.msn.com (accessed 11 March 2013).

News 24. 23 July 2012 (2012a). More no-fee schools in SA—SAIRR. News24. Available from http://www.news24.com (accessed 8 March 2013).

News 24. 20 September 2012 (2012b). 2 children murdered every day. News 24. Available from http://www.news24.com (accessed 5 March 2013).

Pillay, Verashni. 28 August 2012. ANCWL defends Zuma after "sexist" complaint. *Mail and Guardian*. Available from http://mg.co.za (accessed 7 March 2013).

Posel, Dorit, Daniela Casale, and Claire Vermaak. 2013. The unemployed in South Africa: Why are so many not counted? Econ3x3. Available from http://www.econ3x3.org (accessed 5 March 2103).

Puri, Lakshmi. 2012. *Gender equality and women's empowerment: The power behind successful sustainable development*. Available from www.unwomen.org (accessed 12 June 2013).

Schäfer, Rita. 1 March 2013. Men as agents of change: Role model. D + C. Available from http://www.dandc.eu (accessed 7 March 2013).

Sesanti, Simphiwe. 2011. Equality is an African tradition. In *On African culture and politics: Reflections of a black journalist*, 66–67. Cape Town: Centre for Advanced Studies of African Society.

Sexual Violence Research Initiative (SVRI). 2011. *Mental health responses for victims of sexual violence and rape in resource-poor settings*. Pretoria: SVRI. Available from http://www.svri.org/MentalHealthResponse.pdf. (accessed 4 March 2013).

Sharma, Sudhanshu. 2012. *Rising inequality in South Africa: Drivers, trends and policy responses*. Consultancy Africa. Available from http://www.consultancyafrica.com (accessed 6 March 2013).

Skillsportal. 2012. The sorry state of gender equality in South Africa. Available from http://www.skillsportal.co.za (accessed 5 March 2013).

Smythe, Dee, Lily Artz, Helene Combrinck, Katherine Doolan, and Lorna Martin. 2007. *Caught between policy and practice: Health and justice responses to gender-based violence*. Cape Town: Medical Research Council. Available from http://www.mrc.ac.za (accessed 5 March 2013).

South African Broadcasting Corporation (SABC). 19 April 2012. South Africa—World's rape capital. *SABC News*. Available from www.sabc.co.za (accessed 5 March 2013).

South African Government. 2013a. *Religion*. Available from http://www.info.gov.za (accessed 5 March 2013).

South African Government. 2013b. *State of the Nation Address by His Excellency Jacob G. Zuma, President of the Republic of South Africa on the occasion of the Joint Sitting of Parliament, Cape Town*. Available from http://www.info.gov.za (accessed 6 March 2013).

South African Institute of Race Relations (SAIRR). 2012 February 2009. *Half of the HIV-positive people are women of child-bearing age*. Johannesburg: SAIRR. Available from http://www.sairr.org.za/media/media-releases/10Feb12%20Hiv-Aids%2009Feb12.pdf (accessed 5 March 2013).

South African Police Service (SAPS). 2012. *2012 crime statistics*. Available from http://www.saps.gov.za (accessed 6 November 2013).

Southern African Regional Poverty Network (SARPN). 2008. An overview of poverty and inequality in South Africa. Working Paper prepared for DFID (SA). Southern African Regional Poverty Network. Available from http://www.sarpn.org (accessed 6 March 2013).

Statistics South Africa. 2010. *Social profile of South Africa, 2002–2009*. Pretoria: Statistics South Africa. Available from http://www.statssa.gov.za/publications/Report-03-19-00/Report-03-19-002009.pdf (accessed 6 March 2013).

Studies in Poverty and Inequality Institute. 2008. *South Africa: Poverty, social security, and civil society: Triangulating transformation*. Brot feur die Welt. Available from http://www.spii.org.za (accessed 6 November 2013).

Taylor, Darren. 2012. Inside South Africa's rural healthcare crisis: Lack of medicines and equipment, severe shortages of doctors and nurses retard development. *Voice of America*. Available from http://www.voanews.com (accessed 6 March 2013).

TradingEconomics.com. 2013. South Africa unemployment rate. Available from http://www.tradingeconomics.com (accessed 5 March 2013).

UNDP. 2013a. Current programmes in South Africa. Pretoria: UNDP. Available from http://www.undp.org.za (accessed 5 March 2013).

UNDP. 2013b. MDGs in South Africa. Pretoria: UNDP. Available from http://www.undp.org.za (accessed 6 March 2013).

UNICEF. 2013a. *Alternative care*. New York, NY: UNICEF. Available from http://www.unicef.org/south-africa/protection_6633.html (accessed 9 March 2013).

UNICEF. 2013b. *Women and children in South Africa*. New York, NY: UNICEF. Available from http://www.unicef.org/southafrica/children.html (accessed 12 March 2013).

UN News Centre. 2010. Noting progress to date, ban urges greater efforts against HIV/AIDS. Available from http://www.un.org (accessed 6 March 2013).

UN Office of the High Commissioner of Human Rights (UNOHCHR). 1991. The right to adequate housing. Committee on Economic, Social and Cultural Rights, General Comment 4. Geneva: UN.

# Post-1994 South African Education: The Challenge of Social Justice

By
SALEEM BADAT
and
YUSUF SAYED

The formal end of apartheid was greeted with optimism and expectations. A new Government of National Unity with Nelson Mandela at its head signaled a new just and democratic social order, including social justice in and through education. Twenty years later, formally desegregated yet class-based educational institutions, continuing disparities and inequities, and poor academic achievement are key features of the contemporary educational order. This article considers how far South Africa has come since 1994 in realizing laudable constitutional and policy goals, especially equity, quality, and social justice in education. It argues, however, that, as a consequence of policy, the doors of learning remain firmly shut to the majority of South Africans. Some key strategies to advance social justice are identified. A failure to act now and with urgency to reform South Africa's educational approach betrays constitutional ideals and leaves intact the systemic crisis of education that especially affects South Africa's historically disadvantaged and marginalized peoples.

Keywords: social justice; education; post-apartheid South Africa; affirmative action

Post-1994, a nonracial, democratic South Africa came into being on a rising tide of expectations, legitimacy, and political will. Education was called on to address and respond to the needs of all citizens, and to the social and economic development imperatives of the new state. There was great anticipation that the education system would be fundamentally transformed by dismantling the old apartheid

Saleem Badat is vice-chancellor of Rhodes University. He has served as the CEO of the Council on Higher Education, the policy advisory body to the minister of higher education & training, and as director of the Education Policy Unit at the University of the Western Cape. He is the author of Black Student Politics, Higher Education and Apartheid (Routledge 2002), coauthor of National Policy and a Regional Response in South African Higher Education (James Currey 2004), and coeditor of Apartheid Education and Popular Struggles in South Africa (Ravan Press 1990).

DOI: 10.1177/0002716213511188

order and creating a new system based on the Freedom Charter edict: "The doors of learning and culture shall be open to all." People's Education for People's Power[1] captured the zeitgeist of the immediate post-apartheid educational order. South Africa's new democratic government committed itself in 1994 to transforming education as well as the inherited apartheid social and economic structures and institutionalizing a new social order. Over the past 20 years no domain of education has escaped scrutiny, and there have been a wide array of "transformation"-oriented initiatives.[2]

This article critically considers why, almost 20 years later, there is still a "long walk" to realize the anticipated freedom of education. Why does the "right to learn" ring hollow for many, while for others quality public education is an everyday reality? How and in what ways and to what extent can deep-seated historic and structural inequalities be overcome? There are no simple answers to these questions, but a critical analysis and understanding of the trajectory of post-apartheid South African educational policy are important in the quest for a new educational order predicated on social justice.

In examining such issues, we adopt a social justice perspective that encompasses a number of theses. Colonialism and apartheid were predicated on a racially based system of inequality in which the black majority was denied equal educational opportunities and outcomes. As a consequence, post-1994 education policy is predicated on the principle of equality of opportunity in relation to provision, access, and outcomes. First, equality of treatment and opportunity is a necessary but not sufficient condition for eliminating systemic historical and structural educational inequalities that black South Africans experience as a result of the segregated (and underdeveloped and unequal) institutions that were reserved for them under apartheid. The systemic nature of inequities cannot be redressed by formal equality while it ignores inherited and structurally produced inequalities. Thus, formal equality has to be distinguished from equity: whereas the former refers to the "principle of sameness" and to uniformity and standardization, the latter is concerned with fair and just treatment. Equity is thus essential for achieving substantive equality.

Second, redress requires a state that has the political commitment to institute measures that favor, through positive discrimination, those who were and are disadvantaged.[3] Redress measures are especially critical for ensuring social advancement for individuals from socially disadvantaged and marginalized groups. Third, good quality public education is critical for social justice in and through education. It is a necessary condition for the formation of the intellectual and other capabilities of individuals, their cultivation as lifelong learners,[4] their functioning as economically and socially productive people, and their participation as critical and democratic citizens.

*Yusuf Sayed is a reader in international education at the University of Sussex. He is also a research associate at the Institute of Social and Economic Research (ISER), Rhodes University, South Africa. Previously, he was a senior policy analyst at the EFA Global Monitoring Report, UNESCO; team leader for education and skills, Department for International Development UK; and head of the Department of Comparative Education at the University of the Western Cape, South Africa.*

Fourth, although policies and practices predicated on all four dimensions of social justice noted above would represent a significant advance in educational conditions prior to 1994, they still embody a restricted notion of social justice. A more substantive idea of social justice would recognize that South Africa's economic and social structures, with their attendant class inequalities, significantly constrain equality, equity, redress, good quality education, and social justice for all.

In this article we argue that education in South Africa generally fails to enhance the freedom of all. The idea that "with freedom comes responsibilities" to respect and promote constitutional imperatives to social justice in and through education has not received the full and concerted attention of the government. What is required, in addition to measures of positive discrimination that operate largely in terms of historical rectification and at the level of individuals, is structural change and the institutional transformation of education and society. Positive discrimination is, on its own and in the absence of far-reaching institutional transformation, likely to leave the status quo unchanged (Mamdani 1993, cited in Sikhosana 1993).

In the next section of this article, we outline the intentions and goals of educational change after 1994 in the context of the apartheid inheritance. Then we assess the changes that have occurred during the past two decades under the new democratic government, noting continuities and discontinuities, successes and failures, and shortcomings. Next, we review official efforts to address shortcomings and accelerate progress, and identify some priority issues in need of urgent attention. We conclude that there is a long road ahead to realizing social justice and constitutional imperatives and goals in education.

## The Context of Educational Change in South Africa

Post-apartheid South African education had to deal with two impulses. On one hand, there was the new government's commitment to deal with racial discrimination as the most obvious and visible form of inequality in education. This approach gave rise to a conception of social justice as racial redress, captured in a policy of affirmative action, or positive discrimination. On the other hand, this strategy had to be pursued in a manner that maintained the social order and educational system; that is to say, change was not to rupture radically prevailing educational norms, structures, and policies and practices. In essence, there was a limited conception of social justice, predicated on a pluralist democratic approach where any strong form of social justice, such as redistribution, could only be undertaken with the political consent of the privileged.

Developments in post-1994 education did not occur in a vacuum; change or the lack of change in education was conditioned by the specific nature of the inherited educational order, in particular the apartheid legacy of unequal spending, unequal access, unequal opportunity and outcomes, distorted notions of quality, and so forth. In 1982, the apartheid government spent R146 (on average) educating a black child, but invested R1,211 on a white child (De Waal 2013). The School Register of Needs, commissioned by the Ministry of Education to determine the needs of schools, indicated in 1996 that there were significant infrastructural and other backlogs: 65,380 classrooms were needed, about a 25 percent increase from the total number of classrooms that then existed; 60 percent of schools did not have access to electricity and telephones; 35 percent were without potable water; and 12 percent did not have access to toilets—pit latrines constituted 47 percent of all school toilets.[5] The new government would need to muster enormous resources to overcome the educational legacy of apartheid.

The ability of the new government to address the apartheid legacy was conditioned by the changes that occurred between 1990 and 1994. On one hand, the ruling National Party began the process of transferring control of schools previously reserved for whites to school governing bodies, effectively privatizing them (Carrim and Sayed 1992). On the other hand, the post-1994 state was, as an outcome of the pre-1994 negotiations, a Government of National Unity (GNU) in which the majority party (African National Congress [ANC]), in a coalition led by President Nelson Mandela, emphasized reconciliation. The GNU was reluctant to act decisively to transform the educational system. This result was partly a consequence of the negotiated settlement itself, which created a federalist state and established powerful provincial interest groups that shared concurrent responsibilities for schooling. Implementing redress as a national strategy was thus constrained by relatively autonomous provinces coupled with strong governing bodies in previously white-only schools—what Weiler (1990) refers to as the displacement of conflict and an attempt to secure local-level legitimation. Provincialization also created local-level elite capture as the new provincial parliament and governments, by and large dominated by the ANC, were (and remain) reluctant to cede control to the central state. They fear loss of power, authority, patronage, and accumulation of wealth through control of provincial structures (McGinn and Street 1986). The new national government also had limited policy resources to draw on to articulate a clear and focused strategy for effecting social justice. The policies to which it had recourse, in particular the National Education Policy Investigation documents (1992) and the ANC's 1994/1995 Education and Training Framework and Implementation Plan, were long on values and principles but short on strategy, including finding the right people and finances to effect the transformation of the education system.

South Africa's post-1994 educational goals were explicitly framed in relation to the existing and inherited order, and the 1996 South African Constitution, which set out the character of the society that was envisaged, proclaimed the values of "human dignity, the achievement of equality, and the advancement of human rights and freedoms," and "non-racialism and non-sexism" (Republic of South Africa 1996a, Section 1). The Bill of Rights unambiguously proclaimed that individuals and "the state may not unfairly discriminate directly or indirectly against anyone on one or more grounds, including race, gender, sex, pregnancy, marital status, ethnic or social origin, colour, sexual orientation, age, disability, religion, conscience, belief, culture, language and birth" (Sections 9.3 and 9.4). The Constitution declared the right of all "(a) to a basic education including adult basic education; and (b) to further education, which the state, through reasonable measures, must make progressively available and accessible" (Republic of South Africa 1996a, Section 29a, 29b). The notion of a progressive realization beyond basic education has been the subject of much contestation.

These constitutional commitments were captured in a 1995 White Paper on Education and Training,[6] which directed the state to "redress educational inequalities among those sections of our people who have suffered particular disadvantages" and affirm the principle of "equity" so that all citizens have "the same quality of learning opportunities" (Department of Education [DoE] 1995, 16–17). A year later, the National Education Policy Act of 1996 stated its goal as "the democratic transformation of the national system of education into one which serves the needs and interests of all of the people of South Africa and upholds their fundamental rights" (Republic of South Africa 1996b).

The Constitution and the National Education Policy Act not surprisingly echoed the views of the Mandela-led ANC and its politics of equality of treatment whether in relation to race, gender, or ethnicity. The Freedom Charter statements that "South Africa belongs to all", and that "All national groups shall have equal rights" are manifestations of this commitment to a politics of equal treatment. With the advent of democracy, "equal treatment" was translated into a constitution that guaranteed equality in all spheres of society.

Following the hallmark National Education Policy Act, there was a flurry of policy activity, manifest in the production of green and white papers, acts, and regulations, all seeking to transform the nation's educational system. Between 1994 and 2013, there were about seven white papers, three green papers, twenty-six bills (of which seventeen were amending bills), thirty-five acts, eleven regulations, fifty-two government notices, and twenty-six calls for comments that encompassed basic to higher education (Sayed and Kanjee 2013).[7] During this period, the Ministry of Education was governed by four different ministers.

In 2009, two separate departments were created for basic and higher education, each headed by a minister. In basic education, a new system of school governance was established with the passing of the South African Schools Act in 1997, a more equity-focused form of school financing was promulgated with the National Norms and Standards for School Funding (DoE 1998), curriculum reform was enacted in the form of Outcomes Based Education (1997), and a new regime of continuous assessment was introduced in 1998, followed by Whole School Evaluations in 2001 and Annual National Assessment in 2008.[8]

In higher education, Education White Paper 3 of 1997 proposed a far-reaching transformation of higher education (DoE 1997), and the 2001 National Plan for Higher Education (Ministry of Education 2001) suggested some of the decisive choices of government with respect to higher educational change, including institutional mergers.

All these policies argued that substantive equality was not possible without an active political commitment to favor those who had been disadvantaged. A politics of equal recognition could not be blind to the effects of the legacies of colonialism and apartheid. Nor could it ignore that the advent of democracy was not in itself a sufficient condition for the elimination of historic and structural inequalities in all domains of social life. It was precisely this reality that gave salience to the idea of redress and made it a fundamental and necessary dimension of educational and social transformation. The notion of redress that drives educational policy today is well encapsulated in Education White Paper 3, which proclaimed an intention "to provide a full spectrum of advanced educational opportunities for an expanding range of the population irrespective of race, gender, age, creed or class or other forms of discrimination" (DoE 1997, 1.27). The white paper further states:

> The principle of equity requires fair opportunities both to enter higher education programmes and to succeed in them. It implies, on the one hand, a critical identification of existing inequalities which are the product of policies, structures and practices based on racial, gender, disability and other forms of discrimination or disadvantage, and on the other a programme of transformation with a view to redress. Such transformation involves not only abolishing all existing forms of unjust differentiation, but also measures of empowerment, including financial support to bring about equal opportunity for individuals. (1997, 1.18)

Educational policy changes since 1994 have been framed within the government's wider and contested macroeconomic developmental strategies. Changes in educational policy were initially aligned to the 1994 Reconstruction and Development Programme, which spoke of "meeting basic needs of people"; "developing human resources"; and "democratising the state and society" (Ministry in the Office of the President 1994). Subsequently, from 1996, the Growth, Employment and Redistribution (GEAR) program, described in some quarters as "a neoliberal macroeconomic policy . . . [developed to dismantle] the RDP," began to frame state priorities and also condition educational change (Buhlungu 2003, 195). Later, GEAR was replaced by the Accelerated and Shared Growth Initiative for South Africa (AsgiSA). On the back of a decade of sustained economic growth and stable macroeconomic conditions, AsgiSA projected cutting the unemployment and poverty rates by half by 2014 through various initiatives, including significant investments in public infrastructure, focused attention on "skills and education," and building a "developmental state." Of importance was the acknowledgment that one of the key "binding constraints" on economic and social development was "the shortage of skills—including professional skills such as [the skills among] engineers and scientists; managers such as financial, personnel, and project managers; and skilled technical employees such as artisans and IT technicians."[9] More recently, the National Planning Commission (NPC) diagnosed problems and challenges in South African society generally and in education more specifically. As with AsgiSA, the NPC's National Development Plan 2030 is an attempt to create a macro framework for social change in South Africa. The NPC argues that it seeks to "realise the promise of our future, as it is so aptly captured in the preamble to our Constitution," and to ensure that "by 2030, South Africans should have access to education and training of the highest quality, leading to significantly improved learning outcomes" (NPC 2011, 29, 296). It makes a number of recommendations to achieve this vision and sets ambitious targets for early childhood education, basic education, higher education, and skills development, recognizing that improved education is critical "in building an inclusive society, providing equal opportunities and helping all South Africans to realise their full potential, in particular those previously disadvantaged by apartheid policies, namely black people, women and people with disabilities" (NPC 2011, 296).

Educational policy development after 1994 was framed by the constitutional imperative of cooperative governance—an understanding that the collective good can best be advanced by diverse stakeholders united around a common vision. Yet it is evident that the principle has not been fully realized. First, the state has over time become more directive and dirigiste, as it has become frustrated with the slow pace of change and as the citizenry has grown impatient with the lack of positive change in living standards. The state has sought to intervene in institutional governance in higher education and to impose on schools a culture of testing and performance. These impositions have created tensions between particular education ministers and institutions, between national and provincial ministers, and between stakeholders and the state. Second, in basic education there has been growing frustration with teacher unions perceived as blocking change; such unions are subject to considerable media and public derision and are accused of indefensible self-interests. Third, initial high participation by civil society organizations in policy development was subordinated to technocratic, state-centric, modalities of policymaking.

# The Results of Educational-Change Efforts

Given the extensive policy activity noted above, what has changed in education since 1994? At one level, given the previous salience of race in all aspects of social, economic, and political life, much has changed. Race is no longer a primary determinant and marker of inequity in post-1994 educational policies and strategies. However, race necessarily features in the various educational equity strategies discussed below, given the constitutional commitment to affirmative action.

## Differentiated access

The most visible evidence of change has been the formal desegregation of schools and higher educational institutions, manifest in increased participation in education. In the case of higher education, by 2010, black students composed 80 percent (714,597) of the total student body of 892,943; African students made up 66.7 percent (595,963) of students, and white students 19.9 percent (Council on Higher Education [CHE] 2012, 1). There has also been commendable progress in terms of gender equity. By 2010, women constituted 57.4 percent (512,570) of the total student body (CHE 2012, 1). This compares favorably with the apartheid era: in 1993, whereas black South Africans (Indians, Coloureds, and Africans) constituted 89 percent of the population, black students constituted only 52 percent of the student body of 473,000. African students, although composing 77 percent of the population, made up only 40 percent of enrollments. On the other hand, white students, although only 11 percent of the population, constituted 48 percent of enrollments. Forty-three percent of students were women (Badat 2012, 124). Great progress, then, has been achieved in terms of racial redress in so far as access to universities is concerned. Still, African and Coloured South Africans continue to be underrepresented in higher education relative to their population size (CHE 2012, 2).

However, racial redress is but a small part of the picture. The desegregation of institutions has inadequately addressed the differentiated access to different institutions. Students from the capitalist and middle classes are concentrated at historically white institutions, while those from the working class and rural poor are concentrated at historically black institutions. Despite initiatives to reshape the apartheid institutional landscape through mergers of higher educational institutions and the opening up of public schools, the historical geographical patterns of advantage and disadvantage continue to condition the capacities of historically black institutions to pursue excellence and provide high-quality learning experiences and equal opportunity and outcomes. In short, if equity of opportunity and outcomes were previously strongly affected by race, they are now also conditioned by social class and geography.

The differentiated access to schooling and higher education in post-1994 South Africa parallels the evolution of the English education system, which one scholar described as the two nations educational structure (Simon 1974). In the South African case, the "two nation" educational structure is reflected in a two-tier system of education, resulting in a poorly resourced educational sector serving the poor and mainly black population, while the wealthy have access to private and semiprivate public schools that serve mainly whites and the new black elite, and attend "research" universities. These new geographies of inequality in the schooling sector are the direct results of national policy; in the search to retain the middle class within the public school system, the state created, by design or default, a differentiated and bifurcated educational system that permits the charging of school fees and the control of schools by school governing bodies. Government policy, such as the South African Schools Act, has allowed the middle class to secure control of the historical ex-white school sector, empowering a "new deracialised middle class" to obtain semiprivate education (Sayed and Ahmed 2009).

The bifurcation of schooling is mirrored in higher education if we examine the progress of black and female students. A larger proportion of African students are concentrated in distance education—40.5 percent as compared to 33.3 percent for whites (CHE 2012, 7). African and female students continue to be considerably underrepresented at the postgraduate level and in science, engineering, and technology programs. There has been little improvement in the university participation rates of African and Coloured South Africans.[10] By 2010, the participation rate of Africans increased from 9 percent in 1993 to 14 percent, and that of Coloureds from 13 percent to 15 percent. In contrast, the participation rate of

Indian students increased from 40 percent in 1993 to 46 percent in 2010. The white student participation rate stood at 57 percent in 2010, down from 70 percent in 1993. The overall participation rate (those 18–24) in 2010 was 18 percent (CHE 2012, 3). These statistics, taken together with the patterns of enrollment by fields of concentration, qualifications levels, and modes of study, highlight that the low participation rates of blacks and women in South African higher education has continued.

Perhaps the most visible indicator of differentiated access is shown in pre-primary and early childhood education services. Early childhood education in South Africa before the single year of pre-primary (grade R) education is mainly provided by private for-profit institutions and community-based and nongovernmental organizations through a subsidy for registered centers. However, as the NPC notes, such services are "unevenly distributed and do not yet reach the most vulnerable poor children, especially in rural areas. Fees also inhibit the poorest families from using what services are available. Early childhood development programmes need to expand, with government support, to reach all vulnerable children, including children with disabilities" (NPC 2012, 299). Although there is increasing coverage of pre-primary grade R education (estimates suggest about 81 percent coverage), good quality provision is uneven, and there is a lack of qualified teachers working in grade R classes. Such unequal and differentiated access has inequitable long-term effects. Access to good quality early childhood education is arguably the most important equity measure that can be taken to strengthen South Africa's educational attainments.

## Unequal quality

The weak participation of disadvantaged groups in higher education stems from the ongoing and systemic quality deficiencies associated with South African schooling, especially for students of working-class and rural poor social origins. The data on learning show that although schools may be open and accessible, enrollment is not the same as attendance and attendance does not necessarily imply learning.

Poor quality of learning in South African schools is evidenced by the second Annual National Assessment (ANA)[11] results of learners' mathematics and literacy skills. The results indicated that grade 9 learners across the country achieved an average score of 12.7 percent in mathematics. It also suggests that learners' mathematics ability declines steadily as they progress in school, with grade 1 learners achieving an average score of 68 percent in the mathematics tests and grade 6 learners 27 percent. Significant differences in performance were also noted among the quintile one, two, and three schools,[12] which consist of a high percentage of learners from poor backgrounds; and quintile five schools, which are attended by a high percentage of learners from wealthier families. Across grades 1 to 6, learners in quintile five schools can expect to obtain scores that are approximately 10 to 15 percent higher than their counterparts in the other quintiles.

International tests show disappointing performances among South African learners compared to other countries. In the 2011 Performance in International Literacy Study (PIRLS), 43 percent of South African learners tested in Afrikaans and English were unable to reach the "low international" benchmark, with only 4 percent reaching the "high international" benchmark (Howie et al. 2012). In the 2003 Trends in Mathematics and Science Study (TIMMS), only 29 percent of South African eighth-grade students were able to answer correctly a basic subtraction question. This situation did not improve in the 2011 TIMSS, as South African learners were placed second from the bottom out of a total of forty-four countries for both mathematics and science, despite having tested grade 9 learners while all other countries tested grade 8 learners.[13]

International tests also reveal a marked disparity in learning attainment between rich and poor. South African grade 6 learners participated in the third Southern and Eastern African Consortium for Monitoring Education Quality (SACMEQ) survey, which involved fifteen countries from southern and eastern Africa. The average reading test score for the wealthiest 20 percent of learners was 605, compared to 436 for the poorest 20 percent of learners.[14] Similar disparities were noted for the mathematics test, with averages of 583 and 454, respectively.[15] Moreover, the poorest 20 percent of learners performed far worse than their peers in other African countries. A ranking of the performance of the poorest 25 percent of students places South African learners fourteenth for reading and twelfth for mathematics, both out of fifteen African countries. Similarly, rural South African children fare poorly relative to their peers, ranking thirteenth in reading and twelfth in mathematics out of the fifteen.

Arguably, the most obvious manifestation of poor schooling quality and the bifurcated nature of the South African educational system are the final school leaving examinations results. In 2007, 10 percent of about seven thousand secondary schools—independent schools and public schools previously reserved for white students—produced 60 percent of all university entrance passes. Another 10 percent of mainly historically black schools produced a further 20 percent of all university entrance passes. Thus, in 2007, 80 percent of university entrance passes were generated by only 20 percent of secondary schools, while the remaining 80 percent of secondary schools produced a paltry 20 percent of university entrance passes.[16]

The crisis of schooling is not one of learners alone. It is also one of teachers and teaching, as shown by test results from the SACMEQ III, where teachers were tested in language and mathematics. Although South African teachers performed relatively well on questions requiring the simple retrieval of information explicitly stated in the text (scoring an average of 75.1 percent), scores dropped dramatically as soon as the higher cognitive functions of inference (55.2 percent), interpretation (36.6 percent), and evaluation (39.7 percent) were invoked.[17] Scores on the mathematics test show a similar decline for more complex topics, from a mean of 67.2 percent for basic arithmetic to 49.7 percent for the key topic areas of fractions, and ratio and proportion. A 2008 study that examined teachers on the same test items as that taken by grade 6 learners revealed low levels of performance among teachers. For mathematics, Foundation Phase teachers (up to grade 3) obtained an average score of 53 percent, while their colleagues in the Intermediate Phase (grades 4 to 6) obtained an average of 36 percent. The highest scores were obtained for arithmetic by teachers with postgraduate degrees (Taylor 2011).

Problems of quality in higher education are reflected in the success rates for black and white students. The white student success rate in 2010 was 82 percent at the undergraduate level and 80 percent at the postgraduate level; that of African students was 71 percent and 66 percent, respectively (CHE 2012, 11–12). In so far as graduation rates are concerned, that of Africans was 16 percent in 2010 and 22 percent for whites, with an average of 17 percent, which is low (CHE 2012, 9). In terms of graduation and drop-out rates for a three-year degree at contact institutions, of those students beginning study in 2005, 16 percent of African students had graduated in the minimum three years and 41 percent had graduated after six years, with 59 percent having dropped out.[18] In the case of white students, the comparative figures were 44 percent graduating in the minimum three years and 65 percent graduating after six years, with 35 percent having dropped out (CHE 2012, 51). The figures for three-year diplomas at contact institutions were worse: after six years, 63 percent of African students had dropped out, as had 45 percent of white students (CHE 2012, 50).

## Equal spending but no equality

Financing education was a key concern on the post-1994 agenda to transform education. The most obvious target was the elimination of the racially skewed allocation of resources in schooling and higher education. All institutions and all students in schools and higher educational institutions were allocated resources post-1994 using a common and uniform funding formula in which race was officially no longer a criterion of allocation.

In basic education, equity was built into the funding allocation in two ways. The first was the provincial equitable share formula, which took into account the size of the rural population in each province and the size of the population for social security grants, weighted by a poverty index. The goal was to ensure that every province, whatever its financial standing, would be able to spend an equitable amount on each learner. Since provinces make their own decisions about how to spend their share across social services (education, health, and social welfare), the actual per capita educational expenditure differs from province to province. The second equity measure in financing was related to the National Norms and Standards for School Funding. This strategy ranked schools using a quintile system whereby each school was classified into one of five quintiles based on the socioeconomic status of the surrounding schools. This determination was now a national rather than a provincial function. Using this approach, provinces are expected to direct 60 percent of the available resources to the poorest 40 percent of learners (schools in quintiles one and two). A third measure was what could be classified as targeted and means-tested financing for specific equity interventions (here the principle of affirmative action was most apparent). Such classification included setting up specialist schools in poorer communities. In higher education the obvious manifestations of equity interventions are a formula-based redress factor for universities based on their enrollments of African and Coloured students, the earmarked funding of academic development programs, and the National Student Financial Aid Scheme (NSFAS), which operates on a means-tested basis and has made considerable funding available for indigent (black and white) students.[19]

These efforts to advance equity through financing are laudable, but they fall far short of what is needed. In basic education, equity through financing is beset by two main problems. First, while the new funding formula for basic education does, to some extent, leverage resources for equity, the federalist nature of the polity does not guarantee that school spending is equal, as the actual expenditure on schooling is determined by each province. Equity in education financing is best given through centralized interventions (rather than decentralized efforts). Second, the strategy of using the quintile ranking system to redistribute resources to schools has various weaknesses. For one, the quintile system (and its presumed intake) is not a robust measure of poverty (Chutgar and Kanjee 2009). More fundamentally, the differential allocation of resources through the quintile system only affects operating costs and is not the fundamental driver of inequity; teacher costs and deployment of well-qualified teachers disproportionately benefit schools in the wealthier quintile ranks. While the redeployment and rationalization of teachers initiated in 1995 was perhaps poorly implemented and ultimately defeated in a landmark court case, the intention was laudable as it sought to secure equity through the more equitable deployment of teachers and their expertise.

The greatest problem of equity through financing is that means-tested targeted interventions in South African education are not adequately funded. Thus, for example, the shortage of funds for financial aid and academic development, and limited funding for institutional redress, have compromised attempts both to increase access and to expand equality of opportunity and outcomes for disadvantaged social classes and groups. In the face of the existing needs, the state's equity interventions require a greater commitment of resources if they are to be more meaningful and to achieve their objectives. More fundamentally, targeted means-tested equity interventions insufficiently address deep-seated and historic inequalities that require active redistribution strategies. The equity measures through financing operate on a limited conception of social justice—they ignore the fact that the far-reaching institutional transformation of historically black institutions requires ensuring that they are able to provide equality of opportunity and outcomes. The equity measures discussed above also do not take into account the private contributions of the rich and middle class. Rich and middle-class parents expend substantial financial resources on their children's education, which the poor are unable to do. For example, as a result of income from school fees, the ex-Model C schools[20] perform well notwithstanding the equalized formulae funding. Motala (2006, 2009) argues that when fees are added to the state per capita expenditure per learner, enormous disparities along race and class lines emerge. Her work shows that there are huge differences in per capita learner expenditure that are masked if there is a reliance only on state per capita expenditure data.

## Changing institutional practices and culture

Although adequate funding is important, so too are appropriate institutional cultures of learning and teaching in schools and universities. The white paper on higher education expressed a commitment to increasing the relative proportion of public funding used to support academically able but disadvantaged students and to provide funds for academic development programs, although a call was also made to institutions to "mobilise greater private resources as well as to reallocate their operating grants internally" (DoE 1997, 2.26; 2.24; 2.27). This was an indirect call for changes in learning and teaching to favor historically disadvantaged groups. In this respect, academic development programs were created to address the underpreparedness of students and to facilitate the development of their content knowledge, academic skills, and the literacy and numeracy required for academic success. Over the years institutional approaches to these development programs have changed: they have moved away from being an add-on or supplemental offering to become more institutionally embedded. This shift has moved institutions toward enhancing student learning "across the curriculum" and toward locating initiatives "within a wider understanding of what it means to address student needs framed within the context of a concern for overall *quality*" (Boughey 2005, 36). In this context, it is institutions and not individuals that have to adapt to a changing and more diverse student population.

Institutional cultures, especially at historically white universities, in differing ways and to varying degrees compromise equality of opportunity and outcomes. The specific histories of these institutions—lingering racist and sexist conduct, privileges associated with social class, English as the language of instruction and administration, the overwhelming predominance of white and male academics and white administrators, the concomitant underrepresentation of black and female academics and role models,[21] and limited respect for and appreciation of diversity and difference—combine to produce institutional cultures that black, female, working-class, and rural poor students experience as discomforting, alienating, exclusionary, and disempowering. Such an experience has negative consequences for student outcomes. Even if equality of opportunity and outcomes are not unduly compromised, the overall educational and social experience may be diminished. The existence of class-based, racialized, and gendered institutional cultures also obstructs the forging of social cohesion (Badat 2012, 145).

In sum, the analysis of educational outcomes post-1994 suggests that the cleavages of race, while still noticeable, have become more muted; and inequities of class, gender, and geography have become more apparent. There is a powerful link between the social exclusion of disadvantaged social classes and groups, and equity of access, opportunity and outcomes, and achievement in schools and universities. Without appropriate and extensive interventions on the part of the government significantly to improve the economic and social circumstances of millions of working-class and rural poor (and primarily black) South Africans, the impact of high drop-out rates, poor retention, restricted educational opportunities, and diminished outcomes will be principally borne by those social classes.

The simple reality is that the colonial and apartheid legacies have meant that there is a strong coincidence between class and race, with black South Africans hailing from predominantly working-class and rural poor social backgrounds and white South Africans having their social origins largely in the capitalist and middle classes. (There are, however, also white South Africans of working-class and rural poor origin.) The explicit racial ordering of apartheid has taken on a more class character since 1994 as black elites have joined white elites in historically privileged educational institutions.

The changes noted above suggest that South African education has been characterized by great fluidity and relative stasis; by both ruptures and discontinuities with the past and by continuities in institutions and conditions; by conservation of institutions as well as by the dissolution, restructuring, and reconstruction of institutions; by "small and gradual changes [and] large-scale changes" (Jansen 2004, 293); by modest improvements, more substantial reforms, and deeper transformations; and by successes as well as by failures and shortcomings in policy, planning, strategy, and implementation. There has been no "total, rapid and sweeping displacement" of structures, institutions, policies, and practices (Wolpe 1992, 16). It is also arguable whether there could be, given the post-1994 policy choices of the ANC, constraints on the negotiated political settlement in South Africa, and various other conjunctural conditions and pressures.

## New Pathways

In light of the analysis here, how might key problems that constrain equity and quality in education be tackled, and what might be possible pathways for further advancing social justice in education? The most significant "new" thoughts about this come from three recent documents: the Department of Basic Education's (DBE) *Action Plan to 2014: Towards the Realisation of Schooling 2025* (2010); the Department of Higher Education and Training's (DHET's) *Green Paper for Post-School Education and Training* (2012); and a chapter in the NPC's *National Development Plan 2030* (2012). Collectively, these documents engage with key challenges and propose solutions to them. They generally concur that despite the advances and gains made since 1994, gender, class, racial, and other inequalities persist with regard to access to educational opportunities and outcomes. Their sober assessment of the post-1994 period points to the long road still to be traveled for "the doors of learning" to truly "be opened to all." These documents also recognize the need to hold firmly together the goals of access and quality, and for those to become parallel vectors if there is to be social justice in and through education.

South African educational policy documents tend to be expansive in vision and extremely short on detail. Specifically, establishing priorities and making decisive choices between dearly held goals and attendant social and political dilemmas are critical. For example, the pursuit of social equity and redress, and quality in higher education simultaneously, in the context of inadequate public financing poses a difficult challenge. An exclusive concentration on social equity can lead to its unadulterated privileging at the expense of economic development and quality. Doing so could compromise the goal of producing high-quality graduates with the requisite knowledge, competencies, and skills, and hence result in a slower pace of economic development. Conversely, an exclusive focus on economic development and quality and "standards" (especially when considered to be timeless and invariant and attached to a single, ahistorical, and universal model of higher education) could result in equality being delayed with no, or limited, erosion of the racial and gender character of the national occupational structure. The danger of concentrating purely on social equity or economic development is that such a formulation abstracts from and hinders the development of policies appropriate to contemporary conditions and social and economic imperatives (Badat 2009, 462). Thus, details are needed on how the proposed solutions to the educational challenges as proposed in the various recent documents can mediate among key paradoxes and potentially competing goals. Policymakers have to be more specific not only about the goals and targets (as is happening) but also need to map the journey and indicate concretely the means to get there.

Arguably the biggest challenge in advancing social justice in South Africa is making adequate state funding available for equity; otherwise social justice and development in and through education will be undermined by financial constraints. It is increasingly clear that public funding of basic and higher education is inadequate in the face of the legacy of past inequities and new demands. At least two areas warrant attention. First, there is a need to increase the block funding allocations to schools and universities; in the case of schools, doing so requires a substantial increase in provincial budgets with a ring-fencing of the educational component. Second, equity interventions work best when they are adequately financed, well targeted, and robustly monitored and evaluated. In higher education there is a need to increase the NSFAS budget so that all eligible students are funded fully and there is real equality of access and opportunity; and to increase earmarked funding for high-quality academic development initiatives that enhance equality of opportunity and outcomes, for curriculum innovation and transformation, and to enhance the teaching capabilities of institutions to meet the needs of the national economy and society. Basic education requires specific interventions targeted at struggling or dysfunctional schools, including increasing teacher salaries to attract the best educators, and to provide support for curriculum renewal and additional academic support for students. Without well-funded and effectively targeted equity measures, equality of opportunity for students (largely black) from working-class and impoverished rural social backgrounds will continue to be severely compromised.

Beyond the diagnoses and the proposals of the recent DBE, DHET, and NPC documents, there are several other issues in need of urgent attention. First, the DBE should issue clear and transparent minimum infrastructural norms and standards for all schools. Enacting minimum standards is consistent with Section 5A of the South African Schools Act, which empowers the minister of basic education to promulgate minimum norms and standards for school infrastructure.

The minimum standards should encompass both infrastructure (e.g., classrooms, facilities, water, and sanitation) and an appropriate institutional environment (e.g., policies on safety and a teacher code of conduct). At the very least, the historical infrastructural backlogs that include mud hut schools should be redressed as a matter of utmost priority. The draft standards that the DBE has issued, while welcome, remain inadequate. Clear standards would enable citizens to hold the provincial educational departments accountable. Building on the minimum standards, additional support should be provided to schools serving the poor, including nutrition and health programs.

Second, the NPC calls for early investment and interventions in children's schooling. It commends a range of school-specific interventions as well as health and social welfare programs for children starting from birth. Such multisectoral interventions are critical if the state is to begin to tackle the multidimensional causes of poverty and inequality. Advancing social justice in education requires more programs of this kind, including tying social grants provided by the Department of Social Development more clearly to education.

Third, "qualified, motivated, and committed teachers" are "the single most important determinant of effective learning" (Sayed 2008, 7). To this end, there is an urgent policy need to ensure that schools that educate learners from the most deprived backgrounds have the best teachers—not to do so is to trap the poor into vicious intergenerational cycles of poverty. A range of interventions are required, including paying teachers more in such schools so as to attract well-qualified and experienced instructors. Twinning arrangements between rich and poor schools would also be helpful so that good teachers can be deployed across schools rather than being confined to the wealthy schools.

Fourth, the process of educational decentralization to provinces since 1994 has occurred in a context of great social disparity; as such, policy has exacerbated rather than reduced educational inequity across provinces; the provincial capacity to deliver high-quality education is uneven across the country and is constrained by the legacy of colonialism and apartheid. For example, the Eastern Cape Province, which brings together two of the former Bantustans, shows poor progress across multiple measures of poverty, including education, in precisely those geographical locations that were part of the former Bantustans (Noble, Dibben, and Wright 2010). Provincialization as an outcome of the post-1994 settlement requires rethinking if social justice in education is to be achieved.

Fifth, the policy of charging school fees—an outcome of the school decentralization policy—is probably the most difficult political issue to resolve and yet remains a key source of inequity in education. It is tempting (and indeed popular) to suggest that this policy be abandoned, but doing so could well destabilize a stable and functioning section (the ex-model C schools) of the public school system. An alternative is to ensure more equity-focused measures that share and redirect resources in the private and ex-model C schools to schools that are most in need. One strategy could share well-qualified and experienced teachers across schools. To do so, targeted and attractive incentives need to be provided.

Sixth, a key distinguishing feature between the 10 percent of the historically black schools that produce 20 percent of all senior certificate endorsements and the other 80 percent of public secondary schools that produce only 20 percent is effective leadership and management. Creating visionary, purposeful, and effective educational leadership and management in national and provincial departments of education, district offices, and, especially, schools is crucial.

The idea of a "back to basics" curriculum is problematic. Although curricula reduced to the essentials so as to be (almost) teacher-proof and drilling learners in fundamentals may result in modest and temporary gains, those gains are unlikely to bring about any fundamental transformation in teaching and learning. Reducing the curricula ignores the fact that relative to the poor, the economic, social, and cultural resources of the middle class provide it with considerable advantages with respect to access to and opportunity in education. Rather than inherently biased and narrowly utilitarian approaches to education, the poor need varied and challenging curricula and forms of pedagogy that suit their particular contexts and circumstances.

In higher education a number of areas require attention. First, while there has been significant progress in the representation of both black, especially African, and female students in higher education, this progress masks inequities in their distribution across institutions, qualification levels, and academic programs. The representation of black and female students at specific institutions and qualification levels and, in particular, in academic programs, requires constant attention. Carefully designed interventions are needed to ensure improvements in representation. Second, in light of unacceptably poor pass and graduation rates and high drop-out rates, the enhancement of the academic capabilities of universities and rigorously conceptualized and designed academic development programs to support academics and students are urgent to ensure equity of opportunity and outcome, especially for students of working-class and rural poor social origins. There is knowledge, expertise, and experience at some universities in this regard. This knowledge needs to be harnessed, expanded, and put to work for the benefit of all universities.

Third, with respect to postgraduate education, a major constraint is that both the funding for postgraduate study (especially full-time study), and the size of the awards provided through the National Research Foundation, are severely inadequate. If South Africa is to enhance economic and social development as well as ensure greater opportunities for and participation by black students from indigent backgrounds in postgraduate study, significantly more investment is needed in postgraduate, especially doctoral level, study. At many South African universities the availability and quality of the research infrastructure, facilities, and equipment impedes the enrollment and production of doctoral graduates. This effect is so even at twelve of the twenty-three universities that produce 95 percent of the country's doctoral graduates and also the bulk of peer-reviewed scientific publications[22] (CHE 2008).

The challenge of enhancing institutional capacities is, however, not confined to nor should be reduced to infrastructure, facilities, and equipment. It also relates to a capacity to expand and mount new doctoral programs, the management of doctoral education, the management of research, and the mobilization of funding for doctoral studies and students. There is great scope for interuniversity collaboration, though the nature, terms, and conditions of such collaboration will require careful consideration.

Fourth, as a consequence of apartheid, knowledge production in South Africa has been predominantly the preserve of white men. The democratization of knowledge requires special measures to induct previously excluded social groups, such as blacks and women, into the production and dissemination of knowledge. The NPC notes that "Higher Education South Africa has developed a detailed proposal for a National Programme to develop the next generation of academics for South African higher education" and that it "deserves to be implemented" (NPC 2011, 319). This is a good example of an imaginative and well-developed program constrained by the lack of state funding. Improving the proportion of academics with doctoral qualifications will require a dedicated program, with adequate funding and support for staff though formally supervised development programs, mentoring, and co-supervising students alongside experienced supervisors.

The systematic and progressive transformation of institutional cultures, in congruence with constitutional ideals and values, also remains an important and urgent task, especially at historically white universities. The challenges are to uproot historical cultural traditions and practices that impede the development of more open, vibrant, democratic, and inclusive intellectual and institutional cultures; to respect, affirm, and embrace the rich diversity of the people that today constitute and must increasingly constitute historically white universities; purposefully to create and institutionalize cultures that embrace difference and diversity; and to see these challenges as strengths and powerful wellsprings for personal, intellectual, and institutional development.

Although this article has focused on schooling and universities, there are at least 2.8 million people between the ages of 18 and 24 that are neither employed nor at educational or vocational training institutions—the so-called NEETs (Cloete 2009). The vast majority (1 million) have less than a grade 10 qualification, some 990,000 have a grade 10 to 11 qualification, and almost 600,000 have a grade 12 qualification without exemption. Thus, there is a critical need to reconceptualize and clarify the scope, structure, and landscape of the postschool system and institutions, and to give attention to the spectrum of postschool institutions that are required for economic and social development, as well as to expand opportunities for high quality postschool education and training.

## Conclusion

On the final page of a *Long Walk to Freedom*, Nelson Mandela (1994) writes, "The truth is that we are not yet free; we have merely achieved the freedom to be free, the right not to be oppressed. For to be free is not merely to cast off one's chains, but to live in a way that respects and enhances the freedom of others. The true test of our devotion to freedom is just beginning" (p. 617). While the Constitution, laws, and policies direct the state to realize wide-ranging goals in and through education, our analysis indicates that the post-1994 government's devotion in practice to a strong version of social justice underpinning policy in education is moot, due perhaps to the divergent and even contradictory understandings of equity and redress. On one hand, equity and redress are considered as historical rectifications, as in the uniformity and standardization of basic schooling and the equalization of per-learner expenditures. This entails no redistribution of substantial goods and resources from those who were previously advantaged. On the other hand, equity and redress are considered as distributional justices, as a way of providing resources to those who were most disadvantaged under apartheid. Conceived in this way, equity implies redistribution in the sense of taking away from others, specifically from the privileged white minority.

Ultimately, South Africa's educational failings are neither entirely technocratic nor managerial: they are political, associated with a government increasingly mired in short-term electoral politics that fails to distinguish between party and state. The government appears to lack the will to act courageously and decisively to address problems at the levels of policy, personnel, and performance when it is clear that the apartheid legacy in schooling remains entrenched. As Gill Marcus, Governor of the Reserve Bank, an ANC stalwart, puts it, "South Africa faces significant challenges" that "require a coordinated and coherent range of policy responses"; "the government [needs] to be decisive, act coherently," demonstrate "a coordinated plan of action to address them" and "exhibit strong and focused leadership from the top."[23] Doing so "will go a long way to restoring confidence, credibility, and trust."[24] The heady days and promise of "People's Education for People's Power" are long past. Many prominent anti-apartheid activists have mutated into technocratic bureaucrats, and critics of the broken or forgotten promises have been marginalized or have fallen silent. Teacher unions and the government are simultaneously in alliance and at an impasse, and the anomie at various provincial education departments is a serious hindrance to change. Popular mass and civil society formations have disappeared and sometimes been replaced by professional NGO bureaucracies, and there has been a steady decline of popular participation in educational issues. Direct parental participation in education has come to be framed by a discourse of governors and governance. In this context, there is a need to reinvigorate mass community participation and to forge binding compacts among diverse local and national actors to ensure effective education.

Effective policies to advance redress must secure consent and ensure legitimacy. Implementing a social justice vision in education entails establishing new institutions, reconfiguring old ones, and changing institutional cultures and practices. South Africans have to be educated and trained; equipment and learning materials have to be provided; and funding has to be voted, allocated, and accounted for. And all these advances have to be effectively stitched together by people with the necessary knowledge, expertise, skills and values consistent with those espoused in the national Constitution. Ultimately, achieving social justice in education requires Mandela-like commitment, dedication, and a heightened sense of responsibility. The "long walk" to equity in and through education has not yet ended.

# Notes

1. The concept "People's Education for People's Power" was adopted by the National Education Crisis Committee (NECC), an anti-apartheid education organization, at its conference in 1986. It was an attempt to establish the interconnections between peoples' power and peoples' education and an attempt to shift the education struggle away from the idea of "Liberation Now, Education Later." The NECC saw contesting the running of education intuitions through democratically elected structures, such as parent-teacher-student associations (PTSAs) and student representative councils (SRCs), as an important element in the overall struggle for liberation.

2. We use the term "transformation" since it is how government describes the nature of change that is sought (see DoE 1997, 1998). But see the comments here regarding "transformation."

3. The term "positive discrimination" is equivalent to "affirmative action" in the United States. These terms are used interchangeably throughout the article.

4. In South Africa, students are called "learners." Again, these terms (students and learners) are used interchangeably here.

5. The School Register of Needs cited by the Education Rights Project; see http://www.erp.org.za/htm/issue2-3.htm.

6. This formed the basis for the National Education Policy Act of 1996.

7. See http//:www.education.gov.za.

8. These policies were amended in 2006, which clarified the provisions for school funding by means of quintiles, and the charging and payment of school fees (DoE 2006). A large number of schools were declared as no-fee schools; under the amended policy, these schools were entitled to an increased allocation by the state to offset revenues previously generated through school fees, and fee-charging schools (previously all schools) could apply to their provincial education departments to be declared a no-fee school. This was a grudging acknowledgment that equity and redress in education have been less assured than originally conceived.

9. See http://www.info.gov.za/asgisa/asgisa.htm#challenge (accessed 14 June 2008).

10. Total enrollments in higher education as a proportion of the 20 to 24 age group.

11. ANA is the Annual National Assessment, a census-based assessment of school pupils undertaken by the Department of Basic Education and conducted among 7.2 million pupils at 24,000 schools.

12. Each school in South Africa has a poverty score, which assigns it to a quintile rank that determines the amount of funding it receives. Every school in South Africa is assigned to one of five quintiles with quintile five (Q5) representing the wealthiest (least-poor) schools and quintile one (Q1) the poorest.

13. Botswana and Honduras also test grade 9 learners but are excluded from this comparison.

14. The mean across the international sample was set at 500 and the standard deviation at 100.

15. Analysis of a language comprehension test written by a sample of grade 6 teachers in 2007.

16. Statistics presented at a Development Bank of Southern Africa think-tank on education chaired by Mamphela Ramphele. Badat was a member of the think-tank.

17. Ibid.

18. "Contact" institutions provide face-to-face education, in contrast with open distance learning institutions.

19. Academic development programs are interventions aimed at enhancing the academic literacy, numeracy, and content knowledge of students who are eligible for admission to universities but are deemed to be underprepared in certain areas.

20. Ex-Model C schools are previously whites-only schools. In 1992, all schools that were reserved mainly for the white population were granted autonomy by the then-ruling Nationalist Party. In effect independent school governing bodies thereby secured control over these schools in what is known as the Model C Proposals. The new post-1994 democratic government was thus confronted with a system whereby self-managing school governing bodies in effect controlled the most resourced and privileged schools. This article argues that this unequal legacy still persists in post-apartheid South Africa.

21. Black academics constituted only 44.1 percent of the total permanent academic staff of 16,684 in 2010; they composed less than 20 percent of the academic staff at some historically white universities. Female academics compose 44.1 percent of academics in 2010 (CHE 2012, 41). Women tend to be concentrated at the lower levels of the academic hierarchy.

22. Seven of the twelve universities produce 74 percent of all doctoral graduates.

23. See http://www.bdlive.co.za/economy/2013/06/07/marcus-in-strong-plea-for-decisive-leadership-in-sa (accessed 8 June 2013).

24. Ibid.

# References

African National Congress. 1994. *Implementation plan for education and training*. Braamfontein: Centre for Education Policy Development (CEPD).

African National Congress. 1995. *A policy framework for education and training*. Braamfontein: CEPD.

Badat, Saleem. 2009. Theorising institutional change: Post-1994 South African higher education. *Studies in Higher Education* 34 (4): 455–67.

Badat, Saleem. 2012. Redressing the colonial/apartheid legacy: Social equity, redress and higher education admissions in democratic South Africa. In *Equalizing access: Affirmative action in higher education in India, United States, and South Africa*, eds. Zoya Hasan, and Martha C. Nussbaum. New Delhi: Oxford University Press.

Boughey, Chrissie. 2005. *Lessons learned from academic development movement in South African higher education and their relevance for student support initiatives in the FET college sector*. Commissioned Report. Cape Town: Human Sciences Research Council.

Buhlungu, Sakhela. 2003. The state of trade unionism in post-apartheid South Africa. In *The state of the nation, South Africa 2003–2004*, eds. John Daniel, Adam Habib, and Roger Southall, 184–203. Cape Town: Human Sciences Research Council Press.

Carrim, Nazir, and Yusuf Sayed. 1992. The Model B schools: Reform or transformation? *Work in Progress* 14:5–9.

Chutgar, Amita, and Anil Kanjee. 2009. School funding flaws. *HSRC Review* 7 (4): 18–19.

Nico Cloete, ed. 2009. *Responding to the educational needs of post-school youth: Determining the scope of the problem and developing a capacity-building model*. Cape Town: Centre for Higher Education Transformation.

Council on Higher Education (CHE). 2008. *Post-graduate studies in South Africa: A statistical study*. Pretoria: CHE.

CHE. 2012. *VitalStats: Public higher education 2010*. Pretoria: CHE.

Department of Basic Education. 2010. *Action Plan to 2014: Towards the realisation of schooling 2025*. Pretoria: Department of Education.

Department of Education. 1995. *Education and Training*. White Paper. Government Gazette No. 196. Pretoria: Department of Education.

Department of Education. 1997. *A programme for the transformation of higher education*. Education White Paper 3. Government Gazette No. 18207. Pretoria: Department of Education.

Department of Education. 25 September 1998. *Programme for the transformation of further education and training*. Education White Paper 4. Government Gazette No. 19281, Notice 2188. Pretoria: Department of Education.

Department of Education. 2006. South African Schools Act, 1996 (Act No. 84): Amended National Norms and Standards for School Funding. Government Gazette No. 869. Pretoria: Department of Education.

Department of Higher Education and Training (DHET). 2012. *Green paper for post-school education and training*. Pretoria: DHET.

De Waal, Mandy. 2013. A school journey into Eastern Cape's darkest heart. *Daily Maverick*. Available from http://www.dailymaverick.co.za (accessed 30 April 2013).

Howie, Sarah, Surette van Staden, Mishack Tshele, Cilla Dowse, and Lisa Zimmerman. 2012. *PIRLS 2011: South African children's reading literacy achievement report*. Pretoria: Centre for Evaluation and Assessment, University of Pretoria.

Jansen, Jonathan. 2004. Changes and continuities in South Africa's higher education system, 1994 to 2004. In *Changing class: Education and social change in post-apartheid South Africa*, ed. Linda Chisholm, 293–314. Pretoria: Human Science Research Council Press.

Mandela, Nelson. 1994. *Long walk to freedom*. London: Little, Brown.

McGinn, Noel, and Susan Street. 1986. Educational decentralization: Weak state or strong state? *Comparative Education Review* 30 (4): 471–90.

Ministry of Education. 2001. *National Plan for Higher Education*. Pretoria: Ministry of Education.

Ministry in the Office of the President. 23 November 1994. *White paper on reconstruction and development*. Government Gazette, vol. 353, no. 16085.

Motala, Shireen. 2006. Education resourcing in post-apartheid South Africa: The impact of finance equity reforms in public schooling. *Perspectives in Education* 24 (2): 79–93.

Motala, Shireen. 2009. Privatising public schooling in post-apartheid South Africa—Equity considerations. *Compare* 39:185–202.

National Education Policy Investigation (NEPI). 1992. *The framework report and final report summaries*. Cape Town: Oxford University Press/NECC.

National Planning Commission. 2011. *Diagnostic overview*. Pretoria: The Presidency. Available from http://www.npconline.co.za/MediaLib/Downloads/Home/Tabs/Diagnostic/Diagnostic%20Overview.pdf (accessed 4 May 2013).

National Planning Commission. 2012. Improving education, training, and innovation. In *National development plan 2030*, 294–328. Pretoria: The Presidency. Available from http://www.npconline.co.za/MediaLib/Downloads/Home/Tabs/NDP%202030-CH9-Improving%20education,%20training%20and%20innovation.pdf (accessed 4 May 2013).

Noble, Michael, Christopher Dibben, and Gemma Wright. 2010. *The South African Index of multiple deprivation 2007 at datazone level (modelled)*. Pretoria: Department of Social Development.

Republic of South Africa. 1996a. Constitution of the Republic of South Africa, Act No. 108.

Republic of South Africa. 1996b. National Education Policy Act, Act No. 27.

Sayed, Yusuf. 2008. Education and poverty reduction: Omission, fashions, and promises. In *Education and poverty reduction: Towards policy coherence*, ed. Simon Maeile, 53–68. Cape Town: HSRC Press.

Sayed, Yusuf, and Rashid Ahmed. 2009. Promoting access and enhancing education opportunities? The case of no-fees schools in South Africa. *Compare* 39 (2): 203–81.

Sayed, Yusuf, and Anil Kanjee. 2013. An overview of education policy change in post-apartheid South Africa. In *The search for education quality in post-apartheid South Africa: Interventions to improve learning and teaching*, eds. Yusuf Sayed, Anil Kanjee, and Nkomo Mokubung, 5–38. Cape Town: HSRC Press.

Sikhosana, Mpumelglo. 1993. Affirmative action: Its possibilities and limitations. EPU Working Paper No. 1, Education Policy Unit (EPU), University of Natal, Kwazulu-Natal.

Simon, Brian. 1974. *The two nations and the educational structure: 1780–1870*. London: Lawrence and Wishart.

Taylor, Nick. 2011. *The National School Effectiveness Study (NSES)—Summary for the synthesis report*. Johannesburg: JET Education Services.

Weiler, Hans. 1990. Comparative perspectives on educational decentralization: An exercise in contradiction? *Educational Analysis and Policy* 12 (4): 433–48.

Wolpe, Harold. 1992. Convergence of reform and revolution. *Cooperazione* 117:14–16.

# Developing Possibilities for South African Youth: Beyond Limited Educational Choices?

ANDREW BABSON

The South African government must do more to help learners at all educational levels position themselves for class mobility, economic security, and occupational fulfillment. As of the last quarterly labor force survey of 2012, the national unemployment rate was 24.9 percent. Almost three-quarters of the unemployed are between 15 and 34 years of age; and of them about two-thirds lack a matric qualification (equivalent to high school diploma), about one-third had such qualification but no more, and the remaining few had a tertiary qualification. It is obvious that the macroeconomic causes of structural unemployment need immediate attention; this article also argues that there should be concurrent efforts to promote high school completion rates and expand options for postsecondary education. Specifically, this article explains the yet-untapped power of multilingual education to improve learning and classroom engagement, and also looks to a handful of European postsecondary education models that offer accommodating and worker-friendly paths to occupational flourishing.

*Keywords:* youth; South Africa; social mobility; inequality; possibility development; vocational education; higher education

R esearch in language in education and vocational education suggests that two specific initiatives can offer better learning and, by extension, better social outcomes for youths, including more and better employment for this population. The first initiative is improved implementation of current policy in additive multilingual education, and the second is the adoption of a vocational educational model that goes beyond the acquisition of modular "skills" and "qualifications" and focuses on the attainment of occupational competence and identity.

*Andrew Babson is an educational anthropologist and a lecturer at the University of Pennsylvania's Graduate School of Education. His research with high school graduates in Mankweng, Limpopo Province, South Africa, explores the ways education can position youth from historically disadvantaged communities to be agents of sociocultural change.*

DOI: 10.1177/0002716213514342

The wheels of (social) justice, however, grind slowly. Implementation of these initiatives in South Africa will be slowed passively by inertia and actively by ideological and political resistance. Recent governmental restructuring of postsecondary policies and institutions and recent research on the value and feasibility of additive multilingual education suggest that these initiatives are not only possible and broadly beneficial but also highly cost-effective. Adding more urgency to considering these initiatives, unemployment has disproportionally hit black South African youth (Bhorat 2003, 2004; Bhorat, Mayet, and Visser 2010).

This article does not propose immediate solutions for youth who are unemployed. Rather it suggests purposeful and research-based implementation of existing reform commitments in multilingual and vocational education to achieve results within a three-cohort, 12-year timeframe (Badat and Sayed, this volume). I marshal recent analyses, current demographic statistics, and interview and survey data from my own research with recent high school graduates in Limpopo Province (Babson 2011) in support of this argument.

## The Demographics of South African Youth

As of the last quarterly labor force survey of 2012, the national unemployment rate was 24.9 percent; since 2008 it has been stuck between a low of 21.8 percent (2008 Q4), and a high of 25.7 percent (Q2). If one uses the South African government's "expanded definition" of unemployment to include discouraged job seekers, that rate climbs sharply to 35.9 percent (cf. 39.5 percent in 2002 and 29.2 percent in 1995; Bhorat 2004, 42). During the same timespan (2008–2012), another dishearteningly consistent trend was evident: among the unemployed, the large majority—about two-thirds—lacked a matric qualification;[1] about one-third had such qualification but no more; and the remaining few had a tertiary qualification. The fourth quarter of 2012 was typical: 61.3 percent of the unemployed lacked a matric qualification, 32.1 percent had matric, and 6.2 percent had tertiary qualifications (Stats SA 2012). Moreover, during this quarter, the numbers on youth unemployment were particularly concerning: of the 4.5 million unemployed, 71.1 percent, or 3.2 million, were between 15 and 34 years old. Finally, of youth aged between 15 and 24, 31.6 percent (a little over half [54.9 percent] female) counted as NEETs (not in education, employment, or training).

These data point to the pressing need for action regarding South African youth "possibility development" (to use the phrase of applied psychologist Michael Nakkula [Nakkula and Toshalis 2006]), particularly for those without a matric qualification and NEETs aged 15 to 24.

Labor economist Haroon Bhorat has made numerous arguments for action on youth unemployment across the qualification spectrum. For example, in a 2004 study, Bhorat found that between 1995 and 2002, the unemployment rate among those with tertiary qualifications doubled, led by black African degree holders (Bhorat 2004, 43). And in a recent study, Bhorat and coauthors outlined a clear trend of discrimination against black South African tertiary degree holders on the job market (Bhorat, Mayet, and Visser 2010).

These discouraging trends appear on their face to call for one to choose his or her tertiary path to meet the demands of the market: that is, choosing a bachelor's in engineering rather than in poetry. However, this article takes the view of Allais (2012) and others that more basic macroeconomic and political changes must be made in the national educational system, particularly in how it links learners to the world of work. Bhorat's studies indirectly further this line of argument by showing clearly that no healthy economic system leaves behind so many tertiary degree holders.

This article, then, aims to keep a steady eye on how South Africa's fundamental macroeconomic deficiencies are affecting the greatest number of South African youth. Again, 71.1 percent of the unemployed in Q4 2012 were "youth," that is, those aged 15 to 34 (Stats SA 2012). Furthermore, unemployment disproportionately affects black and Coloured South Africans of working age (15–64). The Q4 2012 unemployment rate among working-age South Africans identifying as black was 28.5 percent; 23.5 percent of those identifying as Coloured reported being unemployed during the same time period, 13 percent for those identifying as Indian/Asian, and 5.6 percent for those identifying as white. Although the precise statistic is not available in the Labour Force Survey from which these data are derived, it stands to reason that black and Coloured South Africans youths, aged 15 to 34, are disproportionately affected by unemployment. What must be done to redress such inequalities?

This article proposes two practical measures—fully implementing extant multilingual education policies and broadening postsecondary options—that might improve the chances of young black South Africans staying in school, completing matric, and getting themselves on an occupational track that is satisfying and offers economic stability. My research on language education and practice in Limpopo Province, South Africa (Babson 2011) suggests that, historically, most black families in the region have considered the regional lack of English education to be political oppression because it blocks the route to opportunity. From this standpoint, the two efforts proposed in this article—primary and secondary education in/of African languages, and postsecondary education culminating in less than a university degree—can easily be perceived in the same light. Nonetheless, as Kathleeen Heugh (2010) has pointed out, when parents demand "English" education, they generally want "quality" education.

During apartheid, extensive and high-quality education either *in* or *of* English, or beyond high school, was almost entirely limited to white learners, most of whom also enjoyed the benefits of elevated class status. Even more to the point is that 20 years after the official end of apartheid, elites of all backgrounds and identifications send their children to the "best" schools, and push their children to complete a university degree. Therefore, the strident demand among non-white South African parents for an education that is English-medium and university-leading is entirely justified by experience.

But—and this is a core proposition of this article—these stances are also limiting. They prevent local awareness of and support for the implementation of, or thorough communication about, either a robust additive multilingual approach to teaching and learning, or a wider range of options for postsecondary education and training. Far from preventing access to rewarding occupational tracks, these two measures would lay the groundwork for better learning generally, contribute to a motivation to stay in school, and empower young people and their families with more options for possibility development.

### Why "possibility development"?

The term "possibility development" asks us to think creatively about tracks, trajectories, and timescales for occupational training, and to modify the design of the educational system accordingly to offer both freedom of choice and support for those choices. This balance between autonomy and support is exemplified in the work of Lev Vygotsky, one of the most influential educational theorists and researchers of the past century, and visible in the curriculum structures of some of the most successful educational systems in the world, notably, Finland (Sahlberg and Hargreaves 2011, xix). Furthermore, the term "possibility development" also avoids the inherent limitations of the term "skill development," that is, too much of a focus on discrete technical aspects of procedural knowledge, and too little attention to the relational and identity concomitants of gaining and using such knowledge. "Occupational development" avoids the limitations of the term "skill development": robust, supportive vocational education systems such as in the Netherlands use this term. However, possibility development illustrates an important aspect of these supportive vocational educational systems, namely, the potential to expand or change one's occupational track and trajectory at any point in time without loss of systemic support. Currently, unlike in comparable economies, South African education and labor structures do not promote possibility development (cf. Cosser 2010).

## Multilingual Education and Possibility Development

There are many potential benefits of multilingual education, especially the cultivation of stable conditions for possibility development. Empirical data across various academic fields strongly suggest that multilingualism confers a wide range of cognitive, sociocultural, and emotional benefits (Bialystok 2011; Dewaele and Oudenhoven 2009; Pavlenko 2014). Related research on multilingual education suggests that use of a local language for at least the first four years of schooling, combined with gradual addition of inter/national language use in the classroom—that is, an "additive" approach—correlates strongly with a wide variety of positive educational outcomes in communities where inter/national languages are not widely used (Heugh 2009; Ball 2011).

Competence in standard forms of the English language is highly valued in South Africa, and for many complex reasons. This competence is particularly valued by those who have historically been denied the right to learn English. The apartheid government's emphasis on first-language education at the expense of English education followed historical precedent in many parts of the country. In most nonwhite sections of urban areas, and especially in rural areas where most blacks were relocated (to "Bantustans"), a plurality of the missionary education there either limited or banned education in English. In this historical perspective, apartheid prevention of English education for nonwhites was congruent with history, but also, as English became the world's lingua franca, a policy tantamount to political oppression.

The commonsense assumption is that this history of limiting English (in) education to nonwhites has shaped current attitudes of parents in these former Bantustan areas toward language-in-education issues. A small number of empirical studies over the past 30 years has confirmed that black parents consider learning or using the standard of the local African language in school to be a waste of time, even a continuation of apartheid (Mawasha 1986, 27; Nelson Mandela Foundation 2005; Vesely 1998; V. De Klerk 2009; see Phiri, Kaguda, and Mabhena [2013, 51] for similar parental rejection in Zimbabwe; see Jones and Barkhuizen [2011, 520] on Kenya).

Although the issue of postsecondary education is addressed later, the connecting theme between both proposals—better implementation of multilingual education policy and more diverse and better-supported postsecondary options—is the willful underfunding of education for black South Africans from the earliest days of apartheid to the present day. Although Bantu Education (BE) and standard curricula for white students were identical, expenditure for BE lagged very far behind spending on education for whites (Kallaway 1984). Due to the overall impoverishment of BE and other compounding factors of the apartheid system, few black students made it past year eight (Standard VI)—the very point at which they could first start to learn in English (Birley 1968; Hartshorne 1995; Hyslop 1999). In 1979, BE was abolished, allowing black students to learn in English from Standard III (U.S. equivalent grade 5) onward. The Bantu Education Act of 1953 extended the use of the "mother tongue" as the language of education from the first four years of school (per missionary policy) to the first eight (Horrell 1969, 120; Rose and Tunmer 1975, 184).

Overall, then, despite the fact that black learners have historically had some access to English in education, current research (limited though it may be) strongly suggests that the quality of this instruction, from colonial times right up to the present, has been uneven at best and inadequate or nonexistent at worst. In sum, English language in education has long been limited to mostly white students in South Africa—students who have already benefitted from well-paid and well-trained teachers and adequately resourced schools. This segregation of English language education, and its subsequent ideological conflation with well-resourced and relatively high-functioning schools, has solidified the stance among black parents that good English education, including the pervasive use of English as medium of instruction, is good education per se. Thus, despite postapartheid improvements, competence in English language use remains, in the words of the late language activist Neville Alexander, "unassailable but unattainable" (Alexander 2000; Brock-Utne and Holmarsdottir 2004, 67).

That English is a world language of commerce and sociocultural practice is undeniable. Yet the conflation of English and good education among black parents has crowded out an ideological space for considering the strong benefits of using African languages in education alongside, rather than in opposition to, English. As stated earlier, South African policy supports this "alongside" or "additive" approach to language use both in schooling and as a general social policy. That is, multilingualism, and concomitant multiculturalism and pluralism, is meant to be a core value of the so-called New South Africa. By officially recognizing nine standard African languages, the South African Constitution of 1996 sent a powerful message about the government's long-term support for the education and use of African languages. The constitution not only enshrines nine African languages as official (along with Afrikaans and English), but also an individual's right to an education in an official language of her or his choice, "where that education is reasonably practicable" (Republic of South Africa [RSA] 1996a, Section 29, Part 2). The purpose of this legislation was to raise the status of African languages while promoting multilingualism and empowering local decisions about language in education. The language-in-education policy (LiEP) of 1996 suggests additive multilingualism in schools, meaning that the mother tongue should be used as the language of learning and teaching (LoLT) as long as possible (RSA 1996b). The LiEP also suggests that "the underlying principle is to maintain home language(s) while providing access to (and effective acquisition of) additional language(s)" (RSA 1996b; cf. Mda 2004; Heugh 2000, 2008).

A problematic aspect of the LiEP is that it suggests additive multilingualism but does not enforce it (Brock-Utne and Holmarsdottir 2004, 72). The South African Schools Act of 1996 mandated that parents, as the heads of school governing boards (SGBs), have final say over the school's LiEP (RSA 1996b). But parental and learner choice, a cornerstone of the decentralized education policy (Naidoo 2005) have been very difficult to enforce at the local level for numerous reasons. In rural areas, for example (the very communities decentralization was meant to "empower"), parents' and learners' educational agency has generally been undermined by traditional rural governance, parental illiteracy, gender inequality, lack of English teachers, and constraints on the time and energy needed to make a difficult, day-to-day living (Biseth 2005; G. De Klerk 2002; Nelson Mandela Foundation 2005; Ntsebeza 2005).

The current policies of decentralization and additive multilingualism strike a dramatic break from the past: Pretoria is not the center of power as it was during apartheid, and English in education is promoted. But although meaning well, these policies together have actually hindered adoption of additive multilingualism in schools. This is because, first, the LiEP has erred on the side of flexibility and customization: it is not prescriptive enough and lacks legal weight. Second, decentralization has allowed Pretoria to hesitate to provide direction, training, and public education about additive multilingualism. Although the research basis for such implementation is strong (Alexander 2000; Heugh 2000; Hornberger 2009; cf. Gupta 1997; Makoni 2003; Pennycook 2002), both local and governmental will is lacking, though for different reasons. This lack of will, and diffidence on the part of the national government to provide structures for implementation, only complicates the already technically and practically difficult task of implementation (Bamgbose 2000). The common thread across these two issues is that, in the drafting of postapartheid policies, local empowerment was given priority ahead of central government structure and guidance. For the decentralization of LiEP decisions really to work, must not the research on additive multilingualism be adequately communicated to local stakeholders? Have the negative associations of "mother tongue" education with political oppression loosened enough to refocus learners and their parents on the potential benefits of an additive multilingual LoLT approach?

In an additive multilingual approach, languages are added to the curriculum without necessarily taking away existing curricular languages. So the addition of English, crucially, does not entail an educational subtraction or abandonment of the local language. This practice allows learners to retain the comfort of using a local language in speaking with teachers and classmates while learning English and gradually using it more. Furthermore, multilingualism allows more possibilities for meaning-making with different linguistic codes, and an impressive body of research has shown the wide benefits for learning and relating that this broader expressive and interpretive range offers (Bialystok 2011; Adesope et al. 2010; Shin 2013; Pavlenko 2007, 2012). Possibility development is an appropriate framing for multilingual education because it only adds potentials for meaning-making practices.

Few policy-makers can credibly argue against so-called mother tongue–medium education for the first two to four years of primary school. The policy evidence for substantial investment in mother tongue education—in terms of increased school dropout rates (Patrinos and Velez 1996; Ndaruhutse 2008; Schwieter 2011), the associated costs of wasted school funding (Grin 2005; Heugh 2006; Sahlberg and Hargreaves 2011, 58), and lower academic performance across the board (Alexander 2011, 323–24; Heugh 2000)—makes a convincing argument for delaying the "switch to English" until at least grade 4. However, as detailed in a compelling study on multilingual education in Kenya, obstacles in implementation may also slow motivation to act (Nyaga and Anthonissen 2012). First, Makoni (2003) and others (see review in Babson 2011) have discussed that many learners would be hard pressed to define clearly their "mother tongue"; nor might the "mother tongue" of all classroom participants—teacher and students alike—match. As Phiri and colleagues' recent Harare-based study shows, sixth-grade participants say that English is so pervasive in their usage of Shona that "they are not even aware that the words they speak are not Shona, but are borrowed, from English" (Phiri, Kaguda, and Mabhena 2013, 50). The standardization and alphabetization of African languages, moreover, has long been a controversial issue mired in debates about local relevance, colonial or European hegemony, and even general theories of what languages are. For example, who decides what variety of a spoken language will be used to develop the written form?

These practical issues and the ideological resistance to mother-tongue education have hampered robust implementation of additive multilingual policies in the very places in which they would be most useful: the mostly rural former "homeland" areas where, traditionally, linguistic variety and diversity have been commonplace. Clearly stated, there is a powerful conflict between learning

English (and in English) on one hand, and learning (in) African languages on the other. Additive multilingualism, a policy supported by a wide range of data (and disciplinary approaches), should be the norm in these communities, but it is not.

## Expanding Postsecondary Options

The term "possibility development" also offers a useful lens through which to consider the need for a broader, yet simultaneously more supportive, system of postsecondary education options for young South Africans. By setting "possibility development" rather than "skills development" as its goal, the postsecondary educational system can relink technical procedural knowledge to occupational relations and identities and give learners support to advance through or change educational tracks at their own pace. Such a linked system would both guide learners along an occupational trajectory and allow for change and development at any point along this path. Such a system possibly could be better described as "educational-occupational," because the education and training that an individual receives is always linked to an occupation and its (inter)personal aspects. Crucially, however, if an individual chooses to change educational-occupational paths, there would be support structures in place; they would not be left to cobble together market-responsive skills (at significant expense), which could later prove redundant.

A model for such an educational-occupational system exists already in the Netherlands. One can choose to become, through "senior secondary" education, a specialist or middle manager in a trade, but can later decide to gain further professional training in the trade at university (Hoffman 2011, 90). Or, if one wished to learn a trade after completing a university degree, one could enroll in a senior secondary school to obtain specialist or middle management qualification.

The Dutch model illustrates how possibility development can serve as the teleological focus for an educational-occupational system that is relatively dynamic and open rather than static and closed. It does offer freedom of choice; however, this freedom does entail a loss of support and guidance, does entail significant personal expense, and does not imply excessive market-dependency on technical procedural knowledge (i.e., skills), as in, for example, the United Kingdom and the United States. Compare this model with what the Finnish system offers students in lower-secondary school: up to two hours of weekly career and academic support (Sahlberg and Hargreaves 2011, 23–27). Possibility development is a fitting term for a system that allows for a wide range of occupational possibilities over time, without leading to vocational incoherence or overexposure to the whims of market imperatives.

In their recent Student Retention and Graduate Destination study, researchers from the Human Sciences Research Council of South Africa (HSRC) begin with an important insight: for most learners everywhere, the secondary to postsecondary transition is hardly as linear or predictable as it is often described (Cosser 2010, 11). A lead author of the study, postsecondary education expert

Michael Cosser, stresses two important findings: one, employability strongly affects choice to pursue higher education, choice of institution, and program of study, about equally across all socioeconomic levels; and two, there is a great lack of guidance, leading to uncertainty and ignorance, concerning postsecondary education options (Cosser 2010, 20–23). Macroeconomic policies and structures play a central role in setting up individual choices about educational training, credentialing, and employment prospects. Educational systems typical of so-called coordinated market economies (Hall and Soskice 2001, 8; cf. Allais 2012, 638), such as Germany and the Netherlands, offer a range of postsecondary options that correspond to occupational tracks with opportunities that are moderately linked to forces of supply and demand (Wood 2001, in Hall and Soskice 2001, 251–52). However, in the "liberalized market economies" of, for example, the United States, Great Britain, and South Africa, employment opportunities are far more linked to the vagaries of the market; in such an unstable system, learners gravitate toward obtaining the most employable credentials, that is, university degrees (Wood 2001, in Hall and Soskice 2001, 251–52).

The new Department of Higher Education and Training (DHET), created in early 2009, represents, both symbolically and substantively, a rare opportunity to address such difficult policy issues head-on. The DHET was established further to distinguish tertiary from primary/secondary educational policy development (Akoojee 2012, 678). One important innovation of the department was to include both sector education and training authorities (SETAs), formerly located in the Department of Labour, and further education and training colleges (FETCs). The twenty-three SETAs were first formed in 1998 to provide sector-specific on-the-job training; FETCs were created to provide "intermediate" trade or artisanal skills development and provide "the backbone of the 'technical and associate professionals' arsenal" (Cosser 2010, 5; cf. Akoojee 2012, 680–81). FET colleges have historically suffered from low investment, quality, and, therefore, low esteem, particularly in relation to universities (Cosser 2010; Letseka et al. 2010). SETAs have also been criticized for defining "skills" rather narrowly and furthering an overly market-responsive approach to educational objectives, in addition to charges of mismanagement (Allais 2012, 633–34).

The mere formation of a singularly focused government department of higher education and training, particularly one that comprises, using market-oriented terms, both "demand" and "supply" sides of the employment equation, constitutes a genuinely positive break from a long and troubled educational past in South Africa (cf. Kraak 2002). As Cosser (2010) writes, the formation of the DHET "has major positive implications for the restructuring of the post-schooling landscape and creating new education and training pathways" (p. 6). Akoojee (2012) declares that the new DHET constitutes a "re-positioning with the potential to shift the entire skills development debate in South Africa and forever change the education, training and skills development system" (p. 679).

Without radical changes in the basic structures and functions of either FET college education or SETA-based internships, however, plans to further integrate the two would not represent a substantial move toward a possibility-development model. Allais (2012) argues that any integration of SETAs and FET colleges would reinforce their shared emphasis on "market-responsiveness" and mutual construal of "skills" as modular "qualifications." Akoojee, however, is fairly optimistic that SETAs can increase the importance of workplace training in the overall process of education (Akoojee 2012, 680–81). He acknowledges the potential for SETAs to dictate too much about how FET colleges operate—the former would likely contribute significant finances to the operation of the latter—but appreciates the constructive step toward closer calibration of education and the employment market (Akoojee 2012, 680–81).

Allais, by contrast, takes a step back to consider how rare the opportunity before South Africans really is, namely, a chance to revolutionize the entire way the relationship between education and work in South Africa is theorized, planned, and established. In short, she proposes a model favorable to possibility development (Allais 2012) that is critical of the notion that "skill" is separate from the personal. Training consultant Nancy Hoffman (2011) does the same in a recent book proposing improvements to the American educational-occupational system. In an international comparison of vocational education systems (Austria, France, Germany, the Netherlands, and Norway), Hoffman emphasizes the success of the Dutch system, particularly the low degree of unemployment among Dutch youth (even since the beginning of the global recession in 2007). She compares how the relationship between work and education is construed in these countries, all of which have robust vocational education systems, and the United States. Fundamental is the contrast of the "Anglo-Saxon" notion of skills versus the Germanic notion of *handelende*, or "performance" and associated behaviors, evident in the Dutch "integrative" approach (Hoffman 2011, 31).

Drawing on the work of Westerhuis, Allais (2012, 636) relates this approach to the present state of postsecondary education in South Africa by asserting that, post-apartheid, South Africa has taken up the Anglo-Saxon notion of skills and qualifications to its detriment. Allais argues that this uptake has coincided with the deterioration of artisanal and trade education and apprenticeships, and the general decline in the quality of FET institutions (cf. Cosser 2010, 5). Ideally, for Allais, a commitment to bolstering the status and quality of FET colleges would be grounded in the broader, more relational, and, literally, "vocational" notion of skills as competences linked to a community of practice (Lave and Wenger 1991), with traditions and specific types of knowledge that, together, constitute a powerful form of identification (Hoffman 2011, 23–43). In addition to shortchanging individuals, however, Allais argues that an overly narrow and market-led system of qualifications, skills, and training also shortchanges society as a whole (2012, 636).

# English Language Use, Local "Roots," and Occupational Identity in Limpopo

Data from interviews with Limpopo high school graduates demonstrate the need for further investment in multilingual education. What is needed is more information that enables parents, educators, and administrators at the SGB level, particularly in rural areas, to feel empowered. This information would include not only a research digest demonstrating the potential benefits of multilingual education but would also address parental concerns: learning in local languages and adding English in grade 3 or 4 benefits their children, and does not put them at a disadvantage compared to sub/urban learners, or those who grow up with English in the home. Furthermore, Limpopo parents could also be encouraged that English language learning does not automatically take their children away from home or weaken family and community relations (Alexander 2000).

An especially crucial step in communicating the benefits of multilingual education and the importance of broadening postsecondary options is recognizing the array of intricate connections between knowledge and identity. Forms of knowledge are ideologically connected to personal, social, and cultural differences that carry specific meaning-potentials. Knowing how to speak English well, for example, has different meaning potentials for identity that vary across contexts. Because English is a global language, knowing how to speak it is generally advantageous; however, English may be more valued in certain interactions than in others. There are further nuances in these meaning potentials: what types of English correspond to certain stereotypes, and for whom? This example illustrates how learning a set of competencies (e.g., using English) is just as much of a personal as it is an epistemological matter. But this insight is not new and important; what is, rather, is this insight's lack of weight in policy discussions about how best to (1) assist young South Africans in developing possibilities for work and work's personal aspects, or at least, how to (2) support and guide young people in their entrepreneurial efforts, as they innovatively combine technical knowledge, social relations, and economic resources.

Hoffmann's recent review of the French, Dutch, German, Austrian, and Norwegian postsecondary systems illustrates how these systems' success is largely due to the ample weight they give to the idea that knowledge and identity are inseparable. These systems have managed to sustain high school graduation rates, minimize youth unemployment, and provide guidance and support for ongoing possibility development. At this moment of policy transition and investment in higher education in South Africa, the newly formed DHET has an exciting opportunity to replicate such a successful model.

Interviews in Limpopo show that the place of English in the lives of Limpopo Province youth aspiring to class mobility (Babson 2011) is important. The interview data suggest that the participants understand the challenges and benefits of gaining knowledge that has great potential to reposition them socially and culturally. Specifically, they understand that for them, "good" use of English is a powerful resource that can be converted into labor marketability and cultural capital (Bourdieu 1986; Lareau 1987), but it can also throw into question one's identity as an "African" (Ngwane 2001). The participants' confidence in the face of sociocultural and linguistic complexity supports the promotion of language in educational policies such as additive multilingualism. Self-reporting among youth has often proven to be overly optimistic (see Lapsley and Hill [2009] for review); nonetheless, the clear evidence of socially mobile youth in Limpopo demonstrating not only a keen awareness of how knowledge and identity are interlinked, but also a genuine desire to hold on to their "roots" (beyond the novel scholarly contribution of these kind of data), invites close consideration for the arguments of this article.

The participants included forty-eight class-mobile, multilingual youth in the Mankweng Township (also called "Turfloop") area. Their reflections, which were collected in June through September before the stock market crash of 2008, reflect a bullish confidence in their ability to learn and use English, among other languages, with ease and fluidity, and importantly, to manage the life consequences of using such powerful knowledge. English education in Limpopo post-apartheid has been economically and socioculturally mobility-enhancing, as English language education and usage had long been relatively scarce in the Limpopo provincial region (Bourdieu 1986, 86). Participants—high-performing products of their local school systems—want to present themselves as evenly invested in using African languages and English on a regular basis, thereby "balancing" both class mobility and, to quote several participants, "sticking to their roots."

The participants' strong interest and confidence in their ability to preserve their "roots" attest to the value in acknowledging the complexity of competences, and how they cannot be neatly extracted from identity. This attestation amounts to an endorsement of additive multilingualism—although English needs to be learned and used, the more that subjects can be taught in a local language, the better (Heugh 2009, 170). What is clear from these data is that multilingual youth know that managing the personal dynamics of knowledge can be challenging, and varies contextually, but they consider themselves up to the task. The metalinguistic understanding of the personal nature of linguistic knowledge and use seems to have given them more confidence to learn and use English without fear of being "lost," a term redolent of the classic Durkheimian *anomie*. But these data suggest a recommendation for parents in Limpopo: namely, that they should take an active role in how their children learn and use language; that is to say, they should understand that their children can use knowledge of African languages for both personal and epistemological reasons. Schools and families should work together to support youth in the "balancing" participants described.

A system that supports more young people in this endeavor, particularly through a robust additive multilingual education model, can only alleviate the known problem in many African communities, as documented by Ndaruhutse (2008): many learners struggle with managing the complexities of language-in-education, and this leads to high drop-out rates.

## Conclusion

The large number of South Africans not in education, employment, or training, as well as the glaring fact that more than 90 percent of the unemployed have no tertiary qualifications, begs consideration of what existing policies can be better implemented to improve high school graduation rates, and what new policies might emerge during this promising period of new investment in higher education.

No parent will accept, as a matter of principle, anything less than the best for his or her child. The framework of possibility development, however, sidesteps the false choice between the "best"—university education after matric—and the "rest"—vocational education. Nonuniversity options actually leave open possibilities on a different timescale. The ideological dominance of preferences for university training does little justice to learners who are still finding their way, or who would prefer a more practical or specialized career path after high school.

As critics of educational neoliberalism have underlined, this false choice between the best and the rest is learned as a matter of cultural participation. This educational neoliberal discourse construes lockstep trajectories, educational competition, individual skill development, and educational winners and losers. As Comaroff and Comaroff (2005) and Giroux (2009) point out, it is a discourse championed in the United States and certain European countries, and it promotes a vision of democratic citizenship that is a far cry from John Dewey's ideals (1899, 13–15). For the new South Africa, this vision provides a disappointing response to countering older policies.

Offering alternative pathways to satisfying, stable occupations and extending the timescale of possibility development allows learners to build their occupational identities, including associated skills and knowledge, beyond the neoliberal vision of identity construction. Possibility development is inherently an ongoing, open process that is ultimately individually guided but supported through robust institutional scaffolding and community, including parental, guidance.

The DHET's development of FET and SETA options should not, in reality or image, be construed as setting up inferior options for disadvantaged youth. They should be available to youth who want or need to take a path to occupational satisfaction and stability that is not determined by a neoliberal discourse of lockstep educational trajectories and timescales, or moral economic visions of individual competitiveness in the "job market."

Allais (2012), citing the German vocational model (p. 635; cf. Hoffman 2011, 28–31), argues for apprenticeship into an occupation, and against training for a specific job or just getting someone "employable." The discourse of "skills" is far too socially atomizing while also overburdening to the individual. As my data from Limpopo illustrate, knowledge and identity are intertwined. Institutional supports are necessary to educate parents and learners about the occupational paths available to them, but these occupational paths need to be better constructed and organized and, from a public communication standpoint, more clearly communicated to all local educational stakeholders. The National Qualifications Framework model has failed in this regard, and within the new DHET, closer and better links between SETAs and FET colleges may ameliorate this glaring problem (Cosser 2010, 4).

Pushing for better implementation of good policies can greatly expand occupational opportunities for South African youth, especially those particularly affected by unemployment and low-quality educational provision. Additive multilingualism and a holistic, occupation-focused vocational education system deserve renewed commitment, but implementation quality is essential.

# Note

1. "Matric," short for "matriculation," refers to completing the final year of South African high school. Those who have completed this final year and their school-leaving examinations are said to "have their matric"—the equivalent of a U.S. high school diploma.

# References

Adesope, Olusola O., Tracy Lavin, Terri Thompson, and Charles Ungerleider. 2010. A systematic review and meta analysis of the cognitive correlates of bilingualism. *Review of Educational Research* 80:207–45.

Akoojee, Salim. 2012. Skills for inclusive growth in South Africa: Promising tides amidst perilous waters. *International Journal of Educational Development* 32:674–85.

Alexander, Neville. 2000. *English unassailable but unattainable: The dilemmas of South African language policy in education.* PRAESA Occasional Papers No. 3. Cape Town: PRAESA.

Alexander, Neville. 2011. After apartheid: The language question. In *After apartheid: Reinventing South Africa?* eds. Ian Shapiro and Kathreen Tebeau, 311–31. Charlottesville, VA: University of Virginia Press.

Allais, Stephanie. 2012. Will skills save us? Rethinking the relationships between vocational education, skills development policies, and social policy in South Africa. *International Journal of Educational Development* 32:632–42.

Babson, Andrew. 2011. The place of English in expanding repertoires of linguistic code, identification and aspiration among recent high school graduates in Limpopo Province, South Africa. PhD dissertation, University of Michigan, Ann Arbor. Available from http://deepblue.lib.umich.edu/handle/2027.42/86351.

Badat, Saleem, and Yusuf Sayed. 2014. Post-1994 South African education: The challenge of social justice. *The ANNALS of the American Academy of Political and Social Science*, this volume.

Ball, Jessica. 2011. *Enhancing learning of children from diverse language backgrounds: Mother tongue-based bilingual or multilingual education in the early years.* Paris: UNESCO.

Bamgbose, Ayo. 2000. *Language and exclusion: The consequences of language policies in Africa.* London: Lit Verlag.

Bhorat, Haroon. 2003. *The post-apartheid challenge: Labour demand trends in the South African labour market, 1995–1999.* Cape Town: Development Policy Research Unit, University of Cape Town.

Bhorat, Haroon. 2004. The development challenge in post-apartheid South African education. In *Changing class: Education and social change in post-apartheid South Africa*, ed. Linda Chisholm, 31–55. London: Zed Books.

Bhorat, Haroon, Natasha Mayet, and Mariette Visser. 2010. Student graduation, labour market destinations and employment earnings. In *Student retention and graduation destination: Higher education and labour market access and success*, eds. Moeketsi Letseka, Michael Cosser, Mignonne Breier, and Mariette Visse, 97–123. Cape Town: HSRC Press.

Bialystok, Ellen 2011. Reshaping the mind: The benefits of bilingualism. *Canadian Journal of Experimental Psychology* 65 (4): 229–35.

Birley, Robert, Sir. 1968. African education in South Africa. *African Affairs* 67 (267): 152–58.

Biseth, Heidi. 2005. Language in education influenced by global trends—South African experiences. Paper presented at NETREED Conference, Beitostølen, Norway.

Bourdieu, Pierre. 1986. The forms of capital. In *Handbook of theory and research for the sociology of education*, ed. John Richardson, 241–58. New York, NY: Greenwood Press.

Brock-Utne, Birgit, and Halla Holmarsdottir. 2004. Language policies and practices in Tanzania and South Africa: Problems and challenges. *International Journal of Educational Development* 24 (1): 67–83.

Comaroff, Jean L., and John Comaroff. 2005. Reflections on youth, from the past to the postcolony. In *Makers and breakers: Children and youth in postcolonial Africa*, eds. Alcinda Honwana and Filip De Boek, 19–30. Oxford: James Currey.

Cosser, Michael. 2010. Uniformity and disjunction in the school-to-higher-education transition. In *Student retention and graduation destination: Higher education and labour market access and success*, eds. Moeketsi Letseka, Michael Cosser, Mignonne Breier, and Mariette Visse, 11–23. Cape Town: HSRC Press.

De Klerk, Gerda. 2002. Mother-tongue education in South Africa: The weight of history. *International Journal of the Sociology of Language* 154:29–46.

De Klerk, Vivian. 2009. Language shift in Grahamstown: A case study of selected Xhosa-speakers. *International Journal of the Sociology of Language* 146:87–110.

Dewaele, Jean-Marc, and Jan Pieter van Oudenhoven. 2009. The effect of multilingualism/multicultural-ism on personality: No gain without pain for third culture kids? *International Journal of Multilingualism* 6 (4) 1–17.

Dewey, John. 1899. *The school in society: Being three lectures by John Dewey supplemented by a statement of the University Elementary School*, eds. George H. Mead and Helen C. Mead. Chicago, IL: University of Chicago Press.

Giroux, Henry A. 2009. *Youth in a suspect society: Democracy or disposability*. New York, NY: Palgrave Macmillan.

Grin, Francois. 2005. Économie et langue: de quelques équivoques, croisements et convergences. *Sociolinguistica* 19:1–12.

Gupta, Anthea Fraser. 1997. When mother tongue education is not preferred. *Journal of Multilingual and Multicultural Development* 18:496–506.

Hall Peter A., and David Soskice, eds. 2001. *Varieties of capitalism: The institutional foundations of comparative advantage*. Oxford: Oxford University Press.

Hartshorne, Kenneth. 1995. Language policy in African education: A background to the future. In *Language and social history: Studies in South African sociolinguistics*, ed. Rajend Mesthrie, 306–18. Cape Town: David Phillip Publishers.

Heugh, Kathleen. 2000. *The case against bilingual and multilingual education*. PRAESA Occasional Papers No. 6. Cape Town: PRAESA.

Heugh, Kathleen. 2006. Cost implications of the provision of mother tongue and strong bilingual models of education in Africa. In *Optimizing learning and education in Africa—The language factor. A stock-taking research on mother tongue and bilingual education in sub-Saharan Africa*, eds. Hassana Alidou, Aliou Boly, Birgit Brock-Utne, Yaya Satina Diallo, Kathleen Heugh, and H. Ekkehard Wolff, 138–56. Paris: Association for the Development of Education in Africa (ADEA).

Heugh, Kathleen. 2008. Language policy and education in Southern Africa. In *Encyclopedia of language and education*, vol.1, 2nd ed., eds. Stephen May and Nancy Hornberger, 355–67. New York, NY: Springer.

Heugh, Kathleen. 2009. Into the cauldron: An interplay of indigenous and globalised knowledge with strong and weak notions of literacy and language education in Ethiopia and South Africa. *Language Matters: Studies in the Languages of Africa* 40 (2): 166–89.

Heugh, Kathleen. 2010. Productive engagement with linguistic diversity in tension with globalised discourses in Ethiopia. *Current Issues in Language Planning* 11 (4): 378–96.

Hoffman, Nancy. 2011. *Schooling in the workplace: How six of the world's best vocational education systems prepare young people for jobs and life*. Cambridge, MA: Harvard Education Press.

Hornberger, Nancy H. 2009. Multilingual education policy and practice: Ten certainties (grounded in indigenous experience). *Language Teaching* 42:197–211.

Horrell, Muriel. 1969. *The African homelands of South Africa*. Johannesburg: South African Institute of Race Relations.

Hyslop, Jonathan. 1999. *The classroom struggle: Policy and resistance in South Africa, 1940–1990*. Johannesburg: University of Natal Press.

Jones, Jennifer M., and Gary Barkhuizen. 2011. "It is two-way traffic": Teachers' tensions in the implementation of the Kenyan language-in-education policy. *International Journal of Bilingual Education and Bilingualism* 14 (5): 513–30.

Kallaway, Peter. 1984. *Apartheid and education: The education of black South Africans.* Johannesburg: Ravan Press.

Kraak, Andre. 2002. Discursive shifts and structural continuities in South African vocational education and training: 1981–1999. In *The history of education under apartheid, 1948–1994: The doors of learning and culture shall be opened*, ed. Peter Kallaway, 74–93. Cape Town: Pearson Education South Africa.

Lapsley, Daniel K., and Patrick L. Hill. 2009. Subjective invulnerability, optimism bias and adjustment in emerging adulthood. *Journal of Youth Adolescence* 39:847–57.

Lareau, Annette. 1987. Social class and family-school relationships: The importance of cultural capital. *Sociology of Education* 56:73–85.

Lave, Jean, and Etienne Wenger. 1991. *Situated learning: Legitimate peripheral participation.* Cambridge: Cambridge University Press.

Moeketsi Letseka, Michael Cosser, Mignonne Breier, and Mariette Visser, eds. 2010. *Student retention and graduate destination: Higher education and labour market access and success.* Cape Town: HSRC Press.

Makoni, Sinfree. 2003. From misinvention to disinvention of language: Multilingualism and the South African Constitution. In *Black linguistics: Language, society, and politics in Africa and the Americas*, eds. Sinfree Makoni, Geneva Smitherman, Arnetha F. Ball, and Arthur K. Spears, 132–51. London: Routledge.

Mawasha, Abram Lekalakala. 1986. Medium of instruction in black education in southern Africa. In *The role of language in black education: Papers presented at the conference on the role of language in black education, Pretoria, 17–18 February 1986*, ed. Human Science Research Council [HRSC], 13–29. Pretoria: HSRC.

Mda, Thobeka. 2004. Multilingualism and education. In *Changing class: Education and social change in post-apartheid South Africa*, ed. Linda Chisholm, 177–94. Pretoria: HSRC Press.

Naidoo, Jordan P. 2005. *Educational decentralisation and school governance in South Africa: From policy to practice.* Paris: UNESCO IIEP.

Nakkula, Michael J., and Eric Toshalis. 2006. *Understanding youth: Adolescent development for educators.* Cambridge, MA: Harvard Education Press.

Ndaruhutse, Susy. 2008. *Grade repetition in primary schools in sub-Saharan Africa: An evidence base for change.* Reading, UK: CfBT Education Trust.

Ngwane, Zolani. 2001. "Real men reawaken their fathers' homesteads, the educated leave them in ruins": The politics of domestic reproduction in post-apartheid rural South Africa. *Journal of Religion in Africa* 31 (4): 402–26.

Nelson Mandela Foundation. 2005. *Emerging voices: A report on education in South African rural communities.* Cape Town: HSRC Press.

Ntsebeza, Lungisile. 2005. *Democracy compromised chiefs and the politics of the land in South Africa.* Leiden, the Netherlands: Brill.

Nyaga, Susan, and Christine Anthonissen. 2012. Teaching in linguistically diverse classrooms: Difficulties in the implementation of the language-in-education policy in multilingual Kenyan primary school classrooms. *Compare: A Journal of Comparative and International Education* 42 (6): 863–79.

Patrinos, Harry Anthony, and Eduardo Velez. 1996. Costs and benefits of bilingual education in Guatemala, a partial analysis. Human Capital Development Working Paper No. 74, World Bank, Washington, DC.

Pavlenko, Aneta. 2007. *Emotions and multilingualism.* Cambridge: Cambridge University Press.

Pavlenko, Aneta. 2012. Affective processing in bilingual speakers: Disembodied cognition? *International Journal of Psychology* 47 (6): 405–28.

Pavlenko, Aneta. 2014. *The bilingual mind: And what it tells us about language and thought.* New York, NY: Cambridge University Press.

Pennycook, Alistair. 2002. Mother tongues, governmentality, and protectionism. *International Journal of the Sociology of Language* 154:11–28.

Phiri, Morrin, Darmarris Kaguda, and Dumoluhle Mabhena. 2013. The "mother tongue as media of instruction" debate revisited: A case of David Livingstone Primary School in Harare, Zimbabwe. *Journal of Emerging Trends in Educational Research and Policy Studies (JETERAPS)* 4 (1): 47–52.

Republic of South Africa (RSA). 1996a. Constitution. Pretoria: RSA. Available from http://www.info.gov .za/documents/constitution/.

RSA. 1996b. Language in education policy. *Section 3(4)(m), National Education Policy Act (27)*. Pretoria: RSA. Available from http://www.info.gov.za/acts/1996/a27-96.pdf.

Rose, Brian, and Raymond Tunmer. 1975. *Documents in South African education*. Johannesburg: Donker.

Sahlberg, Pasi, and Andy Hargreaves. 2011. *Finnish lessons: What can the world learn from educational change in Finland*. New York, NY: Teachers College Press.

Statistics South Africa (Stats SA). 2012. *Labour force survey Q4 2012*. Pretoria: Stats SA.

Schwieter, John W. 2011. Migrant Hispanic students speak up: Linguistic and cultural perspectives on low academic attainment. *Diaspora, Indigenous, and Minority Education* 5 (1): 33–47.

Shin, Sarah J. 2013. *Bilingualism in schools and society: Language, identity, and policy*. New York, NY: Routledge.

Vesely, Rima. 1998. *Multilingual environments for survival: The impact of English on Xhosa-speaking students in Cape Town*. PRAESA Occasional Papers No. 5. Cape Town: PRAESA.

# South Africa's Key Health Challenges

South Africa has an estimated 6.4 million people living with HIV, with more than 2 million already on treatment. The disease emerged in South Africa at the same time as the transition to democracy began in 1990. Although the country has seen considerable advances in many social spheres, the health sector has lagged. This lag is primarily because the HIV/AIDS epidemic results in an increased burden of disease in a cohort of people who would otherwise be healthy. This article warns that the all-pervasive nature of the epidemic will put other areas of development at risk. With economic development come new threats to the health of South Africans, including noncommunicable diseases and environmental change. Service delivery remains a challenge for the government at all levels, and the demands of not only South Africans but of migrants and refugees need to be considered.

*Keywords:*  health; South Africa; HIV; AIDS; transition to democracy

*By*
ALAN WHITESIDE

South Africa has had the benefit of 20 years of democratic rule. It has been a period of some success. Perhaps most significantly, there have been three fair elections, each with less violence than the preceding one, with a fourth scheduled for 2014. The press is free and vocal. Basic services are being provided, and most South Africans are better off today than they were in 1994. The economy has grown, albeit not fast enough to create the employment needed. There are huge challenges, many of which are covered elsewhere in this volume. These include inequality (although it is no longer legally racially determined as it was prior to 1994), the lack of employment, corruption, and of course the HIV and AIDS epidemic.

*Alan Whiteside is the director of the Health Economics and HIV/AIDS Research Division, University of KwaZulu-Natal, and Centre for International Governance Innovation (CIGI) Chair in Global Health Policy, Balsillie School of International Affairs/Wilfrid Laurier University. He has been working on economic and social aspects of AIDS for more than 25 years.*

DOI: 10.1177/0002716213508067

South Africa has an estimated 6.4 million of its approximately 52 million people living with HIV, with more than 2 million already on treatment. The disease emerged in South Africa at the same time as the transition to democracy began in 1990. This article warns that the all-pervasive nature of the epidemic will put other areas of development at risk. With economic development come new threats to the health of South Africans, including noncommunicable diseases (NCDs) and environmental change. Service delivery remains a challenge for the government at all levels, and the demands of not just South Africans but of migrants and refugees need to be considered.

This article focuses on the health challenges facing the nation including, but not limited to, HIV. It is a story in three parts. In 1990, at the time that Nelson Mandela was released from prison, and the country began the fraught process of negotiating the changes that were to lead to a free and democratic nation, HIV was just beginning to make its unwelcome presence felt. The African National Congress (ANC) inherited a fractured health care system with huge needs, and in 1994, at the time of transition to democracy, HIV prevalence among ante-natal clinic attendees stood at 7.6 percent and continued to rise.

The government moved to provide and reform health care but took little notice of the looming AIDS threat until President Thabo Mbeki took charge in 1999. What happened then was quite baffling to scientists and observers of the AIDS epidemic. In October 1999, President Mbeki gave a speech to the National Council of Provinces in which he suggested that the antiretroviral drug AZT was unsafe. His dissident views rapidly became more extreme. He would soon suggest that HIV might not be the cause of AIDS. In May 2000, he established a Presidential Panel to look at the causes of the epidemic. This panel met twice, but almost all mainstream scientists withdrew from any involvement with it. Dissident scientist-members of the panel had bizarre and irrational views about the causes of HIV/AIDS. The minister of health for most of this period was Dr. Manto Tsabalala-Msimang, who famously prescribed garlic, olive oil, and lemon juice as a treatment for AIDS. From 2000, until Mbeki's resignation in 2008, Mbeki's government's health policy was largely consumed by the HIV/AIDS controversy.

Leadership (and its style) in the national government's Department of Health changed when Mbeki resigned.[1] And Kgalema Motlanthe, as acting president, appointed Barbara Hogan as the minister of health. Following the election of President Jacob Zuma in 2009, Dr. Aaron Motsoaledi became the minister of health. Apart from being a medical doctor, he had experience in provincial government and had worked in rural areas. In the early years of his ministry, he was supported by an outstanding deputy, Molefi Sefularo, who was later killed in a traffic accident.

Apart from the HIV epidemic, there are four key areas that pose challenges to the South African population. Given the existence of three spheres of government—national, provincial, and local—the first area is health care delivery and policy. Health policy is developed nationally and adapted to fit provincial needs. Health care funding is allocated to and spent by provincial departments of health. There are great variations in need and delivery, and in governmental and civil service competence, across the provinces.

The second is the growth in NCDs. At a meeting of the South African Medical Research Council (MRC) and the U.S. National Institutes of Health (NIH) in Durban in June 2013, Dr. Debbie Bradshaw of the MRC described South Africa as being in the throes of colliding epidemics, namely, HIV and TB and various NCDs. The risks are immediately determined by a person's background, lifestyle, and environment, and they in turn are influenced by society, culture, and the environment. South Africa faces major issues with regard to the health of its citizens: nutrition, obesity, alcohol consumption, and interpersonal violence.

The third concerns migrants and refugees. South Africa is variously regarded as the economic powerhouse of Africa, the engine of continental growth, and the lodestone for subregional governance. Although the country may try to meet these expectations, it is clear it cannot be the employer and provider of social security for the continent. Ordinary South Africans perceive foreigners as taking away scarce resources, as shown by outbreaks of xenophobia. The final issue is environmental change. There are a series of challenges regarding the climate and its impact on the nation and its health that need to be considered. These include droughts of increasing frequency and magnitude, with consequences for production of and access to food and livelihoods; because of space constraints, however, this issue is not discussed here.

Living through the transition in South Africa, especially 1990 to 1996, was formative. My own work on HIV needs to be located in this temporal context. I joined the University of Natal[2] as a research fellow in the Economic Research Unit in 1983. My initial work was on labor migration within South Africa and from neighboring states. The first AIDS cases came from these groups, and I began to look at the HIV issue through the lens of a development economist. By 1998, health and HIV and AIDS had come to dominate my work. The failure of the government to recognize the potential impact of the disease and respond to its challenges has had, and will have, consequences for decades to come. One of the unfortunate legacies of President Nelson Mandela's administration (which he acknowledged) was its failure to respond to HIV/AIDS.

The recent history of health policy in South Africa tells a story of a nation that made poor choices, causing hundreds of thousands of unnecessary deaths, costing billions of rand in health care, and resulting in a huge number of orphans. There is dislocation in society across South Africa and the region. Mortality, suffering, and expenditure of scarce resources would not have happened if the country had got prevention right from the start. South Africa now has to provide treatment for millions, and the number of infections continues to rise.

In the 1980s there was no evidence of an AIDS epidemic in South Africa. There were surveys among sex workers in the Transvaal in 1986 and among outpatients and ante-natal clinic attendees in Natal in 1987 that found absolutely no HIV infections (Gouws and Abdool Karim 2010, 61). However, the mining industry was experiencing increased illness and death among its workforce and correctly ascribed both to AIDS. In 1986, the Chamber of Mines began testing Malawian migrants and found that nearly 4 percent were infected (Whiteside 1990, 10). In those early days no one knew how far or how fast the disease would spread or what its consequences would be. It was a new event occurring in a fluid political and economic environment.

FIGURE 1
Ante-Natal Prevalence of HIV in South Africa, 1990 to 2011

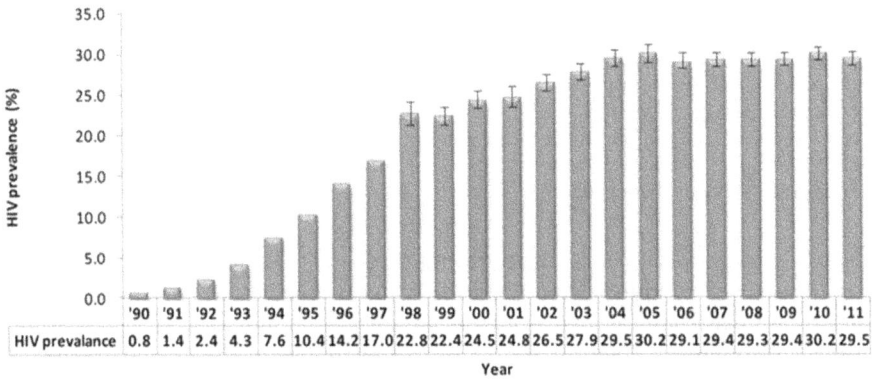

| HIV prevalance | '90 | '91 | '92 | '93 | '94 | '95 | '96 | '97 | '98 | '99 | '00 | '01 | '02 | '03 | '04 | '05 | '06 | '07 | '08 | '09 | '10 | '11 |
|---|---|---|---|---|---|---|---|---|---|---|---|---|---|---|---|---|---|---|---|---|---|---|
| | 0.8 | 1.4 | 2.4 | 4.3 | 7.6 | 10.4 | 14.2 | 17.0 | 22.8 | 22.4 | 24.5 | 24.8 | 26.5 | 27.9 | 29.5 | 30.2 | 29.1 | 29.4 | 29.3 | 29.4 | 30.2 | 29.5 |

Year

SOURCE: Department of Health (2012, 12).

In 1990, the transition to democracy began. It was also the year in which it was certain the HIV epidemic had arrived. The Department of Health carried out the first national survey of ante-natal clinic attendees. The survey found a prevalence of HIV of 0.8 percent (Department of Health 2012). There was to be close to exponential growth over the next decade, and then a stabilization at unacceptably high levels, as shown in Figure 1.

The issue of health was identified as a challenge by the ANC in exile; indeed, it was the subject of a number of conferences. In April 1990, a health and welfare conference was held in Maputo. In May 1990, a workshop, "Towards a South African AIDS Policy," was held in Lusaka (Tsampiras 2012). The ANC came to power with a health plan in existence, evidence that the issue had been considered (ANC 1994). However, the story of health policy in the first 20 years of a democratic South Africa is one of failure, largely caused by the HIV epidemic and South Africa's response to it.

# The 1994 Inheritance

Much has been written about the transition to democracy and the then-new government's inheritance (von Feigenblatt 2008; Wolpe 1995). This section reflects on health, health status, and delivery of services. In 1994, South Africa was a fractured nation. The divisions were deep and covered all aspects of life. Apartheid legislation, which predated but was refined and entrenched by the nationalist government from 1948, was designed to divide and control the population. The country comprised a mosaic of unviable administrative units: the "independent" homelands of Transkei, Ciskei, Bophuthatswana, and Venda; the "self-governing" entities of KwaZulu-Natal, KaNgwane, KwaNdebele, QwaQwa, Gazankulu, and Lebowa; three administrations for Coloureds, Indians, and whites; and four white-ruled provinces of the Cape, Orange Free State, Natal, and Transvaal.

> The roots of a dysfunctional health system and the collision of the epidemics of communicable and non-communicable diseases in South Africa can be found in policies from periods of the country's history, from colonial subjugation, apartheid dispossession, to the post-apartheid period. Racial and gender discrimination, the migrant labour system, the destruction of family life, vast income inequalities, and extreme violence have all formed part of South Africa's troubled past, and all have inexorably affected health and health services. (Coovadia et al. 2009, 817)

South Africa was a militarized frontier society. Historically, in most black tribes, men were inducted into codes of honor that involved toughness. The white ruling class held its place of privilege through coercion and oppression of the black population. White males were conscripted into the armed forces. The consequent levels of violence, and particularly attitudes toward women, were and remain major health challenges (see Bower, this volume).

> Contemporary research has shown that the control of women is a central part of present day constructions of South African masculinity and that the use of physical and sexual violence against women is legitimated when the goal is to secure such control or to punish resistance to it. The historical record suggests that these ideas have long been prevalent. (Coovadia et al. 2009, 821)

# Capitalism, Labor, and Health Consequences

## The legacy of colonialism

South Africa's unique political and economic systems and its labor relations have their roots in the history of the country, and particularly the extraction of mineral wealth. The growth of capitalism and the system of labor migration in southern Africa have their origins in the discovery of diamonds at Hopetown in 1867 and gold on the Witwatersrand in 1886. The mining of these resources required a considerable labor force. Colonial capitalism in the region sought to extract surplus value from the largely unskilled black labor force. The southern African migratory labor movement was the largest in the world, with the longest history and greatest level of organizational sophistication (Crush, Jeeves, and Yudelman 1991). At the level of the individual, the impact of labor migration was, and is, brutal. In 1972, at its height, there were 426,000 men from Botswana, Lesotho, Swaziland, Malawi, and Mozambique employed in South Africa (Whiteside 1986, 25). In addition, there were hundreds of thousands of labor migrants from within South Africa. The most organized labor movement was that of miners, almost all employed on one-year contracts, housed in the most basic of single-sex hostels, with their movement tightly controlled. They were recruited and transported to and from their places of employment by various "labor broking" organizations. The first, the Witwatersrand Labour Organisation (WNLA), began in 1900. In 1912, the Native Recruiting Corporation (NRC) was established. In 1977, these two organizations merged to form The Employment Bureau of Africa (TEBA), still the central recruitment organization for mine workers.

It was not just miners who were employed in South Africa. Labor was needed on the farms and plantations, in industry, and in domestic work. A huge number of migrants traveled from the rural areas and across the borders in search of employment. Black South Africans, especially the men, were an unsettled population, on the move between their workplace and their homes. They were expected to return to their homes between contracts and at the end of their working lives. This was traumatic for families and relationships.

Mobility was in the interest of capital. The reproduction of labor in the rural areas increased the surplus value that could be extracted at the core. Migration was perceived to be in the interest of governments, such as in Lesotho and Malawi, since it meant money was remitted and surplus labor absorbed. This alliance of colonialism, capitalism, and government had disastrous consequences for the health of millions of South Africans (and people across the borders). It continues to do so.

## The legacy of apartheid

Under apartheid, the rights of black South Africans to enter and work in so-called white areas were limited. Apartheid sought to keep the races apart and the black population out of the designated white areas. The draconian legislation of the Nationalist government controlled the movement and the residence of black people. The 1945 Urban Areas Consolidation Act outlined requirements for African peoples' "qualification" to reside legally in white areas. The Natives (Abolition of Passes and Coordination of Documents) Act of 1952 made it compulsory for all black South Africans over the age of 16 to carry a "pass book" at all times in white areas. The law stipulated where, when, and for how long a black person could remain in these areas. Up to 1990 the euphemistically named Department of Cooperation and Development kept detailed records of the number of foreigners (including "citizens" of the "independent" homelands) who could be employed legally in South Africa. In 1985, 1,833,636 people were considered to be migrants.

South Africa was governed primarily for the benefit of the white population. There was great inequality in wealth and, accordingly, discrimination in the provision of health services. A racially divided society, inequality, and widespread poverty were what the ANC government inherited in 1994. However, there were pockets of excellence in health care: this was the country where the world's first successful heart transplant was carried out in 1967. The private medical care system, which covered a small section of the population, was among the best in the world.

It is amazing that the transition to democracy was peaceful and that there was the will to build a new nation (Sparks 2003). However, the free nation was not a healthy one. The physical aspects of this health deficit are discussed below. The psychological scars and dysfunctions of apartheid are a long-term problem and the emergence of AIDS is symbolic of those scars.[3] The spread of HIV was

TABLE 1
South Africa and Comparative Key Health Data: The Past

| Indicator | South Africa | Brazil | Mexico |
|---|---|---|---|
| GNP per capita | 2,560 | 2,940 | 3,030 |
| Life expectancy | 63 | 66 | 70 |
| Infant mortality rate (1991; per 1,000 live births) | 54 | 58 | 36 |
| Maternal mortality rate (1998; per 1,000 live births) | N/A | 140 | 200 |
| Urban population as % of total (1991) | 60 | 76 | 73 |

SOURCE: World Bank (1993).

inevitable under the horrendous governance and economic systems in existence during apartheid. The lack of improvement in health indicators and consequences for other areas of life in South Africa have to be seen in the context of the proliferation of this disease.

## The role of health in developing South Africa

In 1993, the World Bank's sixteenth *World Development Report* was subtitled "Investing in Health." It argued, under the subheading "Why health matters," that

> Good health, as people know from their own experience, is a crucial part of well-being, but spending on health can also be justified on purely economic grounds. Improved health contributes to economic growth in four ways: it reduces production losses caused by worker illness; it permits the use of natural resources that had been totally or nearly inaccessible because of disease; it increases the enrolment of children in school and makes them better able to learn; and it frees for alternative uses resources that would otherwise have to be spent on treating illness. The economic gains are relatively greater for poor people, who are typically most handicapped by ill health and who stand to gain the most from the development of underutilized natural resources. (World Bank 1993, 18)

The arguments for investing in health were expanded in the World Health Organization's (WHO) Commission on Macro-Economics and Health (WHO 2001). For this article, I draw on indicators from the 1993 World Bank report to illustrate what the new government inherited. Table 1 shows key health indicators for South Africa and two other countries with similar development status. It is worth noting that South African data are suspect. The impoverished and badly governed homelands did not collect credible data during apartheid. If anything, the situation was worse than the figures show.

The legacy of apartheid and the problems of the first 15 years of health care in the nation have been excellently captured by a number of authors. Of particular significance is *The Lancet* series on Health in South Africa, published in

TABLE 2
Disability Adjusted Life Years in South Africa

| Disease, Injury, or Condition | Proportion of Total DALYs |
| --- | --- |
| HIV/AIDS | 30.9% |
| Interpersonal violence injury | 6.5% |
| Tuberculosis | 3.7% |
| Road traffic injury | 3.0% |
| Diarrhoeal diseases | 2.9% |
| Lower respiratory infections | 2.8% |
| Low birthweight | 2.6% |
| Asthma | 2.2% |
| Stroke | 2.2% |
| Unipolar depressive disorders | 2.0% |
| Ischaemic heart disease | 1.8% |
| Protein-energy malnutrition | 1.3% |
| Birth asphyxia and birth trauma | 1.2% |
| Diabetes mellitus | 1.1% |
| Alcohol dependence | 1.0% |
| Hearing loss (adult onset) | 1.0% |
| Cataracts | 0.9% |

DALYs = Disability Adjusted Life Years.
SOURCE: Coovadia et al. (2009, 818).

2009.[4] The AIDS epidemic is the most evident, ghastly, and far-reaching of the consequences of this history, and its size and effects are unique to South Africa and the region, especially the Southern African Development Community (SADC) countries. Table 2 shows the burden of disease through the lens of disability adjusted life years. This is a measure of years of "healthy" life lost by virtue of being in a state of poor health or disability.

# Reform, Reconstruction, and Retreat: 1994–2008

The new government faced many challenges: building and uniting a traumatized nation, pulling the economy out of the doldrums, providing services, addressing inequality, and demilitarizing, to mention just a few. The initial plan to address these challenges was encompassed in the Reconstruction and Development Programme, adopted by the ANC government at the time of the transition to democracy. However, in June 1996 a new macroeconomic policy was adopted, due in part to international pressure—the neoliberal Growth Employment and Redistribution (GEAR). This focused on growth aimed to reduce the budget deficit through a mixture of better revenue collection and reduction of government expenditures (see Southall, this volume).

At the transition, the ANC put forward a national health plan that was comprehensive and set out the principles of social justice and equity. The plan recognized the importance of factors outside the biomedical sphere in delivering and ensuring health. For example, obesity leads to diabetes and hypertension and can be averted with lifestyle changes such as proper nutrition and exercise. Specifically for health, the government rapidly rolled out free health care for children and mothers. The White Paper on the "Transformation of the Health System" was endorsed by Parliament in 1997 and provided the foundation for the National Health Act No 61 of 2003. This act aimed to "establish a health system based on decentralised management, on principles of equity, efficiency and sound governance, on internationally recognized research standards, and on a spirit of enquiry and advocacy that encourages participation (Department of Health 2003; see also Delobelle 2013).

*Progress in basic services and social grants*

During the Mandela and Mbeki governments there was a great improvement in the provision of basic services and a massive roll out of social grants, as is shown in Tables 3 and 4. There was, however, little new spending on health and education. These sectors were, and remain, a source of great concern. Much of the literature on the health sector notes the failure to deliver better health, a lack of progress as measured against the Millennium Development Goals, and general reversal of healthiness (Mayosi et al. 2009; Pillay and Jolene Skordis-Worrall 2013).

The attention to basic services and social grants in South Africa is a story of success. The question, therefore, is, Why has the health sector failed? One of the major reasons for the health sector's disappointment was the scale and intractability of the HIV epidemic and the inability of the government to face up to it. There were, however, other contributing factors. Governance was a major issue: the creation of one national Department of Health (DoH) with nine provincial departments was critical. The national DoH sets overall policy; the provinces make provincial policy and deliver public health. The role of the districts and primary health care service, and the responsibility of local government for preventive medicine and health promotion, all created tensions and confusion (Development Bank of South Africa 2008).

Basic primary health care is provided by the state in South Africa. The public sector that treats the majority of people is under resourced. Middle- and high-income earners buy private health care. The problems of health care have been understood and documented, in both academic writings (Delobelle 2013; Coovadia et al. 2009) and in the popular press. The weekly *Mail and Guardian* established a Health Journalism Centre in January 2013.[5]

*The failure in health*

The failure in the health sector can be most clearly seen in the lack of progress toward the Millennium Development Goals. South Africa is only on track with respect to Goal 3—to promote gender equality and empower women. There is

TABLE 3
Social Services in South Africa

| Type | Trend |
| --- | --- |
| Sanitation | In the late 1980s, 62 percent of people living in urban areas had water-borne sewerage, 5 percent had buckets or VIP latrines, and 33 percent had minimal facilities. In rural areas, 14 percent had access to adequate sanitation (VIP or flush toilet). The proportion of households with access to sanitation increased from 50 percent in 1994 to 73 percent in 2007. In 2007, 60 percent of all households had access to a flush or chemical toilet (an increase from 51 percent in 1996). |
| Water | In urban areas in the late 1980s, 59 percent of people had a tap in their house, 14 percent had a tap in the yard, and 7 percent had communal stand pipes. In rural areas, 53 percent had a safe and accessible water supply. Households with access to a water infrastructure meeting RDP standards (a minimum of 25L of potable water per person per day within 200m of household) increased from 62 percent in 1994 to 87 percent in 2007. In 2011, 89.5 percent had access to tap water, although there are provincial disparities. |
| Electricity | Only 35 percent of the South African population had access to electricity in the late 1980s. Households with access to electricity increased from 76.8 percent in 2002 to 82.7 percent in 2011. |
| Housing | Between 1996 and 2007, the proportion of households living in formal dwellings increased from 64 percent to 71 percent; with declines from 16 percent to 15 percent in households not in formal dwellings, and from 20 percent to 12 percent in households living in traditional structures. |
| Literacy | Adult literacy rate increased from 70 percent in 1995 to 74 percent in 2006. In 2011, 91.9 percent of South Africans were literate. |
| Social grants | Between 1996/07 and 2007/08, beneficiaries of social grants increased from 2.4 million to 12.4 million. The new child support grant reached 8.2 million beneficiaries; recipients of the disability grant, which is payable to people with AIDS, doubled to 1.4 million; and old age pensioners rose from 1.6 million to 2.2 million. The number of people benefiting from social grants increased from 12.9 percent in 2002 to 29.6 percent in 2011. |
| Subsidized access and affordability | Water, sanitation, and electricity services have to be paid for by consumers. The government has provided the poorest households with free water and electricity to meet the most basic needs. However, many households are still unable to afford proper access to water and electricity. |

SOURCE: Coovadia et al. (2009, 825).

insufficient progress on Goal 2—achieving universal primary education; Goal 4—reducing child mortality; and Goal 6—combatting HIV/AIDS, malaria, and other diseases. There has been no progress on Goal 5—improving maternal health. On Goal 1—eradicating extreme poverty and hunger—one of the indicators, the percentage of underweight children under five, has actually seen a decline (Department of Health 2012; Statistics South Africa 2012).

TABLE 4
Social Grants in South Africa

| Grant | Amount/ Month | Number of Recipients | Eligibility |
|---|---|---|---|
| Grant for older persons | R1,260 (60 years); R1,280 (>75 years) | 2,663,997 | SA citizen/permanent resident, 60 years old, no other grant, not cared for in a state institution, spouse must comply with the means test, earnings < R49,200/annum, assets <R831,600 |
| Disability | R1,260 | 1,194,901 | SA citizen/refugee, 18–59 years old, no other grant, not cared for in a state institution, assessment report (less than 3 months old), spouse must comply with the means test, earnings <R49,200/annum, assets <R831,600 |
| War veterans | R1,280 | 966 | SA citizen/permanent resident, 60 years old/disabled, fought in the Second World War or the Korean War, not cared for in a state institution, no other grant, spouse must comply with the means test, earnings <R49,200/annum, assets <R831,600 |
| Foster child | R800 | 500,188 | Applicant and child resident in SA, child <18years, court order indicating foster care status, foster parent must be SA citizen/permanent resident/refugee, child must remain in the care of foster parent(s) |
| Child support | R290 | 10,282,531 | Primary care giver must be a SA citizen/permanent resident, the applicant and the child must reside in SA, applicant must be the primary care giver of the child/children concerned, child/children born after December 31, 1993, applicant and spouse must meet the requirements of the means test, cannot apply for more than six nonbiological children, child cannot be cared for in state institution, earnings <R34,800/annum |
| Care dependency | R1200 | 111,334 | SA citizen/permanent resident, applicant and child must be resident in South Africa, child <18 years, medical/assessment report confirming permanent/severe disability, applicant and spouse must meet requirements of the means test, care-dependent child/children must not be permanently cared for in a state institution, earnings <R151,200/annum |
| Grant-in-aid | R280 | 57,040 | Be in receipt of a grant for older people, disability grant or war veteran's grant, require full-time attendance by another person due to physical or mental disability, must not be cared for in an institution that receives subsidy from the state for the care/housing of such beneficiary |

SOURCE: South African Social Security Agency (2011).

In the 2009 *Lancet* series, Chopra and colleagues note the "paradoxical lack of health improvement." The country, they say,

> launched a concerted national and state response to public health challenges, mostly through policy and legislative change, but also by substantial expansion of the number and range of health programmes, especially in primary health-care settings. . . . Data published in 2008 suggest that differences in public health expenditure between rich and poor health districts have substantially narrowed, with greatly increased expenditure in poor districts. Yet a recurring theme across all reports in *The Lancet's* Series on South Africa is the paradox of persistently poor health outputs and outcomes despite high health expenditure and many supportive policies. (Chopra et al. 2009, 1025)

*The Lancet* series identified five main areas to explain the contradiction between the investment in health and poor health outcomes. The first was centralization versus decentralization. Successful central or national policies do not get delivered at the dysfunctional points of care, and in South Africa there has not been a sufficient investment in primary health care. This may be a governance problem—giving resources away from the center is usually problematic for those in control. The second issue is that the private sector provides for about 16 percent of the population but more than 44 percent of the health expenditure takes place in this sector (Mills et al. 2012, 128). If the public sector is indeed subsidizing the private sector, there is an issue, but simply seeing private medicine as a bad thing is a gross oversimplification. Third, too much is spent and invested in tertiary care as opposed to primary care. Fourth, there is a need for multisectoral investments in health. This need is particularly pertinent given the changing burden of disease and the growth in NCDs. The fifth and last issue identified is the fact that so much money has been invested in HIV/AIDS instead of being spread across the health sector.

> The energy, resource mobilisation, and innovation catalysed by the response to the HIV epidemic must be harnessed to achieve a strengthening of the rest of the health system. . . . The country urgently needs a broadened vision of health care in which treatment and preventive programmes for HIV and other disorders are incorporated into a comprehensive primary health-care system and are supported by detailed planning, assessment, and monitoring. (Chopra et al. 2009, 1027)

# Consequences of the HIV and AIDS Epidemic

The country, politicians, policy-makers, and most academics underestimated the financial, human resource, and psychological costs of HIV/AIDS. The failure to wake up to the issue and put in place preventive measures and messages will have a long-term impact.

An estimated 6.4 million people, the largest number in any country, were living with HIV and AIDS in South Africa in 2012. In 2011 (the last year for which there are data), 270,190 South Africans died of AIDS-related causes; there were more than 340,000 new cases (Statistics South Africa 2012; UNAIDS [Joint

United Nations Programme on HIV/AIDS] 2012.) Prevalence, the number of people living with HIV as a percentage of the entire population, rose from 10.6 percent in 2008 to 12.3 percent in 2012. The highest level is in KwaZulu-Natal, where 27.6 percent of the 15–49 age group are infected; the lowest level is in the Western Cape at 9.2 percent (Shisana 2013).

In earlier years, data came from ante-natal clinics, and there was some justification to regard the information skeptically. However, there have been a number of surveys that have confirmed how deep the crisis is. The South African National HIV Prevalence, Incidence, Behaviour and Communication Survey, conducted by the Human Sciences Research Council in 2002, was repeated in 2005, 2008, and 2012. The first survey was

> a watershed cultural and demographic survey, commissioned by former President Nelson Mandela, and it came up with some surprising results! This study sampled a thorough cross-section of 9 963 South Africans from all walks of life. It shows 11 per cent are HIV+, 15.2 per cent of them aged between 15 and 49. Contrary to previous estimates, provinces with large urban informal settlements have the highest incidence of HIV infection. . . . Women are more at risk of infection than men. (Shisana and Simbayi 2002, 2)

These data confirmed what scientists and epidemiologists feared on the basis of the ante-natal data. Nevertheless, South Africa's leadership was already actively arguing that there was no HIV epidemic (and even if there was it was not the cause of the increase in deaths, which was not happening anyway).[6] The Mbeki-led denial of the HIV epidemic has been extensively documented (see, for example, Nattrass 2012; Fourie 2006; Cullinan and Thom 2009). Sadly, political leaders not only buried their heads but also tried to silence those scientists and academics who wanted to face the existing reality and prepare for the inevitable increase in illness and death.

Many of the failures in health can be traced to HIV and the stigma and powerlessness associated with it. It was the unfortunate confluence of a sexually transmitted disease, primarily in the black adult population, in a patriarchal society in denial, that resulted in a disregard for the importance of health and demoralized health workers. As is shown in this article, the blame for failures in the health sector in the first 20 years of the new government can be laid at the door of the AIDS epidemic.

# A Health Report Card: 2013

The health successes in South Africa were undercut by the HIV epidemic. The country, which had been racially divided, now faces a division between those who are affected by AIDS and those who are not. This is still partly a racial division: HIV prevalence in the white, Coloured, and Asian populations is low. It is also increasingly a division across wealth, place of residence, and gender.

The overall health report card shows that as far as political will and policy go, South Africa is doing well. The investment in social grants and the roll out of

TABLE 5
South Africa and Comparative Key Health Data: The Present

| Indicator | South Africa | Brazil | Mexico | Botswana |
|---|---|---|---|---|
| GNI per capita $U.S. | 6,960 | 10,720 | 9,420 | 7,470 |
| Life expectancy | 53 | 73.4 | 76.9 | 53 |
| Infant mortality rate (2011; per 1,000 live births) | 34.7 | 13.9 | 13.4 | 20.3 |
| Urban population as percentage of total (2011) | 62 | 84.6 | 78.1 | 61.6 |
| HIV prevalence 15–49 | 17.3 | 0.3 | 0.3 | 23.4 |

SOURCE: World Bank (2012).

basic services have improved health outcomes. The failure is at the stage of deliv-ery, and with the willingness of people to take responsibility for their own health. The structural drivers of ill-health are critical—but the nation needs to move beyond identifying the problem to come up with solutions. As Table 5 shows, compared to countries such as Brazil and Mexico, South Africa's development has been slow and its health indicators are depressing. However, when compared to the countries with similar levels of HIV infection, the relevant indicators are similar.

Between the writing of the first draft of this article and its publication, the 2012 Human Sciences Research Council (HSRC) survey data were released at the 6th SA AIDS Conference in Durban. The title of the plenary speech by Olive Shishana, the CEO of the HSRC "HIV/AIDS in South Africa: At Last the Glass Is Half Full," summed up the complex and extremely challenging situation. More women than men are infected, and the peak age of infection has risen to between 30 and 34. The epidemic is aging because antiretroviral (ARV) treatment cover-age has increased dramatically. The 2012 survey shows that 2,006,593 people are receiving ARV drugs. This fact and the patients' consequent survival account for the greater number of infections and the aging of the epidemic. An estimated 44 percent of all South Africans know their HIV status, up from 24.7 in 2008. There has been real success in bringing down mother to child transmission rates, from 32 percent in 2000 to just 3.5 percent in 2012.

The bad news, according the HSRC data, is condom use "at last sex" has fallen in all age groups, most significantly from 85.2 percent to 67.4 percent among men aged 15 to 24 and from 66.5 percent to 51 percent among women of the same age group. At the same time, between the 2008 and 2012 surveys, the num-ber of multiple sexual partners has risen in all age groups. In addition, the aver-age age of sexual debut has fallen. All these data suggest that behavior change is not occurring. The growing number of people receiving treatment is putting a strain on the health care system and the national treasury. The South African government covers the bulk of the expenditure. The HIV/AIDS annual budget is R22 billion, of which R5 billion is from donors—mainly the Global Fund for

AIDS, TB and Malaria, and the U.S. President's Emergency Plan for AIDS Relief (PEPFAR). This foreign funding cannot be guaranteed in the future; indeed, PEPFAR plans to reduce its allocation from $500 million in 2013 to $250 million by 2017 (U.S. Department of State 2012).

# The Challenges for Health Care in South Africa: The Third Decade

South Africa has had the benefit of 20 years of democratic rule. The leadership (and its style) in the national government and in the Department of Health changed when Mbeki was forced to resign in September 2008. There are five key areas that South Africa needs to address in the years ahead to deliver health care to its population.

## Delivery and policy

Health policy is developed nationally and adapted to fit the diverse provincial needs. Under the heading of delivery and policy, consideration must be given to human resources for health, which are a significant limitation on the country's ability effectively to deliver good health outcomes. Progress has been made. The number of public sector doctors increased from 10,880 in 2002 to 17,439 in 2011, and the number of nurses from 97,111 to 131,592 (Whiteside, Cohen, and Strauss 2013). However, there is an uneven distribution of human resources for health across provinces, between urban and rural areas, and between the public and private sector. Only 12 percent of the country's doctors and 19 percent of its nurses work in rural facilities, serving 43.6 percent of the population. Attrition due to HIV/AIDS and migration has worsened the ratio of professional and enrolled nurses and doctors within the public sector (Whiteside, Cohen, and Strauss 2013).

Although South Africa's health care infrastructure has improved since 1994, regional and sectoral discrepancies persist. The fragility of the health system was clearly illustrated in December 2012 when Médecins Sans Frontières had to step in to supply ARVs for 50,000 HIV-infected patients who were dependent on the Mthatha medical depot. This depot is responsible for supplying drugs to a part of the Eastern Cape Province. An estimated 5,494 adults taking ARVs went at least one day without treatment due to severe drug supply and delivery disruptions.

Overall expenditure on public health grew from R16.4 billion in 2008/09 to R26 billion in 2011/12. A key component of the expanded health budget is the National Health Insurance (NHI) plan. This is intended to be phased in over 14 years. The NHI model will restructure and strengthen the public health system and improve the quality of care. The implementation of the NHI is one of the key challenges facing the health ministry and the nation. It will require significant financial expenditure. NHI-related public spending increased from

R119.3 million in 2008/09 to R162.6 million in 2011/12, and is expected to increase to R670.2 million by 2015/16. The plan's affordability is contested: the costs of administration may be underestimated and economic growth predictions optimistic. Health, though, is, and must remain, a priority for NHI.

# Noncommunicable Diseases

NCDs are conditions that are noninfectious and nontransmissible. They include autoimmune diseases, heart disease, stroke, many cancers, asthma, diabetes, chronic kidney disease, osteoporosis, and Alzheimer's. These diseases are sometimes (incorrectly) called chronic diseases, but should be distinguished by their noninfectious cause, not their duration. According to the WHO, NCDs are the leading global cause of mortality. "Of the 57 million global deaths in 2008, 36 million were due to NCDs" (WHO 2013). That is approximately 63 percent of total deaths worldwide. If HIV (and linked with it, TB) were to be controlled in South Africa, the major causes of death and disability in the country would be stroke, diabetes, and heart disease. Thirteenth and fourteenth on the list of conditions accounting for years of life lost would be chronic kidney disease and hypertensive heart disorders.

These risks are determined by a person's background, lifestyle, and environment. In 1993 South Africa adopted stringent tobacco control legislation; the benefits of this shift will be felt in the years ahead. There are still major issues of diet, obesity, alcohol consumption, and high blood pressure, however. These problems are set to increase in severity. The Institute of Health Metrics and Evaluation (2010) notes,

> Overall, the three risk factors that account for the most disease burden in South Africa are alcohol use, high body-mass index, and high blood pressure. The leading risk factors for children under 5 and adults aged 15–49 years were suboptimal breastfeeding and alcohol use. (p. 3)

Other issues facing South Africa include interpersonal violence; road traffic accidents; and mental illnesses, including depression and anxiety. It is worth noting that the prevalence of depression and anxiety among people who are living with HIV and AIDS is almost double that of uninfected individuals; the risk of suicide is elevated among this population as well (Govender and Schlebusch 2013, 58). Addressing these issues and the underlying causes of NCDs means looking at lifestyle choices. Lifestyle questions in turn raise questions about structural determinants—housing, sanitation, access to clean water, diet, and access to health services. Great strides have been made in these areas since 1994. Nevertheless, people need to feel invested in their society and that they have the power to improve their lives and those of their children. These concepts have been discussed by a number of authors (James 2007; Wilkinson and Pickett 2009).

# Migrants and Refugees

According to the United Nations High Commission for Refugees (UNHCR) at the end of 2011, some 220,000 asylum-seekers were registered in South Africa. They were mainly from Bangladesh, the Democratic Republic of the Congo (DRC), Ethiopia, Somalia, and Zimbabwe. South Africa has the highest annual number of asylum applications worldwide, with 106,904 applications in 2011. The UNHCR notes there was a reduction from 2010 and suggests that the reduction has come about because of "a more stable political and socio-economic situation in Zimbabwe and the imposition of restrictive measures by countries in the sub-region and beyond to reduce mixed-migration movements" (UNHCR 2013, 118). By December 2011, 63,000 people, mainly from Angola, Burundi, the DRC, Rwanda, and Somalia, were recognized as refugees with freedom of movement, permission to work, and the right to access basic social services through grants. They are required to have documentation, but the sheer number of asylum applications make it difficult to ensure that the refugee status determination process is fair and efficient (UNHCR 2013).

The UNHCR planning figures for 2013 estimated that there would be 480,520 refugees and asylum-seekers in January 2013. Of these, 396,000 are asylum-seekers, the vast majority (261,000) from Zimbabwe (UNHCR 2013). The actual number of refugees and economic and political and illegal migrants is much higher. The number of illegal (undocumented) immigrants in South Africa ranges between 2 million and 8 million (Mwakikagile 2008, 217). Exact figures are difficult to ascertain. The *Mail & Guardian* (2013) reports that deporting illegal immigrants costs the South African government about R90 million per year, and this has prompted calls to legitimize their stay. The majority of these illegals are Zimbabweans, and deportations were reported to have increased by 48 percent between January and May 2013, with between 100 and 200 deportations per day (*The Herald* 2013).

Refugees with disabilities, the elderly, and children in foster care qualify for government grants but face obstacles in obtaining them (UNHCR 2013). In South Africa, people with refugee status are accorded the same rights as South African citizens, except for the right to vote (Department of Home Affairs 2013). The South African Refugees Act of 1998[7] names these rights as the right to full legal protection as stipulated in Chapter 2 of the national constitution, to an identity document, to a South African travel document, to seek employment, to basic health services, and to a basic primary education.

South Africa is the economic powerhouse of the region. Its role in providing health care for the region needs to be further examined. The political leadership recognizes that border communities, particularly from Zimbabwe, Swaziland, and Mozambique will seek health care in South Africa. Refugees have an entitlement to care. Questions will arise, however, if there is an increase in the number of people moving to South Africa in search of health services.

# Conclusion

Changes in South Africa since 1994 have been, for the most part, revolutionary. A country that faced an uncertain future managed a successful transition to democracy. However, huge challenges remain, one of the main ones being the provision of social services. In that category, health services are critical.

There is a known HIV prevalence and a fairly certain projected incidence going forward. The number and needs of those who are infected can be predicted. The main drivers of ill health and the HIV epidemic are social and psychological, and they require a transformation of society. A major concern for South Africa is the high level of unemployment (especially among youths) and the need to find sources of income for the poor of the nation. An answer might surely be to build an "AIDS economy," where we recognize the realities and look at ways to address them that meet political and social needs.

A slightly daring and likely unpopular position to take is that health provision and access to health care are part of a social contract between government and its citizens. There must be public provision of health care services. Such a social contract would mean that citizens undertake to stay healthy in exchange for a health care system. People receiving ARV therapy would be expected and encouraged to engage with society as caregivers, community development workers, and in a myriad of other ways (and they should get paid for doing so).

The international community is phasing out its development assistance to South Africa, and doing so is reasonable. It could, however, consider supporting innovative ideas. South Africa was and is exceptional. AIDS is exceptional. The coincidence of the political transition in 1994 and the spread of the disease was more than unfortunate. The challenge now is to face up to the long-term implications of the AIDS epidemic for South Africa.

## Notes

1. Perhaps optimistically, some of us believe that his bizarre reaction to AIDS played a part in his losing power.

2. The Universities of Natal and Durban Westville merged in 2004 to form the University of KwaZulu-Natal.

3. The role of sexually transmitted diseases and their being a bell weather for the ills of society have been captured in a seminal paper by Sydney Kark (1949).

4. See http://www.thelancet.com/series/health-in-south-africa.

5. See mg.co.za/article/2013-02-19-mg-health-journalism-centre-1.

6. It is impossible to convey the "Through the Looking Glass" world we lived in. There was a sense of disbelief among scientists and activists. The tomes written since to try to explain the positions taken by the leadership are informative, but we need the people involved actually to explain their reasoning. Sadly, this probably will not happen, partly because we regard the period as one of embarrassment, best forgotten.

7. Refugees Act of 1998, Act No. 130. (1998).

# References

African National Congress (ANC). 1994. *A national health plan for South Africa*. Available from http://www.anc.org.za/show.php?id=257 (accessed 15 June 2013).

Bower, Carol. 2014. The plight of women and children: Advancing South Africa's least privileged. *The ANNALS of the American Academy of Political and Social Science*, this volume.

Chopra, Mickey, Joy E. Lawn, David Sanders, Peter Barron, Salim S. Abdool Karim, Debbie Bradshaw, Rachel Jewkes, Quarraisha Abdool Karim, Alan J. Flisher, Bongani M. Mayosi, Stephen M. Tollman, Gavin J. Churchyard, and Hoosen Coovadia. 2009. Achieving the health Millennium Development Goals for South Africa: Challenges and priorities. *The Lancet* 374:1023–31.

Coovadia, Hoosen, Rachel Jewkes, Peter Barron, David Sanders, and Diane McIntyre. 2009. The health and health system of South Africa: Historical roots of current public health challenges. *The Lancet* 374:817–34.

Crush, Jonathan, Alan Jeeves, and David Yudelman. 1991. *South Africa's labour empire: A history of black migrancy to the gold mines*. Boulder, CO: Westview Press; and Cape Town: David Philip.

Cullinan, Kerry, and Anso Thom. 2009. *The virus vitamins and vegetables: The South African AIDS mystery*. Johannesburg: Jacana.

Delobelle, Peter. 2013. The health system in South Africa: Historical perspectives and current challenges. In *South Africa in focus: Economic, political and social issues*, ed. C. C. Wolhuter, 159–96. New York, NY: Nova Science.

Department of Health. 2003. *National Health Act No 61 of 2003*. Cape Town: Government Printers.

Department of Health. 2012. *The National Ante-natal Sentinel HIV & Syphilis Prevalence Survey in South Africa, 2011*. Pretoria: Department of Health. Available from http://www.doh.gov.za/docs/presentations/2013/Antenatal_Sentinel_survey_Report2012_final.pdf (accessed 15 June 2013).

Department of Home Affairs. 2013. *Refugee status & asylum*. Available from http://www.home-affairs.gov.za/index.php/refugee-status-asylum.

Development Bank of South Africa. 2008. *A roadmap for the reform of the South African health system: A process convened and facilitated by the Development Bank of South Africa*. Midrand: Development Bank of South Africa.

Fourie, Pieter. 2006. *The political management of HIV and AIDS in South Africa: One burden too many?* Basingstoke, UK: Palgrave Macmillan.

Govender, Romona Devi, and Lourens Schlebusch. 2013. A suicide risk screening scale for HIV-infected persons in the immediate post-diagnosis period. *South African Journal of HIV Medicine* 14 (2): 58–63.

Gouws, Eleanor, and Qurraisha Abdool Karim. 2010. HIV infection in South Africa: The evolving epidemic. In *HIV/AIDS in South Africa*, 2nd ed., eds. Salim S. Abdool Karim and Qurraisha Abdool Karim, 55–72. Cambridge: Cambridge University Press.

*The Herald*. 2013. Zimbabwe: Deportations up 48 percent. Available from http://allafrica.com/stories/201305100703.html (accessed 17 May 2013).

Institute of Health Metrics and Evaluation, University of Washington. 2010. *GBD profile: South Africa*. Available from http://www.healthmetricsandevaluation.org/sites/default/files/country-profiles/GBD%20Country%20Report%20-%20South%20Africa.pdf (accessed 17 June 2013).

James, Oliver. 2007. *Affluenza*. London: Vermilion.

Kark, Sydney L. 1949. The social pathology of syphilis in Africans. *South African Medical Journal* 23:77–84.

*Mail & Guardian*. 17 May 2013. Zimbabwe wants SA to keep its citizens. *Mail & Guardian*. Available from http://mg.co.za.

Mayosi, Bongani M., Joy E. Lawn, Ashley van Niekerk, Debbie Bradshaw, Salim S. Abdool Karim, and Hoosen M. Coovadia, for The Lancet South Africa Team. 2009. Health in South Africa: Changes and challenges since 2009. *The Lancet* 380:2029–43.

Mills, Anne, John E. Ataguba, James Akazili, Jo Borghi, Bertha Garshong, Suzan Makawia, Gemini Mtei, Bronwyn Harris, Jane Macha, Filip Meheus, and Di McIntyre. 2012. Equity in financing and use of health care in Ghana, South Africa, and Tanzania: Implications for paths to universal coverage. *The Lancet* 380:126–33.

Mwakikagile, Godfrey. 2008. *South Africa and its people*. Pretoria: New Africa Press.

Nattrass, Nicoli. 2012. *The AIDS conspiracy: Science fights back*. New York, NY: Columbia University Press.

Pillay, Timesh D., and Jolene Skordis-Worrall. 2013. South African health financing reform 2000–2010: Understanding the agenda-setting process. *Health Policy* 109:321–31.

Shisana, Olive. 2013. HIV/AIDS in South Africa: At last the glass is half full. Plenary speech given at the 6th South African AIDS Conference, 20 June, Durban, South Africa.

Shisana, Olive, and Leickness Simbayi. 2002. Abstract. In *Nelson Mandela/HSRC study of HIV/AIDS: South African national HIV prevalence, behavioural risks and mass media: Household Survey 2002*. Pretoria: Human Sciences Research Council. Available from http://www.hsrc.ac.za (accessed 17 June 2013).

South African Social Security Agency (SASSA). 2011. *Annual report. 2011/2012*. Pretoria: SASSA. Available from www.sassa.gov.za (accessed 17 June 2013).

Southall, Roger. 2014. Democracy at risk? Politics and governance under the ANC. *The ANNALS of the American Academy of Political and Social Science*, this volume.

Sparks, Allister. 2003. *Beyond the miracle inside the new South Africa*. Chicago, IL: University of Chicago Press.

Statistics South Africa. 2012. Mid-year population estimates. Pretoria: Statistics South Africa. Available from http://www.statssa.gov.za/publications/P0302/P03022011.pdf (accessed 20 May 2013).

Tsampiras, Carla Zelda. 2012. Politics, polemics and practice: A history of narratives about, and responses to, AIDS in South Africa, 1980–1995. D. Phil thesis, Rhodes University, Grahamstown, South Africa.

UNAIDS (Joint United Nations Programme on HIV/AIDS). 2011. *HIV and AIDS estimates*. Geneva: UNAIDS. Available from http://www.unaids.org (accessed 17 June 2013).

United Nations High Commissioner for Refugees (UNHCR). 2013. Planning figures for South Africa. Geneva: UNHCR. Available from http://www.unhcr.org/cgi-bin/texis/vtx/page?page=49e485aa6 (accessed 17 June 2013).

U.S. Department of State. August 2012. *Partnership framework implementation plan in support of South Africa's national HIV, STI & TB response 2012/13–2016/17*. Washington, DC: U.S. Department of State. Available from http://photos.state.gov/libraries/southafrica/231713/Pepfar_001/PFIP_August_2012.pdf (accessed 9 September 2013).

von Feigenblatt, Otto F. 2008. The South African transition: A holistic approach to the analysis of the struggle leading to the 1994 elections. *Journal of Alternative Perspectives in the Social Sciences* 1 (1): 48–80.

Whiteside, Alan. 1985. *Some aspects of labour relations between the Republic of South Africa and neighbouring states. Part 1: Legislation and agreements*. Pretoria: Human Sciences Research Council.

Whiteside, Alan. 1986. *Some aspects of labour relations between the Republic of South Africa and neighbouring states. Part 2: Economic implications*. Pretoria: Human Sciences Research Council.

Whiteside, Alan. 1990. *AIDS in Southern Africa: A position paper for the Development Bank of Southern Africa*. Durban: Development Bank of Southern Africa.

Whiteside, Alan, Jamie Cohen, and Mike Strauss. 2013. Making hard choices in AIDS: The role of economics in reconciling a science and policy divide. Unpublished manuscript.

Wilkinson, Richard, and Kate Pickett. 2009. *The spirit level: Why equality is better for everyone*. London: Penguin.

Wolpe, Harold. 1995. The uneven transition from apartheid in South Africa. *Transformation* 27:88–101.

World Bank. 1993. *World development report 1993: Investing in health*. Oxford: Oxford University Press. Available from http://files.dcp2.org/pdf/WorldDevelopmentReport1993.pdf.

World Bank. 2012. *World development report 2012: Gender, equity, and development*. Washington, DC: World Bank. Available from http://siteresources.worldbank.org/INTWDR2012/Resources/7778105-1299699968583/7786210-1315936222006/Complete-Report.pdf.

World Health Organization (WHO). 2001. *Macroeconomics and health: Investing in health for economic development*. Report of the Commission on Macroeconomics and Health. Geneva: WHO.

World Health Organization (WHO). 2013. Global Health Observatory, Deaths from NCDs. Available from http://www.who.int/gho/ncd/mortality_morbidity/ncd_total_text/en/index.html.

# Curbing the Killing Fields: Making South Africa Safer

ELRENA VAN DER SPUY
and
CLIFFORD SHEARING

South Africa is often held up as an enviable example of a country that avoided a full-blown civil war. Twenty years into the new constitutional democracy, however, the continuation of social conflict and criminal violence begs the question as to whether South Africa deserves to be described as "postconflict." In this article, we take stock of contemporary conversations about crime. First, key dimensions of South Africa's crime problem are described, drawing on a composite report on violent crime published in 2009 by the Centre for the Study of Violence and Reconciliation (Johannesburg). We then focus on three recent episodes to illustrate some of the dimensions of violence in South Africa's multifaceted society. Finally, we take stock of some select approaches to dealing with violent criminality and review ideas for containing crime and making South Africa safer.

*Keywords:* South Africa; violent crime; safety; policing; crime policy

## The Killing Fields in South Africa in Broad Perspective[1]

South Africa has always been a violent, crime-ridden country. The inauguration of the new government under President Nelson Mandela of the African National Congress (ANC), elected by universal franchise in April 1994, was a time of near universal euphoria. This democratic transition led many to hope that the

*Elrena van der Spuy is a professor in the Department of Public Law and a member of the Centre of Criminology at the University of Cape Town.*

*Clifford Shearing is the chair of Criminology and director of the Centre of Criminology, Faculty of Law at the University of Cape Town. He holds the South African National Research Foundation Chair in Security and Justice.*

NOTE: Thanks to Jeffrey Lever for his many critical comments along the way.

DOI: 10.1177/0002716213513540

popular legitimacy bestowed by a democratic regime would bring about much higher levels of social harmony, including a sharp reduction in the rate of violent crime. It did not happen. Instead, as political conflict subsided, violent crime rates continued ever upward (a trend that had with hindsight become evident in the rate of homicide since 1985) (Shaw 1997).

From the mid-1990s the "crisis in crime" in the new South Africa became the subject of heated debate. Rates of violent crime were not only rising from an already high base, but the criminality itself seemed malevolently brutal (Altbeker 2007). Homicide as a proxy indicator of violent crime illustrates the point. In a United Nations study involving calculations of average homicide rates for the 20-year period 1980 to 2000, Shaw, van Dijk, and Rhomberg (2003, 44) found the global average homicide rate to be 7 per 100,000. For the same time period, the comparable rates for South Africa and Columbia were 59 and 68, respectively, that is, eight to nine times the global average. But it was not just murder. Using police-recorded data for 2002 to arrive at a comparison of countries included in another survey, the South African rate of reported rape topped the list of countries at 116 per 100,000 compared to 24 for the United States and 22 per 100,000 for England/Wales (Harrendorf, Heiskanen, and Malby 2010, 25).

This crime trend began to reverse itself in 2004. That it has indeed begun to decline significantly from that date seems indisputable. Statistics released by the South African police reveal quite large reductions in some of the national rates of serious crime for the eight-year period between 2004 and 2012. Comparable data from other sources confirm that the trend is downward. The reductions hold sway for almost all categories of crime except nonresidential robberies. For example, assault with grievous bodily harm declined by almost a third from 535 to 381 per 100,000. Robbery with aggravating circumstances had been reduced by 30.5 percent, from 272.2 to 200.1 per 100,000. Murders have been reduced by 27.6 percent, which translates into a reduction per 100,000 of the population from 40.3 to 30.9 between 2004 and 2012 (South African Police Service [SAPS] 2012a).

These declining rates in homicide support both positive and negative interpretations. The good news is that the homicide rate has dropped sharply over an eight-year period;[2] but, on the other hand, South African figures remain four-and-a-half times higher than the (available but very incomplete) global average of 6.9 murders per 100,000 (Parker 2012).

The reduction in police-recorded crimes, however, has not translated into radically improved perceptions of safety among South Africans. Fear of crime has declined somewhat, but a country-wide survey of households conducted by Statistics South Africa (2012, 2) found that 35 percent of households were of the opinion that crime had increased, 30 percent indicated that crime had stayed the same, and 37 percent believed that both violent and nonviolent crime in their neighborhoods had decreased. Fear of home burglary in particular remains rampant; it was described by 57.4 percent of households as the most feared crime, followed by street robbery (29.6 percent), murder (38.8 percent), and sexual assault (23.6 percent).

From its inception in 1994, the ANC government found the high rates of violent crime an unexpected but unavoidable major policy challenge. The first phase of ANC rule followed an idealistic course. High-minded policy documents directed the administration's sweeping liberal reforms. The ensuing reality check, however, was not far ahead—along came the rise in the rates of violent crime. Policies regarding crime, policing, and the criminal justice system came under heavy pressure. The original policy reform included reversal of the coercive and race-based measures of the old regime and the replacement of personnel. Having been more or less forced to abandon long-standing socialist approaches before its advent to power, the ANC government had adopted a seemingly radical policy document of socioeconomic reform—the Reconstruction and Development Program (RDP). Facing state bankruptcy by 1996, the government was forced to adopt a domestic equivalent of the structural adjustment programs that the International Monetary Fund (IMF) had imposed on Africa since the 1980s. Numerous reform programs fell by the wayside, including extensive reform of the South African police. Another casualty was an overarching National Crime Prevention Strategy (NCPS), embracing all relevant ministries that had been adopted just as budget cuts took effect. Thereafter, government strategy alternated between the coercive and punitive and the more liberal ideas that continued to flow from Western consultants. We consider some of these developments here.

Neither reform nor punishment had brought immediate gains on the crime front by the mid-2000s. Consequently, the criminal justice cluster under the Ministry of Safety and Security engaged a respected Johannesburg-based research institution, the Centre for the Study of Violence and Reconciliation (CSVR), to conduct research and provide recommendations on how to combat crime. Experienced researchers, using up-to-date criminological knowledge, produced a report that was extensive and well informed (CSVR 2007, 2008a, 2008b, 2008c, 2008d, 2010).

When the CSVR conclusions were made public, an uproar ensued. The ministry and its secretariat, together with parliamentarians, felt that the CSVR had failed to provide what had been wanted. For example, the Police Secretariat, Jenni Irish-Qhobosheane remarked, "There was nothing incredibly new that hit us in the face or took us by surprise, for example, the recommended innovations and suggestions are not anything new" (Defence Web 2010).

The truth of the matter is, however, that the CSVR's researchers had conscientiously gone through a mass of material, thoroughly assembled frightening statistics in all their detail (while observing correctly just how unsatisfactory the country's, and especially the police's, data collection was), and responded with an analysis that reflected mainstream conventional wisdom in academia in South Africa, and elsewhere, about why young men commit so much violent crime. The "legacy of apartheid" still weighed heavily on the country, with widespread poverty, deprivation, social exclusion, and social dislocation (CSVR 2010, 5). The result was a "culture of violence" fed by unmet expectations and a highly materialistic and exhibitionist culture.

The CSVR study was concerned almost solely with what might be termed run-of-the-mill violent crime. But the violence that so wracks the country is by no means limited to such crime. Indeed, while the researchers were busy collecting historical data, the country experienced one of its most pronounced outbreaks of mass violence since democracy in 1994. In May 2008, sixty-two people were killed in mob violence in several major cities. These were the so-called xenopho-bia riots. The victims were from mostly other African countries (Kapp 2008, 1986).

In addition, from 2008 onward, "collective violence" on a much less lethal scale had already become widespread. Three forms of this violence were pre-dominant. First, there was violence associated with strike action. A second form represented a sort of rerun of mass action that was so prevalent in the 1980s and that involved local communities expressing their violent dissatisfaction with one or another expected provisions of state services, or what are now simply termed "service delivery protests" (von Holdt et al. 2011). Both of these forms of protest are now so common that they pass hardly remarked on beyond the areas affected. The third form has been commonly termed "vigilantism," in which groups of (mostly) township residents turned on alleged mis-doers and killed them.

## Crime, Justice, and Policing: Three Recent Episodes

South Africa's killings fields are spread across a wide frontier, both spatially and socially. They traverse the border between the private and public domain, and stretch from urban localities into the rural hinterland. The protagonists in the violent dramas—be they perpetrators, victims, or bystanders—include a cosmo-politan spread of South Africans. And yet identities forged along race, class, gender, and age lines converge in such a way that predominantly poor young black and Coloured men and women are pushed to the forefront of the crime drama, in their capacities as both perpetrators and as victims. In the background looms a state operating often ineptly, albeit in a difficult environment. The fol-lowing three sketches attempt to provide more concrete illustrations of the kinds of insecurities South Africans confront and to whom or what they turn for com-fort. The three crime stories offer no more than snapshots of the bigger picture of injury and violence in South Africa.

### Bredasdorp: Lethal rape and acquaintance violence

Concern about sexual violence dominates South African discussions on the topic of violent crime. But even to a public hardened by frequent media reports of rape, what occurred in February 2013 in the small rural town of Bredasdorp, about 180 kilometers from Cape Town, was hard to digest. In the early morning of February 2, Anene Booysen was found on a construction site. Just five hours earlier she had been socializing with friends at a local pub. She suffered a terrible death. She was gang raped, her fingers and legs broken, her throat slit, a broken glass bottle lodged in her stomach, and her entrails plucked out and covered in sand (*Die Burger* 2013).

It was in this unfortunate way that fame came to Anene Booysen. President Jacob Zuma described the incident as "shocking," "cruel," and "inhumane" (SAPA 2013). In the days and weeks that followed Booysen's death, the scourge of rape was debated. The endemic nature of abuse in intimate relationships was reemphasized and much was made about the link between sexual violence and wider societal violence (Lancaster 2013). Several months after the brutality, there was also not much consolation to be derived from the criminal justice system. Several of her "acquaintances" had been arrested, but only one was held on criminal charges.

When it comes to sexual violence in South Africa, dramatic terms are often used to describe the state of affairs. For example, one of the six CSVR reports was titled: "A State of Sexual Tyranny" (CSVR 2008c). The report documented the widespread incidence of sexual assault, in particular rape, against women in South Africa. It made a point to say that such victimization of women (the bulk of them under the age of 20) is not confined to the major urban areas but appears to be common in various rural locales. It estimated that rape is probably reported to the police approximately one in four times, and argued on this basis that it can be estimated that 300,000 rapes take place per annum (CSVR 2008c, 28). The majority of male sexual assailants are men known to the victim, though "stranger" rape is not infrequent in the urban areas. Gang rape, too, the report noted, is frequently encountered.

Research into the problem of sexual violence has proliferated over the past two decades. Estimations of risk vary from one dataset to another, but all concur that for South African women the risk of sexual violence is extremely high. According to official police statistics, 64,514 sexual offences were reported in 2011/2012 (which incidentally constitutes a decrease of 6.7 percent from 2004/2005) (SAPS 2012a). The total number of sexual offences for that year amounted to 179 per day, or seven every hour. The picture worsens when we review research conducted by a number of leading field organizations. One study in Gauteng revealed that one in four of the women whom they interviewed had experienced sexual violence (Gender Links and Medical Research Council 2010). Overall, only one in twenty-five women who had been raped reported it to the police. Data also capture that at 8.8 per 100,000, South Africa has the highest reported intimate female homicide rate in the world (Norman et al. 2007, 697). Research targeting men as potential offenders paints a further worrisome picture. In a study using a randomly selected sample of men, aged between 18 and 49, from the general population of the Eastern Cape and KwaZulu-Natal provinces, Jewkes et al. (2010, 23) established that 27.6 percent of the 1,686 men had forced a woman to have sex, and the majority had done so more than once. In exploring the motivations underlying rape, researchers have found that feelings of sexual entitlement, a desire to have fun, or anger were key motivations. Such findings led Jewkes et al. (2010) to comment, "What we see here is a set of attitudes reflecting men's views that they are legitimate in the use of violence against women, and women in many respects acquiescing to this."[3]

However, in its analysis of the problem, the CSVR report does not go beyond the standard explanations, reporting that there is an all-pervasive "culture of patriarchy" and sexual entitlement on one hand (CSVR 2008c, 83), and a "crisis in masculinity" ("insecurity and threatened masculinity") (CSVR 2008c, 90) among lower-class men on the other. Here, the CSVR report simply echoes the explanatory constructs used in other leading research on the topic (see Jewkes et al. 2010; Moffett 2006). In such discussions, the crisis in masculinity is linked to the unsettling experiences of "structural exclusion" and "relative deprivation" in the post-apartheid order. In its recommendations, the CSVR report argued that an investigation into the sources of men's insecurity would go some way toward "understanding" the psychosocial dynamics at play among emasculated men in the postcolony.

### Marikana: A platinum mine, striking workers, and lethal force

After 1870 the major driver of South Africa's industrial revolution was mining of the country's abundant mineral resources. Indeed, without the discovery of the extensive diamond and gold fields between the 1860s and 1890, it is hard to conceive how the country could ever have become sub-Saharan Africa's leading industrial economy. After diamonds and gold came coal and platinum. The mining industry attracted international capital, entrepreneurial ability, skilled labor, and an almost unquenchable demand for tens of thousands of cheap workers doing the dirty work at the mining seam-face.

Along with the rise of the mining industry came unionization, industrial turmoil, and violent clashes between workers and state law and order forces, not to mention the institutionalization of a captive migrant black labor force. A century or so after the initial discoveries, mechanization, de-racialization, and more sophisticated managerial techniques appeared to have brought stability to the mines. The majority of the massive bloc of black miners had united behind one organization, the National Union of Mineworkers (NUM).

Appearances were, however, deceptive. As the established union and affiliate of the ANC-aligned trade union federation—the Congress of South African Trade Unions (Cosatu)—the NUM had grown lax and unresponsive to the most vociferous voices in its ranks (Southall 2012). A rival yet unrecognized body began to build support among leading sectors of mine workers. The Association of Mineworkers and Construction Union (AMCU) challenged the hegemony of the NUM. On the platinum mines, the AMCU gained the key support of machine rock drillers, behind whom many of the lesser-skilled rank-and-file miners lined up. For reasons that are hard to fathom, management, the NUM, or the state itself did not position themselves to defuse a looming crisis.

As an unrecognized union, AMCU was unable to call on available industrial reconciliation mechanisms. The resulting strike at the Marikana platinum mine near Rustenburg grew totally out of hand. The rock drillers were striking for a two-fold wage increase at a time when the global demand for platinum had decreased and lower prices had been eating into the industry's profits (Southall 2012). Before long, the strike turned violent. In the first week, ten people died; six were mineworkers, two security guards, and two policemen. The policemen were hacked to death. Then a large group of miners assembled on a small hill outside the mine overlooking the waiting police cordon. The strikers held spears and sticks in their hands. They advanced and the police opened fire with automatic weapons. When the police ceased firing, there were thirty-four dead strikers. Just how they all died immediately became controversial. Allegations arose that only sixteen died when police first opened fire and that the rest were killed as police pursued fleeing strikers outside the glare of the media (Chapple and Barnett 2012). Immediately, the killings became public. The national commissioner of police, Riah Phiyega, appeared on national TV and made the injudicious comment that no one should point fingers or assign blame. But of course fingers were pointed at the police, who deployed deadly force at dispersing strikers instead of using less lethal strategies of crowd management (Bruce 2012). Soon there was talk of a "toxic collusion" between "state and capital," which had paved the way for state violence (Alexander et al. 2012). Further allegations of police tampering with the crime scene cast additional aspersions on the role of the police (Hlongwane 2012). Shortly after the shooting, the president appointed the Farlam Commission to examine the role of the mining company, the labor unions, the workers, and the security forces in escalating the conflict and to examine the police's use of lethal force. The Farlam Commission hearings revealed a security organization under stress and in considerable disarray.

### Khayelitsha: Informal settlement, police inefficiency, and self-help justice

The sprawling township of Khayelitsha, east of Cape Town, combines extreme density, socioeconomic underdevelopment, and high rates of unemployment, all of which affect its youth population. Population estimates for the area vary considerably, but even the lower end of the scale estimates that 600,000 people are squashed into an area of 6 square kilometers. Incidents of violent crime are, by national comparison, high in the area.

In October 2011, five hundred Khayelitsha residents gathered outside the office of Helen Zille, Premier of the Western Cape Province, calling for a commission of inquiry into the state of policing in that province. A consortium of NGOs active in the area (Equal Education, Social Justice Coalition, and the Treatment Action Campaign), represented by the Women's Legal Centre, had started to lobby for official action some time before this demonstration (Davis 2012). Zille referred the issue to the office of the provincial commissioner and later to Phiyega, the newly appointed national police commissioner. Phiyega acknowledged receipt of the complaints in June 2012 and requested a three-week delay to investigate them.

The heart of the petitions was that the police response to incidences of widespread criminal victimization in Khayelitsha had long been inadequate. The submission that the Women's Legal Centre prepared for the office of the premier argued that widespread perceptions of police indifference, incompetence, and corruption had contributed to a loss of community faith in the police. The gap left by the police had been filled by self-help "justice." Anticrime vigilante killings, so the argument went, had shown a steady increase in recent years. During the course of 2012 alone, twenty anticrime mob killings—often termed "vigilantism"—occurred in the informal settlements of the area (Nombembe 2012; John 2012). Civil society spokespersons argued that such killings, often spontaneous, were symptoms of much deeper issues related to the state neglect and police inefficiency, which had resulted in a consequent breakdown of trust in the police (De Waal 2012).

Shortly after the inquiry into policing in Khayelitsha, politicking began. The minister of safety and security sought a court interdict, which questioned the constitutionality of the inquiry. The minister's reaction was hardly surprising given the fierce contestation between an ANC-aligned national ministry and the Democratic Alliance's control of the Western Cape provincial government. To subpoena the provincial police to appear before the commission was deemed a direct attack on the national ministry. In January 2013, the High Court dismissed the interdict, paving the way for public hearings.[4] The ministry then indicated that it would appeal the case to the Constitutional Court.

Interestingly enough, from documentation submitted to the commission, it appears that the police did in fact appoint a task team to make a "qualitative assessment" of the allegations that civil society made. During July 2012, inspections were held at three police stations in Khayelitsha: Site B, Harare, and Lingelethu West. The report of the task team (marked confidential) paints a picture of institutional disarray. All three stations had benefited from infrastructural upgrades, which flowed from the presidential police station plan, an initiative dating back to 1999. Over the past decade, the police in the area had received increases in both personnel and vehicles. Despite being "relatively well resourced," noted the task team, the police were not meeting the expectations of the community. There were high rates of absenteeism (almost a third on any given day), poor record keeping, and weak investigative action (SAPS 2012b, 8–9). In all three of the stations a large number of police personnel had been subjected to internal disciplinary procedures, some repeatedly, for various incidences of misconduct (SAPS 2012b, 15). Relations between community police forums and police management, conceded the task team, were indeed adversarial and trust was low.

The issues raised by the Khayelitsha case study have much wider implications. First, the case provides a stark reminder of the kinds of safety challenges that confront the poor across South Africa—an enduring feature of criminalization that first emerged with some clarity from a pioneering enquiry by Louw and Shaw in 1997. Second, the Khayelitsha case also serves as a reminder that in the absence of a capable public guardian, the poor will devise self-help strategies of which vigilantism may be one. Self-help is not new. Organized community action and self-help justice can be traced at least as far back as the 1930s among urban working-class populations. What makes the incidents since the late-1990s somewhat different is the extent to which organization was lacking, and how what in the past had been termed "vigilantism" has deteriorated into on-the-spot reactive mob violence (von Holdt et al. 2011).

To expect anything much from a public enquiry into the state of the police in Khayelitsha would be unwise, although the background research that the commission has requested into demographic trends and socioeconomic conditions in the area may have great potential. Its capacity to spur physical and economic growth is, of course, minimal, but the report may bring some relief regarding the safety concerns of residents and do something to energize the police.

## The State of Policing and the State Police

Questions about the quality of police and policing in South Africa is a central theme running through these three crime stories. The commissions of inquiry—whether focusing on police community relations in Khayelitsha or the Marikana massacre—focus very directly on the national crisis of police (dis)organization. The decline in specialist policing expertise in various areas has long been a source of worry. Decisions that led to the disbanding of specialist police units have undermined dedicated police capacity in areas such as public order, organized crime, anticorruption, and sexual violence. Add to this already long list the corrosive influence of corruption (big and small) involving the top, the middle, and the bottom of the police organization. Furthermore, even among senior officials within the police, there is now open admission of a yawning deficit in command and control throughout the organization.

A program of "en masse" recruitment initiated in 2002 led to a rapid rise in the number of police. It has been described as a costly policy choice. During the 10-year period 2002 to 2012, the number of police personnel increased by 65 percent. Such a rapid increase in personnel has had debilitating effects on all systems of administration from recruitment to selection through to training and deployment (Bruce 2013). Then–Commissioner of Police Bheki Cele conceded in 2010 to the relevant parliamentary portfolio committee that "we have not been big on quality, we have been big on quantity. People have been thrown in by chasing quantity rather than quality" (Newham and Lancaster 2012). Organizational woes extend to electronic data capturing systems, as well—in 2013 only 79 of 1,125 police stations had access to the electronic docket system, which was established over a 10-year period at a cost of R418 million (Newham and Lancaster 2012).

In a presentation to the Portfolio Committee on Police (26 March 2013), researchers based at the Institute for Security Studies produced damning answers to the question, Does the SAPS have a problem with abuse of power? (Newham 2013). The presenter noted that over a period of 10 years there had been a 313 percent increase in the number of brutality-related criminal cases opened up against police officials by the Independent Police Investigative Division. During 2011–2012, SAPS charged 1,050 of its own members with corruption-related offences. Total civil claims against the police have doubled over 2012–2013. Abuse of police power has increased as internal control and disciplinary systems for investigating police misconduct have weakened (Newham 2013).

After 20 years of concerted efforts to modernize systems and democratize procedures, the South African police are still not professionalized. Drawing on public opinion surveys, two-thirds of the adult South African population think that corruption is a widespread problem in the police, 41 percent of the population do not trust the police, and a third interviewed in another study (Futurefact

2013) indicated that they were scared of the police. To all this, one could add indications of growing political interference in the operational mandate of the police—an issue that the Farlam Commission explored (Bruce 2012). But the sources of institutional malaise emanate in part from outside the organization. Political pronouncements of a "war on criminals"—or in the strident words of a former deputy minister of safety and security, a pronouncement to "kill the bastards" and worry about the legal consequences later—have created an environment conducive for police excess (Burger 2013). For many, Marikana occurred because of ill-trained and ill-disciplined police encouraged by the inflammatory "war on crime" rhetoric from a political elite increasingly nervous about manifestations of social disorder.

In informal settlements, such as in Khayelitsha, the failure of the police to respond to the ordinary safety concerns of the poor mirrors the deficiencies of service delivery by the state in areas such as education and health. The risk of criminal victimization is shared unevenly among South Africans. National victimization studies reiterate that it is much more dangerous to live in a lower-class poverty-stricken neighborhood than in a middle-class suburb. As Shaw and Louw (2008, 10) put it, "Race—and its overlay with class—are key determining factors of who is affected by crime." And unlike their middle-class counterparts who have long turned to the private security industry to service their safety needs, the poor will have to make do with the informal resources at their disposal.

## Making Sense of Social and Criminal Violence

### Conventional social science in South Africa: The CSVR reports

Making sense of competing and overlapping perspectives on social and criminal violence is a particular challenge in the conversation about crime. There is no shortage of these perspectives. Commentators have little difficulty in reciting the many factors that structure antisocial motivations and actions. For example, the final report by the CSVR, Tackling Armed Violence, captures academic wisdom on the topic (CSVR 2010). "The core of the problem of violent crime," the report states, "is a culture of violence and criminality" (CSVR 2010, 18). This culture of violence is "associated with young men who tend to be invested in some kind of criminal identity" (CSVR 2010, 7). What then underlies this "culture"? The same report lists the following as the answers: the high-level or "structural" issues of "inequality, poverty, unemployment, and social exclusion, and marginalisation." One derives from these factors "values relating to crime and violence . . . inadequate child rearing and inappropriate youth socialisation," together with "weaknesses of the criminal justice and aligned systems" (CSVR 2010, 10).

At first sight there is an almost self-evident validity to these propositions. Most criminologists will assent to the claim that "young men" (between the ages of 15 and 34, or thereabouts) make up the bulk of violent perpetrators (Seekings and Thaler 2010; CSVR 2008b).This is an assertion of fact, and empirical data bear it out almost universally. Yet there seems to be very little agreement about why this is true. The CSVR reports lean heavily on the fact that young men experience a "crisis of masculinity" as the reason. More plausible explanations draw from multidisciplinary "life-cycle" theories. These have the virtue of transportability across locales. Then there are arguments outside the social sciences that propose that young men tend to be the risk takers, and that those with the least to lose—that is, with the least valuable social and economic assets that translate into reproductive success—will raise the stakes by engaging in crime and violence. In terms of theoretical and empirical depth, the CSVR choice to cite the structural issues as the problem fares badly.

It seems altogether obvious that inequality, poverty, unemployment, social exclusion, and marginalization would generate the underlying psychosocial mechanisms that might turn people against the dominant mores. But in a study by Seekings and Thaler (2010), data suggest that the interconnections are not at all straightforward. Much more research is required before finer distinctions can be made about the particular category of young men driven or attracted to violent crime.

Finally, it should be noted that the concept of a "culture of violence" has not gained strong empirical support since it was first articulated by Marvin Wolfgang and Franco Ferracuti in 1967.[5] Interestingly, the first report of the CSVR (2007) stated that "violence has come to be regarded as a valid means of self-assertion, and of gaining cooperation, respect, and compliance from others, especially among other young men" (p. 170). In the section titled "Normalisation of Violence," the authors of the CSVR report articulate the idea of a culture of violence, describing "a situation where violence is regarded as a viable and legitimate way of resolving problems or protecting one's interests" (p. 169). A "viable and legitimate way of resolving problems" by violence would on the face of it constitute a veritable culture of violence. Nevertheless, the report provides no sound evidence (such as survey data) to support this conclusion. The point could still be valid, however, if persons in this "culture" were indeed "in that condition which is called Warre; and such a warre, as is of every man against every man" (Hobbes 1651/1968, 185). To put it another way, groups so situated are effectively "stateless," lacking the protection, and the preemption of retributive violence, that began with modern state-building (Pinker 2011, 101). There are persuasive reasons, to which the first CSVR report refers, to think that large sections of the population in twentieth-century South Africa were more or less stateless, in somewhat the same way that the people in the lowest strata of industrialized states were. Insofar as large sections of the poor continue to experience structural exclusion from the spoils of the post-apartheid state and its economy, violence will continue to appeal as a means to protect and advance personal interests.

## The burden of the past

The CSVR study refers to the past mainly in its first report. There is a rich (and perhaps a too neglected) historical literature concerning crime and violence in South Africa. Gary Kynoch (2005, 2013) is only one of the more recent historians who has argued that too much attention has been given to the recent past, thereby ignoring the structural continuities that characterized much of the twentieth century. His argument questions the view that contemporary violence is mostly a by-product of political transition in South Africa and the social "looseness" that it introduced. Other work from much earlier in the twentieth century had made more or less the same point. A masterly study in the 1949 edition of the *Handbook on Race Relations in South Africa* that Ellen Hellmann (1949) edited, in a chapter by Jack Simons (1949) on "Law and its Administration," documented the dislocations and disorder that afflicted the urban black population—mining-led industrialization, control of movement, poverty, and harsh policing. Their work was taken further by a new generation of scholars from the 1970s onward. Phillip Bonner (1988), for example, pointed out the extent of youth unemployment, the growth of urban gangs, and the growing impact of a new consumer culture on black youth between 1939 and 1955. Bonner made much use of the concept of "social dislocation" to indicate the way in which family life and a more cohesive value system were being shattered. Clive Glaser (2000) in his study of gangs in Soweto did for that area what Don Pinnock (1984) had done for the Cape Flats in his work on the gang culture there. Pinnock and others also highlighted the rise of self-help justice by township residents attempting to act as "civic guards." Goodhew (1993) traced the emergence of a "People's Police Force" in the Western Areas township on the Rand from 1930 onward. He sounded what became a familiar note in the older literature on the cleavages among the black population, with the older, more educated generations attempting to combat the tide of "youthful violence" (Goodhew 1993, 451).

Kynoch's 2013 study probes the very nature of the "transition" violence that accompanied political changes after 1990. In this study, he offers a revisionist account of political conflict and challenges the overly simplified and deeply romanticized depiction of political violence against a repressive state. A "more inclusive, morally fraught picture emerges from the voices of those who survived the township wars" (p. 7).

## The problem of the present

In the run-up to 1994, and for some years after, the ANC and its intellectual allies set out a program of policing reform based on the argument that a democratic government would enjoy a public legitimacy that the apartheid state could never have achieved. What was needed was a transformation of the state police from a coercive force to a community-supported force. Enjoying popular legitimacy, the police would no longer be viewed as the enemy; through such mechanisms as community policing (as embodied constitutionally in such institutions as community-police forums, the rule of law, and an effective police oversight board), the masses would work together with beat officers to combat crime. Subsequent ethnographic studies on everyday policing in the new century by scholars such as Jonny Steinberg (2008), Antony Altbeker (2005), and Andrew Brown (2008) painted not altogether unflattering pictures of the new police in action. The general tone was that the cops indeed had a difficult job but "that even the worst among them" did more good than the usual public do-gooder

(Altbeker 2005, xiv). Still, it was not easy going. Steinberg concluded that "the consent of citizens to be policed is a precondition of policing" and that it was not always forthcoming (Steinberg 2008). A later article by the same author paints an altogether bleaker picture: the quality of policing had deteriorated (Steinberg 2012) and the SAPs was widely viewed among poorer communities as corrupt and unresponsive to public grievances.

In contrast to the argument about the absence of a normative contract, others approach the crime problem from a situational point of view. They take as a point of departure the commonplace criminological lore that a small proportion of the population is responsible for the bulk of crime. The quotations from the CSVR report to which we referred earlier imply this proposition. Altbeker (2007) makes the point more stridently as he turns to South Africa's "crisis of crime." He argues that focusing on crime prevention in crime policy just after 1994 was a grave mistake. It meant that "those parts of the criminal justice system devoted to finding and punishing criminals have suffered the cruel neglect of the ugly stepchild." What is required is a complete policy reversal, that is, a reorientation away from fighting "crime" and the underlying social conditions toward fighting "criminals" (Altbeker 2007, 142). The immediate task at hand is "to find and to prosecute people who commit crimes" (p. 147). Investigative and prosecutorial efforts need to get "the worst offenders behind bars" (p. 151). An aggressive program aimed at incarcerating a substantially larger number of violent offenders (despite the social costs) would have positive spinoffs. Altbeker's argument in favor of refocusing criminal justice energies on processing criminals runs up against old criminological wisdom, however. Society gets the crime that it deserves; inequality and all the usual social inequities lead inexorably to the killing fields that we now see today (Dixon 2012). Or do they?

## Safety and Security: Future Prospects?

As this volume makes clear, there are many ways in which Mandela's legacy might be conceived. If it is conceived as embodying a profound optimism for a better future that inspired South Africans, the security policies of the 1990s might be regarded as a feature of Mandela's legacy.

The central thrusts of these policy proposals were remarkably consistent. This consistency was embodied in two features.

- First, the policies sought to ensure that South Africa had an effective and accountable police force (and broader criminal justice system) that would focus its attention on doing what police do best. Namely, successfully and legitimately, applying what Egon Bittner (1970) has termed "non-negotiable coercive force" or the credible threat of such force (Shearing and Leon 1977), by agents of the state that would restore peace in the face of threats to it. Bittner (1974, 30) expressed this sense of force as a source of peace when he argued that police were, and should be, an agency to which people

can confidently turn when something serious that "ought-not-to-be-happening-and-that-someone-had-better-do-something-about-now" has occurred.
- Second, these policy statements argued that safety could not be realized through police action alone. Rather, achieving safety required a holistic societal response that enabled the identification, mobilization, and coordination of a wide range of resources.

Achieving these intentions was left to the new, and democratically elected, government to accomplish. The government decided in 2000 to shift away from these policy directions and to implement policy that has led to a very different South Africa than was envisaged during the 1990s.

In reviewing, and seeking to understand, these developments, a useful place to start is with the National Crime Prevention Strategy (Department of Safety and Security 1996). Bold in spirit, this strategy articulated a vision of a post-apartheid engagement with citizen safety as opposed to state security—a turn toward what was beginning to be captured internationally by the concept "human security." Its thrust was clear and concise—what was required for a safe, and just, South Africa was a competent police force along with an active citizenry who shared a common vision of a country in which its citizens live, work, and play in peace.

Other, related policy documents developed throughout the1990s shared this vision. These included the report of the Goldstone Commission that established the framework for the policing of South Africa's first democratic election in 1994 (Heymann 1992)—a policy that was translated into practice and that had much to do with the success of that election (see Kinnes [2013] for an analysis of what transpired in public order policing later; see also Marks 2005).

The National Crime Prevention Strategy was presented as heralding a "new beginning" for the governance of security within South Africa that was to be achieved through whole-of-society and whole-of-government "policing webs" (Brodeur 2010). These plans never materialized. In the words of the National Planning Commission (2011):

> Although this strategy incorporated cutting-edge international thinking and was widely recognised as sound, it was never fully institutionalised as a holistic and comprehensive strategy that focused on all the factors that produced crime and insecurity. (p. 357)

Indeed, as early as the end of the 1990s there was an explicit shift that distanced the South African government from its initial post-apartheid vision (Hornberger 2013). The more combative discourse—that saw the police as occupying the full range of policing roles and portrayed criminals as legitimate targets of a more "forceful" approach—advocated an approach that in its twenty-first-century guise has come to be associated with a "shoot to kill" policy.

Again the 2011 National Planning Commission is instructive.

> In March 2000, the National Crime Combating Strategy superseded this policy [the 1996 policy] and advocated a very different approach, focusing more on criminal justice

resources. As a result, the police were inappropriately envisaged as an all-purpose agency, rather than a highly specialised resource to be deployed strategically. This led to a police agency stretched beyond its capacity, with a mandate that is impossible to fulfil, and disenchanted police officers with fragile authority and legitimacy. (p. 357)

Hornberger (2013), in a wonderfully nuanced analysis, has, along with Steinberg (2011), explored how the widening of the police mandate to include crime prevention broadly understood (the role that a policing web was initially envisaged as pursuing) has worked to further the alliance that was already emerging at the end of the 1990s between a frustrated public and a police that was generalizing the use of force to a wide range of policing functions from prevention to detention.

Despite the government's turn away from the National Crime Prevention Strategy's focus on a policing web, elements of such a web can be found across South Africa, albeit often operating in far from ideal conditions. These elements have emerged as citizens, across all socioeconomic levels, have looked for, and taken up, spaces that have enabled these citizens to act to preserve their safety— sometimes in perfectly legitimate ways but often through violent initiatives that mirror and extend the combative actions of police. Both sorts of initiatives have been documented (e.g., Baker 2002; Buur 2006).

The National Development Plan focuses its attention on how legitimate initiatives might be encouraged and integrated to form elements of policing webs. The plan considers large-scale developmental projects such as Violence Prevention through Urban Upgrade (VPUU). VPUU was introduced by the City of Cape Town in 2005 in partnership with the German Federal Ministry (BMZ) and the German Development Bank (KfW). VPUU utilizes a "holistic" and "community-based approach" to violence prevention that is realized through the improvement of urban infrastructure and services.[6]

Another example of a web-based approach to safety that the plan identifies, this time spearheaded by the Federation de Internationale de Football Association (FIFA), was the policing of the 2010 World Cup, which adopted an explicitly whole-of-society approach (Berg, Nakueira, and Shearing 2014). A similar approach, that also included police within a wider policing web, is the way in which, in several areas, police and community initiatives were integrated to respond to the xenophobic violence of 2008 (Igglesden 2008). Other examples of legitimate community initiatives that were drawn into policing webs include the Community Safety Volunteer Programme, operating in Gauteng and the Western Cape and KwaZulu-Natal—all mentioned in the National Development Plan. In addition to these better known examples, there are many other illustrations of regulated subterranean policing webs that have existed, and still exist, in communities across the country that have acted legitimately to promote the public good of security, including, for instance, a dispute resolution project that resolved tens of thousands of local disputes a year before it closed down because of lack of government support (Froestad 2013). To this array of community-focused programs must be added the equally vast landscape of private sector initiatives, including those of the private security industry—an industry that, on a per capita basis, is among the largest in the world (Berg and Nouveau 2011). For a safe South Africa to be realized, the plan argues, a wider range of state and nonstate capacities need to be mobilized at all levels, which requires shifting to an integrated approach, with active citizen involvement and coresponsibility (National Planning Commission 2011, 356).

At present, the likelihood of this vision being realized is remote. There have been indications that the government does not intend to adopt the plan's policing vision. In 2013, a draft Green Paper on policing was released by the Civilian Secretariat for Police, located within the ministry of police. This paper, although it was short on specific recommendations, suggests that the government might do well to re-endorse the thinking in the National Crime Combatting Policy (SAPS 2000). Hornberger, writing before the Green Paper, argues that the powerful alliances that gave birth to the combative strategy of 2000 continued to hold sway 13 years into the twenty-first century. She argued that criticizing the state for its support of the combative policies of the police "misses its mark [as] it reifies the state as cause, instead of seeing how the state is permeated by popular social forces" (Hornberger 2013, 15). What Hornberger's analysis makes clear is that the vision set out in the National Development Plan finds little support within the political environment of an ANC-dominated South Africa. What is much more likely is that there will be more of the same.

This is not a hopeful note on which to conclude this article. More promising is the Independent Commission on Policing for Northern Ireland (Patten 1999), which was established to transform a violent and oppressive policing regime that had strong resonances with South Africa. The Patten Commission proposed an architecture for policing reform premised on three design principles that, if and when an appropriate political climate emerges in South Africa, would work to institutionalize the National Development Plan's proposals.

The first is a "whole-of-society" principle. This principle calls for the recognition that effective policing requires governments to enable the emergence of policing webs that identify, mobilize, and coordinate a range of societal resources (public, private, and civil). The second principle recognizes that to establish effective policing webs, governments should establish policing budgets, rather than police budgets, that enable them to support and coordinate a range of policing capacities. The third principle requires the establishment of civilian oversight mechanisms, such as policing boards, that are responsible for monitoring the activities of policing webs on behalf of citizens and providing governments with advice on how to facilitate their effective and legitimate functioning.

If this limited set of guidelines—what the Patten Commission conceived of as a "golden thread"—were adopted, it would make fundamental changes to the architecture of South African policing. The critical question is, When might a political configuration emerge that would find such a transformation desirable? In 2013, such a time seemed to be some way off.

# Notes

1. The Oxford English Dictionary defines a killing field as a "place of warfare or unrest associated with heavy loss of (civilian) life, esp. as the result of massacre or genocide; (also, in extended use) any place in which a murder or other killing occurs. Popularized as the name of the film *The Killing Fields* (released 1984), concerning events in Cambodia (or Kampuchea, as it was then named) under the Khmer Rouge regime." Available from www.oed.com (accessed 28 October 2013).

2. The reasons underlying such decline, however, remain ill understood. Altbeker (2008) has argued that the key to variations in murder rates seem to lie in variations in robbery rates. Others again postulate that the decline in homicide is a function of the very steep decline in firearm homicides, which in turn may be linked to fundamental changes in the regime of firearm controls after 2000.

3. See also Smith (2012).

4. *Minister of Police and Others v. Premier of the Western Cape and Others*, Case CCT 13/13 (2010).

5. Part of the reason may be that "culture" itself is such a fuzzy notion, but insofar as it implies normative consent to the employment of violence, the evidence is not very supportive for the subcultural group to which Wolfgang referred. But that was in the United States, and cross-cultural tests are not to be found. If by "culture" it is meant that people imitate and internalize what they see around them, there must be incentives to perpetuate what is inherently risky activity (unless one is referring to only victims who cannot retaliate).

6. See http://www.capetown.gov.za/en/DesignCapital/Documents/BIDBOOK_CS_1_1_CS_1_1.pdf.

# References

Altbeker, Antony. 2005. *The dirty work of democracy: A year on the streets with the SAPS.* Johannesburg: Jonathan Ball.

Altbeker, Antony. 2007. *A country at war with itself: South Africa's crisis of crime.* Johannesburg: Jonathan Ball.

Altbeker, Antony. 2008. Murder and robbery in South Africa: A tale of two trends. In *Crime, violence and injury prevention in South Africa: Data to action*, eds. Ashley van Niekerk, Shanaaz Suppla, and Mohammed Seedat, 131–55. Tygerberg: Medical Research Council, University of South Africa Crime, Violence and Injury Lead Programme.

Alexander, Peter, Thapelo Lekgowa, Botsang Mmpoe, Luke Sinwell, and Bongani Xezwi. 2012. *Marikana: A view from the mountain and a case to answer.* Johannesburg: Jacana.

Baker, Bruce. 2002. Living with non-state policing in South Africa. *Journal of Modern African Studies* 40 (1): 29–53.

Berg, Julie, Sophie Nakueira, and Clifford Shearing. 2014. Global non-state auspices of security governance. In *The Routledge handbook of international crime and justice studies*, eds. Heather Bersot and Bruce Arrigo. New York, NY: Routledge.

Berg, Julie, and Jean-Pierre Nouveau. 2011. Towards a third phase of regulation: Re-imagining private security in South Africa. *South African Crime Quarterly* 38:23–32.

Bonner, Philip L. 1988. Family, crime and political consciousness on the East Rand, 1939–1955. *Journal of Southern African Studies* 14 (3): 393–420.

Bittner, Egon. 1970. *The functions of police in modern society.* Washington, DC: U.S. Government Printing Office.

Bittner, Egon. 1974. Florence Nightingale in pursuit of Willie Sutton: A theory of the police. In *The potential for reform of criminal justice*, ed. Herbert Jacob, 17–44. Newbury Park, CA: Sage Publications.

Brodeur, Jean-Paul. 2010. *The policing web.* New York, NY: Oxford University Press.

Brown, Andrew. 2008. *Street blues.* Cape Town: Zebra Press.

Bruce, David. 14 September 2012. Justice for Marikana: Farlam Commission not up to the task. SACSIS/APCOF. Available from http://sacsis.org.za/site/article/1425 (accessed 18 April 2013).

Bruce, David. 2013. New blood: Implications of en masse recruitment for the South African Police Service. *South African Crime Quarterly* 43:17–28.

Burger, Johan. 16 April 2013. The National Development Plan can improve policing in South Africa. *ISS Today*. Available from www.issafrica.org (accessed 29 April 2013).

Buur, Lars. 2006. Reordering society: Vigilantism and expressions of sovereignty in Port Elizabeth's townships. *Development and Change* 37 (4): 735–57.

Centre for the Study of Violence and Reconciliation (CSVR). 2007. *The violent nature of crime in South Africa: A concept paper prepared for the Justice, Crime Prevention and Security Cluster*. CSVR component one. Braamfontein: CSVR.

CSVR. 2008a. *Adding injury to insult: How exclusion and inequality drive South Africa's problem of violence*. CSVR component four. Braamfontein: CSVR.

CSVR. 2008b. *Case studies on perpetrators of violent crime*. CSVR component five. Braamfontein: CSVR.

CSVR. 2008c. *A state of sexual tyranny: The prevalence, nature and causes of sexual violence in South Africa*. CSVR component three. Braamfontein: CSVR.

CSVR. 2008d. *Streets of pain, streets of sorrow: The circumstances of the occurrence of murder in six areas with high rates of murder*. CSVR component two. Braamfontein: CSVR.

CSVR. 2009. *Supplementary report: Why does South Africa have such high rates of violent crime?* CSVR component seven. Braamfontein: CSVR.

CSVR. 2010. *Tackling armed violence: Key findings and recommendations of the study on the violent nature of crime in South Africa*. CSVR component six. Braamfontein: CSVR.

Chapple, Irene, and Errol Barnett. 14 September 2012. What's behind South Africa's mine violence? *CNN News*. Available from http://edition.cnn.com (accessed 28 October 2013).

Davis, Rebecca. 14 December 2012. Khayelitsha policing inquiry comes to the court. *Daily Maverick*. Available from www.dailymaverick.co.za (accessed 26 April 2013).

Defence Web. 9 November 2010. Police release violence report, adds it leaves main question unanswered. Defence Web. Available from www.defenceweb.co.za (accessed 25 April 2013).

Department of Safety and Security. 1996. *National crime prevention strategy*. Pretoria: Department of Safety and Security.

De Waal, Mandy. 22 March 2012. Vigilante violence: The smoke that calls. *Daily Maverick*. Available from www.dailymaverick.co.za (accessed 26 April 2013).

*Die Burger*. 7 February 2013. Bredasdorp-verkragting—Zuma vra "swaarste vonnis." Available from www .dieburger.com (accessed 26 April 2013).

Dixon, Bill. 2012. Understanding pointy face. *South African Crime Quarterly* 41:3–9.

Froestad, Jan. 2013. *Security governance, policing, and local capacity*. With Clifford Shearing. Advances in Police Theory and Practice Series. Boca Raton, FL: CRC Press.

Futurefact. 2013. "I am scared of the police." Futurefact. Available from http://www.futurefact.co.za (accessed 25 June 2013).

Gender Links and the Medical Research Council. 2010. *Gauteng gender violence prevalence study*. Johannesburg: Gender Links. Available from http://www.genderlinks.org.za/article/gauteng-gender-violence-prevalence-study-2010-11-22 (accessed 8 May 2013).

Glaser, Clive. 2000. *Bo-tsotsi: The youth gangs of Soweto, 1935–1976*. Cape Town: David Philip.

Goodhew, David. 1993. The people's police-force: Communal policing initiatives in the western areas of Johannesburg, circa 1930–1962. *Journal of South African Studies* 19 (3): 447–70.

Harrendorf, Stefan, Markku Heiskanen, and Steven Malby, eds. 2010. *International statistics on crime and justice*. HEUNI Publication Series No. 64. Helsinki: European Institute for Crime Prevention and Control.

Hellmann, Ellen, ed. 1949. *Handbook on race relations in South Africa*. Cape Town: Oxford University Press.

Heymann, Philip. 1992. *Towards peaceful protest in South Africa: Testimony of multinational panel regarding lawful control of demonstrations in the Republic of South Africa*. The Goldstone Commission. Pretoria. HSRC.

Hlongwane, Sipho. 16 November 2012. Marikana Commission: Spotty police evidence continues. *Daily Maverick*. Available from www.dailymaverick.co.za (accessed 26 April 2013).

Hobbes, Thomas. 1651/1968. *Leviathan*. Harmondsworth, UK: Penguin.

Hornberger, Julia. 2013. From general to commissioner to general—On the popular state of policing in South Africa. *Law & Social Inquiry* 38 (3): 598–614.

Igglesden, Vicky. 2008. *Xenophobic violence in South Africa in May 2008*. Witwatersrand: University of Witwatersrand, Force Migration Studies Programme.

Jewkes, Rachel, Yandisa Sikweyiya, Robert Morrell, and Kristin Dunkle. 2010. Why, when and how men rape: Understanding rape perpetration in South Africa. *South African Crime Quarterly* 34:23–31.

John, Victoria. 24 October 2012. Khayelitsha faces fresh vigilante, police problems. *Mail & Guardian*. Available from http://mg.co.za (accessed 26 April 2013).

Kapp, Clare. 2008. South Africa failing people displaced by xenophobia riots. *The Lancet* 371 (9629): 1986–87.

Kinnes, Irvin. 2013. *Public order policing in South Africa: Capacity, constraints and capabilities*. Cape Town: Open Society Foundation for South Africa.

Kynoch, Gary. 2005. *We are fighting the world: A history of the Marashea gangs in South Africa, 1947–1999*. Athens, Ohio, and Scottsville, South Africa: Ohio University Press and University of KwaZulu-Natal Press.

Kynoch, Gary. 2013. Reassessing transition violence: Voices from South Africa's township wars, 1990–4. *African Affairs* 112 (447): 283–303.

Lancaster, Lizette. 25 March 2013. Is South Africa an inherently violent country? *ISS Today*. Available from http://www.issafrica.org/iss-today (accessed 28 October 2013).

Louw, Antoinette, and Mark Shaw. 1997. *Stolen opportunities: The impact of crime on South Africa's poor*. Monograph No 14. Braamfontein: Institute for Security Studies.

Marks, Monique. 2005. *Transforming the Robocops: Changing police in South Africa*. Pietermaritzburg: University of KwaZulu-Natal Press.

Moffett, Helen. 2006. "These women, they force us to rape them": Rape as narrative of social control in post-apartheid South Africa. *Journal of Southern African Studies* 32 (1): 129–44.

National Planning Commission. 2011. *National Development Plan: Vision for 2030*. Pretoria: National Planning Commission.

Newham, Gareth. 26 March 2013. Warning lights flashing: Policing in South Africa 2013/14. Presentation to the Portfolio Committee on Police. Pretoria: Institute for Security Studies.

Newham, Gareth, and Lizette Lancaster. 2012. *The 2012 South African budget reveals big shifts in police personnel trends*. Pretoria: Institute for Security Studies. Available from http://www.issafrica.org (accessed 25 June 2013).

Nombembe, Philani. 12 June 2012. Khayelitsha mob rule raises fear. *Times Live*. Available from www.timeslive.co.za (accessed 26 April 2013).

Norman, Rosana, Richard Matzopoulos, Pat Groenwald, and Debbie Bradshaw. 2007. The high burden of injuries in South Africa. *Bulletin of the World Health Organization* 85 (7): 695–702.

Parker, Faranaaz. 20 September 2012. Crime statistics show marginal improvement. *Mail & Guardian*. Available from http://mg.co.za (accessed 25 June 2013).

Patten, Chris. 1999. *A new beginning for policing in Northern Ireland: The report of the Independent Commission on Policing for Northern Ireland*. Belfast: HMSO.

Pinker, Steven. 2011. *The better angels of our nature: A history of violence and humanity*. London: Penguin.

Pinnock, Don. 1984. *The brotherhoods: Street gangs and state control in Cape Town*. Claremont, South Africa: New Africa Books.

SAPA. 7 February 2013. Zuma condemns Bredasdorp rape as shocking, cruel and inhumane. *Mail & Guardian*. Available from http://mg.co.za (accessed 25 June 2013).

Seekings, Jeremy, and Kai Thaler. 2010. Socio-economic conditions, young men and violence in Cape Town. Centre for Social Science Research Working Paper 285, Cape Town, University of Cape Town.

Shaw, Mark. 1997. *South Africa: Crime in transition*. Occasional Paper No. 17. Braamfontein: Institute for Security Studies.

Shaw, Mark, and Antoinette Louw. 2008. *Environmental design for safer communities: Preventing crime in South Africa's cities and towns*. Monograph 24. Pretoria: Institute for Security Studies.

Shaw, Mark, Jan van Dijk, and Wolfgang Rhomberg. 2003. Determining trends in global crime and justice. *UNODC Forum on Crime and Society* 3 (1–2): 35–63.

Shearing, Clifford, and Jeffrey Leon. 1977. Reconsidering the police role: A challenge to a challenge of a popular conception. *Canadian Journal of Criminology and Corrections* 19 (4): 331–45.

Simons, H. Jack. 1949. The law and its administration. In *Handbook on race relations in South Africa*, ed. Ellen Hellmann. Cape Town: Oxford University Press.

Smith, David. 25 November 2012. One in three South African men admits to rape, survey finds. *The Guardian*. Available from http://www.guardian.co.uk (accessed 22 March 2013).

South African Police Service (SAPS). 2000. *National crime combating strategy. South Africa*. Pretoria: SAPS. Available from http://www.saps.gov.za/ (accessed 25 June 2013).

SAPS. 2012a. *Crime statistics overview RSA 2011/2012*. Pretoria: SAPS. Available from http://www.saps .gov.za (accessed 25 June 2013).

SAPS. 2012b. *Report on the complaint regarding alleged inefficiency and a breakdown in police-community relations in Khayelitsha, Cape Town*. Pretoria: SAPS.

Southall, Roger. 2012. *South Africa's massacre: Peeling the onion*. London: Open Democracy. Available from http://www.opendemocracy.net (accessed 25 June 2013).

Statistics South Africa. 2012. *Victims of Crime Survey 2012*. Statistical release PO341. Pretoria: Statistics South Africa.

Steinberg, Jonny. 2008. *Thin blue: The unwritten rules of policing*. Cape Town: Jonathan Ball Publishers.

Steinberg, Jonny. 2011. Crime prevention goes abroad: Policy transfer and policing in post-apartheid South Africa. *Theoretical Criminology* 15 (4): 349–64.

Steinberg, Jonny. 2012. Security and disappointment: Policing, freedom and xenophobia in South Africa. *British Journal of Criminology* 52:345–60.

von Holdt, Karl, Malose Langa, Sepetla Molapo, Nomfundo Mogapi, Kindiza Ngubeni, Jacob Dlamini, and Adele Kirsten. 2011. *The smoke that calls: Insurgent citizenship, collective violence and the struggle for a place in the new South Africa*. Braamfontein: Centre for the Study of Violence and Reconciliation, Society, Work and Development Institute.

Wolfgang, Marvin, and Franco Ferracuti. 1967. *The subculture of violence: Towards an integrated theory in criminology*. London: Tavistock Publications.

# Accountability and the Media

*By*
ANTON HARBER

Two decades of contestation over the nature and extent of transformation in the South African news media have left a sector different in substantive ways from the apartheid inheritance but still patchy in its capacity to fill the democratic ideal. Change came fast to a newly open broadcasting sector, but has faltered in recent years, particularly in a public broadcaster troubled by political interference and poor management. The potential of online media to provide much greater media access has been hindered by the cost of bandwidth. Community media has grown but struggled to survive financially. Print media has been aggressive in investigative exposé, but financial cutbacks have damaged routine daily coverage. In the face of this, the government has turned its attention to the print sector, demanding greater—but vaguely defined—transformation and threatened legislation. This has met strong resistance.

*Keywords:* media; ANC; transformation; print; broadcasting; Internet; ownership

The ANC signaled early on in the post-1990 transition that the media would get their particular attention as both a sector in need of change and a vehicle for transformation in other sectors. In its 1992 Ready to Govern document, the ANC outlined:

> At the core of democracy lies the recognition of the right of all citizens to take part in society's decision-making process. This requires that individuals are armed with the necessary information and have access to the contesting options they require to make informed choices. An ignorant society cannot be democratic.

> The ANC asserts that freedoms must be underpinned by an equitable distribution of media

*Anton Harber is Caxton Professor of Journalism at the University of the Witwatersrand, Johannesburg, author of* Diepsloot *(Jonathan Ball 2011), and coeditor of* Troublemakers *(Jacana 2010). He was a founding coeditor of the* Mail & Guardian *and chair of the Freedom of Expression Institute.*

DOI: 10.1177/0002716213515154

resources, development programmes and a deliberate effort to engender a culture of open debate. This requires politics of affirmative action to redress the inequalities in our society. (ANC 1992)

The then-soon-to-be president, Nelson Mandela, was less circuitous when he laid out the issue in Prague in 1992:

> I cannot overemphasise the value we place on a free, independent and outspoken press. . . . Such a free press will temper the appetite of any government to amass power at the expense of the citizen. . . . The reality is that today . . . conglomerates, drawn exclusively from the white racial group, dominate the print media of our country. . . . The senior editorial staffs of . . . South Africa's daily newspapers are cast from the same racial mould. They are all white, they are all male, they are all from a middle-class background and tend to share a very similar life experience.

> The ANC has no objection in principle to editors with such a profile. What is disturbing however, and in our view, harmful, is the threat of one dimensionality this poses for the media of our country as a whole. It is clearly unacceptable that a country . . . is serviced by media whose principal players have no knowledge of the life experience of the majority. (Mandela 1992)

Mandela echoed these remarks at the International Press Institute Congress in Cape Town in February 1994, on the eve of his ascendancy to the presidency (see Mandela 1994).

The ANC defined "change" in regard to the media primarily as the need to make the media more racially representative at all levels, but there was also widespread recognition of a need to address the structure of the industry, to better serve the needs of democracy. With broadcasting overwhelmingly dominated by a state broadcaster that had served apartheid, and with the print media dominated by a handful of companies that had either been strongly supportive or weakly oppositional (with the demise of most of the antiapartheid "alternative" presses in the 1980s), there was a keen need to avoid the perpetuation of old patterns in the new order.

A new media order required the balancing of different media functions: the basic democratic need for information exchanges between government and citizens to enable informed decision-making; the empowerment of communities through local, more participative media; and the watchdog function of ensuring transparency in government—the element that was so clearly missing in most postindependence African countries. What was envisaged was for the three media sectors—the public, the private, and the community—to fill these needs in different proportions. The public sector, primarily in the form of the national broadcaster, the SABC, which had so loyally served apartheid, was to be turned into a true public service; the private media, responsible for most of the country's watchdog reporting, needed greater diversity of ownership and staffing; and the community media barely existed and needed to be built up.

Pursuing reform across these three sectors meant creating or reforming three institutions that are foundational to democratic media in South Africa: the SABC, which dominated broadcasting and was the major news and information source for most South Africans, was to be turned into a public service operation; the new independent regulator, at first called the Independent Broadcasting Authority, later the Independent Communications Authority of SA (Icasa), which was tasked with opening up the broadcasting arena, had to be written into law, mandated, and staffed; and the Media Development and Diversity Agency (MDDA) was to be set up as a statutory body to promote and build community media. These were institutional pillars of a new order, envisaged in the new constitution to open up the media arena, operate at arm's length from government, and promote diversity.

## The Private Media after 20 Years

Twenty years of democracy, therefore, the media system is significantly different from in 1994. If one were to assess the news media by its boisterousness; its freedom to speak out critically; and its ability to engage in vigorous public debate, confront authority, and expose wrongdoing, then it scores highly.

In *Troublemakers,* a collection of investigative pieces that celebrated the boom in accountability reporting in South Africa, I described how newspapers remained critical and outspoken in a situation where many of the other independent institutions of democracy were faltering:

> Parliament and the prosecuting authorities backed off from probing the arms deal shenanigans, but some newspapers stuck with the story. The presidency seemed to go soft on corruption, dismantling the Scorpions, and shackling the National Prosecuting Authority, but at least some journalists were relentless in pursuing tales of corruption. The prison authorities failed to act when the president's friend and convicted fraudster Schabir Shaik was shown to be flouting his parole; but reporters and photographers stuck with the story and splashed it over the front pages. When the government shunned a Cosatu call for "lifestyle audits" of political leadership that would show who was using their power to enrich themselves, the media did it anyway. The Judicial Service Commission faltered in calling to account judges who had political clout but flexible ethics, but the media watched their every move.
>
> For all its faults and inadequacies, the private media has become the primary institution holding the government and the private sector to account, exposing corruption and the abuse of power, and keeping a torch shining into the dark areas of our society. Far from being the enemy of democracy described by many of its critics, the media, in its reluctance to accept facile calls for national unity and to insist on the value of its muckraking, has become a bulwark against the potential abuse of power by a dominant ruling party. (Harber and Renn 2010, xxvi–xxvii)

Or, as the judges in the annual Taco Kuiper (TK) Award for Investigative Reporting put it:

> In their determination to shine light in dark spaces, to make public officials account for their actions and decisions, and to highlight complex social problems, our investigative reporters are making an inestimable contribution to the realisation of the constitutional goals of transparency and accountability, and thus to the health of our democracy. (TK Awards 2012)

A glance at the more outspoken of newspapers—notably *Mail & Guardian, Sunday Times*, and *City Press*—indicates no reluctance to exercise the freedom to speak out strongly and critically. Although there has been harassment—*Mail & Guardian* staff has been investigated, the *Sunday Times'* Mzilikazi wa Africa was arrested under strange circumstances, telephones appear to be regularly bugged, and there have been calls to boycott critical newspapers or withdraw government advertising—the freedom to publish remains largely intact. Judging by the size and tone of headlines week after week, at least some South African newspapers are uninhibited in their muckraking and make robust use of their freedom to probe and criticize. The press played a key role in the jailing of one commissioner of police (Jacqui Selebi, exposed in the *Mail & Guardian* and *Sunday Times* and sentenced in 2010 to 15 years for his corrupt relationship with major criminal figures) and the firing of another (Bheki Cele, dismissed in 2012 after being exposed in the *Sunday Times* for dishonest dealings), the dismissal of at least one cabinet minister (Dina Pule, let go as communications minister after a *Sunday Times* exposé about lavish and questionable spending), and the sidelining of a number of lower-level officials accused of corruption or mismanagement.

Less positive is the capacity of the media to cover everyday news. Newsroom cutbacks across the board in recent years have taken a heavy toll on day-to-day reporting. The Independent Group (owners of eighteen titles including the *Star, Cape Times*, and *Daily News*) has cut its total staff from six thousand to a reported fifteen hundred; Media24 (the biggest newspaper and magazine publisher in the country, including of the *Daily Sun, City Press*, and all the Afrikaans titles) has had as many as seven rounds of retrenchments (Daniels 2013); *Business Day's* newsroom in Johannesburg has also shrunk considerably in personnel due to financial pressures. At all these groups, there have also been significant moves to cut costs by merging news-gathering operations into group teams across newspaper titles: Media24 has created one news team for all four of its Afrikaans titles; Independent has merged parts of its reporting and production staff on different newspapers; and *Business Day* and the *Financial Mail* have merged their editorial staffs (Wright 2013). In some respects, this pooling of resources may strengthen coverage when it creates opportunities for specialist reporters that individual newspapers cannot afford on their own. Media24 has been able to build a strong and well-resourced investigations team that serves all its newspapers, for example. In general, however, mergers lead to homogeneity among newspapers and less local or regional diversity among different newspapers of different character in a single group. What has been lost is regular coverage of areas such as city politics and the courts, and specialist reporting.

Critics of the media contest the concentration of ownership in the media, specifically the continued dominance of white ownership in the print media, partly because this continuation impedes the entry of new owners who might be more sympathetic to the ANC. Libby Lloyd writes that the South African media market is among the most concentrated in the world, quoting the Colombia Institute for Tele-Information (Lloyd 2013). This assessment, however, is distorted by the inclusion of the telecoms sector; the report gives insufficient detail to assess the claim of undue concentration.

*Media ownership*

Most media sectors (newspapers, magazines, books, Internet, pay television) are overwhelmingly dominated by Media24, the local arm of what is now a global conglomerate, Naspers. Naspers has a market value around sixty times the size of the next biggest media company, and its South African operation is the largest in the pay-TV, newspaper, book, magazine, and Internet sectors, whether measured by the number of titles or its share of advertising and audience (Harber 2013). It claims a combined South African audience of 25 million people through all its outlets, or half the population (and this number excludes its pay-TV audience, as Multichoice does not operate through Media24). The only areas in which it is not strong are those it is excluded from by regulation: free-to-air radio and television broadcasting. So the private media market is dominated by one major company, ironically the one with the closest historical alliance to apartheid. There are three other companies at the next level (Caxton, Times Media, and the Independent Group), and some smaller ones snapping at their heels (Kagiso, HCI).

How this concentration impacts on choice in the marketplace is complex. South Africa has eighteen daily and thirteen weekly newspapers. Johannesburgers wake up to nine newspapers a day in three languages from five different owners.[1] Capetonians can choose among nine papers in two languages from four different owners.[2] Durbanites have eight newspapers in two languages from four different owners.[3] On Sunday, nationally, there is a choice between six newspapers,[4] and there are also five regional papers.[5] The *Mail & Guardian* publishes nationally on Fridays. Overall, this provides a substantial choice, and the papers range from the fiercely independent (*Mail & Guardian*) to the deeply conservative (*Citizen*) to the ardent supporters of government (*New Age*). Notably absent from this roster is a voice of the Left, particularly of those in the powerful trade union movement.

The arrival of *New Age* in 2010 brought the first unequivocal ANC-supporting newspaper into the fold, putting to rest the (always dubious) ANC complaint that it had no newspaper support. More recently, the Independent Group—the country's second largest newspaper company—was bought by a consortium of businesspeople close to the ANC and eager to secure more business from the government (Harber 2013).

The launch of the *Daily Sun* in 2002—which very quickly became the largest-circulation daily—brought a new wave of tabloid journalism; for the first time in decades a newspaper was aimed toward a working-class market, bringing faces and voices to the news that had been largely absent from the media. It was followed by the *Daily Voice* and the *Sun*, as well as various Sunday papers.

Also adding to diversity of availability are flourishing isiZulu newspapers, of which there are now three. All are among the very few whose circulation has grown in recent years: *Isolezwe* (Independent group), *Ilanga* (the oldest, at over 100 years, linked to the Inkatha Freedom Party), and *UmAfrika* (a small independent).[6] Absent are newspapers, other than very local community publications, in the eight official languages other than English, Afrikaans, and isiZulu.

The issue of race and ownership is complex and constantly shifting. An MDDA research report was able to identify only 14 percent black ownership of the major media groups, but this statistic treats state and pension fund money as "white," so is an incomplete figure (MDDA 2009). The Public Investment Corporation (PIC), representing government pension funds, is now the biggest shareholder in three of the major media groups, Naspers, TMG, and Independent News and Media, and it is unclear how this factor should be counted in the empowerment stakes.

To indicate the ownership flux, TMG (formerly Avusa/Johncom), owners of the giant *Sunday Times*, the *Times, Sowetan*, and *Business Day*, was part of an early empowerment deal in the mid-1990s. This deal collapsed under the burden of debt and poor performance, however, and ownership swung back to private equity funds and banks. Control moved back into black hands when Tokyo Sexwale's Mvelepandhe group became a lead shareholder, but it changed again in 2012 and control swung back to private equity and the PIC. In May 2013, TMG claimed 55 percent black ownership, and 13.5 percent black female ownership, though little detail was given of how this was defined or calculated (TMG 2013).

Independent News and Media, and Caxton were once both solidly white owned, though control of the Independent passed to black owners in 2013. Naspers is a pyramid company tightly controlled by a small handful of owners, led by CEO Koos Bekker. But its local South African arm, Media24, has 107,000 black shareholders who hold 15 percent of the company through its Welkom Yizani scheme. Naspers claims 20 percent black ownership (Harber 2013).

## Diversity

Research in 2012 showed significant shifts in the racial make-up of newsrooms, though the makeup varies across titles, and the research points to some papers still having a predominance of whites in senior positions (Daniels 2013). Most companies have diversified significantly since 1994, when editorial, management, and staffing were overwhelmingly white and male. TMG reported to the Print and Digital Media Industry Transformation Task Team (PDMITT) in 2013 that its top manager in the media division was black and its top editorial manager was black; among senior management, nine of seventeen (just over half) were black, and seven of eleven senior editorial managers (64 percent) were black (TMG 2013).

Independent reported that 60 percent of its editorial staff was black and around 30 percent were black female. Of its nineteen titles (including local community papers), ten have black editors (over 50 percent), eight are women, and three of these women are black. Of its four major business divisions, two have black managers, and one is female. For the company as a whole, 31 percent of its senior management is black (Independent 2013).

Media24's presentation showed less change, which it attributed to the difficulty of recruiting black candidates for its Afrikaans titles. It reported that 480 of its 704 newspaper journalists (68 percent) were white, 24 of its 30 newspapers editors (80 percent) were white, 284 of their 398 magazine journalists (71 percent) were white, and 37 of its 45 magazine editors (82 percent) were white. Of its online journalists, 28 of 53 (54 percent) were white; and of its online editors,

8 of 9 (90 percent) were white (Media24 2013) The fourth major group, Caxton, did not supply its figures (Jenkins 2013).

## The Public, Broadcasting Sector

While ownership and diversity issues have plagued the print sector, the opening up of broadcasting meant that the government could favor, as a matter of policy, new empowerment owners and managers in the issuing of licenses and thereby accelerate change. The ANC has hailed the broadcasting sector as the one that has moved most quickly from apartheid structures (ANC 1997, 1992).

Under a new board and new management, SABC went through a rapid transformation in the demographic makeup of its staff and management and its ability to represent the nation, and it recast its programming to be more in line with the expectations of public broadcasting. It sold off commercial regional stations, which in turn facilitated the emergence of new black empowerment media owners, such as Kagiso Media (which bought a number of radio stations). This purchase was followed by the regulator issuing of a number of new radio licenses and a free-to-air television license, again promoting a new group of owners—such as Hoskens (HCI, which launched eTV and Yfm)—and stimulating a more vibrant and competitive industry. By the end of the first decade of transition, the broadcasting sector had changed at many levels: ownership, management, staffing, policy, and content (OSF 2007).

Over time, however, this process stalled. The SABC was faced with a deep structural conundrum: because of its failure over the years to collect license fees, its revenue was overwhelmingly commercial, with some 82 percent coming from advertising and sponsorship. Only 17 percent came from licenses and a tiny amount from the government. It had to compete with an invigorated private sector, and was therefore constantly caught between the demand of commercialism and extensive public service obligations, including broadcasting in all eleven official languages. The SABC could do neither properly, which meant that it was not strong commercially and offered a half-baked public service, causing a continual tension in the organization.

ANC conference resolutions in 2002 and again in 2007 called for a new funding model that would reduce the SABC's dependence on advertising and boost public service broadcasting, but this approach did not draw the attention of the national treasury and has not been pursued (ANC 2002, 2007). Public service broadcasting was not high on a spending agenda under constant pressure from every side, from the housing and health ministries through to military equipment.

In addition, the SABC became the center of power struggles both within the ANC and between the ANC and its rivals. The SABC board—the essential protector of the organization's independence—is appointed by the president, acting on the recommendations of a parliamentary committee that invites, receives, and filters public nominations. The ANC's domination of Parliament gives it effective control over board nominations and this power has allowed the wholesale implementation of the ANC's deployment strategy—designed to put its cadres into positions of power and influence—at the national broadcaster. The extent to which appointments were decided by the ANC executive became apparent when, in 2011, it emerged that the parliamentary committee had dropped its own board recommendations in favor of a list of names handed down from ANC headquarters (SOS 2011). This practice meant also that the process became entangled in the bitter intraparty battles for leadership, which infested the workings of the SABC board and its senior management.

In addition, the minister of communications negotiated an agreement with the board that, as representative of the sole shareholder, gave her veto power over key appointments (SOS 2011). This control was hugely controversial, as it fell outside of the Broadcasting Act and is seen by many observers and commentators to be contrary to the constitutional guarantee of the independence of public media. It allowed cadre deployment to filter down through the organization and, for example, the appointment of a CEO with no background in broadcasting and news executives who were partisan in ANC leadership struggles.

The independence of the organization was compromised, and it was saddled with ineffectual leadership and management. The result was the collapse of the board twice in as many years, a deterioration in corporate governance, and a series of controversial news decisions that appeared to be politically motivated. By 2010, the SABC was wracked by financial and political crises, and had to be bailed out by the state to the extent of 1 billion rand. The organization was therefore weakened, discredited, and unable effectively to implement its difficult and complicated mandate.

The result was that the country's biggest news organization, and the one institution with the resources to provide comprehensive news coverage, provided patchy service. At its worst, it resorted to the kind of coverage of the government that typified the old state broadcaster; at its best it was tepid and overly timid. The quality of its coverage deteriorated consistently. The poverty of the SABC's public service and professional ethic was most apparent in the build-up to the ANC's heated Mangaung conference in 2012, when a ruling was made that no radio talk show could take place on the matter without the ANC's official participation—an entirely impractical rule that took the most cautious, narrow, and impractical view of how to achieve journalistic balance. In 2011/2012, SABC television news bulletins were shedding their audience rapidly to a private station, eTV. A bold attempt to start an Africa-wide 24-hour news service collapsed in 2011 at great expense, and eTV stepped in to claim this valuable territory. And an extraordinary 30 percent of households moved to pay-TV.

However, long delays in the arrival of digital terrestrial television, which has the potential to open up the broadcasting market significantly to more competition and diversity, have also clogged the system. It did not help that the regulator, Icasa, proved too weak and underresourced to monitor license compliance. Icasa was affected by reduced budgets, making it almost impossible for it to fulfill a wide-ranging mandate, and it had to do without the personnel, skills, or equipment to monitor licensees. A detailed look at Icasa's capacity to meet its mandate in 2007 described it as "historically underfunded (as acknowledged by the government)" (OSF 2007). Add to this palpably weak leadership—again a factor of ANC cadre deployment policy; the organization was doomed to falter in a way that burdened the whole industry. The rate of issuing new licenses, for example, slowed down considerably after 1999, as did the move to digital terrestrial broadcasting.

# Community Media

The third of the foundational institutions came a little later, in 2003. Government created the Media Development and Diversity Agency to "promote access to the media by marginalised groups and to enhance media diversity" through support for small, local, and community media in underserved areas. Its vision was that "each and every South African citizen should have access to a choice of a range of diverse media" (MDDA 2012). It negotiated with the private media sector to match core state funding.

The agency was small and budgets were limited. An original needs assessment in 2001 was that community and small media would need R500 million over five years. The actual budget though, was half that, and it naïvely assumed that this amount could decrease after five years "due to a significant decline in the need for support." But the original budget was not met: in 2005 the MDDA spent R14 million, and this had risen to R33 million in 2010 and R53 million in 2011. The MDDA report for 2011/2012 said it had spent R201 million since 2004 on some 413 media projects, trained 1,764 people, and created about 301 jobs, directly and indirectly. During 2011/2012, these efforts included twenty-six projects in community broadcasting at R40 million, one project in community television at R1.6 million, eight community print projects at R170,000, twenty-three small commercial print projects at R17.5 million, and R4 million on program production.

The Department of Communication also set in place a scheme to build studios for community stations. It did so directly, rather than through the MDDA. In 2010 it amounted to R6 million to assist with infrastructure at fifteen stations, with R10 million also given to support the development of content (mostly in the form of sponsorship to communicate government activity) (DOC 2012).

The MDDA, in the words of researcher Libby Lloyd, herself a former MDDA executive director, "has undoubtedly made a difference—ensuring the survival of many community broadcasters and local newspapers"—but "has not lived up to the original ANC promises" (Lloyd 2013). The issue is not just financial, though. The blockages to community radio are multifold, and the sustainability of such stations highly questionable. State support is for start-ups only. This has led many stations onto a commercial path; those that succeed are those that are most beholden to advertising and sponsorship, which weakens their community ties. A survey of community radio stations in 2010 indicated how few are able to generate their own local news and information: "Community stations are generally failing to meet their mandate in the critical area of providing original, local news," it concluded (Krüger 2011).

*The community press*

The Independent Publishers Association lists 245 titles primarily located in rural and disadvantaged areas, 97 of them publishing at least some content in indigenous languages. There is tremendous flux in this market, with 50 titles having been closed or sold (to larger commercial operators) in the last five years and 18 new applicants for membership in 2012.[7] Where they exist, these papers have added to local voices and news, but like their radio station counterparts, they have few reporting resources and little impact on the national media.

# ANC Criticism of the Media

It was against this background that ANC attention shifted after 2000 toward the private print media, the one area over which it has had least direct influence. There were strong hints of a growing antagonism regarding the press in the 2002 ANC annual conference document:

> Sections of the media continue to act in a manner, which resist meaningful transformation of our country. . . .

> There is an overwhelming perception that the media in general has failed to come to terms with the political changes that placed a predominantly black party to lead our country. Within this environment the state and other organs of society are perceived in terms and roles designed for an illegitimate state. Activities of the state and its representative are viewed with suspicion, if not with open hostility. Although subtle, there lurks the ever-present racial stereotyping and compartmentalization of the South African population. . . .

> Most often than not, it is the opponents of the transformation agenda of government who find space to articulate their views. Instead of debate, media is dominated by sound bytes from the political parties that are opposed to the ANC programme. Thus being independent in media circles is seen as being anti-ANC. Proponents of this approach have consistently disguised this hostility to the organs of society and the ANC as no more than the traditional role of the media as a watchdog over the behaviour of state institutions and their representatives.

> This so-called watchdog role needs to be interrogated. There is overwhelming evidence of sections of the media treating government with open hostility because of its political programme. A true watchdog would provide space for the correct reporting of events and developments that shape the national life rather than partisan positions. Fundamentally, the media ignores the critical issues of transformation and consequently, does not give space to representatives of societal organs to articulate the choices that confront South Africans. . . .

> Most probably, it is in South Africa alone where a political movement that enjoys almost two thirds of electoral support does not have any media outlet that supports its programmes and functions editorially within its political ambit.

The ANC's attitude to the print media moved between a substantive critique of its shortcomings and a discomfort with critical reporting, and the two concerns were blurred. The critique was generalized, with little distinction among different newspapers or any recognition of exceptions: "[The media] is intrusive, embarrassing, irresponsible, disruptive, vulgar, brash and uniformed. Undoubtedly the media is all of the above things some of the time" (ANC 2002). No doubt, that critique fed the hostility of those who were uncomfortable with an independent, critical, and even hostile media.

The core criticism was that:

– Ownership was still too concentrated and white;
– The newspapers were overly hostile to the ANC and its transformation project;
– Newspapers were guilty of ethical misconduct, through intrusions into privacy and dignity; and
– There was deterioration in the quality of reporting.

Some of this criticism reflects global patterns of news media grappling with financial and new technology pressures, leading to cutbacks in newsrooms, and quality and ethical issues. And some of it reflects a discomfort with a robust and critical media. Certainly, elements of the media have been bold and persistent in their criticism of the ruling party.

Two events in particular fueled debates over journalistic ethics—notably around sensitive issues of dignity and privacy. The first was the *Sunday Times'* publication of leaked (or stolen, as the ANC put it) medical records of the highly controversial Manto Tshabalala-Msimang, minister of health from 1999 to 2008. Msimang had courted controversy over her HIV and AIDS skepticism and her reputation for bibulousness. When she was admitted for a kidney transplant, the publication of her medical records indicated that she was still drinking, even while in hospital. The invasion of privacy infuriated the ANC, even though a judge ruled that the publication served the public interest.

Second, the publication by the *City Press* of a painting depicting President Jacob Zuma as a Lenin-like character, with caricatured genitals exposed, brought furious protests, threats, court action, and calls from ANC officials for a boycott of the newspaper. At issue here were conflicting views of the balance between the right to satirize the president and his sense of dignity. At the ANC's Polokwane conference of 2007, the language, and the sense of an ANC facing an implacably hostile media grew strong:

> The ANC is faced with a major ideological offensive, largely driven by the opposition and fractions in the mainstream media, whose key objective is the promotion of market fundamentalism, control of the media and the images it creates of a new democratic dispensation in order to retain old apartheid economic and social relations. This offensive against our movement, in its content and form, is part of a global offensive against progressive values and ideas.

They talked of "antidemocratic elements" in the media. With it came the threat of state intervention into private media.

This was a significant shift, for the ANC, until this point, had been critical of the private media, and had pushed for change, but had behaved in a hands-off manner. First came attacks on the adequacy of the press' self-regulatory mechanisms (a Press Council and Ombudsman) and a call for an investigation into a statutory appeals body to supersede these structures. Second, a Protection of State Information Bill, quickly dubbed the "Secrecy Bill," which would have stifled leaks from official sources, with very heavy penalties for anyone possessing or publishing a wide range of documents that would be deemed secret. At the same time, a new push was made to encourage "transformation" with parliament's call for the introduction of an industry charter, along the lines of other major industries. The charter was resisted on the grounds that it opened the door to state interference in the private media.

It was at the ANC's Polokwane conference that a call was made for Parliament to address the inadequacy of press self-regulation. A statutory tribunal that would be a final court of appeal inserted above the existing Press Council and Ombudsman system was proposed. No detail was given of how such a tribunal would operate, and Parliament never moved to legislate. In response, the print media set up a public inquiry under former Chief Justice Pius Langa to examine the effectiveness of the existing system. He recommended a move to what was called coregulation. This phrase usually refers to a system of media regulation run jointly by the state and the private sector, as in India, but Langa was only suggesting greater public participation in the Press Council. His proposal, however, gave the ANC a way out of the corner into which they had put themselves, and its leadership moved quickly to accept the Langa recommendations.

The "Secrecy Bill" emerged in 2011 from the state security sector's desire to stem the leaks that were feeding investigative journalists. A draconian clampdown on anyone publishing or possessing a wide range of documents that could be deemed secret was desired. The definition of what could be secret was all-embracing and the power to decide it given to thousands of state officials. Two years later, after about thirty drafts, and in the face of growing public protest, the bill that was eventually passed by Parliament in 2013 was watered down, with the worst restrictions removed, though it was still criticized by free speech proponents for its chilling effects on investigative reporting. By mid-2013, the bill had not been signed into an act, and a review by the Constitutional Court was likely.

The next push came from the parliamentary communications committee. It called a series of hearings on transformation in the print media industry. Again, the print sector formed its own commission, the Print and Digital Media Industry Transformation Task Team (PDMITT), to hold hearings on the issue and to seek a solution with which both the government and the industry could live. In mid-2013, this commission made recommendations to accelerate and monitor transformation.

It was while this focus was on the private media that the Marikana shootings claimed the lives of thirty-four striking platinum miners at the hands of the police in August 2012. It became clear that the gradual build-up to this incident had been largely overlooked by a media—private and public—that offers very little labor coverage and therefore was not plugged into the trade union and labor dynamics in the critical Rustenberg region. But it was not only the lacunae in reporting that were apparent, it was the absence from the public arena—before, during, and after Marikana—of voices that are politically important but marginalized in public debate.

In an analysis done shortly after the event, Jane Duncan of Rhodes University showed that of 153 articles about Marikana or Lonmin, the mining company involved, in the week of the shootings only 3 percent of sources quoted were miners themselves, and only on one occasion was a miner quoted on what actually happened on that fateful day (Duncan 2012). Duncan blamed journalists, but she failed to take account of the many attempts by reporters to speak to miners without success, often blocked by the workers' own unions. There were also notable attempts by some media to humanize the victims of the shootings by telling their and their families' stories.[8] But what did become clear was imbalances in coverage and media access, which had hidden the growing crisis from the public eye and masked the decline of the National Union of Mineworkers, a key ANC ally. It was a dramatic demonstration of the impact of a media that mirrored wider social and economic inequalities and contributed to the marginalization of those outside of center of power and their exclusion from democracy's public sphere.

The call for media transformation has largely been focused on an attempt to de-racialize media ownership, management, and production and has barely addressed the historical exclusion of large parts of the country from media coverage. The ruling party and its allies have a voice, as do organized business and labor and civil society, but the large number of South Africans outside of these institutions are almost as marginalized in the media as ever, covered only as causes for concern and welfare when they pose a threat to stability because of strikes or service delivery protests, for example. These imbalances are seen in the South African media constantly: potholes in suburban roads get more coverage in much of the media than the absence of passable roads in informal settlements, for example; and service delivery issues are seldom covered by most (but not all) media outside of outbreaks of protest. To make it into the media, most of those on the fringes of the economy have to rely on a visit from a political celebrity or resort to crime or violence (Harber 2011).

# The Media and Democracy

This marginalization of many from our media goes to the heart of the deliberative nature of our democracy, as envisaged in the constitution. Parliament is instructed to "make rules and orders concerning its business, with due regard to representative and participatory democracy, accountability, transparency and public involvement" (South African Government 1996, Section 57). It must "facilitate public involvement in the legislative and other processes of the Assembly and its committees; and conduct its business in an open manner, and hold its sittings, and those of its committees, in public" (Section 59). These principles apply to "administration in every sphere of government," "organs of state," and "public enterprises" (Chapter 10).

In practice, the media plays a central role, as in any representative democracy, in conveying the workings of parliament and other centers of power to citizens, and the diverse views of citizens back to parliament and the executive—in particular for those who do not have the resources for lobbying. In South Africa, the views of the ruling elite dominate the media, and those with the least resources are only infrequently heard.

South Africans seeking to create a unified country can celebrate the absence (largely) of an ethnic media, which in some other African countries (notably Kenya in its recent conflicts) has contributed to divisive identities and tensions, but the fact that English is increasingly dominant as the language of national debate, business, and politics excludes many, and notably a disproportionate number of its poorer, less educated citizens. In other words, the language of the media is further marginalizing those already on the nation's social fringes.

## South Africa in the digital age

As does technology, digital networked media may have the potential to allow for much greater interaction, to break down the gate-keeping of traditional media and the censorship of governments, to provide powerful tools for deliberative and participative politics, and to lower the cost of entry into the media world, but achieving this result depends on availability and access. But where bandwidth remains slow and expensive, it has the opposite effect—widening the chasm between those with information access and those without it, or with only limited access. The most recent research shows an upswing in Internet access: having hovered around 10 percent of the population for some years, this number has risen quickly to about 30 percent on the back of mobile access. Usage, however, remains severely limited by cost.

## The national conversation

The result of this perpetuation of inequalities in media access is a limited national conversation, one that draws a restricted range of citizens into the all-important debate about the allocation of the country's resources. The South African nation gathers only occasionally around television and radio for events such as the president's annual State of the Nation speech at the opening of Parliament, Nelson Mandela's death, or—most commonly—sporting events. Sport may be the one area where there has been a conscious attempt to break traditional class, race, language, and gender divides (international rugby coverage is often available in three or four languages), drawing South Africans together around an issue of national pride.

Again, this audience fragmentation is a global phenomenon, driven by technologies. The Internet allows for and encourages media targeting of smaller and smaller niches, even individuals. In the face of this factor, mass media all around the world—where national conversations have traditionally happened—are giving way to smaller communities reading niche media where the conversation is increasingly between like-minded individuals. For example, in the United States the ritual of a nation gathering for the evening network news—where the news culture was one of professional fairness and objectivity—is rapidly being displaced by individuals choosing cable channels that are more opinionated and partisan and selected on the basis of political affiliation, or on the Internet where audiences are defined by a set of common interests and viewpoints.

In South Africa, this trend is superimposed on a foundation of social inequality. The result is a distortion in the public sphere: we conduct parallel conversations of different social, economic, and language groups, rarely overlapping, with the exclusion of a large part of the country from the media.

## A Partial Transformation

South Africa now has more media serving more people thanks to the rise of tabloid presses; local, community media; and the opening up of the broadcasting and digital markets. And there have been changes in the demographics of ownership, management, and newsrooms, though this outcome is uneven across the industry. But there is still a large part of the country that does not have access to the media, and whose voices and faces are seldom heard and seen in any form except as victims in need of help. In a country with large scale unemployment and high levels of inequality along historically racial lines, those included in the public sphere are now more racially diverse, while those excluded are still poor, black, and marginal. Shortcomings in the building of public and community media have meant a failure to address this issue.

If one were to assess the South African news media against the democratic functions outlined earlier in this article, one would have to say that the media is a watchdog, an enforcer of public accountability, and that the private media in particular stands out. In providing a conversation and a flow of information between government and citizens, the news media is less successful, largely because finances have impaired the capacity to do daily reporting. The drive to empower marginalized communities to join the national debate, and participate in the democratic process—so strongly argued for in early ANC policy papers—has faltered along with the weakening of the SABC, the regulator Icasa, and a failure adequately to support community media.

## Notes

1. *Star, Isolezwe* (Independent newspapers); *Business Day, Sowetan, The Times* (TMG); *Citizen* (Caxton); *Beeld, Daily Sun* (Media24); *New Age* (New Age Publishers).

2. *Cape Argus, Cape Times, Daily Voice* (Independent newspapers); *Business Day, The Times* (TMG); *Burger, Daily Sun, Son* (Media24); *New Age* (New Age Publishers).

3. *Daily News, Mercury, Isolezwe* (Independent newspapers); *Business Day, The Times* (TMG); *Daily Sun, Witness* (Media24); *New Age* (New Age Publishers).

4. *Sunday Times, Sunday World* (TMG); *Sunday Independent* (Independent); *Rapport, City Press, Sunday Sun* (Media24).

5. *Sunday Tribune, Isolwezwe ngeSonto* (Independent); *Son op Sondag, Sondag* (Media24); *Ilanga Langesotot* (IFP).

6. See www.abc.org.za.

7. See http://www.aip.org.za/.

8. Most notably *City Press's* multimedia Faces of Marikana, for which reporters, photographers, and videographers traveled rural areas for weeks tracking down the stories, winning them a number of awards and citations. See http://www.m24i.co.za/facesofmarikana/.

# References

ANC. 1992. *Ready to govern: ANC guidelines for a democratic South Africa*. Policy document. Available from http://www.anc.org.za/show.php?id=227 (accessed 10 November 2013).

ANC. 1997. *50th National Conference: Strategy and tactics—As amended by conference*. Available from http://www.anc.org.za/show.php?id=2424 (accessed 10 November 2013).

ANC. 2002. *51st National Conference: Discussion documents—Media in a democratic South Africa*. Available from http://www.anc.org.za/show.php?id=2504 (accessed 10 November 2013).

ANC. 2007. *52nd National Conference: Adopted strategy and tactics of the ANC*. Available from http://www.anc.org.za/show.php?id=2535 (accessed 10 November 2013).

Daniels, Glenda. 2013. *State of the newsroom South Africa 2013: Disruption and transitions*. Johannesburg: Wits Journalism. Available from www.journalism.co.za.

Department of Communications (DOC). 2012. *Annual report*. Pretoria: DOC.

Duncan, Jane. 2012. Where were the miners' voices at Marikana? Available from www.journalism.co.za.

Harber, Anton. 2011. *Diepsloot*. Johannesburg: Jonathan Ball.

Harber, Anton. 2013. *The Big gorilla* [E-book]. Johannesburg: Mampoer. Available from www.mampoer .co.za.

Harber, Anton, and Renn Margaret. 2010. *Troublemakers*. Johannesburg: Jacana.

Howard, Tony, and Khathu Mamaila. 26 April 2013. Presentation to the PDMITT on behalf of Independent News and Media, South Africa. Unpublished.

Jenkins, Paul. 25 April 2013. Presentation to the Print and Digital Media Industry Transformation Task Team (PDMITT) on behalf of Caxton, Johannesburg. Unpublished.

Krüger, Franz. 2011. News broadcasting on South African community radio. *Ecquid Novi: African Journal Studies* 32 (3): 61–79.

Lloyd, Libby. 2013. *South Africa's media 20 years after apartheid*. Washington, DC: Center for International Media Assistance.

Mandela, Nelson. 26 May 1992. Address by Comrade Nelson R Mandela to the International Federation of Newspapers Conference, Prague. Available from www.nelsonmandela.org.

Mandela, Nelson. February, 1994. Address to International Press Institute Conference. Available from www.saha.org.za.

Media Development and Diversity Agency (MDDA). June 2009. *Trends of ownership and control*. Parktown: MDDA. Available from www.mdda.org.za.

MDDA. 2012. *Annual report, 2011/2*. Parktown: MDDA. Available from www.mdda.org.za.

Media24. 25 April 2013. Presentation to the PDMITT, Johannesburg. Unpublished.

Open Society Foundation (OSF). 2007. *Meeting their mandates?* Cape Town: OSF.

South African Government. 1996. Constitution of the Republic of SA (No 108 of 1996).

SOS. 2011. SABC shareholder pact. Available from www.supportpublicbroadcasting.co.za.

TK Awards. 2012. Judges' remarks. Available from www.journalism.co.za.

Times Media Group. 26 April 2013. Presentation to the PDMITT, Johannesburg. Unpublished.

Wright, Joanna. June 2013. Afrikaans newspapers continue centralising drive. Johannesburg: The Media Online. Available from www.themediaonline.co.za.

# South Africa and Africa

By
CHRIS SAUNDERS

This article examines aspects of the complex relationship between South Africa and the rest of Africa from the presidency of Nelson Mandela through those of Thabo Mbeki and Jacob Zuma, showing how the relationship changed over time and exploring the influences that shaped South Africa's policy on and toward the continent—a policy that has largely been determined by the presidency rather than the Department of Foreign Affairs/International Relations and Co-operation. To understand the changing relationship between South Africa and the rest of the continent, it is necessary to consider, first, the history before 1994, then the dramatically altered situation that the transfer of power in South Africa brought about, Thabo Mbeki's interventionist approach to Africa in general, and Jacob Zuma's ambiguous involvement in continental affairs. The article concludes with some speculative thoughts on the role that South Africa may play on the continent in the future.

Keywords: South African foreign policy; Mandela; Mbeki; Zuma

South Africa's relationship with the rest of Africa has long been ambiguous. The country's apartheid rulers usually saw South Africa as separate from the rest of the continent, a white-ruled enclave increasingly threatened by hostile forces but with strong ties to the West. Today, some leaders in other African countries still view South Africa as being a country apart from the rest of the continent because of its large non-black African population and its special links to other parts of the world, now both West and East. South Africa does have by far the largest minority groups originally from out-

Chris Saunders is an emeritus professor at the University of Cape Town, where he taught in the Department of Historical Studies until the end of 2008. After leaving the university, he worked as a part-time consultant for the Centre for Conflict Resolution for two years. He has written on many aspects of Southern African history and historiography, and has recently begun publishing on South Africa's foreign policy since 1994.

DOI: 10.1177/0002716213512986

side the continent, and the largest, most diverse, and most developed economy in Africa, with the continent's most significant manufacturing sector, which developed on the back of mineral exploitation. But since the transfer of power to the black majority in 1994, South Africa has identified itself as an African country, has asserted that its relations with other African countries lie at the center of its foreign policy, and has claimed to speak and act as one of the leading countries on the continent. The prime goal of the government's Department of International Relations and Co-operation (DIRCO), proclaims its website, is to have "an African continent which is prosperous, peaceful, democratic, non-racial, non-sexist and united," and DIRCO and government spokespeople make constant reference to South Africa's "African agenda."[1] The relevant chapter in the country's much-heralded National Development Plan (NDP), published in 2012 and subsequently confirmed as the centerpiece of government policy, begins, "We are Africans. We are an African country. . . . We are an essential part of our continent" (National Planning Commission 2012, 15).[2]

What is this "African agenda"? How has the relationship between South Africa and the rest of the continent evolved since the presidency of Nelson Mandela (1994 to 1999) and how may it change in the future? What leadership role should South Africa play on the rest of the continent? To explore such questions, this article examines mainly political aspects of the history of the complex relationship between South Africa and the rest of the continent since 1994. Though that relationship was shaped by a wide variety of factors, domestic and global, the South African presidents played a leading role, and so this article focuses on the three main presidencies since 1994 before concluding by considering aspects of the current relationship between South Africa and the rest of the continent, and suggesting how it may evolve in the future.

## Pre-1994

Until the end of the 1980s the relationship between apartheid South Africa and the rest of the continent was, mostly, an antagonistic one (cf. Rotberg 2002), though the Southern African Customs Union (SACU), born in 1910, brought together South Africa and the three British High Commission territories that ultimately became independent in the 1960s as Botswana, Lesotho, and Swaziland. South African–ruled South West Africa was a de facto member of SACU before becoming a formal member when independent Namibia was born in 1990. The near neighborhood apart, however, most South African government policy-makers in the apartheid era believed that South Africa was somehow sui generis. Despite the attempts that were made to gain ties with certain countries in tropical Africa, there was no thought that "Africa," meaning the rest of the continent, should lie at the center of the country's foreign policy. In the early 1970s, the South African government engaged in a so-called outward policy, focused on developing friendly relations with key African countries (Nolutshungu

1975), but that ended with South Africa's invasion of Angola in 1975, and the Constellation of Southern African States that Prime Minister P. W. Botha proposed in 1979 never got off the ground. The 1980s saw South Africa attempt to destabilize a number of countries in southern Africa and fight a major war in southern Angola. It was only as this era ended in the late 1980s that the other Botha, Foreign Minister Pik Botha, began both to urge that South Africa should see itself primarily as an African country and to argue that South Africa should work with other African countries to solve problems without interference from outside the continent (Papenfus 2010, 626–58).

On the other hand, the very name African National Congress (ANC), adopted in 1923 by what had until then been called the South African Native National Congress (SANNC), suggested that the organization that was to emerge as the leader of the resistance to apartheid had long wished to associate itself with the rest of the continent. In the 1920s, this association was influenced by the Pan-Africanism of Marcus Garvey. When forced into exile in the 1960s, the banned ANC initially had its main base in what was then Tanganyika, later moving its headquarters to Lusaka, Zambia, and its military wing to camps in Angola. It received crucial support from the Liberation Committee of the main continental body, the Organisation of African Unity (OAU), which helped to fund the ANC's armed struggle. In its decades of exile, the ANC forged close ties not only with the governments of a number of independent African countries, but also with liberation movements that later came to power in Angola, Mozambique, Zimbabwe, and Namibia (Thomas 1996; Ellis 2012; Southall 2013a). As the ANC itself approached power in the early 1990s, and began to think about what foreign policy it would adopt when in government, it was, not surprisingly, deeply influenced by its past interactions with African countries and with the OAU (South African Democracy Education Trust 2013, esp. 249–76).

While the ANC was based in exile, its diplomacy was largely anticolonial and anti-Western in its orientation (Thomas 1996), because of its links to the Soviet Union, which provided it with the means to conduct its armed struggle, and the refusal of Western countries to take significant steps against apartheid. But as the ANC moved closer to power in the early 1990s, in what was then the new post–Cold War era, it sought to build ties with Western countries. Mandela published an influential article in the United States–based journal *Foreign Affairs* in which he stated, partly from personal conviction, but also to secure broad international approval, that when the ANC became the government of the new South Africa it would place human rights at the center of its foreign policy (Mandela 1993). In early 1994, officials of the apartheid government joined leading members of the ANC on a visit to a number of countries in tropical Africa to develop a new set of postapartheid relations with those countries (Graham 2011). This visit eased the transition from the old order to the new, for despite the dramatic shift in South Africa's relations with the rest of the continent that the transfer of power made possible, and the enthusiasm for a new relationship with other African countries among many former apartheid bureaucrats, there were also continuities between the old order and the new (Landsberg 2010a).

# The Mandela Presidency, 1994–1999

Within months of Nelson Mandela being sworn in as president, South Africa had become a member of both the OAU and the main regional body in southern Africa, the Southern African Development Community (SADC). SADC had its roots in the Front Line States and the Southern African Development Co-ordinating Conference (SADCC), both formed in opposition to apartheid South Africa (Khadiagala 1994, 2012). Like the OAU, SADC included states of vastly different geographies and economies. From the formation of the OAU in 1963 there were those who questioned the value of having a continental organization, given Africa's great diversity.[3] SADC—the headquarters of which remained in Gaborone, Botswana, even after South Africa joined—included countries that were not near neighbors of South Africa, such as Tanzania, Malawi, and Angola, which in the 1990s continued to be wracked by civil war. Lesotho is entirely surrounded by South Africa, and Swaziland was then, and continues to be, ruled autocratically by a hereditary monarch. In 1998, South Africa supported the addition to SADC's membership of the very large Democratic Republic of the Congo (DRC), despite its distance from South Africa and despite its being so undeveloped that some have called it only a notional state (Herbst and Mills 2013). Though most people in the various SADC countries spoke a Bantu language, these countries' very different colonial experiences had left their peoples speaking different European languages. There was a long history of people moving across the region—the diamond and then the gold mines in South Africa had attracted labor from what is now Malawi, from southern Mozambique, and from the territories adjacent to South Africa that Britain led to independence in the 1960s—but no common set of values that could bind such a diverse region together. While some SADC countries had emerged from colonialism peacefully, others had had to endure bitterly fought armed struggles and postindependence civil wars. In the case of Angola, civil war continued until 2002.

The relative strength of the South African economy meant that South Africa became SADC's most important member and a leading member of the OAU. South Africa was known internationally for having passed through a "miraculous" transition from apartheid to liberal democracy relatively peacefully, and for the generosity of spirit that Mandela showed as president, beginning in 1994. Though Mandela's inspirational leadership and South Africa's remarkable Truth and Reconciliation Commission gave the country great moral standing and a role on the world stage, other southern African countries remained concerned about South Africa's overwhelming economic dominance in the region and suspicious of its intentions, for they could not immediately forget apartheid South Africa's aggression in the region. Therefore, the regional role that the new South African government could play after 1994 was limited, and it was sensitive to the need not to assert its power as the regional hegemon. President Robert Mugabe of Zimbabwe, who had become a leading figure in SADCC, now saw Mandela usurping his role in SADC. From the time that South Africa joined the regional organization in 1994 there were tensions between it and other SADC members

(Nathan 2012), though relations between South Africa and the other countries in the region and beyond varied greatly from country to country. The ANC was conscious of owing a debt to other African countries, particularly those in the southern African region, for supporting its struggle against the apartheid regime.

Though it was conscious not to be seen to be either a continental or a regional bully, the new government nevertheless asserted that Africa was its main foreign policy priority. The number of South African embassies in other African countries quickly increased from four under apartheid to twenty-one (Pfister 2000). Mandela had pressing problems to face at home, including threats from right-wing elements unhappy with the country's abandonment of apartheid, but he told the OAU in Tunis only a month after coming into office that the new South Africa intended to play a leading role on the African continent, though he provided no specifics.[4] The first foreign policy document adopted by the new government, a "Framework for Co-operation in Southern Africa," approved by the cabinet in August 1996, held out a vision for the southern African region of "the highest possible degree of economic cooperation, mutual assistance where necessary, and joint planning of regional development initiatives, leading to integration consistent with socio-economic, environmental and political realities" (Department of Foreign Affairs 1996). When he visited Tanzania in 1996, Mandela said that his presence there underlined "the centrality of Africa and Southern Africa in the foreign policy of [South Africa's] new democracy" (Barber 2004, 171).[5]

Though the new South Africa soon realized the limited effectiveness of both the OAU and SADC, it paid its dues to both, hosting a SADC summit meeting as chair of the regional organization in 1996, and signing most of the relevant protocols. Mandela, striding the global stage, sometimes seemed to forget African countries that had supported the ANC's liberation struggle or had hosted it in exile, but he cultivated relations with President Muammar Qaddafi's Libya in particular, in part as a source of funds for the ANC's election campaigns. South Africa agreed to requests from the OAU and then the successor African Union (AU), as well as from the United Nations (UN), to contribute to peacekeeping missions elsewhere on the continent and, when asked, was willing to mediate in a number of conflict situations. Despite his immense moral authority, Mandela was often unsuccessful in his conciliation efforts elsewhere on the continent. In 1996, he failed to prevent the Nigerian military junta led by President Sani Abacha from executing the activist Ken Saro Wiwa. Elsewhere, he applied the South African experience of a government of national unity to situations in which it was not appropriate. For example, his attempt to broker a peace deal between then-President Mobutu Sese Seko of Zaire/Congo and his rival Laurent Kabila came to naught, while South Africa's attempts to bring about reconciliation between the Popular Movement for the Liberation of Angola (MPLA) and the Union for the Total Independence of Angola (UNITA) led by Jonas Savimbi only aroused the hostility of the MPLA government.

When war escalated in the DRC in 1998, Mandela did not join Angola, Namibia, and Zimbabwe in sending South African troops there, but that year the new South African National Defence Force (SANDF), with a few Botswana troops in tow, was sent into Lesotho to prevent its government from being over-thrown, and only retrospectively was this operation called a SADC effort. Although the intervention itself was inept, its goal was achieved, for the situation was stabilized and the intervention was followed by a lengthy mediation by South Africa to bring into effect a revised electoral system that combined the "first past the post" one inherited from Britain with proportional representation. This reform eventually made possible a peaceful transition to a coalition government in Lesotho in 2012 (Saunders 2013). South Africa's unilateralism was also shown in 1998 when it ignored the concerns of the other members of SACU and signed a bilateral Trade Development and Cooperation Agreement (TDCA) with the European Union (EU). Overall, the record of the Mandela presidency in relation to other countries in Africa was a mixed one that did not measure up to the lofty ambitions that it espoused. While Mandela sought to use soft power, drawing on his immense moral authority, as president, he increasingly handed over aspects of work involving other African countries to Thabo Mbeki, his deputy. In his most successful personal intervention in tropical Africa, Mandela mediated the inter-nal conflict in Burundi—another African country far from South Africa and in which South Africa had no obvious direct interest (Daniel 2006)—after vacating the presidency.

## The Mbeki Presidency, 1999–2008

In his most famous speech, delivered to the South African Parliament in 1996, Thabo Mbeki identified himself as "an African," which meant, in part, his identi-fying with all who lived on the continent (Mbeki 1998). Favoring an intervention-ist approach on the continent, Mbeki was more of a Pan-Africanist than his predecessor. In calling for an African Renaissance, he explicitly drew on the famous speech delivered at Columbia University in 1906 by Pixley Seme, who six years later was the main founder of SANNC (Odendaal 2012). Mbeki took over as president of South Africa in 1999 with a determination to promote his own version of Ghanaian President Kwame Nkrumah's pan-African dream. He pushed ahead rapidly with a highly ambitious African agenda that involved the transformation of the OAU, much criticized for its lethargy, into what he hoped would be a more active AU; and the introduction of a raft of new continental measures to improve governance on the continent. These included the African Peer Review Mechanism (APRM), "a mutually agreed instrument voluntarily acceded to by the member states of the AU as an African self-monitoring mecha-nism,"[6] and the New Economic Partnership for Africa's Development (NEPAD). Though he wanted to reduce the role of Western powers in Africa, Mbeki saw NEPAD as a means to attract new funding that would help to develop Africa as a whole. He played a major role in the creation of the Pan African Parliament, which was then given a home in South Africa, and in designing the AU's Peace and Security Council as a key part of the new continental African security and institutional architecture. With his eyes fixed on such continental schemes,

Mbeki tended not to accord special priority to the southern African region, seeing it as but one part of his broader African agenda (cf. Pottinger 2009; Glaser 2010).

For a time, Mbeki's proactive role on the continent seemed to be strikingly successful: he forged a close relationship with President Olusegun Obasanjo of Nigeria, and after addressing Rwanda's security fears, he brought together the parties to the conflict in the DRC at an inter-Congolese dialogue held in South Africa that ushered in a new dispensation for that war-ravaged country (Khadiagala 2006). South Africa deployed a force in Burundi to safeguard the return of political exiles to that country, after which a power-sharing deal was reached between the rebel forces and the government, thanks in part to the efforts of Jacob Zuma, Mbeki's deputy president (Bentley and Southall 2005).

Mbeki was criticized for his "quiet diplomacy" toward Zimbabwe, his favoring Mugabe against the opposition Movement for Democratic Change (MDC), and his failure to criticize the human rights abuses committed by the Zimbabwe African National Union-Patriotic Front (ZANU-PF) government (e.g., Adelmann 2004; Hamill and Hoffman 2009; Southern African Liaison Office 2013),[7] but he did encourage a process of dialogue that led in September 2008 to the signing of a Global Political Agreement (GPA) between the ruling ZANU-PF and the two MDC formations. The GPA provided for the formation of a so-called unity government, at the cost of President Mugabe remaining in office.

By the time that Mbeki was forced to resign as president, shortly after the signing of the GPA, many of his initial hopes, including the APRM and NEPAD, had largely been dashed, as resources from outside the continent failed to materialize and processes to enhance accountability within Africa had little effect; states could too easily ignore the criticisms made in the APRM review reports (e.g., Cilliers 2011).[8] And despite all the talk of "African solutions to African problems" and the idea of creating an African Standby Force to deal with continental conflicts, African leaders recognized that the UN would need to remain in charge of most peacekeeping missions in Africa, in the absence of the necessary funding and capacity in Africa itself. As one of the five components of the African Standby Force, a SADC brigade was launched with some fanfare in August 2007, in Lusaka, Zambia. South Africa's role in that force was crucial from the start, but although the SADC brigade was initially supposed to be operational by 2010 (Saunders 2012), as of 2013 it remained bedeviled by many problems, not least of which was interoperability among its component parts. The new target date for it to be operational is 2015. Both during his presidency and after, Mbeki made a number of attempts to mediate in the conflict in the Ivory Coast (Côte d'Ivoire), but these were unsuccessful in part because of his bias toward the incumbent ruler and because he aroused the ire of Nigeria, which did not appreciate South African involvement in a region in which it was the hegemon. For all of Mbeki's many failings, however—and it may be argued that he was much too ambitious in what he tried to bring about on the continent (e.g., Glaser 2010)—more than any other postapartheid president of South Africa he had a vision of his country playing a leading role in a revived Africa.

# The Zuma Presidency, 2009–

Having ousted Mbeki from the presidency of the ANC at the organization's 2007 Polokwane conference, Jacob Zuma took over as president of South Africa in 2009. When he did so, many commentators expected him to withdraw from the kind of continental engagements that Mbeki had supported (e.g., Landsberg 2010b). Zuma chose Angola as the first African country to visit as president. The ANC's armed wing had been based there, and Zuma sought to improve relations with President Eduardo dos Santos's regime, for relations with Angola had been strained under both Mandela and Mbeki.[9] Zuma seemed keen to emphasize the ties between the ANC and the other former liberation movements that had fought armed struggles and were now ruling southern African states. Besides the MPLA in Angola, these were the Front for the Liberation of Mozambique (FRELIMO), the South West Africa People's Organisation (SWAPO) in Namibia, and ZANU-PF, though the ANC had not had close ties with the last during the liberation struggle.[10] The view that some expressed, that SADC was little more than an "old boy's club" of veterans of armed struggle, aiming to protect the interests of those in power in the countries of the region, appeared to be further validated when the SADC heads of state agreed to suspend, then disband, SADC's own tribunal, after that body ruled against the Zimbabwean government in a celebrated land case involving white farming rights. The chief judge of the tribunal was then very critical of South Africa for not using "its power as the SADC's largest state and its 'moral authority' to prevent the tribunal from being emasculated."[11] But by then the country's moral authority had dissipated, not least because Zuma had come into office after numerous corruption charges against him had been dropped in a highly dubious manner (e.g., Southall and Daniel 2009).

The xenophobic attacks in South African townships in May 2008, which led to the deaths of more than sixty people, further damaged South Africa's reputation in the eyes of Africans to the north. South Africa had received a very large number of refugees from other African countries, especially from Zimbabwe but also from as far away as Somalia, and reports on the manner in which such refugees were treated in South Africa were often extremely negative. This was another example in which South Africa squandered the goodwill that other African countries had initially had toward the ANC (based on its struggle in exile against apartheid and its actions in its first years in government). There can be no doubt that South Africa's concern with peace and stability elsewhere on the continent was driven in part by the realization that instability elsewhere was likely to increase the flow of refugees to South Africa, and that there was a limit to the number of refugees the country could absorb when so many of its own citizens were unemployed and impoverished.

Like the other states in SADC, South Africa remained opposed to any transfer of national sovereignty to the regional body, wishing to ensure that its "national interests" remained paramount at all times,[12] but South Africa was ready to use SADC in its own interests: in 2011 Zuma persuaded all the other SADC countries to back what he presented as a SADC bid to elect South Africa's Nkosazana Dlamini-Zuma as chair of the AU Commission, the key post in the continental organization. South Africa continued its campaign until it was successful, despite the antagonism that it aroused elsewhere on the continent (e.g., Handy and Kjeldgaard 2011, 2012).

By the time Dlamini-Zuma was eventually elected in Addis Ababa in July 2012, Zuma had scored what he and DIRCO presented as another coup, by having South Africa admitted as a member of the Brazil-Russia-India-China (BRIC) group of countries. He achieved this in part by presenting South Africa as the "gateway" to the rest of Africa and as a country that was in some way the natural leader of Africa and one able to speak on behalf of the continent as a whole. Becoming a member of BRICS emphasized South Africa's special position on the continent—it was the only African country also to be a member of the G20—but naturally aroused animosity elsewhere. When the fifth BRICS summit, the first to be held in Africa, took place in Durban in March 2013, South Africa tried to downplay its special role, choosing as the theme of the summit "BRICS and Africa: Partnership for Development, Integration and Industrialisation" and inviting leaders of other African countries to interact with its BRICS partners.[13] But South Africa's special relationship with China—which has become South Africa's single most important trading partner—further fuelled tension between South Africa and other African countries, those vying for Chinese attention and those more critical than South Africa of China's intentions in Africa. For example, the vice president of Zambia, Guy Scott, was reported to have made some very disparaging remarks at the beginning of May 2013 about South Africa and its pretensions to represent Africa on the global stage (Smith 2013).

Though he did so in a more ad hoc fashion, Zuma continued much of Mbeki's Africa policy. He succeeded Mbeki as chief "facilitator" for Zimbabwe, though with less focus and attention to detail. His efforts to persuade the Zimbabweans to make the GPA work met with little success, and he was unable to secure the necessary reforms that would have enabled a free and fair election to take place in that country in July 2013 (e.g., Zondi and Bhengu 2011). He agreed that South Africa should play a role in mediation in Madagascar after the coup that took place there in 2009 and South Africa was able to help persuade both leading figures to agree that neither would contest the first postcoup election, initially scheduled to take place in July 2013 but postponed. No SADC or AU sanctions were imposed on Madagascar, however, to ensure that the terms of the roadmap drawn up to return that country to constitutionalism were respected.

Zuma continued—and gave greater emphasis to it than Mbeki had—the drive to link SADC to the Common Market for Eastern and Southern Africa (COMESA) and the East African Community (EAC) in a tripartite free trade area, which is supposed to come into being by 2015.[14] A consensus politician who was reluctant to take issue with his peers, Zuma dismissed the criticisms of those who wanted South Africa's foreign policy to be based primarily on human rights. He went along with SADC's decision in effect to destroy the very tribunal it had set up (Nathan 2012).[15] In early 2013, there was some evidence that he was adopting a more proactive and interventionist stance toward the rest of Africa, though the suggestion by Chris Alden and Maxi Schoeman that "the defensive posturing which characterized much of the African National Congress's (ANC) post-apartheid foreign policy" was being "replaced by an unashamed claim to African leadership" is overstated (Alden and Schoeman 2013, 111; cf. Fabricius 2013b). At the end of April 2013, Maite Nkoana-Mashabane, the minister of international relations and co-operation, did, however, say that because South Africa was an integral part of the African continent, it had to say "yes to preventive diplomacy. . . . When it is called upon to intervene, [South Africans] will always be there."[16]

South Africa wished to project an image that it was a responsible member of the international community, not least in the hope that doing so would help it to secure a permanent seat on a reformed and enlarged UN Security Council. But in its two terms as a nonpermanent member of that council (2007–2008 and 2011–2012), its voting record was much criticized. It refused to support resolutions targeted at rogue states, and though it voted for a resolution approving all necessary measures to prevent the Libyan government from suppressing civilian opposition, it then became a strong critic of the NATO operation there on the grounds that NATO wanted regime change (Centre for Conflict Resolution 2013). South Africa was again critical of external intervention on the continent when French troops helped oust the incumbent in the Ivory Coast. While there was clearly no alternative to French intervention in Mali in March 2012 to prevent a possible rebel advance on Bamako, in its aftermath Zuma engaged with the rulers of both Nigeria and Algeria to determine what steps could be taken to avoid further external intervention (e.g., Mbeje 2013), and he then gave stability as the prime reason for South Africa's own intervention in the Central African Republic (CAR).

Additional South African forces were sent to the CAR in January 2013 at a time when the autocratic leader of that country, Francois Bozizé, under pressure from rebels, asked for help. There was speculation that this intervention, supposedly based on a Memorandum of Understanding that provided for South African help in training a CAR military force, was intended to keep France from sending troops to the CAR, as it had to Mali. Perhaps Zuma feared that instability in the CAR might spread into the DRC next door. If there were economic reasons for the intervention, it was not clear what they were. The return of the bodies of thirteen South African National Defence Force (SANDF) soldiers from the CAR in March 2013 raised new doubts among South Africans about what their country was doing in distant tropical Africa, and led to many questions being asked— among a public mostly ignorant about the rest of the continent—about what South Africa's role in Africa should be.

After the SANDF deaths, the remaining South African forces were withdrawn from the CAR, at the request of the Economic Community of Central African States. But not long afterward, South Africa readied one thousand troops to go, with forces from Malawi and Tanzania, to the eastern DRC as part of an activist international intervention force under UN authority (e.g., Fabricius 2013a). When President Goodluck Jonathan of Nigeria made an official state visit to South Africa in early May 2013, he and Zuma agreed to work together on issues affecting the continent as a whole. If such united action were to become effective, it would be likely to increase the fears of other sub-Saharan countries of the dominant role that these two giants might play on the continent.

## Toward a Conclusion: What Should South Africa's Leadership Role Be on the Continent?

Through its involvement in numerous countries, from the Darfur region of the Sudan to Lesotho, South Africa has arguably done more than any other African country since 1994 to promote peace on the continent. South Africa's role in the rest of Africa, nevertheless, remains controversial and contested. As a member of SADC, it should work within its structures, including its Standby Force. If it intervenes unilaterally, either in the southern African region or farther in Africa, such intervention is likely to be seen, as that in the CAR was by some, as an unwarranted move by the "big brother from the south." To counter any perception elsewhere in Africa that it is pushing itself forward as a self-elected continental leader, South Africa will need to be careful to act only when asked to, and, wherever possible, with others.[17] While South Africa may wish to offer its resources to help promote stability, development, and democracy elsewhere, this can best be done as a member of SADC or of the AU. Instead of continuing its divisive campaign for its own permanent seat on the UN Security Council, South Africa should argue for a permanent seat for Africa on the council. South Africa has long since lost the moral capital that it accumulated under Mandela, and whether a successor to Zuma can regain at least some of the country's former moral prestige remains to be seen.

An Afro-optimist scenario for Africa's future sees development and democracy spreading through the continent; an Afro-pessimist one anticipates continuing and increasingly serious crises arising from poor governance, competition for scarce resources, the adverse effects of climate change, food insecurity, and other factors. Given Africa's great diversity, elements of both scenarios are likely. While some South African businesses have flourished in other African countries, such as the mobile-phone giant MTN in Nigeria, others have found the environments difficult and have withdrawn (e.g., Daniel and Lutchman 2006). Such stories of success and failure are likely to continue, but a network of organizations—from, say, the Association of African Universities to the Association of African Central Banks—now link people across the continent, and the fact that students from across most of sub-Saharan Africa now study at universities in South Africa creates networks that tie South Africa to other countries on the continent.

A working group that DIRCO set up in 2010 to help define South Africa's national interest has to date failed to come up with any consensus on what it is.[18] Any country may of course have various national interests, and they are likely to change over time. According to the minister of international relations and co-operation, the cornerstone of South Africa's foreign policy toward the rest of the African continent, as elsewhere, is the country's domestic interest

(Nkoana-Mashabane 2013). Central to the policy is the need to grow the size of the market for South African goods. Instability elsewhere, especially in the southern African region, is not in South Africa's interests, not least because it is likely to increase further the flow of refugees southward. Though South Africa remains committed to working through the structures of SADC, that body has so far proved ineffective in dealing with problems of governance in member-states. It has not produced any clear strategic policy on what to do about undemocratic regimes, whether in Zimbabwe, Swaziland, or Angola. Even if instability, or foreign intervention, in North Africa does not have any direct consequences for South Africa, South Africa needs to be concerned with all of Africa because it is seen as part of the continent in the global imagination, and negative developments anywhere in Africa affect South Africa's image as an African country. That may well, however, be insufficient justification for South Africa contributing troops to, say, the AU mission in the Darfur region of the Sudan.

South Africa does contribute to development on the rest of the continent in many different ways. South African companies such as MTN and Shoprite cater to middle-class needs in many African countries. In May 2013, Eskom, South Africa's national power company, agreed to be the anchor client for hydroelectric power that will be generated from the still-to-be-constructed Grand Inga dam in the DRC, promising to buy 2,500 megawatts of the initial 4,800-megawatt out-put. The Development Bank of Southern Africa, based in South Africa, has now agreed to help finance the project (Norbrook 2013). Zuma has himself been involved, on behalf of both the AU and SADC, in promoting a number of conti-nental infrastructural projects, of which the best-known is the north-south cor-ridor to link the port of Durban in South Africa with the Copperbelt in the DRC and Zambia, with a spur to Dar es Salaam in Tanzania.[19]

Will South Africa develop a clearer strategic vision than it has had for its future relationship with Africa? There is all too little expertise on the rest of Africa in South Africa. The government authorities in South Africa are not nurturing what knowledge there is, and the demise of South African think-tanks that have worked in other African countries does not bode well for the future.[20] In conclu-sion, let me set out some elements of a possible approach for South Africa. The South Africa government should not view any intervention by the West—recently in Libya, the Ivory Coast, and Mali—as imperialist and, therefore, against African interests. The ideas from the Cold War era about the world that linger on in the ANC-SACP-COSATU tripartite alliance should be jettisoned. South Africa should give priority, more than it has to date, to its neighboring countries; it should strengthen SACU by, inter alia, renegotiating the revenue-sharing for-mula; it should stand firm for free and fair elections without violence in Zimbabwe and for democratic reforms in Swaziland;[21] it should persuade SADC to resurrect its tribunal, and ensure that the SADC Standby Force is operational by 2015. It should recognize that Nigeria will take the lead in promoting develop-ment and stability in West Africa, Chad in Central Africa, Kenya in East Africa, and Ethiopia in the Horn of Africa. Nigeria and Kenya are already challenging South Africa's claim that it is "the gateway" into the continent, and South Africa should accept that it is but one among a number of major countries on the continent. There is no reason why all fifty-five African countries should speak with one voice, let alone why South Africa should be that voice.[22]

South Africa should, therefore, recognize its limitations and, in the words of its National Development Plan, "focus on what is practically achievable, without over-committing to possibilities of regional and continental integration." Foreign policy should be regularly evaluated to "secure and promote national interests" (National Planning Commission 2012, 243), which include the tackling of unemployment, inequality, and poverty at home. At the same time, issues such as climate change may need to be addressed regionally or continentally.

# Notes

1. See http://www.dfa.gov.za/department/index.html.

2. DIRCO said its mission was to promote "South Africa's national interests and values, the African Renaissance and the creation of a better world for all." See www.dfa.gov.za/department/index.html.

3. For a recent strong critique of the pan-African vision of the OAU and the AU, see Zachary (2011).

4. Citing Mandela's speech, Frank Chikane, a minister in the presidency under both Mandela and Mbeki, has recently stressed what he sees to be the continuities between the two presidencies. See Chikane (2013).

5. Barber's (2004) book provides the best account of Mandela's policy toward Africa and the region in chapters 14 and 15, but compare also the 418 items listed in Pfister (2000); Adebajo, Adedeji, and Landsberg (2007); Blumenfeld (2010); and Landsberg (2010a).

6. See http://aprm-au.org.

7. Mbeki's deputy minister of foreign affairs has written recently of the need to consider the real world rather than human rights; see the preface in Landsberg and van Wyk (2012, vii). Mbeki echoed Mugabe in characterizing the MDC as Western puppets, seeking to reintroduce colonial rule. In a letter to Tsvangirai on November 22, 2008, Mbeki wrote, "It may be that, for whatever reason, you consider our region and continent as being of little consequence to the future of Zimbabwe, believing that others further away, in Western Europe and North America, are of greater importance" (Chikane 2013, 30).

8. For a recent strong critique of NEPAD as a neoliberal project based on market fundamentalist principles and an endorsement of the global capitalist order, see Makgetlaneng (2013, esp. 75 and 84).

9. President Jose Eduardo dos Santos reciprocated by making, in December 2010, his first state visit to South Africa since 1994.

10. The former liberation movements continue to meet, most recently at Freedom Park in March 2013: *Weekend Argus*, 9 March 2013. The ANC worked with ZAPU, not ZANU, in the 1960s and 1970s.

11. See, for example, http://www.safpi.org/news/article/2013/selfish-jz-allowed-mugabe-kill-sadc-tribunal. Cf. Nathan (2012).

12. Laurie Nathan has argued that this reluctance to transfer sovereignty to the regional body stemmed in part from the fact that sovereignty, acquired relatively recently through a process of decolonization, remained fragile. See Nathan (2011).

13. See www.brics5.co.za.

14. It was agreed in 2008 to form such a free trade area, which would bring together twenty-six countries. It was argued that this would expand South Africa's market from 50 million to 600 million and, therefore, give it a market similar in size to that of some of its BRICS partners. But the free trade agreement that SADC in theory implemented in 2008 did not do much to increase South Africa's market, not least because Angola and the DRC were not involved in it.

15. The tribunal began work in Windhoek, Namibia, in November 2005. The government of Zimbabwe rejected its judgment in the case of *Mike Campbell v. the Republic of Zimbabwe*, which challenged the expropriation of agricultural land in that country by its government, and refused to compensate the farmers concerned. See Nathan (2012).

16. *Business Day*, 30 April 2013.

17. Cf. editorial in *Mail and Guardian*, 9 May 2013.

18. Cf. Landsberg and van Wyk (2012) and email to this author from Dr. Eddy Maloka, 2 May 2013. Roger Southall concludes a section of *New South African Review 3* on South Africa and the wider world by saying that no one can doubt that the country's "national interest" is now that of the ANC (Southall 2013b, 296). There has certainly been a massive conflation of the ruling party with the country.

19. See http://www.icafrica.org/en/topics-programmes/north-south-corridor/.

20. IDASA, which had reinvented itself as a think-tank with African expertise, closed its doors in March 2013, and at the same time there were plans to merge the Africa Institute of South Africa, based in Pretoria, with the government's Human Sciences Research Council.

21. On Swaziland, the ANC has on occasion, in championing such reforms, moved ahead of the government.

22. Fifty-four if Morocco is excluded; Morocco is not a member of the AU.

# References

Adekeye Adebajo, Adebayo Adedeji, and Chris Landsberg, eds. 2007. *South Africa in Africa: The post-apartheid era*. Pietermaritzburg, South Africa: University of KwaZulu Natal Press.

Adelmann, Martin. 2004. Quiet diplomacy: The reasons behind Mbeki's Zimbabwe policy. *Afrika Spectrum* 39 (2): 249–76.

Alden, Chris, and Maxi Schoeman. 2013. South Africa in the company of giants: The search for leadership in a transforming global order. *International Affairs* 89 (1): 111–29.

Barber, James. 2004. *Mandela's world: The international dimension of South Africa's political revolution 1990–99*. London: James Currey.

Bentley, Kristina, and Roger Southall. 2005. *An African peace process: Mandela, South Africa and Burundi*. Cape Town: HSRC Press.

Blumenfeld, Jesmond. 2010. South Africa: "In Africa" but still not "of Africa"? *Focus: The Journal of the Helen Suzman Foundation* 58 (September): 14–21.

Centre for Conflict Resolution. 2013. *Africa, South Africa, and the United Nations' security architecture*. Cape Town: Centre for Conflict Resolution.

Chikane, Frank. 2013. *The things that could not be said: From A(IDS) to Z(imbabwe)*. Johannesburg: Picador Africa.

Cilliers, Jackie. 2011. *Peace and security through good governance: A guide to the NEPAD African peer review mechanism*. Institute for Security Studies Paper 70. Pretoria: Institute for Security Studies. Available from http://hdl.handle.net/123456789/31270.

Daniel, John. 2006. Soldiering on: The post-presidential years of Nelson Mandela, 1999– 2005. In *Legacies of power: Leadership change and former presidents in African politics*, eds. Roger Southall and Henning Melber, 26–50. Cape Town: HSRC Press.

Daniel, John, and Jessica Lutchman. 2006. South Africa in Africa: Scrambling for energy. In *State of the nation: South Africa 2005–2006*, eds. Sakhela Buhlungu, John Daniel, Roger Southall, and Jessica Lutchman, 484–509. Pretoria: HSRC Press.

Department of Foreign Affairs. 1996. *Framework for co-operation in Southern Africa*. Pretoria: Department of Foreign Affairs. Available from www.dfa.gov.za/foreigin/multilateral/Africa/sadc.html.

Ellis, Stephen. 2012. *External mission: The ANC in exile 1960–1990*. Johannesburg: Jonathan Ball.

Fabricius, Peter. 3 February 2013 (2013a). Tension over regional force in DRC. *Weekend Argus*.

Fabricius, Peter. 2 May 2013 (2013b). Are we seeing the emergence of a new "Zuma doctrine" on Africa? Institute for Security Studies Newsletter, Pretoria.

Glaser, Daryl, ed. 2010. *Mbeki and after: Reflections on the legacy of Thabo Mbeki*. Johannesburg: Wits University Press.

Graham, Matthew. 2011. Coming in from the cold: The Transitional Executive Council and South Africa's reintegration into the international community. *Commonwealth and Comparative Politics* 49 (3): 359–78.

Hamill, James, and John Hoffman. 2009. Quiet diplomacy or appeasement? South African policy towards Zimbabwe. *The Round Table: The Commonwealth Journal of International Affairs* 98 (402): 373–84.

Handy, Paul-Simon, and Stine Kjeldgaard. 11 December 2011. SA bid for AU chair a dicey one. *The New Age*.

Handy, Paul-Simon, and Stine Kjeldgaard. 27 January 2012. State's bid for the AU top job—Right move, wrong timing? *Afronline*. Available from http://www.afronline.org/?p=22383.

Herbst, Jeffrey, and Greg Mills. 7 July 2013. The DRC is "only a notional state." *Sunday Argus*.

Khadiagala, Gilbert M. 1994. *Allies in adversity: The frontline states in southern African security, 1975–1993*. Athens, OH: Ohio University Press.

Khadiagala, Gilbert M., ed. 2006. *Security dynamics in Africa's Great Lakes region*. Boulder, CO: Lynne Reiner Publishers.

Khadiagala, Gilbert M. 2012. The SADCC and its approaches to African regionalism. In *Region-building in southern Africa*, eds. Chris Saunders, Gwinyayi Dzinesa, and Dawn Nagar, 25–38. London: Zed Books.

Landsberg, Chris. 2010a. *The diplomacy of transformation: South African foreign policy and statecraft*. Johannesburg: MacMillan.

Landsberg, Chris. 2010b. The emerging Africa strategy of the new Jacob Zuma administration. In *The future of South Africa's foreign policy: Continuity and change?* eds. Siphamandla Zondi and Lesley Masters, 29–41. Pretoria: Institute for Global Dialogue.

Landsberg, Chris, and Jo-Ansie van Wyk, eds. 2012. *South African foreign policy review*, vol. I. Pretoria: Institute for Global Dialogue.

Makgetlaneng, Sehlare. 2013. Is the new partnership for Africa's development an appropriate programme for African continental integration? *Africa Insight* 42 (4): 71–90.

Mandela, Nelson. 1993. South Africa's future foreign policy. *Foreign Affairs* 72 (5).

Mbeje, Mzwandile. 15 April 2013. AU to form centre of discussions between Zuma and Bouteflika. *SABC News*. Available from http://www.sabc.co.za.

Mbeki, Thabo. 1998. *Africa: The time has come. Selected speeches*. Cape Town: Tafelberg.

Nathan, Laurie. 2011. *Community of insecurity: SADC's struggle for peace and security in southern Africa*. Andover, MA: Ashgate.

Nathan, Laurie. 2012. *Solidarity triumphs over democracy: The dissolution of the SADC tribunal*. Available from http://repository.up.ac.za/bitstream/handle/2263/19451/Nathan_Solidarity%282011%29.pdf?sequence=1.

National Planning Commission. 2012. *National Development Plan 2030: Our future—Make it work*. Pretoria: The Presidency.

Nkoana-Mashabane, Maite. 4 July 2013. Foreign policy has reached a turning-point. *Business Day*.

Nolutshungu, Sam. 1975. *South Africa in Africa: A study in ideology and foreign policy*. Manchester, UK: Manchester University Press.

Norbrook, Nicholas. 11 June 2013. DRC: Grand Inga, world's biggest dam in the offing. *Africa Report*. Available from http://www.theafricareport.com.

Odendaal, Andre. 2012. *The founders*. Auckland Park, South Africa: Jacana.

Papenfus, Theresa. 2010. *Pik Botha and his times*. Pretoria: Litera Publications.

Pfister, Roger. 2000. South Africa's post-apartheid foreign policy towards Africa. *Electronic Journal of Africana Bibliography* 6. Available from http://ir.uiowa.edu/ejab/vol6/iss1/1.

Pottinger, Brian. 2009. *The Mbeki legacy*. 2nd ed. Cape Town: Zebra Press.

Rotberg, Robert I. 2002. *Ending autocracy, enabling democracy: The tribulations of Africa 1960–2000*. Washington, DC: Brookings Institution Press.

Saunders, Chris. 2012. Peacekeeping: From the United Nations to the SADC standby force. In *Region-building in southern Africa*, eds. Chris Saunders, Gwinyayi Dzinesa, and Dawn Nagar, 92–106. London: Zed Books.

Saunders, Christopher. 2013. Lesotho: Modern history. In *Africa South of the Sahara 2013*, 42nd ed., ed. Iain Frame. New York, NY: Routledge.

Smith, David. 2 May 2013. Zambian vice-president: "South Africans are backward." *The Guardian*. Available from http://www.guardian.co.uk.

South African Democracy Education Trust. 2013. *The road to democracy in South Africa*, vol. 5. Pretoria: UNISA Press.

Southall, Roger. 2013a. *Liberation movements in power: Party and state in southern Africa*. Scottsville, South Africa: University of KwaZulu Natal Press.

Southall, Roger. 2013b. South Africa at large. In *New South African Review 3: The second phase—Tragedy or farce?* eds. John Daniel, Prishani Naidoo, Devan Pillay, and Roger Southall, 294–96. Johannesburg: Wits University Press.

Southall, Roger, and John Daniel. 2009. *Zunami! The South African elections of 2009.* Auckland Park, South Africa: Jacana Media.

Southern African Liaison Office. 2013. *South Africa-Zimbabwe Relations*, vol. I, *Pre-colonial to 2006.* Auckland Park, South Africa: Jacana Media.

Thomas, Scott. 1996. *The diplomacy of liberation: The foreign relations of the ANC since 1960.* London: I. B. Taurus.

Zachary, G. Pascal. 24 October 2011. As Qaddafi died, so did his craziest dream and mistake: Pan-Africanism. *Atlantic.*

Zondi, Siphamandla, and Zandile Bhengu. 2011. *The SADC facilitation and democratic transition in Zimbabwe.* Pretoria: Institute for Global Dialogue.

# The Need for Strengthened Political Leadership

By
ROBERT I. ROTBERG

South Africa desperately needs newly recommitted leadership capable of serving the entire nation, not a ruling class or a cohort of robber barons. It is conceivable that political leadership capable of building upon Mandela's legacy and uplifting the nation and its people could come from within the ranks of the Democratic Alliance, from Agang, or from South Africa's several other national political parties. But it is more likely to arise within the ANC, possibly through the deputy presidential and eventual presidential efforts of Cyril Ramaphosa or others within the dominant ANC not yet fully dedicated to assuming national leadership. But from wherever it comes, South Africa is ready and anxious to be renewed.

*Keywords:* leadership; Mandela; Mbeki; Zuma; Ramaphosa; renewal

"Listen to me . . . I am your leader. I am going to give leadership. . . . As long as I am your leader, I will tell you, always, when you are wrong." That was vintage Nelson Mandela, counseling his African National Congress (ANC) supporters in Katlehong, east of Johannesburg, at the height of vicious battles on the East Rand in 1993, in which followers of

*Robert I. Rotberg is the founding director of the Program on Intrastate Conflict, Harvard Kennedy School; president emeritus of the World Peace Foundation; fellow of the American Academy of Arts & Sciences; Fulbright Professor at both the Paterson School of International Affairs (Carleton University) and the Balsillie School of International Affairs (University of Waterloo); and senior fellow of the Centre for International Governance Innovation. His most recent book is* Africa Emerges: Consummate Challenges, Abundant Opportunities *(Polity 2013).*

NOTE: A revision of this article greatly benefited from Roger Southall's written critique and the oral comments of other participants in an authors' meeting about this volume at Steenberg, Western Cape Province, South Africa, in May 2013. This article draws on the relevant sections of my *Transformative Political Leadership: Making a Difference in the Developing World* (Chicago University Press 2012).

DOI: 10.1177/0002716213514163

the Inkatha Freedom Party (IFP) and the ANC combatants vied for authority over the nation and the townships.

On the dais, where Mandela was to give his talk, was a stark message: "No peace, do not talk to us about peace. We've had enough. Please, Mr. Mandela, no peace. Give us weapons. No peace." Mandela, tossing aside his prepared text, agreed that it was hard to tell angry people that they must still remain nonviolent. "But the solution is peace, it is reconciliation, it is political tolerance." The responsibility for stopping the internecine fighting in the townships of the East Rand was the government's, he said, but "it is also our responsibility. . . . If you are going to kill innocent people you don't belong to the ANC. Your task is reconciliation" (Mandela quoted in Lodge 2006, 179–80).

Mandela had a vision, which he carefully articulated occasion after occasion. He knew what was moral. He knew that he could only retain the hearts and minds of his angry followers by showing courage as well as integrity of purpose and belief. He also needed to be intellectually honest—one of the components of effective and responsible leadership—if he hoped to strengthen his existing aura of legitimacy and to build mightily upon it for the future of the new rainbow nation and the ANC as a liberation movement.

The Katlehong speech also demonstrates Mandela's finely tuned leadership instincts. More demagogic, populist, irresponsible leaders might have raised their fist, chanted fight songs, and otherwise egged on their supporters. But Mandela knew how to meet not the needs of the moment but the requirements of the future. He understood the importance of leading, rather than of shirking responsibility. He appreciated that among the many tasks of consummate leadership were those of instruction and mobilization for good. He had learned on Robben Island, if not before, the importance of modeling a tough guiding role. He had fought on the island to become a robust, fully legitimate leader. He, therefore, always believed, no less in Katlehong and no less throughout the 1993–1994 campaign for full independence, that his leadership competencies and vision could guide South Africans successfully to the promised land of national and individual freedom, and also give each and every South African a sense of belonging to a larger, worthy human enterprise. That last enterprise—a mark of consummate leadership—was one he made his own.

# The Force of Leadership

Outcomes for the citizens of the developing world, and for South Africa, depend greatly on the actions and determinations of political leaders and on critical political leadership decisions. Nothing else—not contingency, not structure—may be so important in determining a nation's success. As set out at length in *Transformative Political Leadership*, such provocative conclusions apply with unusual relevance to the South African situation today and tomorrow (Rotberg 2012).

This appraisal tends to fly in the face of conventional wisdom—and tilts against traditional scholarly emphases on the primary salience of structures and

institutions. It also appears to contradict older research suggesting that little vari-
ance in performance could be attributed to individuals and individual differences
(Lieberson and O'Connor 1972; Cohen and March 1974). It may even unwit-
tingly differ from those who prefer to emphasize structure and contingency
rather than the importance of individual agency in the conduct of human affairs.
Yet leadership capabilities matter as much as do many external influences, internal structures, and institutional constraints in shaping nation-state policy and in
influencing the ways in which beneficial results are pursued across diverse
national cultures.

Fortunately, recent corporate and empirical psychological studies support
such conclusions. Those studies show that leaders do "have a substantial impact
on performance" (Podolny, Khurana, and Besharov 2010, 73, 93, 95). Those who
have examined the role of leadership particularly in the foreign policy realm
conclude that individual agency matters (Hermann and Hagan 1998, 124, 135).
Leaders (not necessarily situations or structures by themselves) largely create
peace and war. Leaders even help signally to guide their people into or out of
poverty. For example, Jones and Olken (2005) established in a path-breaking
econometric study with robust evidence that national political leaders, irrespective of institutions and context, influence economic growth attainments. Leaders
help to overcome geographical, climatic, and resource limitations. As close attention to the political history of independent Asia, Africa, and the Caribbean will
show, human agency has the capacity to strengthen or fail nation-states, uplift or
oppress citizens, and unleash or stifle the talents and aspirations of all manner of
followers (Rotberg 2004, 1–45). Should it be any different in South Africa?

Indeed, studies of twins, identical versus fraternal, indicate that there could
plausibly be a genetic basis for leadership. Research shows a predisposition for
and against taking up the leadership baton. Some were born to lead—born with
"an innate set of skills that makes us good candidates for directing a group of
people toward a goal" (Shane 2010, 123–24). Moreover, research shows that
genes predispose not only to leadership, but to whether the ambition to lead is
achieved, and sometimes at what level. In the South African context, identifying
possible political leaders via the genome is possibly a task for the future. But the
more serious task for the present is to strengthen and embolden embryonic
national talents for responsible, nationally focused political leadership.

National founders or the rebuilders (after revolutions or dramatic societal
breaks) have almost everywhere in the developing world helped to set a dramatic
course. The influence of human agency appears at least suggestive. If Lee Kuan
Yew had not been born to a Singaporean elite family, coming of age during the
Japanese occupation, would Singapore have been led effectively and developed
so extraordinarily after 1959? If Kemal Ataturk had not been a radical-thinking
Turkish officer under the Ottomans at the time of the empire's collapse, would
there today be a powerful, modern Turkey? If a person such as a Govan Mbeki
(Bundy 2013), a Walter Sisulu, or an Oliver Tambo (all distinct personalities, with
different ideological profiles and personal trajectories)—not Nelson Mandela—
had grasped the leadership of South Africa after the demise of apartheid, would

independent South Africa have avoided a revanchist race war or have been so peacefully, even magisterially, launched? Ambitious left-leaning nationalists could even have substituted themselves for Seretse Khama in Botswana and have ignored some of the traditional and religious foundations of what became democratic rule under Khama and his successors. If Khama had been born a Tanzanian and rose there to political prominence, would Tanzanians now be much wealthier per capita, and much less corrupt? Paul Kagame has vigorously altered the trajectory of postgenocidal Rwandan development. So, for good or ill, have and did Evo Morales in Bolivia, the late Hugo Chavez in Venezuela, the late Meles Zenawi in Ethiopia, Yoweri Museveni in Uganda, and the late Muammar Qaddafi in Libya. Robert Mugabe (not Joshua Nkomo) in Zimbabwe channeled and channels followers' energies and placed an undeniable personal stamp on the remaking of his people and nation.

What, it is also important to ask, accounts for the different outcomes in India and Pakistan after partition? Obviously, size and resources were important. So was religion, and how religion was employed to mobilize electors, a critical factor. But how the first postpartition leaders responded to the different hands that they were dealt mattered massively, too. Arguably, today's India owes its messy but secure democratic political culture and strong institutions as much to Jawaharlal Nehru's formative guidance as it does to the British Raj and the long decades of prepartition Indian Congress Party socialization to democratic norms. As Huntington concludes sensibly, "Economic development makes democracy possible; political leadership makes it real" (Huntington 1991, 316).

The colonial experience, like the Raj in India and Pakistan, conceivably conditioned the growth of developing world leadership. Yet comparisons show that whether the imperial example was Belgian, British, Dutch, French, Italian, or Spanish, in modern times it has mattered little which metropole tutored and controlled (Rotberg 1997, 198–217). All oppressed, conditioned, discriminated, and withheld opportunity and full human advancement until compelled by the rise of nationalism and changing times to respond positively. British rule, sometimes thought more benign, spawned Robert Mugabe, Idi Amin in Uganda, Hastings Banda in Malawi, a series of Nigerian tyrants, and many others. It also gave us excellent leaders such as Seretse Khama and his successors, Sir Seewoosagur Ramgoolam of Mauritius and his successors, and Lee Kuan Yew in Singapore, among others. Britain's much vaunted representative institutions only last where leaders embraced them and made them work.

French rule brought Jean-Bédel Bokassa, the Central African emperor; Omar Bongo of Gabon; Gnassingbé Eyadéma of Togo; and many other autocratic despots. Félix Houphouët-Boigny in Côte d'Ivoire and Léopold Sédar Senghor in Senegal may provide somewhat more tolerant and democratic examples, but the more definitively positive French postcolonial examples are all in the Caribbean or in Oceania. Belgian oversight, abetted by the United States, prepared Congolese for Mobutu Sese Seko's long tyranny. Portuguese colonialism led equally to the superb modern governance experience of Cape Verde and the corrupt authoritarianism of Angola. Italian colonial rule was a precursor to Siad Barre's hegemony in Somalia, and what has since occurred there, and to the rise of Muammar Qaddafi in Libya. Spain's legacy is Teodoro Obiang Nguema Mbasogo in Equatorial Guinea, one of the worst despotisms in the developing world.

Idiosyncratic behaviors of individual leaders arguably mattered more, whether in Sri Lanka, Jamaica, or Côte d'Ivoire, than whatever their ex-colonies' received legacies. Despite more representative and participatory institutions at independence in ex-British colonies than in the former dependencies of the other colonial powers, their subjects fared no better on average during the independence period than the citizens of ex-Belgian, ex-Dutch, ex-French, ex-Italian, and ex-Spanish territories. Whether a colonial experience was more or less consultative mattered little in terms of postindependence leadership and governance results. Unconscionable tyrants flourished then and now equally in common law and Napoleonic systems. Greed, and a preference for preying and looting, depended and depends more on the designs and integrities of a new state's first leader (or a later leader coming to power after a major crisis) than it does on any colonial inheritance. Likewise, excellent and reasonably good governance in Asia and Africa has flowed from leadership action, not adherence to a colonial model or the existence or absence of ethnic plurality, geographical constraints, arbitrary borders, navigable rivers, tropical diseases, allocations of natural resources, or foreign assistance levels. Compare across decades the two postcolonial wealthy British colonies—Uganda and Ghana—and comparable French outposts like Côte d'Ivoire and, say, Mali. In times of plenty and in times of scarcity, in times of ample rainfall and in times of drought, leaders help to shape the lives of their citizens and respond poorly or well to the crises and needs of their parlous states.

Likewise, the quality of the political institutions that have been inherited or that exist within a given polity, its literacy and educational levels, the quality of its health care, and overall standards of living levels have had and have less influence on national outcomes and leadership results than such underlying motivators as individual and group senses of what is right and wrong and what is responsible, sheer avarice, the gaining and keeping of power, and formidable senses of entitlement.

Are these conclusions consistent with what we know intimately about South Africa? Does South Africa's astute political leadership by Mandela and its lack of gifted political leadership ever since conform to this paradigm?

# Political Leadership

Political leadership is a "social construction" that acts within a particular historical and social context, as a multidimensional activation that is a peculiar mixture of contingent situation and personal intervention, and as the impact of individual style and creativity on political challenges and opportunities. Equally, "too great a focus on . . . context robs the notion of leadership of its core" (Avery 2004, 8). This generalization applies directly to South Africa.

In recent years the study of the political leadership variable has been neglected in mainstream social science. However, the relevance of human agency to the direction of the affairs of nations, particularly in emerging nations such as South Africa, is old news that nonetheless deserves to be highlighted. Such important theorists as Weber, Merriam, Shannon, Seligman, Pye, Easton, Rustow, Burns, Paige, and many others sought to persuade students of politics and political trans- formation that leadership was a crucial variable in the study of politics; they tried in their different ways to emphasize its primordial centrality—to stress the sig- nificance of leadership for an understanding of how politics really worked. For Seligman, political leadership was essential to the creation and maintenance of democracy. For Rustow, political leadership expressed itself as the interplay between private personality and public performance. He advocated the "system- atic rediscovery of leadership as a central political process." Paige suggested a reasonable all-encompassing definition: "Political leadership is the behavior of persons in positions of authority." Political leaders influence everything around them and, Paige reminded us, even external and exogenous influences come through them, being mediated by leadership decisions and determinations. In politics, leaders can often change not only the rules of the game, but how people play. "The choices they make or fail to make seemingly affect everything" (Paige 1977, 1; see Weber 1948, 77–78; Seligman 1950; Easton 1965, 212–16; Pye 1967, 43; Rustow 1970, 687). The average South African, African, Asian, or Latin American worker, farmer, or voter likely would consider such insights obvious.

They would also be familiar with Burns's important but controversial distinc- tion between power wielders and leaders. The former (Hitler, Stalin, Mao, Idi Amin, Pol Pot, Mugabe) treat people as things; the latter "may not." Naked power overrides competition and conflict while leadership always is exercised amid conflict and competition—leaders appeal to the "motive bases" of potential followers. Burns's full articulation, very helpful in the context of this article, is: "Leadership over human beings is exercised when persons with certain motives and purposes mobilize, in competition or conflict with others, institutional, politi- cal, psychological, and other resources so as to arouse, engage, and satisfy the motives of followers" (Burns 1978, 18). The last phrase is critical because Burns insists, rightly, that leadership is the employment largely of informal means to induce followers and citizens together with the leader to achieve mutual goals and joint purposes. Leaders do not make people do what they do not want to do. They persuade them (Neustadt 1990, 11). They cajole them. They allow them to maximize their own interests by believing in and endorsing the policies and articulated goals expressed by their leaders. The genius of political leadership melds leadership drives and followership aspirations and beliefs.

Stated simply, leaders cannot exist without followers. Kellerman reminds us that there are as many kinds of followers—isolates, bystanders, activists, and diehards primarily—as there are varieties of leaders (Kellerman 2008, 23). Each type of follower plays a role in the unfolding drama of political engagement and nation-building. Followers have power because should they stop following, the leader cannot achieve his or her goals, including the basic one of maintaining his or her position, unless he or she turns to the naked use of coercive power to eliminate competition. It is the modern political leader's task to interact effec- tively and successfully, preferably responsibly, with the changing cast of citizens and followers. She wins their trust. She gains legitimacy. They follow her and sometimes exert meaningful influence. The tension between leader and led, follower and ruler, remains critical to outcomes especially and obviously in democracies, but also in autocracies.

The actions of political leaders in at least the developing world are therefore determined more by their creative interaction with (and sometimes their manipulation of) their followers than they are narrowly inhibited by socioeconomic circumstance, global trends, resource constraints, and so on. Political leaders, especially but not exclusively in the developing world, are able more than others to override structural constraints and act largely autonomously. Sometimes, bolstered by a core of dedicated followers, they go so far as to disregard economic or global realities, big power or world order strictures, and internal public opinion (on the causes of HIV/AIDS, say). These leaders focus on the deployment both of noncoercive power (the usual mechanisms of informal power) and various kinds of co-optive and occasionally coercive power (components of formal power that many developing world leaders use to buttress their personal power and authority) (Blondel 1987, 74).

In the developing world, at least, the syllogism is straightforward: leadership begets governance, governance in turn begets political culture and, only over time, begets institutions. That is why much of sub-Saharan Africa is preinstitutional, awaiting the development of a democratic political culture. President Obama said that Africa "needed strong institutions," not strong men (quoted in *The Economist* 2009). The sentiment and the intent were correct. But the analysis was incomplete. After independence, or after traumatic postconflict transitions, leaders fashion the ways in which the nation-state and its residents respond to external and internal challenges. They, either alone or together with a cohort of senior officials—and in tension with their followers—help to determine the direction of the nation-state. They govern, and the methods of governing that are chosen early create precedents and practices that shape the nature and course of a nation-state's governance. Indeed, personally influential, even inspirational leaders, or innovative leaders with transformational impulses, flourish more readily in new countries before there are institutions, in periods of extreme crisis, or before institutional safeguards have been developed and matured except on paper (Willner 1984, 46–47).

Good leadership separates endeavors that succeed from those that fail. Imaginative political leadership—excellent and all-consuming political leadership—is especially important, more necessary, and often more lacking even in comparatively mature new countries such as South Africa. Effective statecraft depends on considered leadership. Careful and far-sighted leadership is necessary, particularly amid dangerous times or unsettled neighborhoods. Economic advances rely on skillful leadership, especially in such places as South Africa. Poverty can hardly be alleviated without a leadership that understands the close connections among macroeconomic prudence, increased employment opportunities, good governance, the rule of law, media openness, attracting foreign direct investment, and strengthened prosperity. The delivery of essential political goods—the political goods of security, rule of law, and so on that citizens expect and insist upon and that compose good governance—is most easily achieved by the Mandelas and Khamas and other accomplished leaders who have appeared rarely in the developing world in the last half century. Where such effective leaders have gained power, they have made incomparable positive advances in terms of the material and social attainments of their peoples.

In a country such as South Africa, the critical variable of leadership makes much more of a difference in every realm, particularly in the political realm, than it does in the developed world where value systems of democracy are fully rooted, where political institutions such as legislatures and judiciaries are independent, where the reality of good governance is taken for granted, and where open economic practices are common. In other words, the value added of responsible, enlightened leadership is much greater in those regions of the globe where political cultures and political institutions are still embryonic or growing, where political life is largely preinstitutional. Human capacity is also much more limited in the developing than in the developed world. A tiny, fully literate country such as Norway can provide innumerable potential leaders. A much poorer African country with roughly three times the population (but far less literacy), such as Malawi or Zambia, can produce many fewer potential leaders of stature. In the developing world of which South Africa is a part, both the prevailing methods of political recruitment and the corrosive quality of political competition inhibit the development of broadly based leaders entering politics from the private sector or from civil society. (Cyril Ramaphosa could prove an exception to this rule.) Thus, for those and a host of other reasons, emerging as an independently minded leader responsive to national rather than sectoral or narrow party needs is exceedingly difficult in South Africa, the rest of Africa, Asia, and other developing regions. This is among the many developing world leadership traps into which South Africa has fallen.

## The Differences Leaders Make

It is in less well privileged places that political leadership is more rather than less essential. In such surroundings, leadership quality matters severely, and matters intensely. Who leads makes a bigger difference in the fractured, scrabbling nation-states than it does in settled, stable ones. The differing results of leadership in South Africa by Nelson Mandela, Thabo Mbeki, or Jacob Zuma are instructive. Likewise, the contrasts in governmental outcomes between a country led by a Jerry Rawlings or a John A. Kufuor (in Ghana) are notable. Or contrast what Sukarno did to retard Indonesia to the work of the more developmentally and socially effective actions of his successors, especially Susilo Bambang Yudhoyono, the country's current president. Pairing in that manner dramatizes the presumed effects of good leadership and demonstrates once more that in countries where institutions are young and threatened and democratic political cultures are still being created, leadership quality is an independent variable that matters greatly to human outcomes (cf. Mills 2010).

Responsible or effective political leaders in the developing world generally share a number of characteristics. National heads of state and heads of government such as Kemal Ataturk, Seretse Khama, Lee Kuan Yew, and Nelson Mandela mostly adhered to positive methods of governing because they believed such approaches had proven or would prove more successful in uplifting and building their nations, or because they wanted to emulate successful models of governance developed in North America, Europe, or elsewhere in Asia and Africa. But those who today or in recent decades learned from Lee or Mandela, and emulated their competencies, are in the minority; too much of Asia and Africa since World War II (and since 1960 in Africa) has been led by men and women who have preyed on their citizens for private, chauvinistic gain. Even when elected freely to high office, they undermined nominal democratic procedures and, like Sukarno, Suharto, Nkrumah, Mobutu, and now Mugabe, violated all the textbook good leadership behavioral rules.

The task of political leadership is to help citizens to "create and achieve shared goals . . . reinforce group identity and cohesion . . . and mobilize collective work" (Nye 2008, 18–20). Citizens are followers, of course, but followers especially in the new nations of the developing world need leaders that highlight common and collective, or perhaps more accurately joint, goals that go beyond narrow group, ethnic, or sectarian interests and identifications. Leadership is indeed impossible without followership, but followers remain politically inchoate without leaders who periodically emerge and offer new visions and new approaches around which to mobilize. Such leaders often employ mixtures of emotional, political, and contextual intelligence and demonstrate varieties of hard, soft, and co-optive power. They develop reciprocal dependencies with followers.

## The Key Leadership Competencies

Citizens and followers seek leaders who are inspirational and appeal emotionally. They follow leaders who articulate appealing visions, are courageous, and remain legitimate. They can be mobilized and empowered by such dynamic persons, and are comfortable with and respond much more enthusiastically to leaders who exhibit high orders of integrity, inspire trust, appear to labor for all citizens (not narrow ethnic groups or lineages), and offer strong reasons to enable citizens to believe in the future of a new or a posttransitional state. Such leaders need not be charismatic (Rotberg 2012, 36–38).

Successful leaders are consummate visionaries, know expertly how to mobilize followers and citizens behind their visions, and intuitively understand that to turn a vision and a mobilized following into a transformational force they, as leaders, must retain that difficult to define quality known as legitimacy. In turn, stores of legitimacy grow and shrink according to follower perceptions of leader accomplishments and talents (growing the economy, reducing unemployment, and debating well), but they mostly depend on whether followers believe that the leader is trustworthy, has integrity, is personally and intellectually honest, faces challenges squarely, and avoids even the appearance of sleaze (cf. Bennis 1989, 161, 192–98). The implied social contract between ruled and ruler is that trust once given will not be abused. But it very often is.

The relationship between performance and perception is not perfect, and neither is the relationship between leader characteristics and competencies and either performance or perception. Nonetheless, there are identifiable competencies that are the behaviors and skills that followers look for in their leaders.

The five key behavioral competencies of compelling political leadership include being able to create a transformational vision; to mobilize followers behind it; to appear or be fully legitimate; to gain a population's trust; and to persuade citizens and constituents that they are an integral part of what is or what will be a noble, uplifting, purposeful enterprise. Political courage is important. So is a high degree of emotional intelligence—the ability to be empathic and to listen. Legitimacy in a leader is enhanced by what Adam Smith called a sense of personal mastery and prudence (A. Smith 1976, 237). Personal integrity, or integrity of person, is obviously important, especially in South Africa despite its traditional acceptance of polygamy and adultery. (President Jacob Zuma has been weakened by a loss of moral authority because of his nonchalance about HIV/AIDS and allegations concerning his personal profits from the South African arms procurement deals of the 1990s.) Another distinguishing characteristic of high-quality political leadership is intellectual honesty. To succeed, transformational leaders need that competency. Transactional leaders, by far the majority in the world, need neither be honest personally, intellectually sound, nor even more than passably legitimate.

Transformational leaders are supreme motivators. They challenge settled expectations and demand new, higher levels of national and governmental performance. They "wake people out of inertia" (Kanter 2003). They elevate their followers' level of consciousness about proposed outcomes, encourage citizens to embrace national rather than self-interested personal goals, empower their constituents to excel, and themselves enunciate high-value objectives by which followers can be inspired. They drive a nation forward to new achievements, and to new views of itself. They instill pride. In the best of cases, a nation's citizens come to internalize a transformational leader's vision in a manner that is sustainable and actionable. Transformational leaders provide a sense of transcendence within the nation and among its peoples. Mandela did so magnificently.

Transactional leaders, on the other hand, are incrementalists—"business as usual" politicians focusing on the mechanisms of statecraft and on perpetuating themselves and their parties in office. They exchange mutual self-interests with their followers and hence are primarily engaged in transactions. Such leaders— Zuma is one—operate within existing frameworks; transformative leaders like Mandela alter the frameworks and the governing paradigms. Transactional leaders govern, sometimes well, but absent a grand design (Burns 1978, 4). As Lee describes transactional leaders, "If you just do your sums—pluses, minuses, credit, debit—you are a washout" (Minchin 1986/1990, 343).

# Mandela's Methods

As president of South Africa from 1994 to 1999, Mandela sought to overcome all the intense societal challenges that he and his government had inherited from decades of apartheid-permeated governance. For a year or two, he ran cabinet meetings and gave clear instructions to his ministers. But Thabo Mbeki, his deputy president and presumed heir, more and more held the operational reins of government, day to day. Mandela concerned himself progressively less with the details, preferring instead to focus primarily and intensely on a few larger issues: ensuring economic growth and modernization, fostering harmony at home and peace abroad, and resetting South Africa's tone and its mode of discourse. His became a "somewhat removed" presidency that for the most part attempted to reframe the dialogue of the new South Africa and to motivate his constituents and people of all backgrounds to forge a new social compact (Sampson 1999, 585; Daniel 2006, 31).

Mandela's first term included foreign policy accomplishments (and some disasters), macroeconomic openness, fiscal responsibility, the sidelining of old socialist nostrums, and an awareness that reducing high levels of unemployment should be a key palliative for prevailing poverty. He stabilized the security establishment and shored up the nation's economic management team.

But it was as a determined inclusionist, as a fervent conciliator, as a bridger of the color divides, and as a determined optimist about human nature that Mandela captured the imagination of his country and the world. By his gestures, by his symbolism (the green Springbok jersey and tea with Prime Minister Hendrik Verwoerd's widow), and by his deft actions locally and internationally, Mandela gave South Africans confidence that their novel national enterprise was fully worthwhile—that their nation-building project was an endeavor that could be pursued confidently by all. Mandela offered to his people and followers a sense of belonging, a sense of being a part of a larger project that promised to uplift them spiritually, if not necessarily materially. It was Mandela's natural gift to lead his nation, and take it and his people as rapidly as possible toward a New Zion (Rotberg 2012, 40–65).

# Mandela's Successors

Unfortunately, the New Zion is still over the next hill. Mandela used his power "not to dominate but to distribute—to convey power to others." As Mandela himself warned Mbeki in 1997, "One of the temptations of a leader who has been elected unopposed is that he may use his powerful position to settle scores with his detractors, marginalize them, in certain cases, get rid of them." He explained of what good leadership consisted: a leader "must keep forces together; but you can't do that unless you allow dissent. People should be able to criticize the leader without fear or favor" (Kanter 2004, 315; Gevisser 2009, 261).

Mandela had begun to transform South Africa. But, as we now know, there is but one Mandela, and the leadership legacy (accomplishments, style, symbolism, tolerance, integrity, and legitimacy) that he bequeathed to his successors was one on which they were unable or incapable of building. Because of their leadership insufficiencies, South Africa is more adrift politically and socially, and certainly less united, than Mandela's presidency left it. The material progress that he hoped would accelerate after his days in office has hardly been realized. Unemployment numbers have been little reduced, matriculation results are barely improved, housing opportunities are insufficient for growing urban populations, inequality between haves and haves-not has grown, industrialization has not moved forward, land ownership issues have not been resolved, and shortages of water and power persist. HIV/AIDs has, however, partially been conquered thanks to policy changes and the availability of antiretroviral medicines. Yet tuberculosis is a bigger killer than before, and pneumonia and diarrheal diseases continue to decimate South Africa's young. Labor strife is becoming more persistent. Most of all, corruption is now rampant even though Mandela specifically warned the ANC in 1997 in Mafikeng against behaving like "predatory elites that [thrive] on the basis of the looting of national wealth" (Sampson 1999, 533). As Archbishop Desmond Tutu told a university audience in 2011, "Our country with such tremendous potential is [being] dragged backwards and downwards by corruption, which is quite blatant" (Tutu 2011).

Can South Africa's downward spiral be attributed to Mandela's successors and their leadership insufficiencies? Those who followed the transformational and nation-building leadership examples of Sir Seretse Khama in Botswana, Lee Kuan Yew in Singapore, and Kemal Ataturk in Turkey have managed to build upon these first leaders' example, and to continue to guide their large and small states in the stellar manner of their founders. Singapore is one of the wealthiest nation-states in the world, per capita, with no natural resources but exemplary governance (if limited free speech). Botswana is mainland Africa's only consistently democratic endeavor, its best governed, and thus (thanks to the discovery of diamonds 10 years into Khama's presidency and its sensible management of that resource, and without Dutch disease), its most prosperous (except for oil-rich, tiny, corrupt Equatorial Guinea). Turkey has finally become a confident regional power, with the second largest army in NATO, and prosperity for its peoples.

But first Mbeki and now Jacob Zuma have squandered the social and political capital that Mandela conveyed to them and to their collective followers. For that reason, South Africa's problems have increasingly come to exhibit the leadership weaknesses of the rest of the continent. Whereas South Africa was once the acknowledged leader of Africa, now it struggles to fulfill that role, and provides one after another poor example. (But see also the article in this volume by Chris Saunders.)

At best, Mandela's successors, like so many of the contemporary heads of state in the developing world, have demonstrated but a minimal vision of national renewal—one that little motivates their followers. By definition and by daily activity they behave and have behaved merely as transactional leaders.

They display little of the self-mastery, the prudence and proportionality, and the integrity of the best world leaders. Along with the majority of their developing world contemporaries, they seem and seemed primarily preoccupied with preserving their own power and power bases and far less—at least only intermittently—with transforming their nation and distributing power widely, and not just through patronage.

### The Mbeki era

No career demonstrates these failings more than Mbeki's. When overtaken by unexpected calamities for which he may have been unprepared, he quickly exhibited that kind of counterfeit leadership of which Mandela had warned. The trust that Mandela had begun to build up for the ANC and the government was rapidly eroded. The integrity of the presidency and the legitimacy of its political leadership were too soon undermined. Mbeki's lack of intellectual honesty also rapidly squandered what remained of the legitimacy with which he had entered upon the national presidency.

Mbeki chose first to deny the importance of the HIV/AIDS epidemic, and then to refute scientific knowledge that HIV/AIDS was a sexually transmitted disease. He followed hunches about other possible causes of the malady, and publicly explored various alternative, mostly preposterous, remedies, thus delaying treatment for myriad sufferers (Daniel 2006, 37). With regard to Zimbabwe, he denied or ignored the blatant seriousness of President Robert G. Mugabe's many crimes and Zimbabwe's massive social and economic deterioration, its wild inflation, and the absurdly pretentious rationalizations of the tyrant. At home, Mbeki condoned or overlooked mounting corruption scandals within the ANC, within the country, and across the provinces, protecting cronies and colleagues. He helped to diminish, or allowed to diminish, democracy within the ANC and within the political movement that Mandela had led. Rather than economically empowering the new nation, as Mandela intended, Mbeki gave rise to the indigenous robber barons. By the time that Mbeki was ousted from office by Zuma and the party for arrogance and incompetence, South Africa had begun its long steady slide from Mandelan pride and hope toward cynicism and opportunism, the lot of so many other African and Asian new nations.

### Zuma's leadership

Has Zuma been an improvement? Has he and his administration begun to rebuild upon Mandela's vaunted legacy? Possibly the best one could conclude is that Zuma as president has focused far less on articulating a vision than he has on being thoroughly transactional. He has also attempted to redeem himself from many personal missteps, although the foray into massive villa building for himself in KwaZulu-Natal hardly speaks to a major paradigmatic shift. Only intermittently decisive, Zuma has rarely been uplifting, visionary, or transformational. Nor, perhaps, does he need to perform as a navigator if he swims with sure strokes and stays afloat.

Many of Zuma's local critics accuse him of presiding over an "incapacitated" nation—a nation adrift without a plan or a program and without any knowledge of how best to retrieve Mandela's legacy. Under Zuma, as other articles in this collection explain, a large number of Africans still have no hope of gaining formal employment. Young persons particularly find themselves devoid of the possibility of meaningful formal sector jobs. The South African economy has grown very slowly, at half or less of the desired rate. Moreover, the wage gap between rich and poor Africans widened considerably under Mbeki and now under Zuma. This growing gulf has been exacerbated by rigid and constraining labor laws, by the elite approach of the main trade unions, and by a dearth of new foreign direct investment. South Africa's economic competitiveness is no greater than it was a decade ago.

Foreign investors stay away in part because under Zuma educational attainments and medical treatment possibilities have both deteriorated, crime rates remain among the highest in the world, energy is short (although improved from 2008), foreign policy mishaps are frequent, and the great rainbow nation of Mandela's early days has become less coherent and less united than before. (On education and health, see the articles in this volume by Saleem Badat and Yusef Sayed, Andrew Babson, and Alan Whiteside.) Zuma, presiding over potentially the richest and most mature of the nation-states of Africa, is but another so-so developing world leader. He demonstrates few of the required competencies, especially as inevitably compared to Mandela.

In the foreign policy realm, as Saunders' article in this volume explains, Zuma has vacillated. He was for the Libyan intervention before he was against it. He tried to assist an autocrat in the Central African Republic to resist being overthrown, and then welcomed regime change. He was against the French intervening decisively in Mali, and then backed the result. Regarding Zimbabwe, first he cracked down on Mugabe's arrogant political grandstanding at SADC's meeting in Livingstone in 2011. Then he promised Mugabe's opponents and foreign powers that he would bring Mugabe to heel and preside over a true resurgence of democracy in Zimbabwe. But he failed to deliver such changes at a Kinshasa meeting of SADC in 2012, and despite the active oversight of Mugabe and Zimbabwe by Lindiwe Zulu and Mac Maharaj, deputizing for Zuma, he let Mugabe persist in defying SADC both at a Maputo meeting in 2013 and in the critical run-up to the decisive 2013 presidential and parliamentary elections in Zimbabwe in July. Indeed, after Mugabe complained to Zuma that Zulu—someone whom Mugabe publicly called an "idiotic street woman"—was opposing his high-handed preelection efforts, Zuma sidelined Zulu and essentially let Mugabe and his associates free before the elections to do what they could to prevent a free and fair poll (Campbell 2013a).

Within the ANC, Zuma has had sharp elbows, first for Mbeki, then for other rivals, such as Tokyo Sexwale, a sometime cabinet minister. He was uncharacteristically forceful in sidelining Julius Malema, a strident youth leader. He put key loyalists into judicial positions where they could be helpful to him and to the ANC. He marginalized some of Mbeki's key associates, such as Trevor Manuel, and usefully behaved tolerantly toward various ANC miscreants and cronies who happened to be felons.

But beyond the ANC, Zuma has largely dithered, providing no steady or inventive policy directions to his ministers or to the party. He is the big chief, for sure, but with few effective educational, medical, social welfare, agricultural, or infrastructural initiatives to his credit. Where is the leader who promises his people positive change and delivers results? Where is the leader who reassures his nation about its future, or instills in them a sense of self-worth and of being involved in an all-encompassing national project of renewal, even transformation?

President Jacob Zuma said recently that "the legacy of apartheid [ran] too deep and too far back for the democratic administration to reverse it in so short a period" (Torchia 2013). Although he and the ANC sought rapid improvements, 20 years was too short a period for "comprehensive change" to have occurred, he said. Thus inequality had grown, housing availabilities had not kept pace with population increases and urbanization, educational goals had not been met, and the ranks of the unemployed had hardly been diminished, or so Zuma implicitly admitted.

Afrobarometer opinion surveying in 2011 in South Africa found that only 28 percent of South Africans "trusted" Zuma "a lot," and a further 35 percent trusted him "somewhat." Thirteen percent trusted him "not at all" and 24 percent "just a little." And all but 9 percent of South Africans believed that the presidency was riddled with corruption. Nevertheless, 49 percent of South Africans "approved" the performance of Zuma (Graham and Alpin 2012). Whether these numbers would be so positive in 2013 or 2014 is hard to say. Anecdotally, and from press accounts, the "passing grade" that Zuma received in 2011(Graham and Alpin 2012) might be much lower now.

# The Gathering Critiques

"The country of our dreams has unfortunately faded," says Mamphela Ramphele. Poverty and destitution persist too commonly. South African society is "increasingly unequal." "Instead of the people governing, party bosses are governing, that's the fundamental flaw. So you can have a corrupt person being reappointed to either a government position or a parliamentary position because there is no cost, no accountability." When launching her Agang Party in March 2013, Ramphele admitted that her generation had "to confess to the young people" of South Africa that it had failed them. She blamed successive ANC governments for failing to build an education and training system to prepare South Africa's youth for "life in the twenty-first century." Moreover, "Our society's greatness is being fundamentally undermined by a massive failure of governance. Our country has lost the moral authority and international respect it enjoyed when it became a democracy," Ramphele said (D. Smith 2013). Her more progressive and productive leadership would, she promised, offer better outcomes than those achieved by the "bankrupt" ANC. Its leadership since Mandela left office had simply failed to advance the rainbow nation materially or spiritually.

Archbishop Desmond Tutu wants South Africa, "for goodness' sake," to try hard to "recover the spirit that made us great." South Africa, says Tutu, is both more unequal and more violent than it was under apartheid (Torchia 2013). Moreover, South Africa is morally adrift, thanks to a lack of legitimate leadership.

Trevor Manuel, minister in the presidency in charge of the National Planning Commission and former minister of finance, believes that South Africa's leaders should assume full responsibility for the problems of the nation and "resist the temptation" to blame apartheid for the current regime's failures of governance. Those failures include a "faltering" educational enterprise, a diminution of the delivery of essential services, and the kinds of widespread corruption and cronyism that would cause any public to lose faith in the legitimacy of national leadership and government.

Lesiba Seshoka, of the South African National Union of Mineworkers, asserts that "there is still a long way to go." Robert Schrire believes "the honeymoon is pretty much over." The dominant ANC has forfeited the loyalties of at least some of its followers by failing to produce a meaningful post-apartheid dividend in terms of plentiful jobs, available housing, improved educational opportunity, health care, and the rest. ANC supporters, says Schrire, feel "angry and betrayed" (Raghavan 2012). "Despair about the leadership of . . . Zuma is at fever pitch," says Jonny Steinberg (Steinberg 2013).

After Zuma endorsed Mugabe's victory in Zimbabwe's 2013 elections despite cries of massive cheating and blatant fraud by internal civil society monitoring groups, Botswana, Australia, Britain, and the United States, the Democratic Alliance denounced his profound lack of leadership: "By congratulating Robert Mugabe on his stolen election, President Zuma has failed Zimbabwe, failed Zimbabweans, and failed the South African Development Community by not providing the leadership that the region desperately required" (Campbell 2013b). These are all tough but widely acknowledged indictments of the ANC's guidance of South Africa since Mandela's presidency, and also of the lack of visionary, legitimate, and intellectually honest leadership of the party and the nation.

As other articles in this volume indicate, South Africa has created very few net new jobs in the past 30 years. The economy has never achieved the 6 percent annual GDP growth per year that is asserted to be necessary to begin to reduce massive unemployment (officially 25 percent, unofficially 33 percent). Too few majority South Africans obtain their matriculation certificate (graduate from high school) each year, and too few qualify at those examinations to enter university. Moreover, there is a massive shortage of skilled artisans; large artisanal vacancies—as many as a reputed six hundred thousand—go unfilled. (See the articles in this volume by Ann Bernstein and Nicoli Nattrass.)

Corruption (as the introductory article in this volume tells us) is rife. In the provincial administrations, fake jobs and fake purchases are frequently discovered, as in Limpopo Province. There, in 2012 and before, provincial ANC politicians overspent their official budgets by many hundreds of millions of rand, much of the expenditures having been doled out in the form of special payments to cronies. Lucrative contracts were awarded without fair tendering; nearly 10 percent of the province's teachers drew salaries but did not exist. "We thought that South Africa could be different," concluded the head of Limpopo's branch of the South African Communist Party. Moeletsi Mbeki's damning comment was that such corrupt dealings were hardly unique to Limpopo. "It is all over the country." "It is a general form of self-enrichment by the politically connected" (Polgreen 2012).

President Zuma is dogged by scandal and conflict of interest, first with regard to suspected under-the-table payoffs by French and other European arms suppliers eager to sell their fighter jets, helicopters, tanks, submarines, frigates, and other military wares to the South African security forces (a $7 billion deal), second because of the $27 million in official funding that was being spent in 2013 to upgrade his private residence in his home village in KwaZulu-Natal, and third because of the privileges he and his administration gave in 2013 to wealthy patrons of the ANC. Not to be outdone, in the past parliamentarians have padded their expense accounts and traveled expensively. Every week in 2013 brought a new alleged scandal involving the ANC and its members to the fore. The moral climate in South Africa in 2013 was hardly what it was in 1999, when Mandela left the presidency.

In the national police establishments, commissioners and other top officials have fiddled property accounts, consorted with drug lords, and thwarted inconvenient investigations. A Gauteng police commander indicated that six hundred of his own officers had been arrested in 2011–2012 for murder, assault, blackmail, and burglary. In 2012, Zuma discharged both his national police chief and the head of the crime intelligence unit for "dirty tricks, political machinations, and even [alleged] murder." In the previous year, nearly six thousand complaints were laid against the national police for assault and attempted murder. Transparency International claims that 68 percent of urban South Africans say that the police are "extremely corrupt." Many motorists report having been shaken down by the police (*The Economist* 2013; see also the introduction to this volume).

The killing of striking platinum miners by police in 2012 caused widespread alarm and focused renewed attention on the ANC government's reputed neglect of the nation's poor and its leaders' moral insufficiencies. The 2013 dragging by the police of a Mozambican taxi driver through the streets of Daveyton testified, many observers thought, to additional leadership weaknesses. The "noble" enterprise notion has long ceased to be accepted widely.

## The Low and High Roads

As much as President Mandela uplifted and rejuvenated South Africa, by force of character, creating a plausible rainbow nation out of the wreckage and despair of an apartheid-damaged country, all of these and many other critiques inside and outside the ANC, and inside and outside South Africa, testify to the leadership failures of his successors, and of the leaders of the ANC more generally. Mandela took the high road, his successors the lower roads. Whereas Mandela was decidedly transformational in his ability to lead South Africans out of and beyond apartheid, his successors seemed directed less by Mandela's consummate vision than by the narrow battles for power and primacy within the party, and only partly within the nation. Mandela made it clear that he served all the people and the entire nation. His successors increasingly seemed and have seemed primarily to serve themselves and their coteries. They became transactional leaders, obsessed by place and position, less by how they could and can lead their people toward the promised land of prosperity, sustainable social and economic growth, and justice for all.

South Africa desperately needs newly recommitted leadership capable of serving the entire nation, not a ruling class or a cohort of robber barons. It is conceivable that political leadership capable of building upon Mandela's legacy and uplifting the nation and its people could come from within the ranks of the Democratic Alliance, from Agang, or from South Africa's several other national political parties. But it is more likely to arise within the ANC, possibly through the deputy presidential and eventual presidential efforts of Cyril Ramaphosa or others within the dominant ANC not yet fully dedicated to assuming national leadership. But from wherever it comes, South Africa is ready and anxious to be renewed. None of the challenges raised in this volume can be met successfully without the kind of national leadership that Mandela exemplified and his successors, so far, have provided largely in the breach.

The articles in this volume of *The ANNALS* have described the problems and prescribed a variety of remedies. But improved governance, a key ingredient of prosperity and national uplift, hardly happens on its own. Nor does it occur by chance. Only dedicated leadership—usually individuals at the top, sometimes an entire cadre within a party or a movement—can right a vessel of state that has foundered. South Africa is ready for such new visionary, transformational leadership. Where and when will it arise? And will it come in time?

# References

Avery, Gayle C. 2004. *Understanding leadership: Paradigms and cases*. London: Sage Publications.

Bennis, Warren. 1989. *On becoming a leader*. New York, NY: Basic Books.

Blondel, Jean. 1987. *Political leadership: Towards a general analysis*. London: Sage Publications.

Bundy, Colin. 2013. *Govan Mbeki*. Athens, OH: University of Ohio Press and Swallow Press.

Burns, James MacGregor. 1978. *Leadership*. New York, NY: Harper & Row.

Campbell, John. 24 July 2013 (2013a). President Zuma's approach to Mugabe and Zimbabwe's elections. *Africa in Transition* [blog], Council on Foreign Relations. Available from blogs.cfr.org/Campbell.

Campbell, John. 5 August 2013 (2013b). Zimbabwe's post-election repression. *Africa in Transition* [blog], Council on Foreign Relations. Available from blogs.cfr.org/Campbell.

Cohen, Michael D., and James G. March. 1974. *Leadership and ambiguity: The American college president*. New York, NY: Carnegie Foundation for the Advancement of Teaching.

Daniel, John. 2006. Soldiering on: The post-presidential years of Nelson Mandela, 1999–2005. In *Legacies of power: Leadership change and former presidents in African politics*, eds. Roger Southall and Henning Melber, 26–50. Cape Town: Human Sciences Research Council.

Easton, David E. 1965. *A systems analysis of political life*. New York, NY: John Wiley & Sons.

*The Economist*. 16 July 2009. How different is his policy?

*The Economist*. 23 June 2013. Something very rotten.

Gevisser, Mark. 2009. *A legacy of liberation: Thabo Mbeki and the future of the South African dream*. New York, NY: Palgrave MacMillan.

Graham, Paul, and Carmen Alpin. 2012. *Public attitudes towards the president of the Republic of South Africa, Jacob Zuma*. Afrobarometer Briefing Paper 104. Accra, Ghana.

256                                                    THE ANNALS OF THE AMERICAN ACADEMY

Hermann, Margaret G., and Joe D. Hagan. 1998. International decision making: Leadership matters. *Foreign Policy* 110:124–35.

Huntingon, Samuel P. 1991. *The third wave: Democratization in the late twentieth century*. Norman, OK: University of Oklahoma Press.

Jones, Benjamin F., and Benjamin A. Olken. 2005. Do leaders matter? National leadership and growth since World War II. *Quarterly Journal of Economics* 120:835–64.

Kanter, Rosabeth Moss. 25 November 2003. *Leadership for change: Enduring skills for change masters*. Harvard Business Review Case Study. Boston, MA: Harvard Business Publishing.

Kanter, Rosabeth Moss. 2004. *Confidence: How winning streaks and losing streaks begin and end*. New York, NY: Crown Business.

Kellerman, Barbara. 2008. *Followership: How followers are creating change and changing leaders*. Boston, MA: Harvard Business Review Press.

Lieberson, Stanley, and James F. O'Connor. 1972. Leadership and organizational performance: A study of large corporations. *American Sociological Review* 37:117–30.

Lodge, Tom. 2006. *Mandela: A critical life*. New York, NY: Oxford University Press.

Mills, Greg. 2010. *Why Africa is poor: And what Africans can do about it*. Cape Town: Penguin.

Minchin, James. 1986/1990. *No man is an island: A portrait of Singapore's Lee Kuan Yew*. London: Unwin Hyman.

Neustadt, Richard E. 1990. *Presidential power and the modern presidents: The politics of leadership from Roosevelt to Reagan*. New York, NY: Free Press.

Nye, Joseph S., Jr. 2008. *The powers to lead*. New York, NY: Oxford University Press.

Paige, Glenn D. 1977. *The scientific study of political leadership*. New York, NY: Free Press.

Podolny, Joel M., Rakesh Khurana, and Marya L. Besharov. 2010. Revisiting the meaning of leadership. In *Handbook of leadership theory and practice*, eds. Nitin Nohria and Rakesh Khurana, 73–96. Boston, MA: Harvard Business Review Press.

Polgreen, Lydia. 18 February 2012. South Africa suffers as graft saps provinces. *New York Times*.

Pye, Lucian W. 1967. *Politics, personality, and nation building: Burma's search for identity*. New Haven, CT: Elliot's Books.

Raghavan, Sadarsan. 3 November 2012. In South Africa, disillusionment with the party that ended apartheid. *Washington Post*.

Rotberg, Robert I. 1997. Peripheral successor states and the legacy of empire: Succeeding the British and French empires in Africa. In *The end of empire? The transformation of the USSR in comparative perspective*, eds. Karen Dawisha and Bruce Parrott, 198–217. Armonk, NY: M. E. Sharpe.

Rotberg, Robert I. 2004. *When states fail: Causes and consequences*. Princeton, NJ: Princeton University Press.

Rotberg, Robert I. 2012. *Transformative political leadership: Making a difference in the developing world*. Chicago, IL: University of Chicago Press.

Rustow, Dankwart A., ed. 1970. *Philosophers and kings: Studies in leadership*. New York, NY: G. Braziller.

Sampson, Anthony. 1999. *Mandela: The authorized biography*. New York, NY: Random House.

Seligman, Lester G. 1950. The study of political leadership. *American Political Science Review* 44:904–15.

Shane, Scott. 2010. *Born entrepreneurs, born leaders: How your genes affect your work life*. New York, NY: Oxford University Press.

Smith, Adam. 1976. *The theory of moral sentiments*, ed. David Daiches Raphael and Alec Lawrence Macfie. Oxford: Oxford University Press.

Smith, David. 18 February 2013. Mamphela Ramphele launches challenge to South Africa's ANC. *The Guardian*.

Steinberg, Jonny 18 October 2013. Hard to lead a party that doesn't want to be led. *Business Day*.

Torchia, Christopher. 13 April 2013. South Africa debates persistent troubles since end of apartheid. *Boston Globe*.

Tutu, Desmond. 9 March 2011. The musings of a decrepit. Lecture, The University of the Western Cape, Cape Town.

Weber, Max. 1948. Politics as a vocation. In *From Max Weber: Essays in sociology*, trans. and eds. H. H. Gerth and C. Wright Mills, 77–128. New York, NY: Routledge.

Willner, Ann Ruth. 1984. *The spellbinders: Charismatic political leadership*. New Haven, CT: Yale University Press.

www.ingramcontent.com/pod-product-compliance
Lightning Source LLC
Chambersburg PA
CBHW072101020426
42334CB00017B/1589